STERLING
Test Prep

OAT
Physics
Practice Questions

3rd edition

www.Sterling-Prep.com

3   2   1

ISBN-13: 978-1-9475562-2-5

Sterling Test Prep products are available at special quantity discounts for sales, promotions, academic counseling offices and other educational purposes.

For more information, contact our Sales Department at:

Sterling Test Prep
6 Liberty Square #11
Boston, MA 02109
info@sterling-prep.com

Dear Student!

Congratulations on choosing this book as part of your OAT preparation!

Scoring well on OAT is important for admission into optometry school. To achieve a high score, you need to develop skills to properly apply the knowledge you have and quickly choose the correct answer. You must solve numerous practice questions that represent the style and content of the OAT questions. Understanding key science concepts is more valuable than memorizing terms.

Physics is a challenging discipline tested on the OAT. This book provides over 850 high-yield practice questions that test your knowledge of all physics topics on the test. The explanations for these questions provide detailed solutions and cover a broad spectrum of concepts that you must be well versed to answer related questions on the test. By reading these explanations carefully and understanding how they apply to solve the question, you will learn important physics concepts and the relationships between them. This will prepare you for the test, and you will significantly increase your score.

All the questions in this book are prepared by physics instructors with years of experience. This team of educators analyzed the content of the OAT exam and designed practice questions that will help you build physics knowledge and develop the skills necessary for your success on the test. The questions were reviewed for quality and effectiveness by our science editors who possess extensive credentials, are educated in top colleges and universities, and have years of teaching and editorial experience.

We wish you great success in your future academic achievements and look forward to being a part of your successful preparation for OAT!

Sterling Test Prep Team

191114gdx

Our Commitment to the Environment

Sterling Test Prep is committed to protecting our planet's resources by supporting environmental organizations with proven track records of conservation, ecological research and education and preservation of vital natural resources. A portion of our profits is donated to help these organizations so they can continue their critical missions. These organizations include:

For over 40 years, Ocean Conservancy has been advocating for a healthy ocean by supporting sustainable solutions based on science and cleanup efforts. Among many environmental achievements, Ocean Conservancy laid the groundwork for an international moratorium on commercial whaling, played an instrumental role in protecting fur seals from overhunting and banning the international trade of sea turtles. The organization created national marine sanctuaries and served as the lead non-governmental organization in the designation of 10 of the 13 marine sanctuaries.

For 25 years, Rainforest Trust has been saving critical lands for conservation through land purchases and protected area designations. Rainforest Trust has played a central role in the creation of 73 new protected areas in 17 countries, including the Falkland Islands, Costa Rica and Peru. Nearly 8 million acres have been saved thanks to Rainforest Trust's support of in-country partners across Latin America, with over 500,000 acres of critical lands purchased outright for reserves.

Since 1980, Pacific Whale Foundation has been saving whales from extinction and protecting our oceans through science and advocacy. As an international organization, with ongoing research projects in Hawaii, Australia, and Ecuador, PWF is an active participant in global efforts to address threats to whales and other marine life. A pioneer in non-invasive whale research, PWF was an early leader in educating the public, from a scientific perspective, about whales and the need for ocean conservation.

With your purchase, you support environmental causes around the world.

Table of Contents

Table of Contents (*continued*)

We want to hear from you

Your feedback is important to us because we strive to provide the highest quality prep materials. Email us if you have any questions, comments or suggestions, so we can incorporate your feedback into future editions.

Customer Satisfaction Guarantee

If you have any concerns about this book, including printing issues, contact us and we will resolve any issues to your satisfaction.

info@sterling-prep.com

We reply to all emails – please check your spam folder

Thank you for choosing our products to achieve your educational goals!

Optometry Admission Test (OAT): General Information

About the OAT

The Optometry Admission Test (OAT) is a standardized multiple-choice, computer-based exam conducted by the Association of Schools and Colleges of Optometry. The exam measures general academic ability and comprehension of scientific information. The OAT is multi-disciplinary in nature and is composed of four sections.

To score well, sufficient content knowledge and competence is required for all four sections. The tested concepts reflect those typically encountered in first-year biology, general chemistry, organic chemistry and physics courses, as well as concepts from statistics and algebra II. The general format of the entire OAT is detailed in the table below.

OAT Format		
Section	**Number of Questions**	**Time Limit**
Optional Tutorial	N/A	15 minutes
Survey of the Natural Sciences	100	90 minutes
Reading Comprehension Test	50	60 minutes
Scheduled Break	N/A	15 minutes
Physics Test	40	50 minutes
Quantitative Reasoning Test	40	45 minutes
Optional Post-Test Survey	N/A	15 minutes
Totals	**280**	**4 hours 50 minutes**

OAT Scoring

The OAT score is composed of separate section scores based on the number of correct answers (incorrect answers and skipped questions are weighed the same); guessing is not penalized. OAT results are reported in terms of scale scores. These scores represent separate assessments for physics, reading comprehension, quantitative reasoning, biology, general chemistry, and organic chemistry. After completing the test, you will receive an unofficial score report printout indicating your scale score for each of the four primary sections of the test. On the OAT, scores range from 200 to 400, in increments of 10. Performance can be compared between two applicants using a scale score.

Official OAT scores are electronically reported between three and four weeks after the exam to the schools indicated on your OAT application. These listed schools (up to five) cannot be retroactively changed after completion of the exam.

Survey of the Natural Sciences

This section covers topics rooted in biology, general chemistry and organic chemistry and is likewise divided into three separate subsections corresponding to each discipline. Five answer choices accompany each question in this section. Given the three subsections and their associated number of questions (see table below), it is advisable to devote approximately 54 seconds per question to finish the section within the allotted 90 minutes.

It is important to know that general chemistry section questions tend to require a greater number of calculations, so plan on allocating sufficient time for it. For your convenience, the OAT computer program provides a periodic table of elements that is accessible during this portion of the exam.

Survey of the Natural Sciences	
Subsection	**Number of Questions**
Biology	40
General Chemistry	30
Organic Chemistry	30

Biology

Biology is the first Survey of Natural Sciences subsection. A listing of the covered knowledge areas and their required topic and skill competencies is outlined in the table below.

It should be noted that individual questions on the exam frequently cover more than one topic or even knowledge area.

Biology		
Area	**Topic / Skill Competencies**	**Portion of Subsection**
Cell and Molecular Biology	Biomolecules, cell metabolism (photosynthesis, enzymology), cell structure, cellular processes, experimental cell biology, organelle structure and function, the origin of life, mitosis/meiosis, thermodynamics	~32.5%
Diversity of Life	Biological organization and the relationship of major taxa (Six-Kingdom, Three-Domain System: animalia, archaea, eubacteria, fungi, plantae, protista) and their relationships	~7.5%

Structure and Function of Systems	Circulatory, digestive, endocrine, immunological, integumentary, muscular, nervous/senses, reproductive, respiratory, skeletal, urinary, etc.	~22.5%
Developmental Biology	Descriptive embryology, developmental mechanisms, experimental embryology, fertilization	~10%
Genetics	Chromosomal genetics, classical genetics, genetic technology, human genetics, molecular genetics	~17.5%
Evolution, Ecology and Behavior	Animal behavior (including social behavior), ecosystems, population genetics/speciation, population and community ecology, natural selection	~10%

In previous years, the biology subsection tended to assess from the reductionist position. That is, the subsection required significant memorization of discrete facts. The current shift, however, emphasizes integrative learning, focusing holistically on systems and their associated interactions. Therefore, it is incumbent to arrive at this subsection with a wide scope of knowledge and an ability to perceive connections. Core basics should still be committed to memory, but not knowing how the separate elements interact will limit your outcome.

General Chemistry

General Chemistry is the second Survey of Natural Sciences subsection. A listing of the covered areas and their required topic and skill competencies are outlined in the below table. Like the biology subsection, individual questions on general chemistry frequently cover more than one topic or knowledge area, so possessing a broad familiarity is the key to success.

General Chemistry		
Area	**Topic / Skill Competencies**	**Portion of Subsection**
Stoichiometry and General Concepts	Balancing equations, calculations from balanced equations, density, empirical formulae, molar mass, moles and molecular formulas, percent composition	~10%
Gases	Boyle's Law, Charles' Law, Dalton's Law, ideal gas law, kinetic molecular theory of gases	~7%

Liquids and Solids	Intermolecular forces, phase changes, polarity, properties, structures, vapor pressure	~10%
Solutions	Concentration calculations, forces, polarity, properties (colligative, non-colligative)	~10%
Acids and Bases	Calculations, Brønsted-Lowry reactions, pH, strength	~10%
Chemical Equilibria	Acid/base, calculations, Le Chatelier's principle, molecular, precipitation	~7%
Thermodynamics and Thermochemistry	Enthalpies, entropies, heat transfer, Hess' Law, laws of thermodynamics, spontaneity	~7%
Chemical Kinetics	Activation energy, half-life, rate laws	~7%
Oxidation-Reduction Reactions	Balancing equations, determination of oxidation numbers, electrochemical calculations, electrochemical concepts, and terminology	~7%
Atomic and Molecular Structure	Atomic theory, bond types, electron configuration, Lewis-Dot diagrams, orbital types, molecular geometry, quantum theory, sub-atomic particles	~10%
Periodic Properties	Descriptive chemistry, periodic trends, representative elements, transition elements	~7%
Nuclear Reactions	Balancing equations, binding energy, decay processes, particles, terminology	~3%
Laboratory	Basic techniques, data analysis, equipment, error analysis, safety	~7%

Having a firm understanding of theoretical concepts and their practical applications is what will increase outcomes in this subsection.

Some questions will require mathematical calculations. Given that each question is weighed the same, and the lack of access to a calculator during this subsection, in the interest of time management, it is best to use estimations instead of precise number-crunching. If you can calculate quickly, then do so.

What is key when it comes to the math components is confidently knowing what each variable represents, the implied proportionalities and the relationship reasoning.

Organic Chemistry

Organic Chemistry is the third Survey of Natural Sciences subsection. A listing of the covered knowledge areas and their respective topics and skill competencies is shown in the table below.

In this subsection, individual questions frequently cover more than one knowledge area or topic.

Organic Chemistry		
Area	**Topic / Skill Competencies**	**Portion of Subsection**
Mechanisms	Energetics, structure (addition, elimination, free radical, substitution mechanisms, other mechanisms, and reactions)	~17%
Chemical and Physical Properties of Molecules	Laboratory theory and techniques (separations, TLC, etc.), spectroscopy (^{13}C NMR, ^{1}H NMR, infrared, multi-spectral), structure (intermolecular forces (boiling point, melting point, solubility, etc.) and polarity.	~17%
Stereochemistry	Chirality, conformations, isomer relationships	~10%
Nomenclature	Functional groups in molecules; IUPAC rules	~7%
	Individual Reactions of the Major Functional Groups & Combinations of Reactions to Synthesize Compounds	~30%
Acid-Base Chemistry	Prediction of products and equilibria, ranking acidity/basicity (pH/pK$_a$ data analysis, structure analysis)	~10%
Aromatics and Bonding	Concept of aromaticity, atomic/molecular orbitals, bond angles/lengths, hybridization, resonance	~10%

As with the above subsections, a more conceptual understanding of the areas (that is, generalizations, patterns, and critical thinking) is needed, rather than demonstrating raw memorization of facts.

Only roughly a third of the subsection's questions assess knowledge on individual (named) reactions. These questions that do solicit reaction analysis can usually be answered by applying causation critical thinking.

Therefore, it is key to focus study efforts on concepts. Take note, however, of the listed topic and skill competencies listed above. For those items, hone a nuanced understanding.

Reading Comprehension Test

This section assesses reading comprehension ability in regard to provided scientific passages. These passages may center on topical areas encountered in optometry school. Given the three subsections, it is advisable to devote no more than approximately 20 minutes for both reading each passage and answering their accompanying 16-17 questions.

Aim for 8 minutes of reading and 12 minutes for question answering, which simplifies to roughly 40-45 seconds per question. Keep in mind to jot down quick notes to streamline reading comprehension. It is advised to hone the ability to both analyze and evaluate.

Further, the questions can be divided into seven categories, which are listed in the table below along with descriptions on how to succeed with them.

Reading Comprehension Test	
Question Type	**Strategy**
Detail	Identify explicitly made statements
Except	Choose the one answer that is incorrect
Function	Assess and evaluate the author's organization of the argument
Global	Demonstrate holistic understanding in relation to the passage's main idea(s), thesis or conclusion
Inference	Using what is explicitly stated in the passage, conclude according to the author's logic
Strengthen / Weaken	Identify the answer choice that most effectively enhances or undermines the argument
Tone	Ascertain the author's implicit bias

Physics Test

This section is premised on assessment of knowledge of college-level physics. The test contains 40 questions, so you should devote around one minute and 15 seconds per question.

The topics tested include: units and vectors, linear kinematics, statics, dynamics, rotational motion, energy and momentum, simple harmonic motion, waves, fluid statics, thermal energy and thermodynamics, electrostatics, D.C. circuits, and optics.

Read all problem set instructions carefully and understand them completely before attempting to answer questions. Measuring devices of any form are not permitted.

Quantitative Reasoning Test

This section assesses abilities to interact shrewdly with quantitative materials, reason with numbers and manipulate numerical relationships. It is divided into two problem set categories (see table below). Also, note that the mathematical problem set covers four content areas.

Given the 45 minutes allowed for this section, you will want to endeavor to devote approximately 1 minute and 7 seconds per question.

Quantitative Reasoning Test	
Problem Sets	**Topics**
Mathematical Problems	Algebra (equations and expressions, inequalities, absolute value, exponential rotation, ratios and proportions, graphical analysis); Data Analysis, Interpretation and Sufficiency; Quantitative Comparison; Probability and Statistics
Applied Mathematics (Word Problems)	(A basic four-function calculator is provided for the Quantitative Reasoning section in the testing computer program.)

For best results, this book should be supplemented by

"OAT Physics Complete Subject Review"

OAT Physics Complete Subject Review provides a detailed and thorough review of topics tested on the physics portion of OAT. The content covers foundational principles and concepts necessary to answer related questions on the test.

· Kinematics & dynamics

· Force, motion, gravitation

· Equilibrium & momentum

· Work & energy

· Rotational motion

· Waves & periodic motion

· Sound

· DC circuits

· Electrostatics

OAT Strategies

Preparation Strategies

- Plan to devote between 3 and 6 months to studying for the OAT before your examination date. The OAT can be challenging even when the appropriate study has been dedicated, so it will be guaranteed to be difficult if preparation has been inadequate. If circumstances require that you hold down a part-time or full-time job, err on the side of giving yourself more versus less time to study. If you can go without employment, 3 months' preparation should be sufficient if you commit to studying as though it were roughly a typical 9-to-5 shift (advice ranges from devoting 6-8 hours a day, 5-6 days a week). Advice concerning the total number of hours needed to prepare ranges from a low of 405 to a high of 1,300; it depends on how strong your prior knowledge background is.

- Do not study too far in advance. This can inadvertently result in poor knowledge retention. Studying more than 6 months ahead of time is usually not advised, provided this is your first time taking the OAT, and you completed all the required coursework successfully.

- During this preparation period, it is wise to temporarily remove or postpone as many distractions as you can from your life. With that in mind, it is also crucial to not completely neglect physical activity or your social life. The goal should be to prepare robustly, but not to jeopardize your health and emotional well-being – balance is key.

- Develop a realistic study and practice schedule. Cramming 12 hours a day is not only unfeasible, but it will also likely burn you out which is detrimental to your intended efforts. Once a realistic study and practice schedule is determined, commit to it.

- When studying, focus on developing an understanding over memorization. The OAT is intended to measure your understanding of concepts.

- When studying, devote blocks of time to each OAT section. At the end of each study block, write a one-page outline of the topics you covered. The act of writing this increases knowledge retention.

- Alternate the days you commit to studying and the days you commit to practicing. This will result in a steady increase in knowledge retention, aid in identifying problematic areas that require further study and accustom you to the challenging nature of the test ahead.

- Consider using homemade flash cards to develop knowledge retention and to quiz what you know. Do not opt for flash cards sold on the OAT books market because the act of making them is very beneficial for retaining knowledge.

- Consider occasionally studying with a friend who is also preparing for the OAT. This can not only be a source of encouragement but also bolster your competence. Explaining concepts to help your study partner comprehend them can improve and fine-tune your degree of understanding.

- Take practice tests. You shouldn't take them too early in your preparation before you develop a broad and deep understanding of concepts, but you should not postpone them to the last couple of weeks before your test. If you find you are not scoring well on practice tests, you want to have enough time left to fill in your gaps without much stress.

- During practice tests, it is a good idea to replicate the test center conditions you might encounter. This includes sitting at a desk and working at a plug-in keyboard computer, wearing earplugs (which are provided at testing centers), eating the sorts of snacks or light meals you will likely bring on your test day, endeavoring to limit your breaks to those allowed by testing centers, not using your cell phone, studying under both hotter and colder temperatures than you prefer (since you cannot control the test center thermostat), etc. It may also be wise to situate yourself in a study environment where background noise is present. During the exam, you will likely hear sniffles, coughs, shifting in seats and pencil or finger tapping, among other noises. Even with available earplugs being provided at the test center, you will want to be adept at tuning these noises out as much as possible.

- During practice tests, develop a consistent pace at which you answer questions. Getting your response time reliably down to the desired target will ensure that you complete the OAT sections on time when you take the official test.

- Develop a healthy sleep, exercise and dietary regimen to optimize your physical and mental condition. Some people require more sleep, others less. The same applies to physical activity and dietary needs. Commit to getting the amount of sleep, exercise, and nutrition appropriate for your personal needs.

Test Day Strategies

- Ensure a restful mental and physical state by getting a full night's sleep before the test.

- Avoid foods and drinks that lead to drowsiness (foods heavy in carbohydrates and protein) and sweets or drinks loaded with sugar.

- Arrive at the testing center early. This will give you ample time to both check-in and arrive at a place of mental calm before the test begins. Starting off the right way is an advantage you should give yourself.

- Uphold a positive attitude and avoid falling to mental spirals of negative emotions. Too much concern can lead to underperformance.

- Do not concern yourself with what other test takers are doing. If some appear to be proceeding rapidly through the test, that should not matter to you. For all you know, they may be guessing on every other question. Focus only on your progress.

- Do not skip the available break. Even if you perceive your stamina to be Herculean, giving yourself these moments of rest will help you finish strong. The test is long and demanding, your mind and body will appreciate the break in the second half.

- Eat a light meal or snack during the allowed breaks to replenish your energy.

- Close your eyes and consider taking a waking-nap or moment of meditation during the allowed breaks to give your eyes and mind a brief respite. Just be sure to rouse yourself when the time approaches to go back in.

Test-taking Strategies

There are strategies, approaches, and perspectives that you should learn to apply on the OAT. On the test, you need to think and analyze information quickly. This skill cannot be gained from a college course, a review prep course or a textbook. However, you can develop it through repetitive practice and focus.

Intimidation by information. Test developers usually select material for the test that will be completely unknown to most test takers. Don't be overwhelmed, intimidated or discouraged by unfamiliar concepts. While going through a question, try to understand all the relevant material available, while disregarding the distracter information. Being exposed to topics and terms that you are not familiar with is normal for this test. Do not feel stressed out if you're not very familiar with the topic. If you have done your preparation, then most other test takers are not familiar with it either. So, stay calm and work through the questions.

Find your pace. Everybody reads and processes information at a different rate. You should practice finding your optimal rate, so you can read fast and still comprehend the information.

If you have a good pace and don't invest too much time in any one question, you should have enough time to complete each section at a comfortable rate. Avoid two extremes where you either work too slowly, reading every word carefully, or act panicky and rush through the material without understanding.

When you find your own pace that allows you to stay focused and calm, you will have enough time for all the questions. It is important to remember, that you are trying to achieve optimal, not maximum, comprehension. If you spend the time necessary to achieve a maximum comprehension of a passage (in the Reading Comprehension section) or question, you will most likely not have enough time for the whole section.

Don't overinvest in one question. The test is timed, and you cannot spend too much time on any one question. Get away from thinking that if you spent just one more minute on the question, you'd get it right. You can get sucked into a question so that you lose track of time and end up rushing through the rest of the test (which may cause you to miss even more questions).

If you spend your allocated per-question time and are still not sure of the answer, select the best option, note the question number and move on. The test allows you to return to any question and change your answer choice. If you have extra time left after you answered all other questions on that section, return to that question and take a fresh look. Unless you have a sound reason to change your original answer, don't change your answer choice.

You shouldn't go into the OAT thinking that you must get every question right. Accept the fact that you will have to guess on some questions (and maybe get them wrong) and still have time for every question. Your goal should be to answer as many questions correctly as you possibly can.

Factually correct, but actually wrong. Often OAT questions are written in a way that the incorrect answer choice may be factually correct on its own but doesn't answer the question. When you are reading the answer choices, and one choice jumps out at you because it is factually correct, be careful.

Make sure to go back to the question and verify that the answer choice actually answers the question being asked. Some incorrect answer choices will seem to answer the question asked and are even factually correct, but are based on extraneous information within the question stem.

Narrow down your choices. Use the process of elimination to narrow the possible answer choices if you cannot identify the one correct answer with certainty. For example, if answer choices "A" and "C" can be quickly identified as incorrect for a particular question, you will have increased your chances of guessing the correct answer from 20% to 33.3%. Using this method as a last possible recourse will increase your likelihood of receiving a higher score.

When you find two answer choices that are direct opposites, it is very likely that the correct answer choice is one of the two. You can typically rule out the other two answer choices (unless they are also direct opposites of each other) and narrow down your search for the correct choice that answers the question.

Experiments. If you encounter a question that describes an experiment, ask some basic questions including:

"What is the experiment designed to find out?",

"What is the experimental method?",

"What are the variables?",

"What are the controls?"

Understanding this information helps you use the presented information to answer the question.

Multiple experiments. The best way to remember three variations of the same experiment is to focus on the differences between the experiments. What changed between the first and second experiment? What was done differently between the second and the third experiment? This will help you organize the information in your mind.

Look for units. When solving a problem that you don't know the formula for, try to solve for the units in the answer choices. The units in the answer choices are your clues for understanding the relationship between the question and the correct answer. Review what value is being sought in the question. Sometimes you can eliminate some wrong answers because they contain improper units.

Don't fall for the familiar. When in doubt, it is easy to choose what you are familiar with. If you recognize a term in one of the four answer choices, you may be tempted to pick that choice. However, don't go with familiar answers just because they are familiar.

Think through the other answer choices and how they relate to the question before making your selection.

Extra Tips

- With fact questions that require selecting among numbers, don't go with the smallest or largest number unless you have a reason to believe it is the answer.

- Do not rely on gut feelings alone to quickly answer questions. Understand and recognize the difference between *knowing* an answer and having a *gut feeling* about the answer. Gut feelings should only be utilized after conducting a process of elimination.

- Use estimation rather than exact computation when possible. In most instances, estimating will enable the correct answer to be identified much more quickly than if exact computations are made.

- Don't fall for answers that sound "clever" and don't go with "bizarre" choices. Only choose them if you are confident that the choice is correct.

- None of these strategies will replace the importance of preparation. However, knowing and using them will help you utilize your test time more productively and increase your probability for successful guessing when you simply don't know the answer.

Common Physics Formulas & Conversions

Constants and Conversion Factors

1 unified atomic mass unit	$1\ u = 1.66 \times 10^{-27}\ kg$
	$1\ u = 931\ MeV/c^2$
Proton mass	$m_p = 1.67 \times 10^{-27}\ kg$
Neutron mass	$m_n = 1.67 \times 10^{-27}\ kg$
Electron mass	$m_e = 9.11 \times 10^{-31}\ kg$
Electron charge magnitude	$e = 1.60 \times 10^{-19}\ C$
Avogadro's number	$N_0 = 6.02 \times 10^{23}\ mol^{-1}$
Universal gas constant	$R = 8.31\ J/(mol \cdot K)$
Boltzmann's constant	$k_B = 1.38 \times 10^{-23}\ J/K$
Speed of light	$c = 3.00 \times 10^8\ m/s$
Planck's constant	$h = 6.63 \times 10^{-34}\ J \cdot s$
	$h = 4.14 \times 10^{-15}\ eV \cdot s$
	$hc = 1.99 \times 10^{-25}\ J \cdot m$
	$hc = 1.24 \times 10^3\ eV \cdot nm$
Vacuum permittivity	$\varepsilon_0 = 8.85 \times 10^{-12}\ C^2/N \cdot m^2$
Coulomb's law constant	$k = 1/4\pi\varepsilon_0 = 9.0 \times 10^9\ N \cdot m^2/C^2$
Vacuum permeability	$\mu_0 = 4\pi \times 10^{-7}\ (T \cdot m)/A$
Magnetic constant	$k' = \mu_0/4\pi = 10^{-7}\ (T \cdot m)/A$
Universal gravitational constant	$G = 6.67 \times 10^{-11}\ m^3/kg \cdot s^2$
Acceleration due to gravity at Earth's surface	$g = 9.8\ m/s^2$
1 atmosphere pressure	$1\ atm = 1.0 \times 10^5\ N/m^2$
	$1\ atm = 1.0 \times 10^5\ Pa$
1 electron volt	$1\ eV = 1.60 \times 10^{-19}\ J$
Balmer constant	$B = 3.645 \times 10^{-7}\ m$
Rydberg constant	$R = 1.097 \times 10^7\ m^{-1}$
Stefan constant	$\sigma = 5.67 \times 10^{-8}\ W/m^2K^4$

Units			Prefixes		
Name	**Symbol**		**Factor**	**Prefix**	**Symbol**
meter	m		10^{12}	tera	T
kilogram	kg		10^9	giga	G
second	s		10^6	mega	M
ampere	A		10^3	kilo	k
kelvin	K		10^{-2}	centi	c
mole	mol		10^{-3}	mili	m
hertz	Hz		10^{-6}	micro	μ
newton	N		10^{-9}	nano	n
pascal	Pa		10^{-12}	pico	p
joule	J				
watt	W				
coulomb	C				
volt	V				
ohm	Ω				
henry	H				
farad	F				
tesla	T				
degree Celsius	°C				
electronvolt	eV				

Values of Trigonometric Functions for Common Angles

θ	$\sin \theta$	$\cos \theta$	$\tan \theta$
0°	0	1	0
30°	1/2	$\sqrt{3}/2$	$\sqrt{3}/3$
37°	3/5	4/5	3/4
45°	$\sqrt{2}/2$	$\sqrt{2}/2$	1
53°	4/5	3/5	4/3
60°	$\sqrt{3}/2$	1/2	$\sqrt{3}$
90°	1	0	∞

Newtonian Mechanics

Translational Motion	$v = v_0 + a\Delta t$	a = acceleration
	$x = x_0 + v_0\Delta t + \dfrac{1}{2}a\Delta t^2$	A = amplitude
	$v^2 = v_0^2 + 2a\Delta x$	E = energy
	$\vec{a} = \dfrac{\sum \vec{F}}{m} = \dfrac{\vec{F}_{net}}{m}$	F = force
		f = frequency
		h = height
Rotational Motion	$\omega = \omega_0 + \alpha t$	I = rotational inertia
	$\theta = \theta_0 + \omega_0 t + \dfrac{1}{2}\alpha t^2$	J = impulse
	$\omega^2 = \omega_0^2 + 2\alpha\Delta\theta$	K = kinetic energy
	$\vec{\alpha} = \dfrac{\sum \vec{\tau}}{I} = \dfrac{\vec{\tau}_{net}}{I}$	k = spring constant
		ℓ = length
Force of Friction	$\left\|\vec{F}_f\right\| \leq \mu\left\|\vec{F}_n\right\|$	m = mass
		N = normal force
Centripetal Acceleration	$a_c = \dfrac{v^2}{r}$	P = power
		p = momentum
Torque	$\tau = r_\perp F = rF\sin\theta$	L = angular momentum
		r = radius of distance
Momentum	$\vec{p} = m\vec{v}$	T = period
Impulse	$\vec{J} = \Delta\vec{p} = \vec{F}\Delta t$	t = time
		U = potential energy
Kinetic Energy	$K = \dfrac{1}{2}mv^2$	v = velocity or speed
		W = work done on a
Potential Energy	$\Delta U_g = mg\Delta y$	system
Work	$\Delta E = W = F_\parallel d = Fd\cos\theta$	x = position
		y = height
Power	$P = \dfrac{\Delta E}{\Delta t} = \dfrac{\Delta W}{\Delta t}$	

Simple Harmonic Motion	$x = A\cos(\omega t) = A\cos(2\pi f t)$	α = angular acceleration
Center of Mass	$x_{cm} = \dfrac{\sum m_i x_i}{\sum m_i}$	
Angular Momentum	$L = I\omega$	μ = coefficient of friction
Angular Impulse	$\Delta L = \tau \Delta t$	θ = angle
		τ = torque
Angular Kinetic Energy	$K = \dfrac{1}{2} I\omega^2$	ω = angular speed
Work	$W = F\Delta r \, \cos\theta$	
Power	$P = Fv \, \cos\theta$	
Spring Force	$\lvert \vec{F_s} \rvert = k\lvert \vec{x} \rvert$	
Spring Potential Energy	$U_s = \dfrac{1}{2} kx^2$	
Period of Spring Oscillator	$T_s = 2\pi\sqrt{m/k}$	
Period of Simple Pendulum	$T_p = 2\pi\sqrt{\ell/g}$	
Period	$T = \dfrac{2\pi}{\omega} = \dfrac{1}{f}$	
Gravitational Body Force	$\lvert \vec{F_g} \rvert = G\dfrac{m_1 m_2}{r^2}$	
Gravitational Potential Energy of Two Masses	$U_G = -\dfrac{Gm_1 m_2}{r}$	

Electricity and Magnetism

		$A = area$
Electric Field	$\vec{E} = \dfrac{\vec{F}_E}{q}$	$B = magnetic\ field$
		$C = capacitance$
Electric Field Strength	$\|\vec{E}\| = \dfrac{1}{4\pi\varepsilon_0}\dfrac{\|q\|}{r^2}$	$d = distance$
		$E = electric\ field$
Electric Field Strength	$\|\vec{E}\| = \dfrac{\|\Delta V\|}{\|\Delta r\|}$	$\epsilon = emf$
		$F = force$
Electrostatic Force Between Charged Particles	$\|\vec{F}_E\| = \dfrac{1}{4\pi\varepsilon_0}\dfrac{\|q_1 q_2\|}{r^2}$	$I = current$
		$l = length$
Electric Potential Energy	$\Delta U_E = q\Delta V$	$P = power$
		$Q = charge$
Electrostatic Potential due to a Charge	$V = \dfrac{1}{4\pi\varepsilon_0}\dfrac{q}{r}$	$q = point\ charge$
		$R = resistance$
Capacitor Voltage	$V = \dfrac{Q}{C}$	$r = separation$
		$t = time$
Capacitance of a Parallel Plate Capacitor	$C = \kappa\varepsilon_0\dfrac{A}{d}$	$U = potential\ energy$
		$V = electric\ potential$
Electric Field Inside a Parallel Plate Capacitor	$E = \dfrac{Q}{\varepsilon_0 A}$	$v = speed$
		$\kappa = dielectric\ constant$
Capacitor Potential Energy	$U_C = \frac{1}{2}Q\Delta V = \frac{1}{2}C(\Delta V)^2$	$\rho = resistivity$
		$\theta = angle$
Current	$I = \dfrac{\Delta Q}{\Delta t}$	$\Phi = flux$
Resistance	$R = \dfrac{\rho l}{A}$	
Power	$P = I\Delta V$	

Current	$I = \dfrac{\Delta V}{R}$
Resistors in Series	$R_s = \displaystyle\sum_i R_i$
Resistors in Parallel	$\dfrac{1}{R_p} = \displaystyle\sum_i \dfrac{1}{R_i}$
Capacitors in Parallel	$C_p = \displaystyle\sum_i C_i$
Capacitors in Series	$\dfrac{1}{C_s} = \displaystyle\sum_i \dfrac{1}{C_i}$
Magnetic Field Strength (from a long straight current-carrying wire)	$B = \dfrac{\mu_0 I}{2\pi r}$

Magnetic Force

$$\vec{F}_M = q\vec{v} \times \vec{B}$$

$$\vec{F}_M = |q\vec{v}||\sin\theta||\vec{B}|$$

$$\vec{F}_M = I\vec{l} \times \vec{B}$$

$$\vec{F}_M = |I\vec{l}||\sin\theta||\vec{B}|$$

Magnetic Flux

$$\Phi_B = \vec{B} \cdot \vec{A}$$

$$\Phi_B = |\vec{B}|\cos\theta\,|\vec{A}|$$

Electromagnetic Induction

$$\epsilon = \dfrac{-\Delta\Phi_B}{\Delta t}$$

$$\epsilon = Blv$$

Fluid Mechanics and Thermal Physics

Density	$\rho = \dfrac{m}{V}$	$A = area$
		$c = specific\ heat$
Pressure	$P = \dfrac{F}{A}$	$d = thickness$
		$e = emissivity$
Absolute Pressure	$P = P_0 + \rho g h$	$F = force$
Buoyant Force	$F_b = \rho V g$	$h = depth$
		$k = thermal\ conductivity$
Fluid Continuity Equation	$A_1 v_1 = A_2 v_2$	$K = kinetic\ energy$
Bernoulli's Equation	$P_1 + \rho g y_1 + \dfrac{1}{2}\rho v_1^2$	$l = length$
	$= P_2 + \rho g y_2 + \dfrac{1}{2}\rho v_2^2$	$L = latent\ heat$
		$m = mass$
		$n = number\ of\ moles$
Heat Conduction	$\dfrac{Q}{\Delta t} = \dfrac{kA\Delta T}{d}$	$n_c = efficiency$
		$N = number\ of\ molecules$
Thermal Radiation	$P = e\sigma A(T^4 - T_C^4)$	$P = pressure\ or\ power$
Ideal Gas Law	$PV = nRT = Nk_B T$	$Q = energy\ transferred\ to$
		$a\ system\ by\ heating$
Average Energy	$K = \dfrac{3}{2}k_B T$	$T = temperature$
		$t = time$
Work	$W = -P\Delta V$	$E = internal\ energy$
		$V = volume$
Conservation of Energy	$\Delta E = Q + W$	$v = speed$
Linear Expansion	$\Delta l = \alpha l_o \Delta T$	$W = work\ done\ on\ a$
Heat Engine Efficiency	$n_c = |W/Q_H|$	$system$
		$y = height$
Carnot Heat Engine Efficiency	$n_c = \dfrac{T_H - T_C}{T_H}$	$\sigma = Stefan\ constant$
		$\alpha = coefficient\ of\ linear$
		$expansion$
Energy of Temperature Change	$Q = mc\Delta T$	$\rho = density$
Energy of Phase Change	$Q = mL$	

Optics

Wavelength to Frequency	$\lambda = \dfrac{v}{f}$	d = separation
		f = frequency or focal length
Index of Refraction	$n = \dfrac{c}{v}$	h = height
		L = distance
Snell's Law	$n_1 \sin \theta_1 = n_2 \sin \theta_2$	M = magnification
		m = an integer
Thin Lens Equation	$\dfrac{1}{s_i} + \dfrac{1}{s_0} = \dfrac{1}{f}$	n = index of refraction
		R = radius of curvature
Magnification Equation	$\lvert M \rvert = \left\lvert \dfrac{h_i}{h_o} \right\rvert = \left\lvert \dfrac{s_i}{s_o} \right\rvert$	s = distance
		v = speed
Double Slit Diffraction	$d \sin \theta = m\lambda$	x = position
	$\Delta L = m\lambda$	λ = wavelength
		θ = angle
Critical Angle	$\sin \theta_c = \dfrac{n_2}{n_1}$	
Focal Length of Spherical Mirror	$f = \dfrac{R}{2}$	

Acoustics

Standing Wave/ Open Pipe Harmonics	$\lambda = \dfrac{2L}{n}$	$f = frequency$
		$L = length$
Closed Pipe Harmonics	$\lambda = \dfrac{4L}{n}$	$m = mass$
		$M = molecular$
		$mass$
Harmonic Frequencies	$f_n = nf_1$	$n = harmonic$
		$number$
Speed of Sound in Ideal Gas	$v_{sound} = \sqrt{\dfrac{yRT}{M}}$	$R = gas\ constant$
		$T = tension$
Speed of Wave Through Wire	$v = \sqrt{\dfrac{T}{m/L}}$	$v = velocity$
		$y = adiabatic$
Doppler Effect (Approaching Stationary Observer)	$f_{observed} = \left(\dfrac{v}{v - v_{source}}\right)f_{source}$	$constant$
		$\lambda = wavelength$
Doppler Effect (Receding Stationary Observer)	$f_{observed} = \left(\dfrac{v}{v + v_{source}}\right)f_{source}$	
Doppler Effect (Observer Moving towards Source)	$f_{observed} = \left(1 + \dfrac{v_{observer}}{v}\right)f_{source}$	
Doppler Effect (Observer Moving away from Source)	$f_{observed} = \left(1 - \dfrac{v_{observer}}{v}\right)f_{source}$	

Modern Physics

		B = Balmer constant
Photon Energy	$E = hf$	
		c = speed of light
Photoelectric Electron Energy	$K_{max} = hf - \phi$	E = energy
		f = frequency
Electron Wavelength	$\lambda = \dfrac{h}{p}$	K = kinetic energy
		m = mass
Energy Mass Relationship	$E = mc^2$	p = momentum
Rydberg Formula	$\dfrac{1}{\lambda} = R\left(\dfrac{1}{n_f^2} - \dfrac{1}{n_i^2}\right)$	R = Rydberg constant
		v = velocity
Balmer Formula	$\lambda = B\left(\dfrac{n^2}{n^2 - 2^2}\right)$	λ = wavelength
		$\emptyset$ = work function
Lorentz Factor	$\gamma = \dfrac{1}{\sqrt{1 - \dfrac{v^2}{c^2}}}$	γ = Lorentz factor

Geometry and Trigonometry

		$A = area$
Rectangle	$A = bh$	
		$C = circumference$
Triangle	$A = \dfrac{1}{2}bh$	$V = volume$
		$S = surface\ area$
Circle	$A = \pi r^2$	$b = base$
	$C = 2\pi r$	$h = height$
		$l = length$
Rectangular Solid	$V = lwh$	
		$w = width$
Cylinder	$V = \pi r^2 l$	$r = radius$
	$S = 2\pi r l + 2\pi r^2$	$\theta = angle$
Sphere	$V = \dfrac{4}{3}\pi r^3$	
	$S = 4\pi r^2$	
Right Triangle	$a^2 + b^2 = c^2$	
	$\sin \theta = \dfrac{a}{c}$	
	$\cos \theta = \dfrac{b}{c}$	
	$\tan \theta = \dfrac{a}{b}$	

OAT Physics

Diagnostic Tests

Diagnostic Test #1

Answer Sheet

#	Answer:					Mark for review	#	Answer:					Mark for review
1:	A	B	C	D	E	___	31:	A	B	C	D	E	___
2:	A	B	C	D	E	___	32:	A	B	C	D	E	___
3:	A	B	C	D	E	___	33:	A	B	C	D	E	___
4:	A	B	C	D	E	___	34:	A	B	C	D	E	___
5:	A	B	C	D	E	___	35:	A	B	C	D	E	___
6:	A	B	C	D	E	___	36:	A	B	C	D	E	___
7:	A	B	C	D	E	___	37:	A	B	C	D	E	___
8:	A	B	C	D	E	___	38:	A	B	C	D	E	___
9:	A	B	C	D	E	___	39:	A	B	C	D	E	___
10:	A	B	C	D	E	___	40:	A	B	C	D	E	___
11:	A	B	C	D	E	___	41:	A	B	C	D	E	___
12:	A	B	C	D	E	___	42:	A	B	C	D	E	___
13:	A	B	C	D	E	___	43:	A	B	C	D	E	___
14:	A	B	C	D	E	___	44:	A	B	C	D	E	___
15:	A	B	C	D	E	___	45:	A	B	C	D	E	___
16:	A	B	C	D	E	___	46:	A	B	C	D	E	___
17:	A	B	C	D	E	___	47:	A	B	C	D	E	___
18:	A	B	C	D	E	___	48:	A	B	C	D	E	___
19:	A	B	C	D	E	___	49:	A	B	C	D	E	___
20:	A	B	C	D	E	___	50:	A	B	C	D	E	___
21:	A	B	C	D	E	___	51:	A	B	C	D	E	___
22:	A	B	C	D	E	___	52:	A	B	C	D	E	___
23:	A	B	C	D	E	___	53:	A	B	C	D	E	___
24:	A	B	C	D	E	___	54:	A	B	C	D	E	___
25:	A	B	C	D	E	___	55:	A	B	C	D	E	___
26:	A	B	C	D	E	___	56:	A	B	C	D	E	___
27:	A	B	C	D	E	___	57:	A	B	C	D	E	___
28:	A	B	C	D	E	___	58:	A	B	C	D	E	___
29:	A	B	C	D	E	___	59:	A	B	C	D	E	___
30:	A	B	C	D	E	___	60:	A	B	C	D	E	___

This Diagnostic Test is designed for you to assess your proficiency on each topic and NOT to mimic the actual test. Use your test results and identify areas of your strength and weakness to adjust your study plan and enhance your fundamental knowledge.

The length of the Diagnostic Tests is proven to be optimal for a single study session.

1. A chipmunk is running along a wire with constant acceleration. If it has an initial velocity of 0.4 m/s and a final velocity of 1.8 m/s after 4 s, how far does the chipmunk run in that time?

A. 2.3 m **B.** 4.4 m **C.** 6.7 m **D.** 9.9 m **E.** 7.2 m

2. An object is moving to the right in a straight line. What happens to the object if the net force acting on the object is also directed to the right, but the magnitude of the force decreases with time?

A. It continues moving to the right with a constant speed
B. It stops and then begins moving to the left with increasing speed
C. It continues moving to the right with increasing speed
D. It continues moving to the right with decreasing speed
E. It moves to the left with increasing speed

3. What is the specific heat capacity of a material if 150 kcal of heat raises the temperature of 3.0 kg of the material by 200 °C?

A. 0.35 kcal/kg·°C
B. 0.5 kcal/kg·°C
C. 0.75 kcal/kg·°C
D. 1.15 kcal/kg·°C
E. 0.25 kcal/kg·°C

4. It takes 40 J of work to push a large suitcase 4 m across a floor. Assuming the suitcase is being pushed in the same direction as it moves, what is the magnitude of the force on the suitcase?

A. 10 N **B.** 4 N **C.** 16 N **D.** 26 N **E.** 34 N

5. A simple pendulum with a length of 58 cm has a period of 2.5 s on Mars. What is the acceleration g due to gravity on Mars?

A. 0.7 m/s^2 **B.** 3.7 m/s^2 **C.** 6.8 m/s^2 **D.** 9.8 m/s^2 **E.** 17.2 m/s^2

6. What is the source of all electromagnetic waves?

A. Crystalline fluctuations
B. Vibrating nuclei
C. Accelerating electric charges
D. Changes in atomic energy levels
E. All of the above

7. How far does a wavefront of an acoustical wave travel in 1 s if it has an f of 800 Hz and a λ of 0.5 m?

A. 400 m **B.** 150 m **C.** 75 m **D.** 300 m **E.** 600 m

8. What is the value of a resistor if, when a 12 V battery is connected to a resistor, 2 A of current flows through the resistor?

    A. 1.5 ohms   **B.** 6 ohms   **C.** 7.5 ohms   **D.** 3 ohms   **E.** 24 ohms

9. What is the result of connecting two identical storage batteries in parallel in a circuit?

    A. Half the voltage and half the total charge compared to a circuit from a single battery
    B. Half the voltage, but the same total charge compared to a circuit from a single battery
    C. The same voltage and the same total charge compared to a circuit from a single battery
    D. The same voltage, but half the total charge compared to a circuit from a single battery
    E. The same voltage, but twice the total charge compared to a circuit from a single battery

10. What is the power of the combination for 5 D and 3 D thin lenses that are positioned near each other?

    A. 1/8 D   **B.** 5/3 D   **C.** 3/5 D   **D.** 8 D   **E.** 8/3 D

11. How long does it take for a rotating object to speed up from 15.0 rad/s to 33.3 rad/s if it has a uniform angular acceleration of 3.45 rad/s^2?

    A. 3.45 s   **B.** 5.30 s   **C.** 8.35 s   **D.** 14.60 s   **E.** 20.80 s

12. A 1,450 kg cannon fires a 90 kg cannonball at 30 m/s. Assuming that frictional forces are negligible and the cannonball is fired horizontally, what is the recoil velocity of the cannon?

    A. 5.1 m/s   **B.** 1.2 m/s   **C.** 3.4 m/s   **D.** 1.9 m/s   **E.** 2.8 m/s

13. An engineer expends 900 J to lift a block to a height h. He then repeats the task using a simple non-motorized pulley system that reduces the input force by half. Using the pulley system, how much work must the engineer perform to lift the block to height h?

    A. 100 J   **B.** 225 J   **C.** 900 J   **D.** 450 J   **E.** 1,400 J

14. A massless, ideal spring projects horizontally from a wall and connects to a 0.1 kg mass. The mass is oscillating in one dimension, such that it moves 0.4 m from one end of its oscillation to the other. What is the amplitude of the oscillation if it experiences 20 complete oscillations in 60 s?

    A. 0.2 m   **B.** 0.4 m   **C.** 0.8 m   **D.** $\sqrt{0.4}$ m   **E.** 4 m

15. What is the wave speed of the standing wave shown, if it is oscillating at 900 Hz on a string?

    A. 280 m/s   **C.** 360 m/s

    B. 170 m/s   **D.** 570 m/s   **E.** 420 m/s

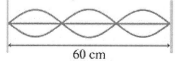

60 cm

16. What is the density of water?

A. 1×10^3 kg/cm³   **C.** 1×10^2 kg/m³

B. 1×10^1 kg/cm³   **D.** 1×10^{-3} g/m³   **E.** 1×10^3 kg/m³

17. Two stationary positive charges of $Q = 10^{-10}$ C are fixed and separated by a distance of $d = 4$ cm. What is the net electrostatic force on a charge $q = -10^{-9}$ C that is placed at a distance of $d / 2$ from each of the charges?

A. 5×10^{-10} N   **B.** 1.5×10^{-9} N   **C.** 0 N   **D.** 2.5×10^{-10} N   **E.** 1×10^{-9} N

18. A capacitor, initially having a charge of Q on the left plate and a charge of $-Q$ on the right plate, is connected to a switch and an inductor.

Assuming that the resistance of the circuit is zero, which statement is true when the switch is closed?

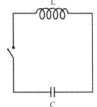

A. Current flows back and forth through the inductor, with the magnitude of the current steadily decreasing and eventually becoming zero

B. Current flows until the left plate of the capacitor has a charge $-Q$, and the current flows in the opposite direction, reversing again when the left plate has a charge of $+Q$. The cycle repeats

C. Charge flows out of the capacitor until the left plate is no longer charged, and then all current ceases

D. Because the switch is closed, the current flows clockwise with a constant magnitude.

E. Current flows back and forth through the inductor, with the magnitude of the current increasing at a constant rate

19. What is observed when sunlight passes through a prism?

   I. Bright spots and lines   II. White light   III. Continuous spectrum

A. I only   **B.** II only   **C.** III only   **D.** I and II only   **E.** I and III only

20. A solid uniform sphere of mass 120.0 kg and radius 1.7 m starts from rest and rolls without slipping down an inclined plane of vertical height 5.3 m; the sphere started at the top of the ramp. What is the angular speed of the sphere at the bottom of the inclined plane? The moment of inertia of a solid sphere is $(2/5)mR^2$.

A. 0.81 rad/s   **C.** 2.9 rad/s

B. 1.7 rad/s   **D.** 4.3 rad/s   **E.** 5.1 rad/s

21. A heat engine performs the reversible cycle *abca* with 9 moles of an ideal gas. Path *ca* is an adiabatic process. The temperatures at points *a* and *b* are 300 K and 500 K, respectively. The volume at point *c* is 0.2 m³. The adiabatic constant of the gas is 1.6. What is the heat absorbed by the gas in path *ca*?

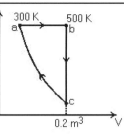

A. −10 kJ   **B.** 16 kJ   **C.** 10 kJ   **D.** 0 kJ   **E.** −16 kJ

22. Forces A, B and C act on a body. A fourth force, *F*, keeps the body in equilibrium. What is the *x* component of the force *F*?

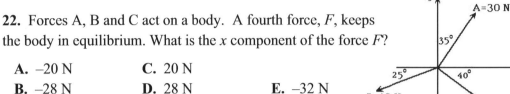

A. −20 N   **C.** 20 N

B. −28 N   **D.** 28 N   **E.** −32 N

23. In an organ pipe (cylindrical 0.2 m long tube 0.02 m in diameter, open at both ends), what is the λ of the 4th harmonic?

A. 0.08 m   **B.** 0.1 m   **C.** 0.05 m   **D.** 0.2 m   **E.** 0.8 m

24. What is the velocity of a fluid in a tube with the diameter 3 mm for a pump that has a piston of 15 cm in diameter that moves 2 cm/s?

A. 50 m/s   **B.** 21 cm/s   **C.** 25 m/s   **D.** 50 cm/s   **E.** 5 cm/s

25. What is the essential difference between microwaves and blue light?

    A. One is a form of radiation while the other is not
    B. Blue light is a beam of photons and microwaves are positrons
    C. One has a positive charge while the other does not
    D. One undergoes refraction while the other does not
    E. There is no essential difference other than frequency and wavelength

26. The resistance of a variable resistor can be adjusted. A battery is connected to a variable resistor. The potential difference across the resistor and the current through it are recorded at variable resistance. Assume that the battery is an ideal potential source in series with an internal resistor. Under which circumstances is it valid to ignore the internal resistance of the battery?

    I. small external resistance   II. large external resistance   III. low total current

A. I only   **B.** II only   **C.** III only   **D.** I and III only   **E.** II and III only

27. Which type of mirror produces an image that is always virtual, erect the same height as the object?

    A. concave   **B.** convex   **C.** plane   **D.** spherical   **E.** none of the above

28. Total constructive interference is observed when two waves with the same frequency and wavelength are at a:

A. 45° phase difference

C. 180° phase difference

B. 90° phase difference

D. –90° phase difference

E. 0° phase difference

29. What is being described when a manufacturer advertises that their car goes *from zero to sixty in 7 s*?

A. Average acceleration

C. Average speed

B. Instantaneous acceleration

D. Change in speed

E. Displacement

30. Two forces are acting on an object as shown, with magnitudes $F_1 = 80$ N and $F_2 = 24$ N. What third force causes the object to be in equilibrium?

A. 3.3 N up

C. 56 N up

B. 3.3 N down

D. 56 N down

E. 124 N up

31. Compared to falling on a wooden floor, a wine glass may not break when it falls on a carpeted floor because of the:

I. lesser impulse in stopping

II. longer time to stop

III. decreased acceleration due to gravity

A. I only **B.** II only **C.** III only **D.** I and II only **E.** I and III only

32. A 6.5 kg bag of groceries is carried 1.1 m above the ground at a constant velocity across a 3.8 m room. How much work was done on the bag in this process?

A. 183 J **B.** 155 J **C.** 0 J **D.** 84 J **E.** 22.7 J

33. A wave that has a lower frequency has a:

A. higher amplitude

C. slower velocity

B. shorter period

D. shorter wavelength

E. longer wavelength

34. A rod has a length 2.0000 m at 20 °C. The length of the rod increases to 2.0005 m when the temperature increases to 40 °C. What is the coefficient of thermal expansion α of the material for the rod?

A. 1.25×10^{-5}/K

C. 0.75×10^{-5}/K

B. 5×10^{-3}/K

D. 2.5×10^{-5}/K

E. 0.75×10^{-3}/K

35. An object is viewed at various distances using a concave mirror with a focal length of 12 m. Relative to the mirror, where is the image when the object is 6 m in front of the mirror?

   A. 12 m behind   **B.** 12 m in front   **C.** 6 m behind   **D.** 6 m in front   **E.** 24 m behind

36. What effect does the addition of resistors in parallel have on a circuit?

   A. Decreases the current   **C.** Decreases the voltage

   B. Increases the current   **D.** Increases the voltage   **E.** No change in the current

37. The electric field at point P due to a point charge of Q a distance R away has a magnitude of E. Which statement is true to double the magnitude of the field at P?

   A. Reduce the charge to $Q/2$
   B. Reduce the distance to R/2
   C. Double the distance to 2R while reducing the charge to $Q/2$
   D. Double the charge to $2Q$
   E. Double the charge to $2Q$ while reducing the distance to R/2

38. If 20% of the volume of a floating buoy is above the surface of a liquid, then the density of the buoy is what percent of the density of the surrounding liquid?

   A. 40%   **B.** 90%   **C.** 60%   **D.** 70%   **E.** 80%

39. A pipe of length L that is open at both ends is resonating at its fundamental frequency. Which statement about the sound is correct?

   A. The λ is $L/2$, and there is a displacement node at the midpoint of the pipe
   B. The λ is $L/2$, and there is a displacement antinode at the midpoint of the pipe
   C. The λ is $2L$, and there is a displacement node at the midpoint of the pipe
   D. The λ is $2L$, and there is a displacement antinode at the midpoint of the pipe
   E. The λ is $4L$, and there is a displacement node at the midpoint of the pipe

40. Wave interference occurs for:

   I. sound waves   II. water waves   III. light waves

   A. I only   **B.** II only   **C.** III only   **D.** I and III only   **E.** I, II and III

41. What is the value of the spring constant if a force of 30 N stretches a spring 0.75 m from equilibrium?

   A. 85 N/m   **B.** 25 N/m   **C.** 35 N/m   **D.** 40 N/m   **E.** 30 N/m

42. In a perfectly inelastic collision, two moving objects of unequal mass (A and B) collide and immediately come to rest. Before colliding, object A was traveling at speed 5 times that of object B. Which is the ratio of the mass of object A to that of object B?

    A. 50 : 1   **B.** 5 : 1   **C.** 1 : 5   **D.** 1 : 50   **E.** $\sqrt{5}$: 1

43. If the mass of an object does not change, a constant net force on the object produces constant:

    I. velocity   II. acceleration   III. speed

    A. I only   **B.** II only   **C.** III only   **D.** I and II only   **E.** I and III only

44. A chestnut falls straight down from a chestnut tree growing on a 20° slope. What is the component of the chestnut's impact velocity parallel to the ground if it hits the ground with a speed of 16 m/s?

    A. 5.5 m/s   **B.** 8.6 m/s   **C.** 4.1 m/s   **D.** 11.4 m/s   **E.** 10.6 m/s

45. In a given reversible process, the temperature of an ideal gas is kept constant as the gas is compressed to a smaller volume. Which statement is correct?

    A. The process is adiabatic   **C.** The gas releases heat to its surroundings
    B. The pressure remains constant   **D.** The gas absorbs heat from its surroundings
                                     E. None of the above

46. A heavy pile driver starting from rest smashes into a pile with a force that depends on the:

    I. distance the pile driver falls
    II. initial potential energy of the driver
    III. initial height of the driver

    A. I only   **B.** II only   **C.** III only   **D.** I and III only   **E.** I, II and III

47. Which of the following is an accurate statement?

    A. The fundamental frequency is the highest frequency at which a system naturally vibrates
    B. The air in an organ pipe can vibrate at an infinite number of frequencies
    C. A system, like a vibrating string, has only one possible frequency
    D. For a singer to break a wine glass by singing, the amplitude of sound must be greater than the amplitude of vibration for a wine glass
    E. None of the above

48. The unit used to measure electrical resistance is:

    A. watts   **B.** ohms   **C.** AC   **D.** volts   **E.** amps

49. A myopic girl wears eyeglasses that allow her to have clear distant vision. The power of the lenses of her eyeglasses is –3 diopters. Without eyeglasses, the far point of the girl is:

A. 0.32 m   **B.** 0.17 m   **C.** 0.75 m   **D.** 0.33 m   **E.** 0.50 m

50. A woman starts her car from rest and accelerates at a constant 2.5 m/s^2 for 8 s to get to her cruising speed. What is her velocity 8 s after beginning her trip?

A. 1.8 m/s   **B.** 5.5 m/s   **C.** 12.5 m/s   **D.** 7.5 m/s   **E.** 20 m/s

51. What is the velocity of the cars immediately after impact for a perfectly inelastic collision between a 2,500 kg car moving North at 7 m/s and a 2,000 kg car moving South at 14 m/s?

A. 2.3 m/s S   **B.** 9.4 m/s S   **C.** 5.4 m/s N   **D.** 9.4 m/s N   **E.** 11 m/s N

52. Grandfather clocks are designed so they can be adjusted by moving the weight at the bottom of the pendulum up or down. Suppose a grandfather clock is running slow. Which of the following adjustments of the weight would make it more accurate?

A. Move weight down   **C.** Remove half the mass from the weight
B. Move weight up   **D.** Add double the mass to the weight
E. Increase the amplitude of swing by a significant amount

53. Why does the paper rise when the air is blown above a paper strip?

A. Air above the paper moves slower, while the pressure remains constant
B. Air above the paper moves slower, and the pressure is higher
C. Air above the paper moves faster, while the pressure remains constant
D. Air above the paper moves slower, and the pressure is lower
E. Air above the paper moves faster, and the pressure is lower

54. If the internal resistance of the battery is 20 Ω, what current flows in a 4 V battery if the circuit is shorted?

A. 5 A   **B.** 3.2 A   **C.** 80 A   **D.** 0.2 A   **E.** 7.3 A

55. Three solid, uniform, cylindrically shaped flywheels, each of mass 65.0 kg and radius 1.47 m, rotate independently around a common axis. Two of the flywheels rotate in one direction at 3.83 rad/s; the other rotates in the opposite direction at 3.42 rad/s. What is the magnitude of the net angular momentum of the system?

A. 168.0 kg·m^2/s   **C.** 456.0 kg·m^2/s
B. 298.0 kg·m^2/s   **D.** 622.0 kg·m^2/s   **E.** 882.0 kg·m^2/s

56. A glass flask has a volume of 450 ml at a temperature of 22 °C. The flask contains 442 ml of mercury at an equilibrium temperature of 22 °C. The temperature is raised until the mercury reaches the 450 ml reference mark. What is the temperature at which this occurs? (Use the coefficients of volume expansion α of mercury = 18×10^{-5} K^{-1} and α of glass = 2×10^{-5} K^{-1})

   A. 103 °C   **B.** 152 °C   **C.** 92 °C   **D.** 135 °C   **E.** 116 °C

57. Which graph represents a constant positive acceleration?

  I.    II.    III.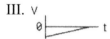

   A. I only   **B.** II only   **C.** III only   **D.** II and III only   **E.** I, II and III

58. A Ferrari accelerates from 0 to 100 km/h in 4.8 s. What force does a 68 kg passenger experience during the acceleration?

   A. 342 N   **B.** 311 N   **C.** 394 N   **D.** 82.0 N   **E.** 7 N

59. What happens to an object if a constant net torque is applied?

   A. Rotates with increasing angular acceleration
   B. Rotates with constant angular acceleration
   C. Rotates with constant angular velocity
   D. Rotates with increasing linear velocity
   E. Increases its moment of inertia

60. What is the focal length of a lens if a candle is placed at a distance of 4 m from the lens and the image is 2 m from the other side of the lens?

   A. –2 m   **B.** –4/3 m   **C.** 3/4 m   **D.** 2 m   **E.** 4/3 m

---

Check your answers using the answer key. Then, go to the explanations section and review the explanations in detail, paying particular attention to questions you didn't answer correctly or marked for review. Note the topic that those questions belong to.

We recommend that you do this BEFORE taking the next Diagnostic Test.

Diagnostic Test #2

Answer Sheet

#	Answer:					Mark for review	#	Answer:					Mark for review
1:	A	B	C	D	E	___	31:	A	B	C	D	E	___
2:	A	B	C	D	E	___	32:	A	B	C	D	E	___
3:	A	B	C	D	E	___	33:	A	B	C	D	E	___
4:	A	B	C	D	E	___	34:	A	B	C	D	E	___
5:	A	B	C	D	E	___	35:	A	B	C	D	E	___
6:	A	B	C	D	E	___	36:	A	B	C	D	E	___
7:	A	B	C	D	E	___	37:	A	B	C	D	E	___
8:	A	B	C	D	E	___	38:	A	B	C	D	E	___
9:	A	B	C	D	E	___	39:	A	B	C	D	E	___
10:	A	B	C	D	E	___	40:	A	B	C	D	E	___
11:	A	B	C	D	E	___	41:	A	B	C	D	E	___
12:	A	B	C	D	E	___	42:	A	B	C	D	E	___
13:	A	B	C	D	E	___	43:	A	B	C	D	E	___
14:	A	B	C	D	E	___	44:	A	B	C	D	E	___
15:	A	B	C	D	E	___	45:	A	B	C	D	E	___
16:	A	B	C	D	E	___	46:	A	B	C	D	E	___
17:	A	B	C	D	E	___	47:	A	B	C	D	E	___
18:	A	B	C	D	E	___	48:	A	B	C	D	E	___
19:	A	B	C	D	E	___	49:	A	B	C	D	E	___
20:	A	B	C	D	E	___	50:	A	B	C	D	E	___
21:	A	B	C	D	E	___	51:	A	B	C	D	E	___
22:	A	B	C	D	E	___	52:	A	B	C	D	E	___
23:	A	B	C	D	E	___	53:	A	B	C	D	E	___
24:	A	B	C	D	E	___	54:	A	B	C	D	E	___
25:	A	B	C	D	E	___	55:	A	B	C	D	E	___
26:	A	B	C	D	E	___	56:	A	B	C	D	E	___
27:	A	B	C	D	E	___	57:	A	B	C	D	E	___
28:	A	B	C	D	E	___	58:	A	B	C	D	E	___
29:	A	B	C	D	E	___	59:	A	B	C	D	E	___
30:	A	B	C	D	E	___	60:	A	B	C	D	E	___

This Diagnostic Test is designed for you to assess your proficiency on each topic and NOT to mimic the actual test. Use your test results and identify areas of your strength and weakness to adjust your study plan and enhance your fundamental knowledge.

The length of the Diagnostic Tests is proven to be optimal for a single study session.

1. Ignoring air resistance, if it takes 16 s for a package to strike the ground, how high above the ground was the package when it was thrown upward from a stationary helicopter at 15 m/s? (Use the acceleration due to gravity $g = 10$ m/s^2)

   A. 920 m   **B.** 740 m   **C.** 1,400 m   **D.** 1,040 m   **E.** 1,800 m

2. What is the mass of the car if a tow truck exerts a force of 3,000 N on a car and accelerates it at 2 m/s^2?

   A. 500 kg   **B.** 1,000 kg   **C.** 1,500 kg   **D.** 2,000 kg   **E.** None of the above

3. A bimetallic strip, consisting of metal A on the top and metal B on the bottom, is rigidly attached to a wall at the left, as shown. The coefficient of linear thermal expansion of metal A is greater than that of metal B. Which statement is true if the strip is heated uniformly?

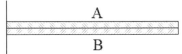

   A. remains horizontal, but increases in length   **C.** curves upward
   B. remains horizontal, but decreases in length   **D.** curves downward
       E. bends in the middle

4. A massless, ideal spring has a spring constant of 4,600 N/m as it hangs from the ceiling. By how much does its potential energy increase if a 30 kg mass is attached to it? (Use the acceleration due to gravity $g = 10$ m/s^2)

   A. 9.8 J   **B.** 6.3 J   **C.** 19.4 J   **D.** 12.4 J   **E.** 4.3 J

5. What is the speed of a water wave if a floating object oscillates up and down two complete cycles in 1 s as the water wave with a wavelength of 6 m passes?

   A. 1 m/s   **B.** 0.17 m/s   **C.** 12 m/s   **D.** 18 m/s   **E.** 3 m/s

6. By what value does the sound level of a wave decrease if the intensity of the sound wave decreases by a factor of 10?

   A. 0.1 dB   **B.** 10 dB   **C.** 1 dB   **D.** 100 dB   **E.** 0.01 dB

7. A piece of wood is floating in a bathtub. A second piece of wood sits on top of the first piece and does not touch the water. If the top piece is taken off and placed in the water, what happens to the water level in the tub?

   A. It remains the same   **C.** It increases
   B. It decreases   **D.** Requires the volumes of the two pieces of wood
       E. Requires the densities of the two pieces of wood

8. A point charge Q_1 has a charge of -1 μC. What is the number of excess electrons in charge Q_1? (Use the charge of an electron $e = -1.60 \times 10^{-19}$ C)

 A. 2×10^{11} **B.** 2×10^{12} **C.** 6.3×10^{12} **D.** 6.3×10^{13} **E.** 2×10^{13}

9. The capacitance of a capacitor depends on its:

  I. energy stored   II. charge   III. potential difference across it

 A. I only   **C.** II and III only

 B. II only   **D.** I and III only   **E.** none of the above

10. What is the radius of curvature for a flat plane mirror?

 A. Imaginary   **B.** Zero   **C.** Infinite   **D.** Negative   **E.** Undefined

11. A cylinder and a sphere are released simultaneously at the top of an inclined plane. Which reaches the bottom first if they roll down the inclined plane without slipping?

 A. The one of smallest diameter   **C.** The disk

 B. The one of greatest mass   **D.** The sphere

               E. They reach the bottom at the same time

12. Consider two uniform solid spheres where both have the same diameter, but one has twice the mass of the other. What is the ratio of the larger moment of inertia to the smaller?

 A. $\sqrt{2} : 1$ **B.** $4 : 1$ **C.** $10 : 1$ **D.** $2 : 1$ **E.** $16 : 1$

13. Using 1,000 J of work, an elevator is raised from the ground to the second floor in 40 s. How much power does the elevator use?

 A. 100 W   **B.** 25 W   **C.** 50 W   **D.** 1,000 W   **E.** 200 W

14. A ball is attached to an ideal spring and oscillates with a period T. What is the new period that is produced if the mass of the ball is doubled?

 A. $T\sqrt{2}$ **B.** T   **C.** T/2   **D.** 2T   **E.** $T/\sqrt{2}$

15. Larry drops a mailing tube to the floor, and the tube produces a musical note. The mailing tube is 1.5 m long with a cylindrical cross-sectional diameter of 3.5 cm. It is sealed at one end and open at the other. What is the wavelength of the third harmonic? (Use speed of sound in air $v = 340$ m/s)

 A. 1.5 m   **B.** 2 m   **C.** 3.5 m   **D.** 4 m   **E.** 7.5 m

16. A compressed gas with a total mass of 115 kg is stored in a spherical container that has a radius of 0.6 m. What is the density of the compressed gas?

   A. 147 kg/m³   **B.** 183 kg/m³   **C.** 151 kg/m³   **D.** 127 kg/m³   **E.** 267 kg/m³

17. Electrons are made to flow in a wire when there is:

      I. a potential difference across its ends
      II. an imbalance between positive and negative charges in the wire
      III. more final kinetic energy than initial kinetic energy in the wire

   A. I only   **B.** II only   **C.** III only   **D.** I and II only   **E.** I and III only

18. A Coulomb per second is the same as a(n):

   A. Newton   **C.** ampere
   B. volt-second   **D.** watt   **E.** volt per second

19. What is observed when an object is placed exactly at its center of curvature in front of a concave mirror?

   A. The image is not seen because it is focused at a different distance
   B. The image is seen, but it appears smaller
   C. The image is seen, but it appears larger
   D. The image is seen as the same size, and it is upright
   E. The image is seen as the same size, but it is inverted

20. What is the angular speed of a flywheel turning at 813.0 rpm?

   A. 8.33 rad/s   **C.** 33.84 rad/s
   B. 56.23 rad/s   **D.** 85.14 rad/s   **E.** 116.48 rad/s

21. The process shown on the pressure vs. volume diagram represents which type of expansion?

   A. Isobaric
   B. Isometric
   C. Isothermal
   D. Adiabatic
   E. Isochoric

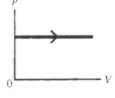

22. A block is on a frictionless table on Earth. The block accelerates at 4 m/s² when a 20 N horizontal force is applied to it. The block and table are then set up on the Moon where the acceleration due to gravity is 1.62 m/s². What is the weight of the block on the Moon?

   A. 11 N   **B.** 9.7 N   **C.** 5.6 N   **D.** 6.2 N   **E.** 8.1 N

23. In the figure, the frequency is:

A. 2 Hz
B. 4 Hz
C. 0.5 Hz
D. 1 Hz
E. 1.5 Hz

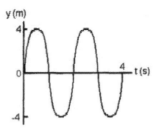

24. Consider a very small hole in the bottom of a tank that is 18 cm in diameter and is filled with water to a height of 80 cm. What is the speed at which the water exits the tank through the hole? (Use the acceleration due to gravity $g = 9.8$ m/s^2)

A. 4 m/s   B. 17 m/s   C. 42 m/s   D. 36 m/s   E. 7 m/s

25. Two charges, $Q_1 = 3.4 \times 10^{-10}$ C and $Q_2 = 6.8 \times 10^{-9}$ C, are separated by a distance of 1 cm. Let F_1 be the magnitude of the electrostatic force felt by Q_1 due to Q_2 and let F_2 be the magnitude of the electrostatic force felt by Q_2 due to Q_1. What is the ratio of F_1 / F_2?

A. 2   B. 1   C. 16   D. 8   E. 4

26. A component with an 18 Ω resistor is rated for use at power levels not exceeding 16 W. How much current can safely flow through the component?

A. 0.12 A   B. 2.8 A   C. 1.31 A   D. 0.94 A   E. 12.1 A

27. How are the wavelength and frequency of light related?

A. Wavelength increases as the frequency increases
B. Wavelength increases as the frequency decreases
C. Wavelength is one-fourth of the frequency
D. Wavelength is four times the frequency
E. Wavelength is not related to the frequency

28. What is the approximate wavelength of a wave that has a speed of 360 m/s and a period of 4.2 s?

A. 85.7 m   B. 1.86 m   C. 1,512 m   D. 288.6 m   E. 422.1 m

29. A merry-go-round is 18 m in diameter with a child sitting on the outer edge. If the merry-go-round makes 8.3 rev/min, what is the velocity of the child?

A. 1.9 m/s   B. 7.8 m/s   C. 3.9 m/s   D. 14.6 m/s   E. 18.3 m/s

30. What is the magnitude of the instantaneous force with which a ball hits a bat if a batter hits a ball pitched with a 1,700 N instantaneous force?

A. Greater than 1,700 N

B. Zero

C. Equal to $\sqrt{1,700}$ N

D. Less than 1,700 N

E. Equal to 1,700 N

31. A 2.8 kg block, moving on a frictionless surface with a speed (v_i) of 8.5 m/s, makes a perfectly elastic collision with a block of mass m at rest. After the collision, the 2.8 kg block recoils with a speed (v_f) of 1.1 m/s. What is the mass of block m?

A. 22.8 kg   **B.** 14.4 kg   **C.** 17.8 kg   **D.** 3.6 kg   **E.** 12.2 kg

32. If the height of a frictionless incline is h, determine the work done by the force due to gravity F as the crate of mass m slides down the incline.

A. $mgh \sin^2$ **B.** mgh **C.** $mgh \cos^2$ **D.** $mgh \sin$ **E.** $mgh \tan$

33. What is the speed of a wave if it has a wavelength of 25 cm and a frequency of 1.6 kHz?

A. 400 m/s   **B.** 1,400 m/s   **C.** 0.4 m/s   **D.** 14 m/s   **E.** 28 m/s

34. A glass beaker of unknown mass contains 60 ml of water. The system absorbs 2,200 cals of heat, and the temperature rises 25 °C as a result. What is the mass of the beaker? (Use specific heat for glass = 0.18 cal/g·°C and specific heat for water = 1.0 cal/g·°C)

A. 675 g   **B.** 540 g   **C.** 460 g   **D.** 370 g   **E.** 156 g

35. What is the radius of curvature for a concave mirror with a focal length of 20 cm?

A. 20 cm   **B.** –40 cm   **C.** 40 cm   **D.** 10 cm   **E.** –20 cm

36. What is the power dissipated in the 2 Ω resistor in the circuit?

A. 6.3 W

B. 5.7 W

C. 3.5 W

D. 7.8 W

E. 8.5 W

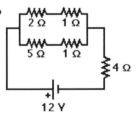

37. What causes an object to become electrostatically charged?

A. Charge is created

B. Protons are transferred

C. Electrons are transferred

D. Protons, and electrons are transferred

E. Charge is destroyed

38. What is the gauge pressure 10 m below the surface of the ocean? (Use the acceleration due to gravity $g = 9.8$ m/s^2, the density of water $\rho = 10^3$ kg/m^3 and $P_{atm} = 1.01 \times 10^5$ Pa)

A. 1.4×10^5 Pa　　　　**C.** 9.8×10^4 Pa

B. 2.3×10^5 Pa　　　　**D.** 6.5×10^4 Pa　　　　**E.** 5×10^6 Pa

39. If a 75 cm string, which is fixed at both ends between two adjacent nodes, supports a standing wave, what is the wavelength λ?

A. 15 cm　　　**B.** 300 cm　　　**C.** 7.5 cm　　　**D.** 200 cm　　　**E.** 150 cm

40. The speed of sound in steel is 4,900 m/s. What is the wavelength of a sound wave in the steel of frequency 640 Hz?

A. 1.3 m　　　**B.** 0.83 m　　　**C.** 7.7 m　　　**D.** 4.2 m　　　**E.** 2.6 m

41. Ignoring the force of friction, what is the work done by Stacey when she carries a 15 kg mass and walks along the *x*-axis for a distance of 100 m with a constant velocity of 2.5 m/s?

A. 0 J　　　**B.** 5 J　　　**C.** 30 J　　　**D.** 50 J　　　**E.** 450 J

42. Hannah is in karate and delivers a swift blow to sever a cement block in two with her bare hand. The magnitude is the same for the:

　　　I. time of impact on both the block and Hannah's hand
　　　II. force on both the block and Hannah's hand
　　　III. impulse on both the block and Hannah's hand

A. I only　　　**B.** II only　　　**C.** III only　　　**D.** I and III only　　　**E.** I, II and III

43. Karen is driving a car along a road when she realizes, almost too late, that she needs to make a left-hand turn. Karen quickly turns the car's steering wheel, and the textbooks that were in the passenger seat go crashing against the passenger door. Which of the following are true?

　　　I. The textbooks were pushed against the door by a centrifugal force
　　　II. The textbooks were pushed against the door by a centripetal force
　　　III. The forces acting on the textbooks when they crashed against the door were
　　　　　gravity, the normal force and a force toward the right

A. I and III only　　　　**C.** III only

B. II and III only　　　　**D.** I, II and III　　　**E.** None of the above

44. How far does a car travel while accelerating if it accelerates from 5 m/s to 21 m/s at a rate of 4 m/s^2?

A. 112 m　　　**B.** 35 m　　　**C.** 71 m　　　**D.** 52 m　　　**E.** 153 m

45. The coefficient of linear expansion of lead is $30 \times 10^{-6} \, K^{-1}$. What change in temperature causes a 10 m long lead bar to change in length by 3 mm?

   A. 7.5 K   **B.** 20 K   **C.** 10 K   **D.** 5 K   **E.** 40 K

46. A constant force of 10 N is applied horizontally for 15 s on a 2 kg toy cart so that the cart begins to move along the level frictionless floor. What is the kinetic energy of the cart just after the 15 s?

   A. 1,540 J   **B.** 2,300 J   **C.** 3,450 J   **D.** 2,985 J   **E.** 5,625 J

47. Mary has tuned the B string of a guitar to the fundamental frequency of an E (680 Hz). The E string is left untuned. When she plucks the B string and the untuned E string together, she hears a note that changes from loud to soft to loud twice per second. What is an allowable fundamental f on the untuned E string?

   A. 2 Hz   **B.** 340 Hz   **C.** 680 Hz   **D.** 682 Hz   **E.** 1,360 Hz

48. A positive reaction charge Q is held fixed at the origin. A positive charge q is on the positive x-axis and released. Assuming no friction, which statement describes the theoretical acceleration of q after its release?

   A. Decreases and then increases
   B. Remains constant for a while and then decreases, eventually reaching zero
   C. Decreases and eventually reaches zero
   D. Decreases forever, but never reaches zero
   E. Acceleration remains unchanged

49. Which statement about a single thin lens is correct?

   A. A diverging lens always produces a virtual upright image
   B. A converging lens sometimes produces a real upright image
   C. A diverging lens sometimes produces a virtual upright image
   D. A converging lens always produces a real upright image
   E. A diverging lens produces a virtual upright image only if the object is located between the lens and its focal point

50. What is the magnitude and direction of the combined vectors A and B if vector A has a length of 5 units and is directed to the North (N) while vector B has a length of 11 units and is directed to the South (S)?

   A. 16 units, S   **C.** 6 units, N
   B. 16 units, N   **D.** 6 units, S   **E.** 2.2 units, N

51. The conservation of momentum is most closely related to:

      I. Newton's First Law   II. Newton's Second Law   III. Newton's Third Law

  A. I only   **B.** II only   **C.** III only   **D.** I and II only   **E.** I and III only

52. At which point in a swinging pendulum's arc does it have the most energy?

      I. At its lowest point, it has the most potential energy
      II. The energy is the same at all points of the arc
      III. At its highest point, it has the most kinetic energy

  A. I only   **B.** II only   **C.** III only   **D.** I and II only   **E.** I and III only

53. If the amount of fluid flowing through a tube remains constant, how does the speed of the fluid change if the diameter of the tube increases from 3 cm to 8 cm?

  A. Increases by a factor of 5   **C.** Decreases by a factor of 5
  B. Increases by a factor of 9   **D.** Decreases by a factor of 7
                               E. Remains the same

54. Voltage can be induced in a wire by:

      I. changing the current in a nearby wire
      II. moving a magnet near the wire
      III. moving the wire near a magnet

  A. I only   **B.** II only   **C.** III only   **D.** II and III only   **E.** I, II and III

55. A machinist turns on the power on to a grinding wheel at time $t = 0$ s. The wheel accelerates uniformly from rest for 10.0 s and reaches the operating angular speed of 96.0 rad/s. The wheel is run at that angular velocity for 40.0 s and then power is shut off. The wheel slows down uniformly at 1.5 rad/s^2 until the wheel stops. For how long after the power is shut off does it take the wheel to stop?

  A. 56.0 s   **B.** 64.0 s   **C.** 72.0 s   **D.** 82.0 s   **E.** 90.0 s

56. A container of an ideal gas at standard temperature and pressure undergoes an isothermal expansion. How much work does it do if its entropy changes by 2.6 J/K? (Use standard temperature = 273 K and pressure = 1 atm)

  A. 1.4×10^3 J   **B.** -1×10^3 J   **C.** 7.1×10^2 J   **D.** 0 J   **E.** -1.4×10^3 J

57. Jack stands on a bridge and throws a rock straight down. The rock leaves Jack's hand at $t = 0$. Which of the graphs represents the velocity of the stone as a function of time?

A.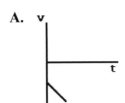

C.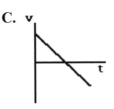

B.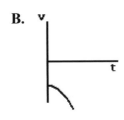

D.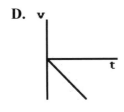

E.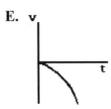

58. A 100 g ball of clay is thrown horizontally with a speed of 50 m/s toward a 900 g block resting on a frictionless surface. It hits the block and sticks. The clay exerts a constant force on the block during the 10 ms it takes for the clay to come to rest relative to the block. After 10 ms, the block and the clay are sliding along the surface as a single system. What is the force of the clay on the block during the collision?

  A. 500 N   **B.** 2,250 N   **C.** 5,400 N   **D.** 4,500 N   **E.** 450 N

59. Cart A (2 kg) and Cart B (2.5 kg) run along a frictionless, level, one-dimensional track. Cart B is initially at rest, and Cart A is traveling 0.6 m/s toward the right when it encounters Cart B. After the collision, Cart A is at rest. What is the final velocity of Cart B?

  A. 0.48 m/s   **B.** 0.36 m/s   **C.** 0.75 m/s   **D.** 0.64 m/s   **E.** 1.1 m/s

60. A girl of height h stands in front of a plane mirror. What must the minimum length of the mirror be so that she can view her entire body?

  A. ¼h **C.** ½h
  B. 2h **D.** h **E.** Depends on her distance from the mirror

---

Check your answers using the answer key. Then, go to the explanations section and review the explanations in detail, paying particular attention to questions you didn't answer correctly or marked for review. Note the topic that those questions belong to.

We recommend that you do this BEFORE taking the next Diagnostic Test.

Diagnostic Test #3

Answer Sheet

#	Answer:					Mark for review	#	Answer:					Mark for review
1:	A	B	C	D	E	___	31:	A	B	C	D	E	___
2:	A	B	C	D	E	___	32:	A	B	C	D	E	___
3:	A	B	C	D	E	___	33:	A	B	C	D	E	___
4:	A	B	C	D	E	___	34:	A	B	C	D	E	___
5:	A	B	C	D	E	___	35:	A	B	C	D	E	___
6:	A	B	C	D	E	___	36:	A	B	C	D	E	___
7:	A	B	C	D	E	___	37:	A	B	C	D	E	___
8:	A	B	C	D	E	___	38:	A	B	C	D	E	___
9:	A	B	C	D	E	___	39:	A	B	C	D	E	___
10:	A	B	C	D	E	___	40:	A	B	C	D	E	___
11:	A	B	C	D	E	___	41:	A	B	C	D	E	___
12:	A	B	C	D	E	___	42:	A	B	C	D	E	___
13:	A	B	C	D	E	___	43:	A	B	C	D	E	___
14:	A	B	C	D	E	___	44:	A	B	C	D	E	___
15:	A	B	C	D	E	___	45:	A	B	C	D	E	___
16:	A	B	C	D	E	___	46:	A	B	C	D	E	___
17:	A	B	C	D	E	___	47:	A	B	C	D	E	___
18:	A	B	C	D	E	___	48:	A	B	C	D	E	___
19:	A	B	C	D	E	___	49:	A	B	C	D	E	___
20:	A	B	C	D	E	___	50:	A	B	C	D	E	___
21:	A	B	C	D	E	___	51:	A	B	C	D	E	___
22:	A	B	C	D	E	___	52:	A	B	C	D	E	___
23:	A	B	C	D	E	___	53:	A	B	C	D	E	___
24:	A	B	C	D	E	___	54:	A	B	C	D	E	___
25:	A	B	C	D	E	___	55:	A	B	C	D	E	___
26:	A	B	C	D	E	___	56:	A	B	C	D	E	___
27:	A	B	C	D	E	___	57:	A	B	C	D	E	___
28:	A	B	C	D	E	___	58:	A	B	C	D	E	___
29:	A	B	C	D	E	___	59:	A	B	C	D	E	___
30:	A	B	C	D	E	___	60:	A	B	C	D	E	___

This Diagnostic Test is designed for you to assess your proficiency on each topic and NOT to mimic the actual test. Use your test results and identify areas of your strength and weakness to adjust your study plan and enhance your fundamental knowledge.

The length of the Diagnostic Tests is proven to be optimal for a single study session.

1. A baseball is projected upward at time $t = 0$ s, from a point 60 m above the ground with an initial velocity of 28.4 m/s. The baseball rises, then falls and strikes the ground. Consider the upward direction as positive. What is the acceleration of the baseball at time $t = 4.3$ s? (Use the acceleration due to gravity $g = 10$ m/s^2)

    A. −5 m/s^2 **B.** 10 m/s^2 **C.** 5 m/s^2 **D.** 0 m/s^2 **E.** −10 m/s^2

2. A 110 kg block is released from rest at the height of 1 m (as shown). What is the mass of the block on the left if it takes 0.95 s for the 110 kg block to reach the floor? (Use acceleration due to gravity $g = 9.8$ m/s^2)

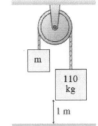

    A. 38 kg   **C.** 56 kg

    B. 81 kg   **D.** 70 kg   **E.** 63 kg

3. An adiabatic and isothermal process are shown on the pressure vs. volume diagram. Which is the isothermal process?

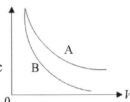

    I. Process A

    II. Process B

    III. Requires knowing if the gas is monatomic or diatomic

    A. I only   **C.** III only

    B. II only   **D.** I and II only   **E.** None are correct

4. A 3 kg cat leaps from a ledge to the ground, which is a distance of 4 meters. What is its velocity just before it strikes the ground? (Use the acceleration due to gravity $g = 10$ m/s^2)

    A. 8 m/s   **B.** 3 m/s   **C.** 9 m/s   **D.** 16 m/s   **E.** 4 m/s

5. A massless, ideal spring is projected horizontally from a wall and is connected to a 0.3 kg mass. The mass is oscillating in one dimension, such that it moves 0.5 m from one end of its oscillation to the other. What is the frequency of the oscillation if it undergoes 10 complete oscillations in 60 s?

    A. 0.17 Hz   **B.** 3.9 Hz   **C.** 3.1 Hz   **D.** 11.2 Hz   **E.** 17.6 Hz

6. An organ pipe is a cylindrical tube open at both ends. The air column is set to vibrate by air flowing through the lower portion of the pipe. The length of the pipe is 0.1 m, and the diameter is 0.2 m. What is the frequency of the fundamental? (Use the velocity of sound $v = 340$ m/s)

    A. 300 Hz   **B.** 600 Hz   **C.** 1,700 Hz   **D.** 800 Hz   **E.** 1,200 Hz

7. A 12-liter volume of oil is subjected to pressure which produces a volume strain of -3×10^{-4}. The bulk modulus of the oil is 6.3×10^9 Pa and is independent of the pressure. What is the change in the pressure of the oil? (Use the conversion of 1 atm = 10^5 Pa)

    A. 26 atm   **B.** 4 atm   **C.** 7 atm   **D.** 19 atm   **E.** 13 atm

8. A charged parallel plate capacitor has, between the plates, an electric field (E_0). $^{20}F^-$ and $^{35}Cl^-$ ions are placed between the plates. The $^{20}F^-$ experiences a force of F_F, and the $^{35}Cl^-$ experiences a force F_{Cl}. Ignoring the force of gravity, how do these forces compare? (Use the charge of a proton $q_p = 1.6 \times 10^{-19}$ C)

    A. $F_{Cl} = 35/9\ F_F$ **C.** $F_{Cl} = F_F$

    B. $F_{Cl} = 4\ F_F$ **D.** $F_{Cl} = 35/36\ F_F$ **E.** $F_{Cl} = 36/9\ F_F$

9. How much power is dissipated by a device that experiences a voltage drop of 4 V across it, while a current of 4 mA flows through it?

    A. 1.8×10^3 W   **C.** 6.4×10^{-3} W

    B. 1.6×10^{-2} W   **D.** 4×10^3 W   **E.** 1.1×10^{-3} W

10. A light ray in glass arrives at the glass-water interface at an angle of $\theta = 48°$ with the normal. The refracted ray in water makes an angle of $\phi = 72°$ with respect to the normal. What is the new angle of refraction ϕ in the water if the angle of incidence is changed to $\theta = 37°$? (Use the index of refraction for water n = 1.33)

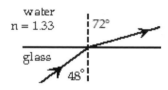

    A. 43°   **B.** 55°   **C.** 37°   **D.** 59°   **E.** 50°

11. A futuristic design for a car is to have a large disk-like flywheel within the car storing kinetic energy. The flywheel has mass 370.0 kg with a radius of 0.500 m and can rotate up to 200.0 rev/s. Assuming all of this stored kinetic energy could be transferred to the linear velocity of the 1500.0-kg car, what is the maximum attainable speed of the car?

    A. 29.6 m/s   **B.** 88.4 m/s   **C.** 162 m/s   **D.** 221 m/s   **E.** 318 m/s

12. After accelerating uniformly from rest at a rate of 3 m/s² for 4 seconds, a 2 kg object collides head-on with a stationary 1 kg object. After the completely inelastic collision, what is the velocity of the two objects?

    A. 6 m/s   **B.** 8 m/s   **C.** 12 m/s   **D.** 10 m/s   **E.** 4 m/s

13. A vertical, hanging spring stretches by 20 cm when a 120 N object is attached. What is the weight of a ball that stretches the spring by 44 cm?

    A. 264 N   **B.** 93 N   **C.** 305 N   **D.** 156 N   **E.** 411 N

14. An object is attached to a vertical spring and bobs up and down between points A and B. Where is the object located when its elastic potential energy is a maximum?

    A. One-fourth of the way between A and B   **C.** Midway between A and B
    B. One-third of the way between A and B   **D.** At either A or B
                                          E. At none of the above points

15. Three tones (D, E and F) are played two at a time. When tones D and E, or when tones E and F, are played together, the beat frequency of 3 Hz is heard in either case. What is the beat frequency when tones D and F are played together?

    A. 0 Hz or 3 Hz   **C.** 3 Hz or 6 Hz
    B. 0 Hz or 6 Hz   **D.** 0 Hz, 3 Hz or 6 Hz   **E.** 0 Hz or 1.5 Hz

16. An ideal, incompressible fluid flows steadily through a pipe that has a change in diameter. The fluid speed at a location where the pipe's diameter is 9 cm is 1.5 m/s. When the diameter narrows to 3 cm, what is the fluid speed at that point location?

    A. 0.72 m/s   **C.** 1.3 m/s
    B. 6.9 m/s   **D.** 21.2 m/s   **E.** 13.5 m/s

17. Suppose a van de Graaff generator builds a negative static charge, and a grounded conductor is placed near enough to it so that 9 μC of negative charge arcs to the conductor. What is the number of electrons that are transferred? (Use Coulomb's constant $k = 9 \times 10^9$ N·m^2/C^2 and charge of an electron = 1.6×10^{-19} C)

    A. 1.6×10^{18} electrons   **C.** 5.6×10^{13} electrons
    B. 43.8×10^{12} electrons   **D.** 7 electrons
                                          E. 4.1×10^{20} electrons

18. Four 6 V batteries are connected in series to power light bulbs A and B in series. The resistance of light bulb A is 60 Ω and the resistance of light bulb B is 30 Ω. How does the voltage drop across light bulb A compare to the voltage drop across light bulb B?

    A. It is greater by a factor of 2   **C.** It is smaller by a factor of 2
    B. It is the same   **D.** It is smaller by a factor of 4
                                          E. It is greater by a factor of 4

19. Is it possible to see a virtual image?

  A. Yes, because the rays that appear to come from a virtual image can be focused on the retina just like those from a real object

  B. Yes, because most objects are virtual since they do not emit light, but only reflect light from another source

  C. No, because virtual images don't exist

  D. No, because the rays that seem to come from a virtual image do not originate from the image

  E. Yes, but only indirectly if the virtual image is formed in a mirror

20. An electrical motor spins at a constant 2,695.0 rpm. If the rotor radius is 7.165 cm what is the linear acceleration of the edge of the rotor?

  A. 707.0 m/s^2 **C.** 3,272 m/s^2

  B. 1,280 m/s^2 **D.** 4,028 m/s^2 **E.** 5,707 m/s^2

21. A substance has a density of 1,800 kg/m^3 in the liquid state. At atmospheric pressure, the substance has a boiling point of 180 °C and a heat of vaporization of 1.4×10^5 J/kg. The vapor has a density of 4 kg/m^3 at the boiling point at atmospheric pressure. What is the work done by 2 kg of the substance, as it vaporizes at atmospheric pressure? (Use atmospheric pressure = 1×10^5 Pa = 1×10^5 N/m^2)

  A. 20 kJ   **B.** 50 kJ   **C.** 10 kJ   **D.** 30 kJ   **E.** 60 kJ

22. An object is dropped from a helicopter. When it reaches terminal velocity, the:

  A. net force is zero

  B. net force reaches its maximum negative value

  C. force of gravity is greater than the force of air resistance

  D. acceleration reaches its maximum value

  E. acceleration decreases

23. A taut 2 m string is fixed at both ends and plucked. If the fundamental has wavelength λ_1, and the second harmonic has wavelength λ_2, what is the ratio λ_1 / λ_2?

  A. 0.5   **B.** 1.5   **C.** 2   **D.** 4   **E.** 3.5

24. A pipe with a 3 cm radius carries water at a velocity of 4 m/s. What is the volume flow rate?

  A. 1.1×10^{-2} m^3/s   **C.** 7.5×10^{-3} m^3/s

  B. 48 m^3/s   **D.** 2.7×10^2 m^3/s   **E.** 4.3 m^3/s

25. Two charged objects attract each other with a certain force. If the charges on both objects are doubled with no change in separation, what is the force between them?

A. Quadruples
B. Halves

C. Doubles
D. Becomes zero
E. Requires knowing the distance between them

26. A proton with speed 2.5×10^5 m/s goes through a potential difference of 110 volts, gaining speed. What is the speed reached? (Use the mass of a proton = 1.67×10^{-27} kg and the charge of a proton = 1.6×10^{-19} C)

A. 4.8×10^5 m/s
B. 8.3×10^5 m/s

C. 4.6×10^5 m/s
D. 2.9×10^5 m/s

E. 1.7×10^6 m/s

27. When light travels from air into water, its:

A. frequency changes, but its velocity and wavelength remain the same
B. velocity and wavelength change, but its frequency remains the same
C. velocity, wavelength, and frequency all change
D. velocity and frequency change, but its wavelength remains the same
E. wavelength and frequency change, but its velocity remains the same

28. The displacement of a vibrating tuning fork and the resulting sound wave is related to:

A. period
B. wavelength

C. resonance
D. frequency

E. amplitude

29. A projectile is fired from the top of a cliff with the height $y = 20$ m. The initial velocity components are $v_{ix} = 480$ m/s and $v_{iy} = 32$ m/s. The projectile reaches a maximum height at point P, then falls and strikes the ground at point Q. What is the y component of velocity of the projectile at point P?

A. 70 m/s
B. −40 m/s

C. −70 m/s
D. 40 m/s

E. zero

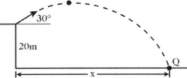

30. An 81 kg mass is affixed to a point on a frictionless table by a massless string with a length of 1.3 m. How long does it take for the mass to make one complete revolution if, while the mass moves in a uniform circle on the table, the tension in the string is 55 N?

A. 6.2 s   B. 8.7 s   C. 9.6 s   D. 7.1 s   E. 3.7 s

31. A 5,000 kg train collides with a stationary 10,000 kg train. The trains stick together upon collision and move with a speed of 3.5 m/s. What was the initial speed of the 5,000 kg train?

A. 1.75 m/s   B. 5 m/s   C. 10.5 m/s   D. 18.5 m/s   E. 15 m/s

32. Ingrid pulls on the strap of a suitcase at an angle 32° above the horizontal. What is the tension in the strap if 880 J of work are done by the strap while moving the suitcase a horizontal distance of 14 m?

    A. 66 N   **B.** 86 N   **C.** 59 N   **D.** 74 N   **E.** 32 N

33. The rotation of the Earth was demonstrated using a 12 m long pendulum. How long does it take for the pendulum to make one complete cycle? (Use acceleration due to gravity $g = 9.8$ m/s^2)

    A. 2.4 s   **B.** 1.8 s   **C.** 5.4 s   **D.** 8.6 s   **E.** 6.9 s

34. 200 kcal of heat raises the temperature of 3 kg of material by 90 °C. What is the material's specific heat capacity?

    A. 0.74 kcal/kg·°C   **C.** 1.42 kcal/kg·°C
    B. 0.33 kcal/kg·°C   **D.** 1.13 kcal/kg·°C   **E.** 0.14 kcal/kg·°C

35. A convex lens has focal length *f*. If an object is placed at a distance beyond 2*f* from the lens on the principal axis, the image is located at a distance from the lens:

    A. between the lens and *f*   **C.** between *f* and 2*f*
    B. of *f*   **D.** of 2*f*   **E.** of infinity

36. The heating element of a 360 W toaster is a long wire of a metal alloy, which heats up when a 120 V potential difference is applied across it. What is the resistance of such a toaster?

    A. 1.4 Ω   **C.** 6.4×10^{-1} Ω
    B. 26 Ω   **D.** 2.8×10^{-1} Ω   **E.** 40 Ω

37. If the distance between two electrostatic charges is doubled, how is the force between them affected?

    A. Increases by 2   **C.** Decreases by √2
    B. Increases by 4   **D.** Decreases by 4   **E.** Remains the same

38. Reynold's number is given by Re $= L\rho v / \mu$, where L is some characteristic length related to the path that the fluid travels (e.g., the length or diameter of the pipe), ρ is the density of the fluid, v is the velocity of the fluid, and μ is the viscosity. A larger Reynold's number for a given flow indicates the increased likelihood of developing turbulence. For water flowing in a pipe, which might reduce the likelihood of turbulent flow?

    A. Raising the temperature   **C.** Increasing the flow rate
    B. Increasing the radius of the pipe   **D.** Increasing the viscosity
                                          E. None of the above

39. A taut 3 m string is fixed at both ends and plucked. The speed of waves on this string is 3×10^4 m/s. If the fundamental has a frequency of f_1, and the second harmonic has a frequency of f_2, what is the ratio f_1 / f_2?

   A. 0.5   **B.** 1   **C.** 2.5   **D.** 4   **E.** 5

40. A fisherman fishing from a pier observes that the float on his line bobs from the highest point to the lowest in 2.4 s. He estimates that the distance between adjacent wave crests is 48 m. At what speed are the waves passing the pier?

   A. 10 m/s   **B.** 5 m/s   **C.** 1 m/s   **D.** 25 m/s   **E.** 40 m/s

41. A 1,500 kg car is moving at 25 m/s on a level road and the driver slams on the brakes. The skid marks are 30 m long. What is the force of the road on the car if the force is constant during the stop?

   A. 1,100 N   **B.** 4,440 N   **C.** 9,250 N   **D.** 18,460 N   **E.** 15,625 N

42. A 0.10-kg baseball is thrown with a velocity of 30 m/s towards a batter. How long are the bat and ball in contact if the batter strikes the baseball with an average force of 5,000 N that results in a velocity of 35 m/s in the opposite direction?

   A. 5.3×10^{-3} s   **C.** 1.2×10^{-2} s

   B. 4.2×10^{-2} s   **D.** 1.3×10^{-3} s   **E.** 2.4×10^{-2} s

43. Brad is pulling Mary in a sled. Mary and the sled are 50 kg. For 4 s, Brad exerts a force that accelerates the sled uniformly from 1.5 m/s to 4 m/s. What is the net force on the sled with Mary?

   A. 31.3 N   **B.** 50 N   **C.** 44.6 N   **D.** 22.2 N   **E.** 90 N

44. A heavy object and a light object are dropped from rest at the same time in a vacuum. Relative to the light object, when does the heavier object reach the ground?

   A. After the lighter object   **C.** Depends on the shape of the objects

   B. At the same time   **D.** Depends on the density of the objects

                            E. Before the lighter object

45. What is the efficiency of a heat engine that receives 8,500 J of heat and loses 4,500 J in each cycle?

   A. 57%   **B.** 47%   **C.** 33%   **D.** 16%   **E.** 29%

46. Which of the graphs illustrates Hooke's Law?

A.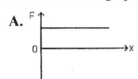

C.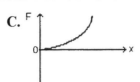

B.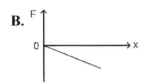

D.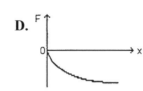

E. None of the above

47. A 4.20 g string, 0.380 m long, is under tension. The string produces a 600.0 Hz tone when it vibrates in the third harmonic. What is the tension in the string? (Use the speed of sound in air $v = 340.0$ m/s)

    A. 183 N   **B.** 210 N   **C.** 255 N   **D.** 324 N   **E.** 360 N

48. A 0.1 m cube consists of six aluminum plates that are insulated from each other. Plates A and D are opposite and maintained at 750 V. Plates B and E are opposite and maintained at 0 V. Plates C and F are opposite and maintained at –750 V. A force moves a charge of 10^{-14} C at constant speed straight across from the center of plate A to the center of plate D. What is the total work done by this force? (Use the elementary charge = 1.6×10^{-19} C)

    A. 7.5×10^{-12} J   **C.** 5.1×10^{-14} J

    B. 0 J   **D.** 7.5×10^{-14} J   **E.** 2.3×10^{5} J

49. If Susan stands in front of a concave mirror, at the same distance from it as its focal length:

    A. her image appears larger and upright
    B. no image is formed
    C. her image appears larger, but upside down
    D. her image appears the same size as her and upright
    E. her image appears the same size as her, but upside down

50. If the fastest Mary can safely drive is 65 mi/h, what is the longest time she can stop for dinner if Mary must travel 460 mi in a total of 9.4 h?

    A. 1.9 h   **B.** 5.1 h   **C.** 3.1 h   **D.** 4.2 h   **E.** 2.3 h

51. A projectile is traveling in a circular path. If the radius of the circular path is doubled without changing the speed of the object, what change in the force is required to maintain the projectile's motion?

    A. Doubled   **C.** Halved

    B. Quadrupled   **D.** Unchanged   **E.** Dependent on mass

52. Two air-filled organ pipes, each closed at one end, have different lengths. Compared to the shorter pipe, the longer pipe resonates at:

    A. the same fundamental frequency, but a longer fundamental wavelength
    B. a higher fundamental frequency, but a shorter fundamental wavelength
    C. a higher fundamental frequency and a longer fundamental wavelength
    D. a lower fundamental frequency and a shorter fundamental wavelength
    E. a lower fundamental frequency, but a longer fundamental wavelength

53. A marble cube is lowered at a steady rate into the ocean by a crane, while its top and bottom surfaces remain parallel with the water's surface. Which graph describes the buoyant force (B) on this cube as a function of time (t), if the cube enters the water at time $t = 0$ s and is lowered until its top surface is well below the water?

A.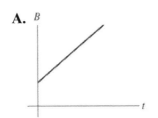

C.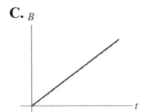

B.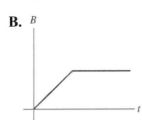

D.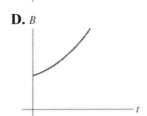

E.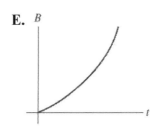

54. A charged parallel-plate capacitor has an electric field E_0 between its plates. A stationary proton and an electron are both between the plates. Ignoring the force of gravity, how does the magnitude of the acceleration of the proton a_p compare with the magnitude of the acceleration of the electron a_e? (Use the mass of an electron $= 9 \times 10^{-31}$ kg, the mass of a proton $= 1.67 \times 10^{-27}$ kg and the charge of a proton $= 1.6 \times 10^{-19}$ C)

    A. $a_p = (1{,}850)^2 a_e$ **C.** $a_p = a_e$
    B. $a_p = 1{,}850 a_e$ **D.** $a_p = (1 / 1{,}850) a_e$ **E.** $a_p = (1 / 1{,}850)^2 a_e$

55. To drive a typical car at 40.0 mph on a level road for one hour requires about 3.2×10^7 J of energy. Suppose one tried to store this much energy in a spinning solid cylindrical flywheel which was then coupled to the wheels of the car. What angular speed would be required to store 3.2×10^7 J if the flywheel has of radius 0.60 m and mass 400.0 kg?

    A. 943.0 rad/s   **C.** 1,822.4 rad/s
    B. 1,384.2 rad/s   **D.** 2,584.5 rad/s   **E.** 5,360.8 rad/s

56. How much heat must be added to a 10 kg block of ice at –8 °C to change it to water at 14 °C? (Use the specific heat of ice = 0.5 kcal/kg·°C, the latent heat of fusion L_f = 80 kcal/kg and the specific heat of water = 1 kcal/kg·°C)

   A. 840 kcal   **B.** 280 kcal   **C.** 440 kcal   **D.** 980 kcal   **E.** 744 kcal

57. A dropped ball falls to the ground from a height of 10 m with a constant acceleration downward of 9.8 m/s². What is the velocity of the ball just before it hits the ground? (Use the acceleration due to gravity g = 10 m/s²)

   A. 9.8 m/s   **B.** 14 m/s   **C.** 19.6 m/s   **D.** 1.4 m/s   **E.** Requires more information

58. A rope pulls on the lower block with a tension force of 18 N. The coefficient of kinetic friction between the lower block and the surface is 0.17. The coefficient of kinetic friction between the lower block and the upper block is also 0.17. What is the acceleration of the 2 kg block? (Use the acceleration due to gravity g = 9.8 m/s², and consider the pulley to be frictionless and massless)

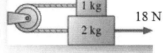

   A. 9.8 m/s²   **C.** 6.7 m/s²
   B. 7.4 m/s²   **D.** 1.3 m/s²   **E.** 3.2 m/s²

59. An ice skater performs a fast spin by pulling in her outstretched arms close to her body. What happens to her moment of inertia about the axis of rotation? Model the skater's arms as a uniform rod with the axis of rotation at her torso.

   A. Increases by radius²   **C.** Remains the same
   B. Increases by √(radius of the circle)   **D.** Decreases
                                         E. Requires more information

60. A blue object appears black when illuminated with which color of light?

   A. Green   **B.** Yellow   **C.** Cyan   **D.** Blue   **E.** None of the above

---

Check your answers using the answer key. Then, go to the explanations section and review the explanations in detail, paying particular attention to questions you didn't answer correctly or marked for review. Note the topic that those questions belong to.

We recommend that you do this BEFORE taking the next Diagnostic Test.

Diagnostic Test #4

Answer Sheet

#	Answer:					Mark for review	#	Answer:					Mark for review
1:	A	B	C	D	E	___	31:	A	B	C	D	E	___
2:	A	B	C	D	E	___	32:	A	B	C	D	E	___
3:	A	B	C	D	E	___	33:	A	B	C	D	E	___
4:	A	B	C	D	E	___	34:	A	B	C	D	E	___
5:	A	B	C	D	E	___	35:	A	B	C	D	E	___
6:	A	B	C	D	E	___	36:	A	B	C	D	E	___
7:	A	B	C	D	E	___	37:	A	B	C	D	E	___
8:	A	B	C	D	E	___	38:	A	B	C	D	E	___
9:	A	B	C	D	E	___	39:	A	B	C	D	E	___
10:	A	B	C	D	E	___	40:	A	B	C	D	E	___
11:	A	B	C	D	E	___	41:	A	B	C	D	E	___
12:	A	B	C	D	E	___	42:	A	B	C	D	E	___
13:	A	B	C	D	E	___	43:	A	B	C	D	E	___
14:	A	B	C	D	E	___	44:	A	B	C	D	E	___
15:	A	B	C	D	E	___	45:	A	B	C	D	E	___
16:	A	B	C	D	E	___	46:	A	B	C	D	E	___
17:	A	B	C	D	E	___	47:	A	B	C	D	E	___
18:	A	B	C	D	E	___	48:	A	B	C	D	E	___
19:	A	B	C	D	E	___	49:	A	B	C	D	E	___
20:	A	B	C	D	E	___	50:	A	B	C	D	E	___
21:	A	B	C	D	E	___	51:	A	B	C	D	E	___
22:	A	B	C	D	E	___	52:	A	B	C	D	E	___
23:	A	B	C	D	E	___	53:	A	B	C	D	E	___
24:	A	B	C	D	E	___	54:	A	B	C	D	E	___
25:	A	B	C	D	E	___	55:	A	B	C	D	E	___
26:	A	B	C	D	E	___	56:	A	B	C	D	E	___
27:	A	B	C	D	E	___	57:	A	B	C	D	E	___
28:	A	B	C	D	E	___	58:	A	B	C	D	E	___
29:	A	B	C	D	E	___	59:	A	B	C	D	E	___
30:	A	B	C	D	E	___	60:	A	B	C	D	E	___

This Diagnostic Test is designed for you to assess your proficiency on each topic and NOT to mimic the actual test. Use your test results and identify areas of your strength and weakness to adjust your study plan and enhance your fundamental knowledge.

The length of the Diagnostic Tests is proven to be optimal for a single study session.

1. Acceleration can be expressed in multiples of g, whereby $g = 9.8$ m/s^2 is the acceleration due to the Earth's gravity. If, in a car crash, a car's velocity changes from 28 m/s to 0 m/s in 0.14 s, how many g are experienced, on average, by the driver during the crash?

    A. 8 g **B.** 6 g **C.** 12 g **D.** 20 g **E.** 26 g

2. Which statement is true when a 15-ton truck collides with a 1,700 lb car and causes damage to the car?

    A. The velocity of the truck did not decrease during the collision
    B. The force of collision on the truck is smaller than the force of collision on the car
    C. The force of collision on the truck is equal to the force of collision on the car
    D. The force of collision on the truck is greater than the force of collision on the car
    E. The velocity of the car did not decrease during the collision

3. How much heat must be added to a 12 kg block of ice at -8 °C to change it to water at 16 °C? (Use the specific heat of ice $= 2,050$ J/kg·°C, the specific heat of water $= 4,186$ J/kg·°C, the latent heat of fusion of ice $L_f = 334,000$ J/kg and conversion of 1 cal $= 4.186$ J)

    A. 2,160 kcal   **C.** 1,460 kcal
    B. 980 kcal   **D.** 1,824 kcal   **E.** 1,196 kcal

4. A crane lifts a 450 kg steel beam vertically upward a distance of 110 m. Ignoring frictional forces, how much work does the crane do on the beam if the beam accelerates upward at 1.8 m/s^2? (Use the acceleration due to gravity $g = 9.8$ m/s^2)

    A. 3.3×10^5 J   **C.** 5.7×10^5 J
    B. 4.2×10^5 J   **D.** 2.4×10^5 J   **E.** 1.2×10^5 J

5. A massless, ideal frictionless spring projects horizontally from a wall and is connected to a 0.5 kg mass. The mass is oscillating in one dimension, such that it moves 1 m from one end of its oscillation to the other. It undergoes 30 complete oscillations in 60 s. What is the energy flow in such a system?

    A. Back and forth from spring PE to KE
    B. Back and forth from spring PE to gravitational PE
    C. KE to PE and then dissipates as heat
    D. PE to KE and then dissipates as heat
    E. PE to heat to KE

6. How long is an organ pipe, open at both ends, if the consecutive harmonic wavelengths occur at 2 m and 2.5 m?

    A. 4 m   **B.** 5 m   **C.** 6 m   **D.** 11 m   **E.** 12 m

7. A 12 L volume of oil is subjected to pressure that produces a volume strain of -3×10^{-4}. The bulk modulus of the oil is 6×10^9 Pa and is independent of the pressure. What is the reduction in the volume of the oil?

A. 1.8 ml   **B.** 2.6 ml   **C.** 4.4 ml   **D.** 3.1 ml   **E.** 3.6 ml

8. A proton is traveling to the right and encounters region Y that contains an electric field where the proton speeds up. In what direction does the electric field in region Y point?

A. To the left   **C.** Down into the page
B. To the right   **D.** Up from the page   **E.** To the left and into the page

9. Four 8 V batteries (A + B + C + D) are connected in series to power lights A and B. The resistance of light A is 45 Ω and the resistance of light B is 25 Ω. What is the current through the wire at a point between battery C and D?

A. 0.46 A   **B.** 0.31 A   **C.** 0.17 A   **D.** 0.84 A   **E.** 1.2 A

10. A 5-foot-tall woman stands next to a plane mirror on a wall. As she walks away from the mirror, her image:

A. is always a real image, no matter how far she is from the mirror.
B. changes from being upright to being inverted as she passes the focal point.
C. has a height less than 5 feet.
D. may or may not get smaller, depending on where she is positioned.
E. remains 5 feet tall.

11. A uniform, solid, cylindrical flywheel of radius 1.4 m and mass 15.0 kg rotates at 2.7 rad/s about an axis through its circular faces. What is the magnitude of the flywheel's angular momentum?

A. 22 kg·m^2/s   **C.** 64 kg·m^2/s
B. 40 kg·m^2/s   **D.** 80 kg·m^2/s   **E.** 140 kg·m^2/s

12. Two carts sit on a level, frictionless track and are connected by a compressed spring and a string. At a certain time, the string is cut, and the carts fly apart. Cart A is 3.5 kg, and cart B is 2.5 kg. After the carts separate, cart A has a velocity of 0.3 m/s to the left. Take the system as carts A and B, and set movement to the right as the positive direction. What is the velocity of cart B after the string is cut?

A. −3.8 m/s   **B.** −0.42 m/s   **C.** 0.6 m/s   **D.** 0.42 m/s   **E.** 0.9 m/s

13. Approximately how far above the ground is a 2 kg mass if it has 40 J of potential energy with respect to the ground? (Use the acceleration due to gravity $g = 9.8$ m/s^2)

   A. 1 m   **B.** 2 m   **C.** 3 m   **D.** 4 m   **E.** 8 m

14. A massless, ideal spring projects horizontally from a wall and is connected to a 2 kg mass. The mass is oscillating in one dimension, such that it moves 1.5 m from one end of its oscillation to the other. It undergoes 10 complete oscillations in 60 s. How does the amplitude change if the spring constant were increased by a factor of 3?

   A. Increases by a factor of 9   **C.** Decreases by a factor of 3
   B. Increases by a factor of 3   **D.** Increases by a factor of $\sqrt{3}$
   E. None of the above

15. In a quiet room, Mary hears an almost inaudible sound of a mosquito one meter away. If a swarm of mosquitoes was 10 m away, what is the minimum number of mosquitoes for her to be able to hear them? (Note: an almost inaudible sound has a value of 10^{-12} W/m^2)

   A. 10   **B.** 100   **C.** 1,000   **D.** 10,000   **E.** 100,000

16. What is the result for temperature, measured in Kelvin, if both the pressure and volume of a given sample of an ideal gas double?

   A. Decreases to one-fourth original value   **C.** Decreases to one-half original value
   B. Quadruples original value   **D.** Doubles original value
                                                        E. Remains the same

17. An electron is initially moving to the right when it enters a uniform electric field that is directed upwards. Which trajectory represents the path of the electron?

   A. W   **C.** Y
   B. X   **D.** Z   **E.** More than one

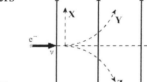

18. Consider the group of charges in the figure. All three charges have $Q = 6.2$ nC. What is their electric potential energy? (Use Coulomb's constant $k = 9 \times 10^9$ Nm^2/C^2).

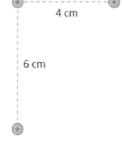

   A. 5.2×10^{-5} J   **C.** 1.9×10^{-5} J
   B. 5.9×10^{-5} J   **D.** 6.1×10^{-5} J
   E. 6.4×10^{-5} J

19. A candle is observed through a converging lens with a focal length of 6 m. The candle is 0.1 m tall and 3 m away from the lens. What is the magnification of the image?

    A. 0.5   **B.** 0.75   **C.** 1.5   **D.** 2   **E.** 1

20. A particular motor can provide a maximum torque of 110.0 N·m. Assuming that all of this torque is used to accelerate a solid, uniform, cylindrical flywheel of mass 10.0 kg and radius 3.00 m, how long will it take for the flywheel to accelerate from rest to 8.13 rad/s?

    A. 2.13 s   **B.** 3.33 s   **C.** 4.65 s   **D.** 5.46 s   **E.** 6.80 s

21. A 9 kg sample of mercury is completely solidified from liquid and liberates 135 kJ of energy. What was the original temperature of the mercury? (Use the specific heat of mercury = 140 J/kg·K, the melting point of mercury = 234 K and the heat of fusion of mercury = 11.3 kJ/kg)

    A. 380 K   **B.** 124 K   **C.** 182 K   **D.** 260 K   **E.** 54 K

22. A 100 kg lion accelerates uniformly from rest to 22 m/s in 10 s. What is the magnitude of the net force on the lion?

    A. 60 N   **B.** 80 N   **C.** 220 N   **D.** 280 N   **E.** 160 N

23. Suppose that a sound source is emitting waves uniformly in all directions. What happens to the frequency of the sound if an observer moves half the distance closer to the source?

    A. One fourth as large   **C.** Four times as large

    B. Twice as large   **D.** Half as large   **E.** Unchanged

24. A change in which of the following will affect the buoyant force experienced by an object that is completely submerged in an incompressible liquid?

        I. Density of the liquid   II. Density of the object   III. Depth of the object

    A. I only   **B.** III only   **C.** I and III only   **D.** I and II only   **E.** I, II and III

25. Why are high voltages used to transmit electrical power over long distances?

    A. Lightning does less damage

    B. Less power is dissipated

    C. Electricity moves faster at higher voltages

    D. A higher voltage requires taller poles, which cover long distances more easily

    E. Electricity moves more slowly at higher voltages

26. What is the speed of an electron that is accelerated from rest through a potential difference of 1,200 V? (Use the mass of an electron = 9.11×10^{-31} kg, the mass of a proton = 1.67×10^{-27} kg and the charge of an electron = -1.6×10^{-19} C)

    A. 4.9×10^7 m/s   **C.** 3.4×10^7 m/s

    B. 1.5×10^7 m/s   **D.** 2.1×10^7 m/s   **E.** 6.6×10^7 m/s

27. Which of the following statements is true?

    A. Violet light has a longer λ than red light

    B. As the λ increases, the f also increases

    C. As the energy increases, the f of radiation decreases

    D. The λ of light is inversely related to its energy

    E. The λ of light is directly proportional to its energy

28. On the Moon, the acceleration of gravity is $g / 6$. If a pendulum has a period T on Earth, what will be the period on the Moon?

    A. 6T   **B.** T/6   **C.** T/√6   **D.** T/3   **E.** T√6

29. To take off an aircraft needs to reach a velocity of 230 km/h. What is the minimum acceleration necessary for the aircraft to take off on a 2,300 m runway?

    A. 0.89 m/s^2 **B.** 0.76 m/s^2 **C.** 0.97 m/s^2 **D.** 1.3 m/s^2 **E.** 2.6 m/s^2

30. Which statement is true for the normal force exerted by a plane on a block if the block is moving down the slope of the inclined plane at constant velocity?

    A. It increases with constant velocity

    B. It is independent of velocity

    C. It decreases with increasing velocity

    D. It increases with increasing velocity

    E. It increases with decreasing velocity

31. A 1.5 kg drone is traveling toward a target at 4 m/s. Another 3 kg drone is traveling at 2.5 m/s in a perpendicular direction. The two drones collide and stick together. What is the magnitude of the final velocity of the two drones?

    A. 2.1 m/s   **B.** 4.8 m/s   **C.** 1.2 m/s   **D.** 0.6 m/s   **E.** 3.6 m/s

32. A massless spring with a spring constant k is connected to a wall and a massless plate. A mass m is sitting on a frictionless surface. The mass m is slid against the plate, and the spring is pushed back a distance x. After release, the mass m achieves a maximum speed v_1. Then, a $6m$ mass is pushed back the same distance x. After release, the $6m$ mass achieves a maximum speed v_2. How does the final KE_1 of mass m compare with the final KE_2 of the $6m$ mass?

A. $6\,KE_1 = KE_2$ **C.** $KE_1 = KE_2 / 3$

B. $9\,KE_1 = KE_2$ **D.** $KE_1 = KE_2$ **E.** $KE_1 = KE_2 + 9$

33. What is the frequency when a weight suspended from a spring bobs up and down over a distance of 1 m in 2 s?

A. 0.5 Hz   **B.** 1 Hz   **C.** 2 Hz   **D.** 0.25 Hz   **E.** 0 Hz

34. Which answer is correct when the first law of thermodynamics, $Q = \Delta U - W$, is applied to an ideal gas that is taken through an isothermal process?

A. $Q = 0$ **B.** $\Delta P = 0$ **C.** $\Delta U = 0$ **D.** $W = 0$ **E.** none are correct

35. A ray in glass is incident onto a water-glass interface at an angle of incidence equal to half the critical angle for that interface. The indices of refraction for water and glass are 1.33 and 1.43, respectively. What is the angle that the refracted ray in the water makes with the normal?

A. 47°   **B.** 26°   **C.** 27°   **D.** 52°   **E.** 37°

36. Three capacitors C_1, C_2 and C_3 have equal capacitance and are connected to a battery as shown. Which capacitor stores the most potential energy?

A. C_3

B. C_1

C. C_2

D. C_2 or C_3

E. All three capacitors store the same amount of energy

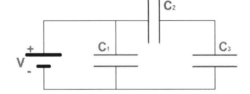

37. The electric field at point P due to a point charge Q a distance R away has magnitude E. What change would double the magnitude of the field at P?

A. Reduce the distance to $R/2$

B. Reduce the distance to $R/4$

C. Double the charge to $2Q$

D. Double the distance to $2R$

E. Double the charge to $2Q$ and at the same time reduce the distance to $R/2$

38. Water undergoes viscous flow in pipes A and B, where pipe B is twice as long as pipe A but has the same diameter. Water is subject to the same pressure difference across the lengths of both pipes. If the flow rate in pipe B is $Q = \Delta V / \Delta t$, what is the flow rate in pipe A?

A. 2Q B. 4Q C. 8Q D. ½Q E. $\sqrt{2}$Q

39. Two speakers, both producing an in-phase sound wave with a wavelength of 0.8 m, are located $L = 2$ m from each other. What kind of point exists exactly 1.3 m to the right of the left-hand speaker? (Use the speed of sound in air $v = 340$ m/s)

A. Neither an antinode nor a node
B. Both an antinode and a node
C. An antinode
D. A node
E. Requires information about the frequency

40. Transverse waves propagate at a speed of 45 m/s in a string that is subjected to a tension of 50 N. If the string is 18 m long, what is its mass?

A. 0.37 kg B. 0.64 kg C. 0.44 kg D. 0.23 kg E. 0.53 kg

41. A husky pulls with a horizontal force F on a sled of mass m. The husky and sled are traveling at a constant speed v on level ground. How much work is done by gravity on the sled in time Δt? (Use acceleration due to gravity $g = 10$ m/s²)

A. $mgv\Delta t$ B. 0 J C. $-mgv\Delta t$ D. $mgv / \Delta t$ E. $mg\sqrt{v}\Delta t$

42. Carts I and II are positioned on a level, frictionless surface in one dimension. Cart I is 5 kg and Cart II is 10 kg, and they are initially at rest. A 3 N force to the right acts on Cart I for 2 s, which then hits Cart II, and they stick together. What is the momentum of Cart I just before the collision?

A. 2.5 kg·m/s B. 4.8 kg·m/s C. 15 kg·m/s D. 8.4 kg·m/s E. 6 kg·m/s

43. A car of mass m is driving up a shallow incline of angle θ with the horizontal when the driver sees a deer and quickly steps on the brakes and the tires lock up (the tires skid along the surface of the road rather than gripping it smoothly). The coefficient of static friction between the tires and the road is μ_s, and the coefficient of kinetic friction is μ_k. What is the magnitude of the net force on the car during the skid?

A. $mg (\mu_s \cos \theta - \sin \theta)$ C. $mg \mu_s \cos \theta$
B. $mg (\mu_s \cos \theta + \sin \theta)$ D. $mg (\mu_k \cos \theta + \sin \theta)$ E. $mg (\mu_k \cos \theta + \sin \theta)$

44. Ignoring air resistance, two objects are thrown from the top of a tall building. With the same initial speed, one is thrown upward, and the other is thrown downward. What is the relationship between their speeds when they hit the street?

  A. It is impossible to determine because the height of the building is unknown
  B. They are traveling at the same speed
  C. The object thrown downward is traveling faster
  D. The object thrown upward is traveling faster
  E. It is impossible to determine because their initial velocities are unknown

45. On a cold winter day, the outside temperature is –10 °C and the inside temperature is maintained at 20 °C. There is a net heat flow of 30 kW through the walls to the outside. What is the change of entropy of the air outside the house from this process after 15 seconds have passed?

  A. 7.6 J/K   **C.** 15.8 J/K
  B. 10.1 J/K   **D.** 5.3 J/K   **E.** 4.2 J/K

46. What is the effect on an object's KE if negative net work is done on an object?

  A. Equals zero   **C.** Remains the same
  B. Increases   **D.** Requires the mass   **E.** Decreases

47. Two transverse waves, with the same amplitude and frequency, travel in the same direction along a stretched string. However, at $t = 0$, where wave A has its maximum positive displacement, wave B has zero displacement. At the point where wave A has zero displacement, wave B has its maximum displacement. What is the phase difference between wave A and wave B?

  A. 45°   **B.** 60°   **C.** 360°   **D.** 180°   **E.** 90°

48. A positive charge Q is held fixed at the origin. A positive charge z is let go from point p on the positive x-axis. Ignoring friction, which statement describes the velocity of z after it is released?

  A. Increases indefinitely   **C.** Increases, then decreases, but never reaches zero
  B. Decreases to zero   **D.** Increases, but never exceeds a certain limit
                           E. Increases, then decreases to zero

49. The objective and the eyepiece of a microscope have focal lengths of 4 mm and 25 mm, respectively. The objective produces a real image 30 times the size of the object. The final image is viewed at infinity. The near point of the microscope user is 25 cm. The overall magnification of the microscope is closest to:

  A. 250   **B.** 300   **C.** 350   **D.** 400   **E.** 450

50. A projectile is fired at time $t = 0$ s, from point 0 at the edge of a cliff. It has initial velocity components of $v_x = 50$ m/s and $v_y = 240$ m/s with time in flight of 60 s. The projectile lands at point P. What is the y coordinate of the projectile when its x coordinate is 1,000 m? (Use the acceleration due to gravity $g = 9.8$ m/s^2)

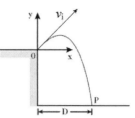

   A. −160 m   **B.** 1,240 m   **C.** 2,840 m   **D.** 850 m   **E.** 1,600 m

51. A 48 kg girl throws a 0.8 kg ball against a wall. The ball strikes the wall horizontally with a speed of 25 m/s and bounces back at the same speed. What is the absolute value of the average force exerted on the wall by the ball if the ball is in contact with the wall for 0.05 s?

   A. 26,500 N   **B.** 55,750 N   **C.** 400 N   **D.** 800 N   **E.** 16,000 N

52. If the frequency of a system undergoing simple harmonic motion doubles, by what factor does the maximum value of acceleration change?

   A. $2/\pi$ **B.** $\sqrt{2}$ **C.** 2   **D.** $\sqrt{2}/\pi$ **E.** 4

53. A tank of water has a hose, filled with water, projecting from the top. The system acts as a siphon as the other end of the hose is below the tank. The end of the hose outside the tank is at height $h = 0$ m. The bottom of the tank is at height h_1, the end of the hose inside the tank is at height h_2, and the top of the water is at height h_3. Assuming that the flow is without viscosity, which is the best expression for the pressure at the bottom of the tank?

   A. $P_{atm} + \rho g(h_3 + h_1)$ **C.** $P_{atm} + \rho g(h_3 - h_1)$

   B. $P_{atm} - \rho g(h_3 + h_1)$ **D.** $P_{atm} - \rho g(h_3 - h_1)$ **E.** $P_{atm} \times \rho g(h_3 - h_1)$

54. What is the resistance for a device obeying Ohm's law?

   A. Proportional to voltage
   B. Zero
   C. Constant
   D. Proportional to current
   E. Proportional to (current)^2

55. A satellite is in a circular orbit around a planet. What is the satellite's orbital speed if the orbital radius is 34.0 km and the gravitational acceleration at that height is 2.3 m/s^2?

   A. 26 m/s   **B.** 150 m/s   **C.** 280 m/s   **D.** 310 m/s   **E.** 390 m/s

56. A heat engine takes 4 moles of an ideal gas through the reversible cycle *abca*, on the pressure vs. volume diagram, as shown. The path *bc* is an isothermal process. The temperature at *c* is 650 K, and the volumes at *a* and *c* are 0.025 m³ and 0.33 m³, respectively.

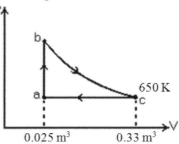

What is the work done by the gas for the path *bc*? (Use molar heat capacity at constant volume of the gas = 18 J/mol·K and universal gas constant R = 8.134 J/mol·K)

    A. −56 kJ   **C.** 56 kJ

    B. −82 kJ   **D.** 82 kJ   **E.** 0 kJ

57. The driver of a car traveling at 26 mi/h applies the brakes, and the car comes to rest in a certain distance. How much farther would the car go had the driver applied the brakes when traveling at 58 mi/h? Assume the force of friction is the same in both cases so that acceleration is the same and constant.

    A. 6.6 times farther   **C.** 3.4 times farther

    B. 4.8 times farther   **D.** 5 times farther   **E.** 2 times farther

58. Two filled cardboard boxes are in contact with each other on a table. Box B has twice the mass of box A. If box A is pushed with a horizontal force *F*, what is the net force experienced by box B?

    A. 2/3 *F*   **B.** 2 *F*   **C.** √*F*   **D.** 3/2 *F*   **E.** √3 *F*

59. What is the magnitude of a flywheel's angular momentum for a uniform, solid flywheel of radius 1.8 m and mass 12 kg that rotates at 2.9 rad/s?

    A. 65.8 kg·m²/s   **C.** 41.7 kg·m²/s

    B. 82.4 kg·m²/s   **D.** 56.4 kg·m²/s   **E.** 75.1 kg·m²/s

60. Which expression describes the critical angle for the interface of water with air? (Use the index of refraction for water n = 1.33 and the index of refraction for air n = 1)

    A. $\sin^{-1}(1/3)$ **B.** $\sin^{-1}(3/4)$ **C.** $\sin^{-1}(2/3)$ **D.** $\sin^{-1}(4/3)$ **E.** $\sin^{-1}(3/2)$

> Check your answers using the answer key. Then, go to the explanations section and review the explanations in detail, paying particular attention to questions you didn't answer correctly or marked for review. Note the topic that those questions belong to.

OAT Physics

Topical Practice Questions

Kinematics and Dynamics

1. Starting from rest, how long does it take for a sports car to reach 60 mi/h if it has an average acceleration of 13.1 mi/h·s?

   A. 6.6 s   **B.** 3.1 s   **C.** 4.5 s   **D.** 4.6 s   **E.** 13.1 s

2. A cannonball is fired with an initial speed of 20 m/s at a 30° angle with the horizontal. Ignoring air resistance, how long does it take the cannonball to reach the top of its trajectory? (Use the acceleration due to gravity $g = 10$ m/s^2)

   A. 0.5 s   **B.** 1 s   **C.** 1.5 s   **D.** 2 s   **E.** 2.5 s

3. Darlene starts her car from rest and accelerates at a constant 2.5 m/s^2 for 9 s to get to her cruising speed. She then drives for 15 minutes at constant speed. She arrives at her destination, which is a straight-line distance of 31.5 km away, exactly 1.25 hours later. What is her average velocity during the interval of 1.25 hours?

   A. 3 m/s   **B.** 7 m/s   **C.** 18 m/s   **D.** 22.5 m/s   **E.** 2.5 m/s

4. Which of the following cannot be negative?

   A. Instantaneous speed   **C.** Acceleration of gravity

   B. Instantaneous acceleration   **D.** Displacement   **E.** Position

5. How far does a car travel while accelerating from 5 m/s to 21 m/s at a rate of 3 m/s^2?

   A. 15 m   **B.** 21 m   **C.** 69 m   **D.** 105 m   **E.** 210 m

6. Acceleration is sometimes expressed in multiples of g, where g is the acceleration due to gravity. How many g are experienced, on average, by the driver in a car crash if the car's velocity changes from 30 m/s to 0 m/s in 0.15 s? (Use acceleration due to gravity $g = 9.8$ m/s^2)

   A. 22 g **B.** 28 g **C.** 16 g **D.** 14 g **E.** 20 g

7. Ignoring air resistance, how many forces are acting on a bullet fired horizontally after it leaves the rifle?

   A. Two (one from the gunpowder explosion and one from gravity)
   B. One (from the motion of the bullet)
   C. One (from the gunpowder explosion)
   D. One (from the pull of gravity)
   E. None; it is in freefall and unaffected by any forces

8. Suppose that a car traveling to the East begins to slow down as it approaches a traffic light. Which of the following statements about its acceleration is correct?

    A. The acceleration is towards the East

    B. The acceleration is towards the West

    C. Since the car is slowing, its acceleration is positive

    D. The acceleration is zero

    E. Since the car is slowing, its acceleration cannot be determined

9. On a planet where the acceleration due to gravity is 20 m/s^2, a freely falling object increases its speed each second by about:

    A. 20 m/s   **B.** 10 m/s   **C.** 30 m/s   **D.** 40 m/s   **E.** depends on its initial speed

10. What is a car's acceleration if it accelerates uniformly in one direction from 15 m/s to 40 m/s in 10 s?

    A. 1.75 m/s^2 **B.** 2.5 m/s^2 **C.** 3.5 m/s^2 **D.** 7.6 m/s^2 **E.** 4.75 m/s^2

11. If the fastest a person can drive is 65 mi/h, what is the longest time she can stop for lunch if she wants to travel 540 mi in 9.8 h?

    A. 1 h   **B.** 2.4 h   **C.** 1.5 h   **D.** 2 h   **E.** 0.5 h

12. What is a racecar's average velocity if it completes one lap around a 500 m track in 10 s?

    A. 10 m/s   **B.** 0 m/s   **C.** 5 m/s   **D.** 20 m/s   **E.** 15 m/s

13. What is a ball's net displacement after 5 s if it is initially rolling up a slight incline at 0.2 m/s and decelerates uniformly at 0.05 m/s^2?

    A. 0.38 m   **B.** 0.6 m   **C.** 0.9 m   **D.** 1.2 m   **E.** 2.4 m

14. What does the slope of a line connecting two points on a velocity vs. time graph represent?

    A. Change in acceleration   **C.** Average acceleration

    B. Instantaneous acceleration   **D.** Instantaneous velocity   **E.** Displacement

15. An airplane needs to reach a speed of 210.0 km/h to take off. On an 1,800.0 m runway, what is the minimum acceleration necessary for the plane to reach this speed, assuming acceleration is constant?

    A. 0.78 m/s^2 **B.** 0.95 m/s^2 **C.** 1.47 m/s^2 **D.** 1.1 m/s^2 **E.** 2.5 m/s^2

16. A test rocket is fired straight up from rest with a net acceleration of 22 m/s^2. What maximum elevation does the rocket reach if the motor turns off after 4 s, but the rocket continues to coast upward? (Use the acceleration due to gravity $g = 10 \text{ m/s}^2$)

    A. 408 m   **B.** 320 m   **C.** 357 m   **D.** 563 m   **E.** 260 m

17. Without any reference to direction, how fast an object moves refers to its:

    A. acceleration   **B.** impulse   **C.** momentum   **D.** velocity   **E.** speed

18. Ignoring air resistance, a 10 kg rock and a 20 kg rock are dropped at the same time. If the 10 kg rock falls with acceleration a, what is the acceleration of the 20 kg rock?

    A. $a / 2$ **B.** a **C.** $2a$ **D.** $4a$ **E.** $a / 4$

19. As an object falls freely, its magnitude of:

    I. velocity increases   II. acceleration increases   III. displacement increases

    A. I only   **B.** I and II only   **C.** II and III only   **D.** I and III only   **E.** I, II and III

20. A man stands in an elevator that is ascending at a constant velocity. What forces are being exerted on the man, and which direction does the net force point?

    A. Gravity pointing downward, normal force from the floor pointing upward, and tension force from the elevator cable pointing upward; net force points upward
    B. Gravity pointing downward and the normal force from the floor pointing upward; net force points upward
    C. Gravity pointing downward and normal force from the floor pointing upward; net force is zero
    D. Gravity pointing downward; net force is zero
    E. Gravity pointing downward, normal force from the floor pointing upward, and tension force from the elevator cable pointing upward; net force is zero

21. A football kicker is attempting a field goal from 44 m away, and the ball just clears the lower bar with a time of flight of 2.9 s. What was the initial speed of the ball if the angle of the kick was 45° with the horizontal?

    A. 37 m/s   **B.** 2.5 m/s   **C.** 18.3 m/s   **D.** 7.2 m/s   **E.** 21.4 m/s

22. Ignoring air resistance, if a rock, starting at rest, is dropped from a cliff and strikes the ground with an impact velocity of 14 m/s, from what height was it dropped? (Use the acceleration due to gravity $g = 10 \text{ m/s}^2$)

    A. 10 m   **B.** 30 m   **C.** 45 m   **D.** 70 m   **E.** 90 m

23. An SUV is traveling at 20 m/s. Then Joseph steps on the accelerator pedal, accelerating at a constant 1.4 m/s^2 for 7 s. How far does he travel during these 7 s?

A. 205 m   **B.** 174 m   **C.** 143 m   **D.** 158 m   **E.** 115 m

24. Which of the following is NOT a scalar?

A. temperature   **B.** distance   **C.** mass   **D.** force   **E.** time

25. Two identical balls (A and B) fall from rest from different heights to the ground. Ignoring air resistance, what is the ratio of the heights from which A and B fall if ball B takes twice as long as ball A to reach the ground?

A. 1 : √2   **B.** 1 : 4   **C.** 1 : 2   **D.** 1 : 8   **E.** 1 : 9

26. How far does a car travel in 10 s when it accelerates uniformly in one direction from 5 m/s to 30 m/s?

A. 65 m   **B.** 25 m   **C.** 250 m   **D.** 650 m   **E.** 175 m

27. Which graph represents an acceleration of zero?

I. v 0 ⊢————— t   II. v 0 ⊢————— t   III. v 0 ⊢————— t

A. I only   **C.** I and II only

B. II only   **D.** II and III only   **E.** I and III only

28. Doubling the distance between an orbiting satellite and the Earth results in what change in the gravitational attraction between the two?

A. Twice as much   **C.** One half as much

B. Four times as much   **D.** One fourth as much   **E.** Remains the same

29. An object is moving in a straight line. Consider its motion during some interval of time: under what conditions is it possible for the instantaneous velocity of the object at some point during the interval to be equal to the average velocity over the interval?

     I. When velocity is constant during the interval

     II. When velocity is increasing at a constant rate during the interval

     III. When velocity is increasing at an irregular rate during the interval

A. II only   **C.** II and III only

B. I and III only   **D.** I, II and III   **E.** I and II only

30. A freely falling object on Earth, 10 s after starting from rest, has a speed of about:
(Use the acceleration due to gravity $g = 10$ m/s^2)

 A. 10 m/s **B.** 20 m/s **C.** 80 m/s **D.** 150 m/s **E.** 100 m/s

31. A truck travels a certain distance at a constant velocity v for time t. If the truck travels three times as fast, covering the same distance, then by what factor does the time of travel in relation to t change?

 A. Increases by 3   **C.** Decreases by √3
 B. Decreases by 3   **D.** Increases by 9   **E.** Decreases by 1/9

32. Assuming equal rates of acceleration, how much farther would Steve travel if he braked from 59 mi/h to rest than from 29 mi/h to rest?

 A. 2 times farther   **C.** 4 times farther
 B. 16 times farther   **D.** 3.2 times farther   **E.** 1.5 times farther

33. What is the average speed of a racehorse if the horse does one lap around a 400 m track in 20 s?

 A. 0 m/s **B.** 7.5 m/s **C.** 15 m/s **D.** 20 m/s **E.** 25 m/s

34. What was a car's initial velocity if the car is traveling up a slight slope while decelerating at 0.1 m/s^2 and comes to a stop after 5 s?

 A. 0.02 m/s **B.** 0.25 m/s **C.** 2 m/s **D.** 1.5 m/s **E.** 0.5 m/s

35. Average velocity equals the average of an object's initial and final velocity when acceleration is:

 A. constantly decreasing   **C.** constant
 B. constantly increasing   **D.** equal to zero
             E. equal to the reciprocal of the initial velocity

36. Ignoring air resistance, compared to a rock dropped from the same point, how much earlier does a thrown rock strike the ground if it is thrown downward with an initial velocity of 10 m/s from the top of a 300 m building? (Use acceleration due to gravity $g = 9.8$ m/s^2)

 A. 0.75 s **B.** 0.33 s **C.** 0.66 s **D.** 0 s **E.** 0.95 s

37. With all other factors equal, what happens to the acceleration if the unbalanced force on an object of a given mass is doubled?

 A. Increased by one-fourth   **C.** Increased fourfold
 B. Increased by one-half   **D.** Doubled   **E.** Remains the same

---

38. How fast an object is changing speed or direction of travel is a property of motion known as:

    A. velocity   **B.** acceleration   **C.** speed   **D.** flow   **E.** momentum

39. Which statement concerning a car's acceleration must be correct if a car traveling to the North (+y direction) begins to slow down as it approaches a stop sign?

    A. Acceleration is positive   **C.** Cannot be determined from the data provided

    B. Acceleration is zero   **D.** Acceleration decreases in magnitude as the car slows

                                 E. Acceleration is negative

40. For the velocity vs. time graph of a basketball player traveling up and down the court in a straight-line path, what is the total distance run by the player in the 10 s?

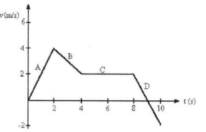

    A. 24 m   **C.** 14 m

    B. 22 m   **D.** 18 m   **E.** 20 m

41. At the same time that a bullet is dropped into a river from a high bridge, another bullet is fired from a gun, straight down towards the water. Ignoring air resistance, the acceleration just before striking the water:

    A. is greater for the dropped bullet   **C.** is the same for each bullet

    B. is greater for the fired bullet   **D.** depends on how high the bullets started

                                   E. depends on the mass of the bullets

42. Sarah starts her car from rest and accelerates at a constant 2.5 m/s² for 9 s to get to her cruising speed. What was her final velocity?

    A. 22.5 m/s   **B.** 12.3 m/s   **C.** 4.6 m/s   **D.** 8.5 m/s   **E.** 1.25 m/s

43. A bat hits a baseball, and the baseball's direction is completely reversed, and its speed is doubled. If the actual time of contact with the bat is 0.45 s, what is the ratio of the acceleration to the original velocity?

    A. –2.5 s⁻¹ : 1   **C.** –9.8 s⁻¹ : 1

    B. –0.15 s⁻¹ : 1   **D.** –4.1 s⁻¹ : 1   **E.** –6.7 s⁻¹ : 1

44. A 2 kg weight is thrown vertically upward from the surface of the Moon at a speed of 3.2 m/s, and it returns to its starting point in 4 s. What is the magnitude of acceleration due to gravity on the Moon?

    A. 0.8 m/s²   **B.** 1.6 m/s²   **C.** 3.7 m/s²   **D.** 8.4 m/s²   **E.** 12.8 m/s²

45. What is the change in velocity for a bird that is cruising at 1.5 m/s and then accelerates at a constant 0.3 m/s² for 3 s?

  A. 0.9 m/s   **B.** 0.6 m/s   **C.** 1.6 m/s   **D.** 0.3 m/s   **E.** 1.9 m/s

46. All of the following are vectors, except:

  A. velocity   **B.** displacement   **C.** acceleration   **D.** mass   **E.** force

> Questions **47-49** are based on the following:

A toy rocket is launched vertically from ground level where $y = 0$ m, at time $t = 0$ s. The rocket engine provides constant upward acceleration during the burn phase. At the instant of engine burnout, the rocket has risen to 64 m and acquired a velocity of 60 m/s. The rocket continues to rise in unpowered flight, reaches the maximum height and then falls back to the ground. (Use the acceleration due to gravity $g = 9.8$ m/s²)

47. What is the maximum height reached by the rocket?

  A. 274 m   **B.** 205 m   **C.** 223 m   **D.** 120 m   **E.** 248 m

48. What is the upward acceleration of the rocket during the burn phase?

  A. 9.9 m/s²   **B.** 4.8 m/s²   **C.** 28 m/s²   **D.** 11.8 m/s²   **E.** 8.6 m/s²

49. What is the time interval during which the rocket engine provides upward acceleration?

  A. 1.5 s   **B.** 1.9 s   **C.** 2.3 s   **D.** 2.1 s   **E.** 2.6 s

50. A car accelerates uniformly from rest along a straight track that has markers spaced at equal distances along it. As it passes Marker 2, the car reaches a speed of 140 km/h. Where on the track is the car when it is traveling at 70 km/h?

  A. Close to Marker 2   **C.** At Marker 1
  B. Between Marker 1 and Marker 2   **D.** Close to the starting point
       E. Before Marker 1

51. What are the two measurements necessary for calculating average speed?

  A. Distance and time   **C.** Velocity and time
  B. Distance and acceleration   **D.** Velocity and acceleration
       E. Acceleration and time

52. A pedestrian traveling at speed v covers a distance x during a time interval t. If a bicycle travels at speed $3v$, how much time does it take the bicycle to travel the same distance?

    A. $t / 3$ **B.** $t - 3$ **C.** $t + 3^2$ **D.** $3t$ **E.** $t + 3^3$

53. Ignoring air resistance, how much time passes before a ball strikes the ground if it is thrown straight upward with a velocity of 39 m/s? (Use the acceleration due to gravity $g = 9.8$ m/s^2)

    A. 2.2 s   **B.** 1.4 s   **C.** 12 s   **D.** 4 s   **E.** 8 s

54. A particle travels to the right along a horizontal axis with a constantly decreasing speed. Which one of the following describes the direction of the particle's acceleration?

    A. ↑   **B.** ↓   **C.** →   **D.** ←   **E.** None of the above

55. Larry is carrying a 25 kg package at a constant velocity of 1.8 m/s across a room for 12 s. What is the work done by Larry on the package during the 12 s? (Use the acceleration due to gravity $g = 10$ m/s^2)

    A. 0 J   **B.** 280 J   **C.** 860 J   **D.** 2,200 J   **E.** 1,125 J

Force, Motion, Gravitation

1. A boy attaches a weight to a string, which he swings counter-clockwise in a horizontal circle. Which path does the weight follow when the string breaks at point P?

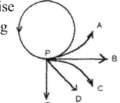

   A. path A   **C.** path C

   B. path B   **D.** path D   **E.** path E

2. A garment bag hangs from a clothesline. The tension in the clothesline is 10 N on the right side of the garment bag and 10 N on the left side of the garment bag. The clothesline makes an angle of 60° from vertical. What is the mass of the garment bag? (Use the acceleration due to gravity $g = 10.0$ m/s^2)

   A. 0.5 kg   **B.** 8 kg   **C.** 4 kg   **D.** 10 kg   **E.** 1 kg

3. A sheet of paper can be withdrawn from under a milk carton without toppling the carton if the paper is jerked away quickly. This demonstrates:

   A. the inertia of the milk carton

   B. that gravity tends to hold the milk carton secure

   C. there is an action-reaction pair of forces

   D. that the milk carton has no acceleration

   E. none of the above

4. A car of mass *m* is going up a shallow slope with an angle θ to the horizontal when the driver suddenly applies the brakes. The car skids as it comes to a stop. The coefficient of static friction between the tires and the road is μ_s, and the coefficient of kinetic friction is μ_k. Which expression represents the normal force on the car?

   A. $mg \tan \theta$ **B.** $mg \sin \theta$ **C.** $mg \cos \theta$ **D.** mg **E.** $mg \sec \theta$

5. A 27 kg object is accelerated at a rate of 1.7 m/s^2. How much force does the object experience?

   A. 62 N   **B.** 74 N   **C.** 7 N   **D.** 18 N   **E.** 46 N

6. How are two identical masses moving if they are attached by a light string that passes over a small pulley? Assume that the table and the pulley are frictionless.

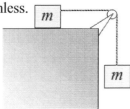

   A. With an acceleration equal to *g*

   B. With an acceleration greater than *g*

   C. At a constant speed

   D. With an acceleration less than *g*

   E. Not moving because the masses are equal

7. An object is moving to the right in a straight line. The net force acting on the object is also directed to the right, but the magnitude of the force is decreasing with time. What happens to the object?

    A. Continues to move to the right with its speed increasing with time

    B. Continues to move to the right with a constant speed

    C. Continues to move to the right with its speed decreasing with time

    D. Continues to move to the right, slowing quickly to a stop

    E. Stops and then begins moving to the left with its speed decreasing with time

8. A crate is sliding down an inclined ramp at a constant speed of 0.55 m/s. Where does the vector sum of all the forces acting on this crate point?

    A. Perpendicular to the ramp   **C.** Vertically upward

    B. Vertically downward   **D.** Across the ramp   **E.** None of the above

9. Consider an inclined plane that makes an angle θ with the horizontal. What is the relationship between the length of the ramp L and the vertical height of the ramp h?

    A. $h = L \sin \theta$ **C.** $L = h \sin \theta$

    B. $h = L \tan \theta$ **D.** $h = L \cos \theta$ **E.** $L = h \cos \theta$

10. Why is it just as difficult to accelerate a car on the Moon as it is to accelerate the same car on Earth?

    I. Moon and Earth have the same gravity

    II. weight of the car is independent of gravity

    III. mass of the car is independent of gravity

  A. I only   **B.** II only   **C.** III only   **D.** I and II only   **E.** I and III only

11. Sean is pulling his son in a toy wagon. His son and the wagon together are 60 kg. For 3 s Sean exerts a force which uniformly accelerates the wagon from 1.5 m/s to 3.5 m/s. What is the acceleration of the wagon with his son?

  A. 0.67 m/s²   **B.** 0.84 m/s²   **C.** 1.66 m/s²   **D.** 15.32 m/s²   **E.** 20.84 m/s²

12. When an object moves in uniform circular motion, the direction of its acceleration is:

    A. directed away from the center of its circular path

    B. dependent on its speed

    C. in the opposite direction of its velocity vector

    D. in the same direction as its velocity vector

    E. directed toward the center of its circular path

13. What happens to a moving object in the absence of an external force?

    A. Gradually accelerates until it reaches its terminal velocity, at which point it continues at a constant velocity

    B. Moves with constant velocity

    C. Stops immediately

    D. Slows and eventually stops

    E. Moves with a constant speed in a circular orbit

14. A force of 1 N causes a 1 kg mass to have an acceleration of 1 m/s^2. From this information, a force of 9 N applied to a 9 kg mass would have what magnitude of acceleration?

    A. 18 m/s^2 **B.** 9 m/s^2 **C.** 1 m/s^2 **D.** 3 m/s^2 **E.** 27 m/s^2

15. Which of the following statements is true about an object in two-dimensional projectile motion with no air resistance?

    A. The acceleration of the object is zero at its highest point

    B. The horizontal acceleration is always positive, regardless of the vertical acceleration

    C. The velocity is always in the same direction as the acceleration

    D. The acceleration of the object is $+g$ when the object is rising and $-g$ when it is falling

    E. The horizontal acceleration is always zero, and the vertical acceleration is always a nonzero constant downward

16. A can of paint with a mass of 10 kg hangs from a rope. If the can is to be pulled up to a rooftop with a constant velocity of 0.5 m/s, what must the tension on the rope be? (Use the acceleration due to gravity $g = 10$ m/s^2)

    A. 100 N   **B.** 40 N   **C.** 0 N   **D.** 120 N   **E.** 160 N

17. What is the magnitude of the force exerted on a 1,000 kg object that accelerates at 2 m/s^2?

    A. 500 N   **B.** 1,000 N   **C.** 1,200 N   **D.** 2,000 N   **E.** 2,200 N

18. A 1,300 kg car is driven at a constant speed of 4 m/s and turns to the right on a curve on the road, which has an effective radius of 4 m. What is the acceleration of the car?

    A. 0 m/s^2 **B.** 3 m/s^2 **C.** 4 m/s^2 **D.** 9.8 m/s^2 **E.** 8 m/s^2

19. A block of mass *m* is resting on a 20° slope. The block has coefficients of friction $\mu_s = 0.55$ and $\mu_k = 0.45$ with the surface. Block *m* is connected via a massless string over a massless, frictionless pulley to a hanging 2 kg block. What is the minimum mass of block *m* so that it does not slip? (Use the acceleration due to gravity $g = 9.8$ m/s^2)

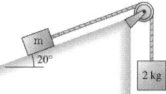

   A. 0.8 kg   **B.** 1.3 kg   **C.** 3.7 kg   **D.** 4.1 kg   **E.** 2.3 kg

20. As shown in the figure to the right, two identical masses, attached by a light cord passing over a massless, frictionless pulley on an Atwood's machine, are hanging at different heights. If the two masses are suddenly released, then the:

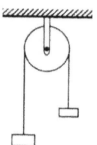

   A. lower mass moves down   **C.** higher mass moves down

   B. masses remain stationary   **D.** motion is unpredictable

                                       E. masses oscillate uniformly

21. When Victoria jumps up in the air, which of the following statements is the most accurate?

   A. The ground cannot exert the upward force necessary to lift her into the air, because the ground is stationary. Rather, Victoria is propelled into the air by the internal force of her muscles acting on her body

   B. When Victoria pushes down on the Earth with force greater than her weight, the Earth pushes back with the same magnitude force and propels her into the air

   C. Victoria is propelled up by the upward force exerted by the ground, but this force cannot be greater than her weight

   D. The Earth exerts an upward force on Victoria that is stronger than the downward force she exerts on the Earth; therefore Victoria is able to spring up

   E. Because gravity is what keeps her on the ground, the internal force of her muscles acting on her body needs to be greater than the force of gravity to propel her into the air

22. If a feather is pounded with a hammer, which experiences a greater force?

   A. The magnitude of the force is always the same on both

   B. If the feather moves, then it felt the greater force

   C. Depends on the force with which the hammer strikes the feather

   D. Always the hammer

   E. Always the feather

23. A block is moving down a slope of a frictionless inclined plane. Compared to the weight of the block, what is the force parallel to the surface of the plane experienced by the block?

A. Greater   **C.** Less than

B. Unrelated   **D.** Equal   **E.** Requires more information

24. A package falls off a truck that is moving at 30 m/s. Ignoring air resistance, the horizontal speed of the package just before it hits the ground is:

A. 0 m/s   **B.** 15 m/s   **C.** $\sqrt{60}$ m/s   **D.** $\sqrt{30}$ m/s   **E.** 30 m/s

25. A carousel with the radius r is turning counterclockwise at a frequency f. How does the velocity of a seat on the carousel change when f is doubled?

A. Increases by a factor of $2r$

B. Increases by a factor of r

C. Remains unchanged

D. Doubles

E. It depends on the mass of the chair

26. What is the mass of a car if it takes 4,500 N to accelerate it at a rate of 5 m/s^2?

A. 900 kg   **B.** 1,320 kg   **C.** 620 kg   **D.** 460 kg   **E.** 1,140 kg

27. Steve is standing facing forward in a moving bus. What force causes Steve to suddenly move forward when the bus comes to an abrupt stop?

A. Force due to the air pressure inside the previously moving bus

B. Force due to kinetic friction between Steve and the floor of the bus

C. Force due to stored kinetic energy

D. Force of gravity

E. No forces were responsible for Steve's movement

28. A plastic ball in a liquid is acted upon by its weight and a buoyant force. The weight of the ball is 4.4 N. The buoyant force of 8.4 N acts vertically upward. An external force acting on the ball maintains it in a state of rest. What is the magnitude and direction of the external force?

A. 4 N, upward

B. 8.4 N, downward

C. 4.4 N, upward

D. 4 N, downward

E. 2 N, downward

---

29. A passenger on a train traveling in the forward direction notices that a piece of luggage starts to slide directly toward the front of the train. From this, it can be concluded that the train is:

A. slowing down

B. speeding up

C. moving at a constant velocity forward

D. changing direction

E. moving at a constant velocity in the reverse direction

30. An object has a mass of 36 kg and weighs 360 N at the surface of the Earth. If this object is transported to an altitude that is twice the Earth's radius, what is the object's mass and weight, respectively?

A. 9 kg and 90 N

B. 36 kg and 90 N

C. 4 kg and 90 N

D. 36 kg and 40 N

E. 9 kg and 40 N

31. A truck is moving at constant velocity. Inside the storage compartment, a rock is dropped from the midpoint of the ceiling and strikes the floor below. The rock hits the floor:

A. just behind the midpoint of the ceiling

B. exactly halfway between the midpoint and the front of the truck

C. exactly below the midpoint of the ceiling

D. just ahead of the midpoint of the ceiling

E. exactly halfway between the midpoint and the rear of the truck

32. Jason takes off across level water on his jet-powered skis. The combined mass of Jason and his skis is 75 kg (the mass of the fuel is negligible). The skis have a thrust of 200 N and a coefficient of kinetic friction on the water of 0.1. If the skis run out of fuel after only 67 s, how far has Jason traveled before he stops?

A. 5,428 m   **B.** 3,793 m   **C.** 8,224 m   **D.** 7,642 m   **E.** 10,331 m

33. A 200 g hockey puck is launched up a metal ramp that is inclined at a 30° angle. The puck's initial speed is 63 m/s. What vertical height does the puck reach above its starting point? (Use acceleration due to gravity $g = 9.8$ m/s^2, the coefficient of static friction $\mu_s = 0.40$ and kinetic friction $\mu_k = 0.30$ between the hockey puck and the metal ramp)

A. 66 m   **B.** 200 m   **C.** 170 m   **D.** 130 m   **E.** 48 m

34. When a 4 kg mass and a 10 kg mass are pushed from rest with equal force:

A. 4 kg mass accelerates 2.5 times faster than the 10 kg mass

B. 10 kg mass accelerates 10 times faster than the 4 kg mass

C. 4 kg mass accelerates at the same rate as the 10 kg mass

D. 10 kg mass accelerates 2.5 times faster than the 4 kg mass

E. 4 kg mass accelerates 10 times faster than the 10 kg mass

35. On a different planet, a person's:

A. weight and mass decrease
B. weight and mass remain the same
C. weight remains the same, but mass changes
D. weight changes, but mass remains the same
E. weight and mass increase

36. Which of the following statements must be true when a 20-ton truck collides with a 1,500 lb car?

A. During the collision, the force on the truck is equal to the force on the car
B. The truck did not slow down during the collision, but the car did
C. During the collision, the force on the truck is greater than the force on the car
D. During the collision, the force on the truck is smaller than the force on the car
E. The car did not slow down during the collision, but the truck did

37. A block is on a frictionless table on Earth. The block accelerates at 3 m/s^2 when a 20 N horizontal force is applied to it. The block and table are then transported to the Moon. What is the weight of the block on the Moon? (Use the acceleration due to gravity at the surface of the Moon = 1.62 m/s^2)

A. 5.8 N   B. 14.2 N   C. 8.5 N   D. 11 N   E. 17.5 N

38. What is the weight of a 0.4 kg bottle of wine? (Use acceleration due to gravity $g = 9.8$ m/s^2)

A. 0.4 N   B. 4 N   C. 40 N   D. 20 N   E. 2 N

39. Car A starts from rest and accelerates uniformly for time t to travel a distance of d. Car B, which has four times the mass of car A, starts from rest and also accelerates uniformly. If the magnitudes of the forces accelerating car A and car B are the same, how long does it take car B to travel the same distance d?

A. t B. $2t$ C. $t / 2$ D. $16t$ E. $4t$

40. A 1,100 kg vehicle is traveling at 27 m/s when it starts to decelerate. What is the average braking force acting on the vehicle, if after 578 m it comes to a complete stop?

A. –440 N   B. –740 N   C. –690 N   D. –540 N   E. –880 N

41. An ornament of mass M is suspended by a string from the ceiling inside an elevator. What is the tension in the string holding the ornament when the elevator is traveling upward at a constant speed?

A. Equal to Mg
B. Less than Mg
C. Greater than Mg
D. Equal to M / g
E. Less than M / g

42. An object that weighs 75 N is pulled on a horizontal surface by a force of 50 N to the right. The friction force on this object is 30 N to the left. What is the acceleration of the object? (Use the acceleration due to gravity $g = 9.8$ m/s^2)

A. 0.46 m/s^2 **B.** 1.7 m/s^2 **C.** 2.6 m/s^2 **D.** 10.3 m/s^2 **E.** 12.1 m/s^2

43. While flying horizontally in an airplane, a string attached from the overhead luggage compartment hangs at rest 15° away from the vertical toward the front of the plane. From this observation, it can be concluded that the airplane is:

A. accelerating forward
B. accelerating backward
C. accelerating upward at 15° from horizontal
D. moving backward
E. not moving

44. An object slides down an inclined ramp with a constant speed. If the ramp's incline angle is θ, what is the coefficient of kinetic friction (μ_k) between the object and the ramp?

A. $\mu_k = 1$
B. $\mu_k = \cos\theta / \sin\theta$
C. $\mu_k = \sin\theta / \cos\theta$
D. $\mu_k = \sin\theta$
E. $\mu_k = \cos\theta$

45. What is the magnitude of the net force on a 1 N apple when it is in free fall?

A. 1 N   **B.** 0.1 N   **C.** 0.01 N   **D.** 10 N   **E.** 100 N

46. What is the acceleration of a 105 kg tiger that accelerates uniformly from rest to 20 m/s in 10 s?

A. 4.7 m/s^2 **B.** 1.5 m/s^2 **C.** 2 m/s^2 **D.** 3.4 m/s^2 **E.** 16.7 m/s^2

47. Yania tries to pull an object by tugging on a rope attached to the object with a force of F. If the object does not move, what does this imply?

A. The object has reached its natural state of rest and can no longer be set into motion
B. The rope is not transmitting the force to the object
C. No other forces are acting on the object
D. The inertia of the object prevents it from accelerating
E. There are one or more other forces that act on the object with a sum of $-F$

48. If a force F is exerted on an object, the force which the object exerts back:

A. depends on the mass of the object
B. depends on the density of the object
C. depends on if the object is moving
D. depends on if the object is stationary
E. equals $-F$

49. What is the mass of an object that experiences a gravitational force of 685 N near Earth's surface? (Use the acceleration due to gravity $g = 9.8$ m/s^2)

   A. 76 kg   **B.** 62 kg   **C.** 70 kg   **D.** 81 kg   **E.** 54 kg

50. Sarah and her father Bob (who weighs four times as much) are standing on identical skateboards (with frictionless ball bearings), both initially at rest. For a short time, Bob pushes Sarah on the skateboard. When Bob stops pushing:

   A. Sarah and Bob move away from each other, and Sarah's speed is four times that of Bob's
   B. Sarah and Bob move away from each other, and Sarah's speed is one-fourth of Bob's
   C. Sarah and Bob move away from each other with equal speeds
   D. Sarah moves away from Bob, and Bob is stationary
   E. Sarah and Bob move away from each other, and Bob's speed is less than one-fourth that of Sarah's

51. Considering the effects of friction, which statement best describes the motion of an object along a surface?

   A. Less force is required to start than to keep the object in motion at a constant velocity
   B. The same force is required to start as to keep the object in motion at a constant velocity
   C. More force is required to start than to keep the object in motion at a constant velocity
   D. Once the object is set in motion, no force is required to keep it in motion at constant velocity
   E. More information is needed about the surface before the amount of force can be determined

52. On the surface of Jupiter, the acceleration due to gravity is about three times that as on Earth. What is the weight of a 100 kg rock when it is taken from Earth to Jupiter? (Use the acceleration due to gravity $g = 10$ m/s^2)

   A. 1,800 N   **B.** 3,000 N   **C.** 3,300 N   **D.** 4,000 N   **E.** 9,000 N

53. Joe and Bill are playing tug-of-war. Joe is pulling with a force of 200 N, while Bill is simply holding onto the rope. What is the tension of the rope if neither person is moving?

   A. 75 N   **B.** 0 N   **C.** 100 N   **D.** 200 N   **E.** 50 N

54. A 4 kg wooden block A slides on a frictionless table pulled by a hanging 5 kg block B via a massless string and pulley system as shown. What is the acceleration of block A as it slides? (Use the acceleration due to gravity $g = 9.8$ m/s^2)

   A. 2.8 m/s^2 **C.** 3.4 m/s^2
   B. 1.6 m/s^2 **D.** 4.9 m/s^2 **E.** 4.1 m/s^2

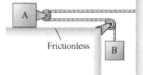

55. Which of the following best describes the direction in which the force of kinetic friction acts relative to the interface between the interacting bodies?

    A. Parallel to the interface and in the same direction as the relative velocity

    B. Parallel to the interface and in the opposite direction of the relative velocity

    C. Perpendicular to the interface and in the same direction as the relative velocity

    D. Perpendicular to the interface and in the opposite direction of the relative velocity

    E. Because kinetic friction depends on movement, there is no way to estimate it unless given a description of a body's velocity

Equilibrium and Momentum

1. When is the angular momentum of a system constant?

  A. When no net external torque acts on the system
  B. When the linear momentum and the energy are constant
  C. When no net external force acts on the system
  D. When the total kinetic energy is positive
  E. When the moment of inertia is positive

2. When a rock rolls down a mountainside at 7 m/s, the horizontal component of its velocity vector is 1.8 m/s. What was the angle of the mountain surface above the horizontal?

  A. 15°   **B.** 63°   **C.** 40°   **D.** 75°   **E.** 9.5°

3. A 200 N sled slides down a frictionless hill at an angle of 37° to the horizontal. What is the magnitude of the force that the hill exerts on the sled parallel to the surface of the hill?

  A. 170 N   **B.** 200 N   **C.** 74 N   **D.** 37 N   **E.** 0 N

4. Water causes a water wheel to turn as it passes by. The force of the water is 300 N, and the radius of the wheel is 10 m. What is the torque around the center of the wheel?

  A. 0 N·m
  B. 300 N·m
  C. 3,000 N·m
  D. 3 N·m
  E. 30 N·m

5. Through what angle, in degrees, does a 33 rpm record turn in 0.32 s?

  A. 44°   **B.** 94°   **C.** 113°   **D.** 32°   **E.** 63°

6. A freight train rolls along a track with considerable momentum. What is its momentum if it rolls at the same speed but has twice the mass?

  A. Zero
  B. Doubled
  C. Quadrupled
  D. Unchanged
  E. Cannot be estimated

Questions **7-9** are based on the following:

Three carts run along a level, frictionless one-dimensional track. Furthest to the left is a 1 kg cart I, moving at 0.5 m/s to the right. In the middle is a 1.5 kg cart II moving at 0.3 m/s to the left. Furthest to the right is a 3.5 kg cart III moving at 0.5 m/s to the left. The carts collide in sequence, sticking together. (Assume the direction to the right is the positive direction)

7. What is the total momentum of the system before the collision?

   A. −2.6 kg·m/s   **C.** 0.6 kg·m/s

   B. 1.4 kg·m/s   **D.** −1.7 kg·m/s   **E.** 1.1 kg·m/s

8. Assuming cart I and cart II collide first, and cart III is still independent, what is the total momentum of the system just after cart I and cart II collide?

   A. −1.7 kg·m/s   **C.** 0.9 kg·m/s

   B. 0.1 kg·m/s   **D.** −0.9 kg·m/s   **E.** −0.11 kg·m/s

9. What is the final velocity of the three carts?

   A. −0.35 m/s   **C.** −0.87 m/s

   B. −0.28 m/s   **D.** 0.35 m/s   **E.** 0.15 m/s

10. A 480 kg car is moving at 14.4 m/s when it collides with another car that is moving at 13.3 m/s in the same direction. If the second car has a mass of 570 kg and a new velocity of 17.9 m/s after the collision, what is the velocity of the first car after the collision?

    A. 19 m/s   **B.** −9 m/s   **C.** 9 m/s   **D.** 14 m/s   **E.** −14 m/s

11. An 8 g bullet is shot into a 4 kg block at rest on a frictionless horizontal surface. The bullet remains lodged in the block. The block moves into a spring and compresses it by 8.9 cm. After the block comes to a stop, the spring fully decompresses and sends the block in the opposite direction. What is the magnitude of the impulse of the block (including the bullet), due to the spring, during the entire time interval in which the block and spring are in contact? (Use the spring constant = 1,400 N/m)

    A. 11 N·s   **B.** 8.3 N·s   **C.** 6.4 N·s   **D.** 12 N·s   **E.** 13 N·s

12. An ice skater performs a fast spin by pulling in her outstretched arms close to her body. What happens to her rotational kinetic energy about the axis of rotation?

    A. Decreases   **C.** Increases

    B. Remains the same   **D.** It changes, but it depends on her body mass

                                           E. It decreases in proportion to $\sqrt{\text{length of her arms}}$

13. A toy car is traveling in a circular path. The force required to maintain this motion is F. If the velocity of the object is doubled, what is the force required to maintain its motion?

A. $2F$ **B.** F **C.** ½F **D.** $4F$ **E.** $\sqrt{2}F$

14. Which of the following are units of momentum?

A. kg·m/s^2 **B.** J·s/m   **C.** N·m   **D.** kg·s   **E.** kg·m^2/s^2

15. The impulse on an apple hitting the ground depends on:

     I. the speed of the apple just before it hits
     II. whether or not the apple bounces
     III. the time of impact with the ground

A. I only   **B.** II only   **C.** III only   **D.** I and III only   **E.** I, II and III

16. A 55 kg girl throws a 0.8 kg ball against a wall. The ball strikes the wall horizontally with a speed of 25 m/s and bounces back at the same speed. The ball is in contact with the wall for 0.05 s. What is the average force exerted on the wall by the ball?

A. 27,500 N   **B.** 55,000 N   **C.** 400 N   **D.** 800 N   **E.** 13,750 N

17. Three objects are moving along a straight line as shown. If the positive direction is to the right, what is the total momentum of this system?

     6 m/s   3 m/s   2 m/s
     •→   •→   ←•
     7 kg   12 kg   4 kg

A. −70 kg·m/s   **C.** +86 kg·m/s

B. +70 kg·m/s   **D.** −86 kg·m/s   **E.** 0 kg·m/s

Questions **18-19** are based on the following:

Two ice skaters, Vladimir (60 kg) and Olga (40 kg) collide in midair. Just before the collision, Vladimir was going North at 0.5 m/s, and Olga was going West at 1 m/s. Right after the collision and well before they land on the ground, they stick together. Assume they have no vertical velocity.

18. What is the magnitude of their velocity just after the collision?

A. 0.1 m/s   **B.** 1.8 m/s   **C.** 0.9 m/s   **D.** 1.5 m/s   **E.** 0.5 m/s

19. What is the magnitude of the total momentum just after the collision?

A. 25 kg·m/s   **C.** 65 kg·m/s

B. 50 kg·m/s   **D.** 80 kg·m/s   **E.** 40 kg·m/s

20. A horse is running in a straight line. If both the mass and the speed of the horse are doubled, by what factor does its momentum increase?

A. $\sqrt{2}$ **B.** 2   **C.** 4   **D.** 8   **E.** 16

21. The mass of box P is greater than the mass of box Q. Both boxes are on a frictionless horizontal surface and connected by a light cord. A horizontal force F is applied to box Q, accelerating the boxes to the right. What is the magnitude of the force exerted by the connecting cord on box P?

A. equal to F **C.** zero

B. equal to $2F$ **D.** less than F but > 0 **E.** equal to $3F$

22. Which of the following is true when Melissa and her friend Samantha are riding on a merry-go-round, as viewed from above?

A. They have the same speed, but different angular velocity
B. They have different speeds, but the same angular velocity
C. They have the same speed and the same angular velocity
D. They have different speeds and different angular velocities
E. Requires the radius of the merry-go-round

23. The relationship between impulse and impact force involves the:

A. time the force acts   **C.** difference between acceleration and velocity

B. distance the force acts   **D.** mass and its effect on resisting a change in velocity

        E. difference between acceleration and speed

24. Angular momentum cannot be conserved if the:

A. moment of inertia changes   **C.** angular velocity changes

B. system is experiencing a net force   **D.** angular displacement changes

        E. system has a net torque

25. A 6.8-kg block is moving on a frictionless surface with a speed of $v_i = 5.4$ m/s and makes a perfectly elastic collision with a 4.8-kg stationary block. After the collision, the 6.8-kg block recoils with a speed of $v_f = 3.2$ m/s. What is the magnitude of the average force on the 6.8-kg block while the two blocks are in contact for 2 s?

A. 4.4 N   **B.** 46.1 N   **C.** 32.6 N   **D.** 29.2 N   **E.** 18.4 N

Questions **26-27** are based on the following:

A 4 kg rifle imparts a high velocity to a small 10 g bullet by exploding a charge that causes the bullet to leave the barrel at 300 m/s. Take the system as the combination of the rifle and bullet. Normally, the rifle is fired with the butt of the gun pressed against the shooter's shoulder. Ignore the force of the shoulder on the rifle.

26. What is the momentum of the system just after the bullet leaves the barrel?

   A. 0 kg·m/s   **B.** 3 kg·m/s   **C.** 9 kg·m/s   **D.** 30 kg·m/s   **E.** 120 kg·m/s

27. What is the recoil velocity of the rifle (i.e., the velocity of the rifle just after firing)?

   A. 23 m/s   **B.** 1.5 m/s   **C.** 5.6 m/s   **D.** 12.4 m/s   **E.** 0.75 m/s

28. A ball thrown horizontally from a point 24 m above the ground strikes the ground after traveling a distance of 18 m horizontally. With what speed was it thrown, assuming negligible air resistance? (Use acceleration due to gravity $g = 9.8$ m/s^2)

   A. 6.8 m/s   **B.** 7.5 m/s   **C.** 8.1 m/s   **D.** 8.6 m/s   **E.** 9.7 m/s

29. An object is moving in a circle at constant speed. Its acceleration vector is directed:

   A. toward the center of the circle
   B. away from the center of the circle
   C. tangent to the circle and in the direction of the motion
   D. behind the normal and toward the center of the circle
   E. ahead of the normal and toward the center of the circle

30. Impulse is equal to the:

       I. force multiplied by the distance over which the force acts
       II. change in momentum
       III. momentum

   A. I only   **B.** II only   **C.** III only   **D.** I and II only   **E.** I and III only

31. A 4 kg object is at the height of 10 m above the Earth's surface. Ignoring air resistance, what is its kinetic energy immediately before impacting the ground if it is thrown straight downward with an initial speed of 20 m/s? (Use the acceleration due to gravity $g = 10$ m/s^2)

   A. 150 J   **B.** 300 J   **C.** 1,200 J   **D.** 900 J   **E.** 600 J

32. A car traveling along the highway needs a certain amount of force exerted on it to stop. More stopping force may be required when the car has:

          I. less stopping distance   II. more momentum   III. more mass

    A. I only   **B.** II only   **C.** III only   **D.** I and III only   **E.** I, II and III

33. A table tennis ball moving East at a speed of 4 m/s collides with a stationary bowling ball. The table tennis ball bounces back to the West, and the bowling ball moves very slowly to the East. Which ball experiences the greater magnitude of impulse during the collision?

    A. Bowling ball
    B. Table tennis ball
    C. Neither because both experience the same magnitude of the impulse
    D. It is not possible to determine since the velocities after the collision are unknown
    E. It is not possible to determine since the masses of the objects are unknown

34. Assume that a massless bar of 5 m is suspended from a rope and that the rope is attached to the bar at a distance x from the bar's left end. If a 30 kg mass hangs from the right side of the bar and a 6 kg mass hangs from the left side of the bar, what value of x results in equilibrium? (Use the acceleration due to gravity $g = 9.8$ m/s^2)

    A. 2.8 m   **B.** 4.2 m   **C.** 3.2 m   **D.** 1.6 m   **E.** 4.5 m

35. A block of mass m sits at rest on a rough inclined ramp that makes an angle θ with the horizontal. What must be true about the force of static friction (f) on the block?

    A. $f > mg \sin \theta$ **C.** $f = mg$
    B. $f = mg \cos \theta$ **D.** $f < mg \cos \theta$ **E.** $f = mg \sin \theta$

36. A 30 kg block is pushed in a straight line across a horizontal surface. What is the coefficient of kinetic friction μ_k between the block and the surface if a constant force of 45 N must be applied to the block to maintain a constant velocity of 3 m/s? (Use the acceleration due to gravity $g = 10$ m/s^2)

    A. 0.1   **B.** 0.33   **C.** 0.15   **D.** 0.5   **E.** 0.66

37. The impulse-momentum relationship is a direct result of:

          I. Newton's First Law   II. Newton's Second Law   III. Newton's Third Law

    A. I only   **B.** II only   **C.** III only   **D.** I and II only   **E.** I and III only

Questions **38-40** are based on the following:

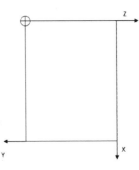

A 0.5 m by 0.6 m rectangular piece of metal is hinged (⊗) (as shown) in the upper left corner, hanging so that the long edge is vertical. A 25 N force (Y) acts to the left at the lower left corner. A 15 N force (X) acts down at the lower right corner. A 30 N force (Z) acts to the right at the upper right corner. Each force vector is in the plane of the metal. Use counterclockwise as the positive direction.

38. What is the torque of force X about the pivot?

   A. 5 N·m   **B.** 3 N·m   **C.** −7.5 N·m   **D.** 0 N·m   **E.** −5 N·m

39. What is the torque of force Z about the pivot?

   A. −10 N·m   **B.** −4.5 N·m   **C.** 4.5 N·m   **D.** 10 N·m   **E.** 0 N·m

40. What is the torque of force Y about the pivot?

   A. −15 N·m   **B.** −3 N·m   **C.** 0 N·m   **D.** 3 N·m   **E.** 7.5 N·m

41. A 50 g weight is tied to the end of a string and whirled at 20 m/s in a horizontal circle with a radius of 2 m. Ignoring the force of gravity, what is the tension in the string?

   A. 5 N   **B.** 10 N   **C.** 50 N   **D.** 150 N   **E.** 20 N

42. A small car collides with a large truck in a head-on collision. Which of the following statements concerning the magnitude of the average force during the collision is correct?

   A. The small car and the truck experience the same average force
   B. The force experienced by each one is inversely proportional to its velocity
   C. The truck experiences the greater average force
   D. The small car experiences the greater average force
   E. The force experienced by each one is directly proportional to its velocity

43. A 10 kg bar that is 2 m long extends perpendicularly from a vertical wall. The free end of the bar is attached to a point on the wall by a light cable, which makes an angle of 30° with the bar. What is the tension in the cable? (Use the acceleration due to gravity $g = 10$ m/s^2)

   A. 75 N   **B.** 150 N   **C.** 100 N   **D.** 125 N   **E.** 50 N

44. Object A has the same size and shape as object B but is twice as heavy. When objects A and B are dropped simultaneously from a tower, they reach the ground at the same time. Object A has greater:

      I. speed   II. momentum   III. acceleration

    A. I only   **B.** II only   **C.** III only   **D.** I and II only   **E.** I and III only

45. Two vehicles approach a right angle intersection and then collide. After the collision, they become entangled. If their mass ratio was 1 : 4 and their respective speeds as they approached were both 12 m/s, what is the magnitude of the velocity immediately following the collision?

    A. 16.4 m/s   **B.** 11.9 m/s   **C.** 13.4 m/s   **D.** 9.9 m/s   **E.** 8.5 m/s

46. A skater stands stationary on frictionless ice. She throws a heavy ball to the right at an angle of 5° above the horizontal. With respect to the ice, if the ball weighs one-third as much as the skater and she is measured to be moving with a speed of 2.9 m/s to the left after the throw, how fast did she throw the ball?

    A. 10.2 m/s   **B.** 7.2 m/s   **C.** 8.73 m/s   **D.** 9.8 m/s   **E.** 8.1 m/s

47. Ignoring the forces of friction, what horizontal force must be applied to an object with a weight of 98 N to give it a horizontal acceleration of 10 m/s^2? (Use the acceleration due to gravity $g = 9.8$ m/s^2)

    A. 9.8 N   **B.** 100 N   **C.** 79 N   **D.** 125 N   **E.** 4.9 N

48. Consider a winch that pulls a cart at constant speed up an incline. Point A is at the bottom of the incline, and point B is at the top. Which of the following statements is/are true from point A to B?

      I. The KE of the cart is constant
      II. The PE of the cart is constant
      III. The sum of the KE and PE of the cart is constant

    A. I only   **B.** II only   **C.** III only   **D.** I and II only   **E.** I, II and III

49. A high-speed dart is shot from ground level with a speed of 140 m/s at an angle of 35° above the horizontal. What is the vertical component of its velocity after 4 s if air resistance is ignored? (Use the acceleration due to gravity $g = 9.8$ m/s^2)

    A. 59 m/s   **B.** 75 m/s   **C.** 34 m/s   **D.** 41 m/s   **E.** 38 m/s

50. What does the area under the curve of a force vs. time graph represent for a diver as she leaves the platform during her approach to the water below?

    A. Work   **B.** Momentum   **C.** Impulse   **D.** Displacement   **E.** Force

51. Strings suspend a rifle of mass 2 kg. The rifle fires a bullet of mass 0.01 kg at a speed of 220 m/s. What is the recoil velocity of the rifle?

    A. 0.001 m/s   **B.** 0.01 m/s   **C.** 0.1 m/s   **D.** 1.1 m/s   **E.** 10.1 m/s

52. How do automobile air bags reduce injury during a collision?

    A. They reduce the kinetic energy transferred to the passenger
    B. They reduce the momentum transferred to the passenger
    C. They reduce the acceleration of the automobile
    D. They reduce the forces exerted upon the passenger
    E. All of the above

> Questions **53-55** are based on the following:

Tim nails a meter stick to a board at the meter stick's 0 m mark. A force I acts at the 0.5 m mark perpendicular to the meter stick with a force of 10 N, as shown in the figure. Force II acts at the end of the meter stick with a force of 5 N, making a 35° angle. Force III acts at the same point with a force of 20 N, providing tension but no shear stress. Use counterclockwise as the positive direction.

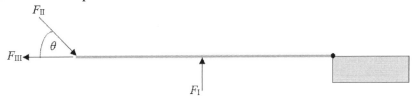

53. What is the torque of Force I about the fixed point?

    A. –5 N·m   **B.** 0 N·m   **C.** 5 N·m   **D.** 10 N·m   **E.** –10 N·m

54. What is the torque of Force II about the fixed point?

    A. –4.8 N·m   **B.** –2.9 N·m   **C.** 4.8 N·m   **D.** 6.6 N·m   **E.** 2.9 N·m

55. What is the torque of Force III about the fixed point?

    A. –20 N·m   **B.** 0 N·m   **C.** 10 N·m   **D.** 20 N·m   **E.** –10 N·m

Work and Energy

1. Consider the following ways that a girl might throw a stone from a bridge. The speed of the stone as it leaves her hand is the same in each of the three cases.

    I. Thrown straight up
    II. Thrown straight down
    III. Thrown straight out horizontally

Ignoring air resistance, in which case is the vertical speed of the stone the greatest when it hits the water below?

  A. I only   **C.** III only
  B. II only   **D.** I and II only   **E.** II and III only

2. A package is being pulled along the ground by a 5 N force F directed 45° above the horizontal. Approximately how much work is done by the force when it pulls the package 10 m?

  A. 14 J   **B.** 35 J   **C.** 70 J   **D.** 46 J   **E.** 64 J

3. Which quantity has the greatest influence on the amount of kinetic energy that a large truck has while moving down the highway?

  A. Velocity   **C.** Density
  B. Mass   **D.** Direction   **E.** Acceleration

4. No work is done by gravity on a bowling ball that rolls along the floor of a bowling alley because:

  A. no potential energy is being converted to kinetic energy
  B. the force on the ball is at a right angle to the ball's motion
  C. its velocity is constant
  D. the total force on the ball is zero
  E. its kinetic energy remains constant

5. A 5 kg toy car is moving along the level ground. At a given time, it is traveling at a speed of 2 m/s and accelerating at 3 m/s². What is the cart's kinetic energy at this time?

  A. 20 J   **B.** 8 J   **C.** 12 J   **D.** 4 J   **E.** 10 J

6. A tree house is 8 m above the ground. If Peter does 360 J of work while pulling a box from the ground up to his tree house with a rope, what is the mass of a box? (Use the acceleration due to gravity $g = 10$ m/s²)

  A. 4.5 kg   **B.** 3.5 kg   **C.** 5.8 kg   **D.** 2.5 kg   **E.** 1.4 kg

7. For an ideal elastic spring, what does the slope of the curve represent for a displacement (x) vs. applied force (F) graph?

A. The acceleration of gravity

B. The square root of the spring constant

C. The spring constant

D. The reciprocal of the spring constant

E. The square of the spring constant

8. A spring with a spring constant of 22 N/m is stretched from equilibrium to 3 m. How much work is done in the process?

A. 33 J **B.** 66 J **C.** 99 J **D.** 198 J **E.** 242 J

9. A baseball is thrown straight up. Compare the sign of the work done by gravity while the ball goes up with the sign of the work done by gravity while it goes down:

A. negative on the way up and positive on the way down

B. negative on the way up and negative on the way down

C. positive on the way up and positive on the way down

D. positive on the way up and negative on the way down

E. requires information about the mass of the baseball

10. Let A_1 represent the magnitude of the work done by gravity as mass A's gravitational energy increases by 400 J. Let B_1 represent the total amount of work necessary to increase mass B's kinetic energy by 400 J. How do A_1 and B_1 compare?

A. $A_1 > B_1$

B. $A_1 = B_1$

C. $A_1 < B_1$

D. $A_1 = 400 B_1$

E. $400 A_1 = B_1$

11. According to the definition of work, pushing on a rock accomplishes no work unless there is:

A. an applied force equal to the rock's weight

B. movement perpendicular to the force

C. an applied force greater than the rock's weight

D. movement parallel to the force

E. force perpendicular to the movement

12. A job is done slowly, while an identical job is done quickly. Both jobs require the same amount of work, but different amounts of:

I. energy II. power III. torque

A. I only **B.** II only **C.** I and II only **D.** I and III only **E.** none are true

13. On a force (F) vs. distance (d) graph, what represents the work done by the force F?

   A. The area under the curve

   B. A line connecting two points on the curve

   C. The slope of the curve

   D. The length of the curve

   E. The maximum F × the maximum d

14. A 3 kg cat leaps from a tree to the ground, which is a distance of 4 m. What is its kinetic energy just before the cat reaches the ground? (Use acceleration due to gravity $g = 10$ m/s^2)

   A. 0 J   **B.** 9 J   **C.** 120 J   **D.** 60 J   **E.** 36 J

15. A book is resting on a plank of wood. Jackie pushes the plank and accelerates it in such a way that the book is stationary with respect to the plank. The work done by static friction is:

   A. zero

   B. positive

   C. negative

   D. parallel to the surface

   E. perpendicular to the surface

16. 350 J of work is required to drive a stake into the ground fully. If the average resistive force on the stake by the ground is 900 N, how long is the stake?

   A. 2.3 m   **B.** 0.23 m   **C.** 3 m   **D.** 0.39 m   **E.** 0.46 m

17. A lightweight object and a very heavy object are sliding with equal speeds along a level, frictionless surface. They both slide up the same frictionless hill with no air resistance. Which object rises to a greater height?

   A. The lightweight object, because the force of gravity on it is less

   B. The heavy object, because it has more kinetic energy to carry it up the hill

   C. The heavy object, because it has greater potential energy

   D. The lightweight object, because it has more kinetic energy to carry it up the hill

   E. They both slide to the same height

18. If Investigator II does 3 times the work of Investigator I in one third the time, the power output of Investigator II is:

   A. 9 times greater

   B. 3 times greater

   C. 1/3 times greater

   D. the same

   E. $\sqrt{3}$ times greater

19. A diver who weighs 450 N steps off a diving board that is 9 m above the water. What is the kinetic energy when the diver strikes the water?

   A. 160 J   **B.** 540 J   **C.** 45 J   **D.** 4,050 J   **E.** 5,400 J

20. A vertical, hanging spring stretches by 23 cm when a 160 N object is attached. What is the weight of a hanging plant that stretches the spring by 34 cm?

    A. 237 N   **B.** 167 N   **C.** 158 N   **D.** 309 N   **E.** 249 N

21. A mule pulls with a horizontal force F on a covered wagon of mass M. The mule and covered wagon are traveling at a constant speed v on level ground. How much work is done by the mule on the covered wagon during time Δt? (Use acceleration due to gravity $g = 10$ m/s^2)

    A. $-Fv\Delta t$ **B.** $Fv\Delta t$ **C.** 0 J   **D.** $-F\sqrt{v}\Delta t$ **E.** $-Fv/\Delta t$

22. Jane pulls on the strap of a sled at an angle of 32° above the horizontal. If 540 J of work is done by the strap while moving the sled a horizontal distance of 18 m, what is the tension in the strap?

    A. 86 N   **B.** 112 N   **C.** 24 N   **D.** 35 N   **E.** 69 N

23. A vertical spring stretches 6 cm from equilibrium when a 120 g mass is attached to the bottom. If an additional 120 g mass is added to the spring, how does the potential energy of the spring change?

    A. the same   **C.** 2 times greater

    B. 4 times greater   **D.** $\sqrt{2}$ times greater   **E.** 3 times greater

24. A Ferrari, Maserati and Lamborghini are moving at the same speed and each driver slams on his brakes and brings the car to a stop. The most massive is the Ferrari, and the least massive is the Lamborghini. If the tires of all three cars have identical coefficients of friction with the road surface, which car experiences the greatest amount of work done by friction?

    A. Maserati   **C.** Ferrari

    B. Lamborghini   **D.** The amount is the same   **E.** Requires more information

25. A hammer does the work of driving a nail into a wooden board. Compared to the moment before the hammer strikes the nail after it impacts the nail, the hammer's mechanical energy is:

    A. the same

    B. less, because work has been done on the hammer

    C. greater, because the hammer has done work

    D. greater, because work has been done on the hammer

    E. less, because the hammer has done work

26. A 1,500 kg car is traveling at 25 m/s on a level road and the driver slams on the brakes. The skid marks are 10 m long. What is the work done by the road on the car?

    A. -4.7×10^5 J   **C.** 2×10^5 J

    B. 0 J   **D.** 3.5×10^5 J   **E.** -3.5×10^5 J

27. A 1,000 kg car is traveling at 4.72 m/s. If a 2,000 kg truck has 20 times the kinetic energy of the car, how fast is the truck traveling?

   A. 23.6 m/s   **B.** 47.2 m/s   **C.** 94.4 m/s   **D.** 14.9 m/s   **E.** 9.71 m/s

28. A 1,500 kg car is traveling at 25 m/s on a level road and the driver slams on the brakes. The skid marks are 30 m long. What forces are acting on the car while it is coming to a stop?

   A. Gravity down, normal force up, and a frictional force forwards
   B. Gravity down, normal force up, and the engine force forwards
   C. Gravity down, normal force forward, and a frictional force backward
   D. Gravity down, normal force forward, and the engine force backward
   E. Gravity down, normal force up, and a frictional force backward

29. A 6,000 N piano is being raised via a pulley. For every 1 m that the rope is pulled down, the piano rises 0.15 m. In this pulley system, what is the force needed to lift the piano?

   A. 60 N   **B.** 900 N   **C.** 600 N   **D.** 300 N   **E.** 6 N

30. What does the area under the curve on a force vs. position graph represent?

   A. Kinetic energy   **B.** Momentum   **C.** Work   **D.** Displacement   **E.** Friction

31. What is the form in which most energy comes to and leaves the Earth?

   A. Kinetic   **B.** Radiant   **C.** Chemical   **D.** Light   **E.** Heat

32. A driver abruptly slams on the brakes in her car, and the car skids a certain distance on a straight level road. If she had been traveling twice as fast, what distance would the car have skid, under the same conditions?

   A. 1.4 times farther   **C.** 4 times farther
   B. ½ as far   **D.** 2 times farther   **E.** 8 times farther

33. A crane hoists an object weighing 2,000 N to the top of a building. The crane raises the object straight upward at a constant rate. Ignoring the forces of friction, at what rate is energy consumed by the electric motor of the crane if it takes 60 s to lift the mass 320 m?

   A. 2.5 kW   **B.** 6.9 kW   **C.** 3.50 kW   **D.** 10.7 kW   **E.** 16.3 kW

34. A barbell with a mass of 25 kg is raised 3.0 m in 3.0 s before it reaches constant velocity. What is the net power expended by all forces in raising the barbell? (Use the acceleration due to gravity $g = 9.8$ m/s^2 and the acceleration of the barbell is constant)

   A. 138 W   **B.** 34 W   **C.** 67 W   **D.** 98 W   **E.** 17 W

35. Susan carried a 6.5 kg bag of groceries 1.4 m above the ground at a constant velocity for 2.4 m across the kitchen. How much work did Susan do on the bag in the process? (Use the acceleration due to gravity $g = 10$ m/s^2)

    A. 52 J   **B.** 0 J   **C.** 164 J   **D.** 138 J   **E.** 172 J

36. A 1,000 kg car experiences a net force of 9,600 N while decelerating from 30 m/s to 22 m/s. How far does it travel while slowing down?

    A. 17 m   **B.** 22 m   **C.** 12 m   **D.** 34 m   **E.** 26 m

37. What is the power output in relation to the work W if a person exerts 100 J in 50 s?

    A. ¼ W   **B.** ½ W   **C.** 2 W   **D.** 4 W   **E.** $\sqrt{2}$ W

38. If a ball is released from a cliff ledge 58 m above the ground, how fast is the ball traveling when it reaches the ground? (Use the acceleration due to gravity $g = 10$ m/s^2)

    A. 68 m/s   **B.** 16 m/s   **C.** 44 m/s   **D.** 34 m/s   **E.** 53 m/s

39. A stone is held at a height h above the ground. A second stone with four times the mass is held at the same height. What is the gravitational potential energy of the second stone compared to that of the first stone?

    A. Twice as much   **C.** One fourth as much

    B. The same   **D.** One half as much   **E.** Four times as much

40. A 1.3 kg coconut falls off a coconut tree, landing on the ground 600 cm below. How much work is done on the coconut by the gravitational force? (Use the acceleration due to gravity $g = 10$ m/s^2)

    A. 6 J   **B.** 78 J   **C.** 168 J   **D.** 340 J   **E.** 236 J

41. The potential energy of a pair of interacting objects is related to their:

    A. relative position   **C.** acceleration

    B. momentum   **D.** kinetic energy   **E.** velocity

42. A spring has a spring constant of 65 N/m. One end of the spring is fixed at point P, while the other end is connected to a 7 kg mass m. The fixed end and the mass sit on a horizontal, frictionless surface so that the mass and the spring can rotate about P. The mass moves in a circle of radius $r = 4$ m, and the centripetal force of the mass is 15 N. What is the potential energy stored in the spring?

    A. 1.7 J   **B.** 2.8 J   **C.** 3.7 J   **D.** 7.5 J   **E.** 11.2 J

43. If electricity costs 8.16 cents/kW·h, how much would it cost you to run a 120 W stereo system 3.5 hours per day for 5 weeks?

    A. $1.11   **B.** $1.46   **C.** $1.20   **D.** $0.34   **E.** $0.49

44. A boy does 120 J of work to pull his sister back on a swing that has a 5.1 m chain until the swing makes an angle of 32° with the vertical. What is the mass of his sister? (Use the acceleration due to gravity $g = 9.8$ m/s^2)

    A. 18 kg   **B.** 16.4 kg   **C.** 13.6 kg   **D.** 11.8 kg   **E.** 15.8 kg

45. What is the value of the spring constant if 111 J of work are needed to stretch a spring from 1.4 m to 2.9 m if the spring's equilibrium position is at 0.0 m?

    A. 58 N/m   **B.** 53 N/m   **C.** 67 N/m   **D.** 34 N/m   **E.** 41 N/m

46. The metric unit of a joule (J) is a unit of:

    I. potential energy   II. kinetic energy   III. work

    A. I only   **B.** II only   **C.** III only   **D.** I and III only   **E.** I, II and III

47. A horizontal spring-mass system oscillates on a frictionless table. Find the maximum extension of the spring if the ratio of the mass to the spring constant is 0.038 kg·m/N, and the maximum speed of the mass is 18 m/s?

    A. 3.5 m   **B.** 0.67 m   **C.** 3.4 cm   **D.** 67 cm   **E.** 34 cm

48. A truck weighs twice as much as a car and is moving at twice the speed of the car. Which statement is true about the truck's kinetic energy compared to that of the car?

    A. The truck has 8 times the KE   **C.** The truck has √2 times the KE
    B. The truck has twice the KE   **D.** The truck has 4 times the KE
                                      E. The truck has √8 times the KE

49. When a car brakes to a stop, its kinetic energy is transformed into:

    A. energy of rest   **C.** potential energy
    B. energy of momentum   **D.** stopping energy   **E.** heat

50. A 30 kg block hangs from a spring with a spring constant of 900 N/m. How far does the spring stretch from its equilibrium position? (Use acceleration due to gravity $g = 10$ m/s^2)

    A. 12 cm   **B.** 33 cm   **C.** 50 cm   **D.** 0.5 cm   **E.** 5 cm

51. What is the kinetic energy of a 0.33 kg baseball thrown at a velocity of 40 m/s?

A. 426 J   **B.** 574 J   **C.** 318 J   **D.** 264 J   **E.** 138 J

52. An object is acted upon by a force as represented by the force vs. position graph below. What is the work done as the object moves from 0 m to 4 m?

A. 10 J   **C.** 20 J

B. 50 J   **D.** 30 J   **E.** 60 J

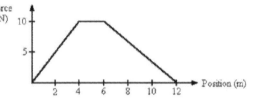

53. James and Bob throw identical balls vertically upward. James throws his ball with an initial speed twice that of Bob's. Assuming no air resistance, what is the maximum height of James's ball compared with that of Bob's ball?

A. Equal   **C.** Four times

B. Eight times   **D.** Two times   **E.** $\sqrt{2}$ times

54. The graphs show the magnitude of the force (F) exerted by a spring as a function of the distance (x) the spring has been stretched. Which of the graphs shows a spring that obeys Hooke's Law?

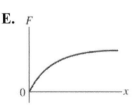

55. If a rocket travels through the air, it loses some of its kinetic energy due to air resistance. Some of this transferred energy:

     A. decreases the temperature of the air around the rocket

     B. is found in increased KE of the rocket

     C. is found in increased KE of the air molecules

     D. decreases the temperature of the rocket

     E. is found in increased PE of the air molecules

Rotational Motion

1. Suppose a uniform solid sphere of mass M and radius R rolls without slipping down an inclined plane starting from rest. The linear velocity of the sphere at the bottom of the incline depends on:

   A. the radius of the sphere
   B. the mass of the sphere
   C. both the mass and the radius of the sphere
   D. neither the mass nor the radius of the sphere
   E. both the mass and the square root of the radius of the sphere

2. A solid, uniform sphere of mass 2.0 kg and radius 1.7 m rolls from rest without slipping down an inclined plane of height 5.3 m. What is the angular velocity of the sphere at the bottom of the inclined plane?

   A. 3.7 rad/s   **B.** 5.1 rad/s   **C.** 6.7 rad/s   **D.** 8.3 rad/s   **E.** 11.9 rad/s

3. A solid uniform ball with a mass of 125.0 g is rolling without slipping along the horizontal surface of a table with a speed of 4.5 m/s when it rolls off the edge and falls towards the floor, 1.1 m below. What is the rotational kinetic energy of the ball just before it hits the floor?

   A. 0.51 J
   B. 0.87 J
   C. 1.03 J
   D. 2.26 J
   E. Requires the radius of the ball

4. David swings a 0.38 kg ball in a circle on a string that is 1.3 m long. What is the magnitude of the ball's angular momentum, if the ball makes 1.2 rev/s?

   A. 0.6 kg·m^2/s
   B. 2.2 kg·m^2/s
   C. 3.6 kg·m^2/s
   D. 4.8 kg·m^2/s
   E. 6.2 kg·m^2/s

5. An ice skater has a moment of inertia of 5.0 kg·m^2 when her arms are outstretched, and at this time she is spinning at 3.0 rev/s. If she pulls in her arms and decreases her moment of inertia to 2.0 kg·m^2, how fast will she be spinning?

   A. 1.8 rev/s   **B.** 4.5 rev/s   **C.** 7.5 rev/s   **D.** 10.5 rev/s   **E.** 12.5 rev/s

6. The angular momentum of a system remains constant when:

   A. its total kinetic energy is constant
   B. the moment of inertia is constant
   C. no net external torque acts on the system
   D. no net external force acts on the system
   E. the linear momentum and the energy are constant

7. A bicycle has wheels that are 60.0 cm in diameter. What is the angular speed of these wheels when it is moving at 4.0 m/s?

A. 0.28 rad/s   **C.** 3.4 rad/s

B. 1.6 rad/s   **D.** 6.7 rad/s   **E.** 13.3 rad/s

8. What is the kinetic energy of a thin uniform rod of length 120.0 cm with a mass of 450.0 g that is rotating about its center along the short axis at 3.60 rad/s? (The short axis is perpendicular to the axis of the rod. Imagine spinning the rod like an airplane propeller.)

A. 0.350 J   **C.** 2.70 J

B. 1.30 J   **D.** 4.96 J   **E.** 6.10 J

9. A rope is wrapped around a wheel of radius R = 2.0 meters. The wheel is mounted with frictionless bearings on an axle through its center. A block of mass 14.0 kg is suspended from the end of the rope. When the system is released from rest, it is observed that the block descends 10.0 meters in 2.0 seconds. What is the moment of inertia of the wheel?

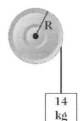

A. 300.0 kg·m^2 **C.** 53.8 kg·m^2

B. 185.0 kg·m^2 **D.** 521.0 kg·m^2 **E.** 88.5 kg·m^2

10. A string is wrapped tightly around a fixed frictionless pulley that has a moment of inertia of 0.0352 kg·m^2 and a radius of 12.5 cm. The string is pulled away from the pulley with a constant force of 5.00 N, causing the pulley to rotate. If the string does not slip on the pulley, what is the speed of the string after it has unwound 1.25 m? Consider the string to be massless.

A. 0.69 m/s   **C.** 3.62 m/s

B. 2.36 m/s   **D.** 4.90 m/s   **E.** 6.12 m/s

11. When a rigid object rotates about a fixed axis, what is true about all the points in the object?

     I. They all have the same angular acceleration
     II. They all have the same tangential acceleration
     III. They all have the same radial acceleration

A. I only   **C.** III only

B. II only   **D.** I and II only   **E.** I, II and III

12. A small mass is placed on a record turntable that is rotating at 33.33 rpm. The linear velocity of the mass is:

A. zero
B. directed parallel to the line joining the mass and the center of rotation
C. independent (in magnitude) of the position of the mass on the turntable
D. greater the closer the mass is to the center
E. greater the farther the mass is from the center

---

13. To drive a midsize car at 40.0 mph on a level road for one hour requires about 3.2×10^7 J of energy. Suppose this much energy was attempted to be stored in a spinning, solid, uniform, cylindrical flywheel. If a flywheel with a diameter 1.2 m and mass 400.0 kg were used, what angular speed would be required to store 3.2×10^7 J?

A. 380 rad/s   C. 940 rad/s

B. 620 rad/s   D. 1,450 rad/s   E. 2,860 rad/s

14. A wheel having a moment of inertia of 5.0 kg·m^2 starts from rest and accelerates for 8.0 s under a constant torque of 3.0 N·m. What is the wheel's rotational kinetic energy at the end of 8.0 s?

A. 29 J   C. 83 J

B. 58 J   D. 112 J   E. 146 J

15. When a rigid object rotates about a fixed axis, what is true about all the points in the object?

     I. They have the same angular speed
     II. They have the same tangential speed
     III. They have the same angular acceleration

A. I only   C. III only

B. II only   D. I and III only   E. I, II and III

16. A uniform, solid cylindrical flywheel of radius 1.4 m and mass 15.0 kg rotates at 2.4 rad/s. What is the magnitude of the flywheel's angular momentum?

A. 11 kg·m^2/s   C. 25 kg·m^2/s

B. 18 kg·m^2/s   D. 35 kg·m^2/s   E. 64 kg·m^2/s

17. A uniform solid disk is released from rest and rolls without slipping down an inclined plane that makes an angle of 25° with the horizontal. What is the forward speed of the disk after it has rolled 3.0 m, measured along the plane?

A. 0.8 m/s   C. 2.9 m/s

B. 1.8 m/s   D. 3.5 m/s   E. 4.1 m/s

18. A tire is rolling along a road, without slipping, with a center-of-mass velocity v. A piece of tape is attached to the tire. When the tape is opposite the road (at the top of the tire), what is its velocity with respect to the road?

A. $2v$ C. $1.5v$

B. v D. $\sqrt{v}$ E. The velocity depends on the radius of the tire

19. A string is wound tightly around a fixed pulley having a radius of 5.0 cm. As the string is pulled, the pulley rotates without any slipping of the string. What is the angular speed of the pulley when the string is moving at 5.0 m/s?

A. 10.0 rad/s   **C.** 75.0 rad/s

B. 25.0 rad/s   **D.** 100.0 rad/s   **E.** 150.0 rad/s

20. A 1.4 kg object at $x = 2.00$ m, $y = 3.10$ m moves at 4.62 m/s at an angle 45° north of east. What is the magnitude of the object's angular momentum about the origin?

A. 1.2 kg·m²/s   **C.** 3.8 kg·m²/s

B. 2.6 kg·m²/s   **D.** 5.0 kg·m²/s   **E.** 8.4 kg·m²/s

21. When a fan is turned off, its angular speed decreases from 10.0 rad/s to 6.3 rad/s in 5.0 s. What is the magnitude of the average angular acceleration of the fan?

A. 0.46 rad/s²   **C.** 1.86 rad/s²

B. 0.74 rad/s²   **D.** 2.80 rad/s²   **E.** 3.62 rad/s²

22. At time $t = 0$ s, a wheel has an angular displacement of 0 radians and an angular velocity of +26.0 rad/s. The wheel has a constant acceleration of –0.43 rad/s². In this situation, what is the time t (after $t = 0$ s), at which the kinetic energy of the wheel is twice the initial value?

A. 48 s   **B.** 86 s   **C.** 115 s   **D.** 146 s   **E.** 185 s

23. A solid uniform disk of diameter 3.20 m and mass 42.0 kg rolls without slipping to the bottom of a hill, starting from rest. If the angular speed of the disk is 4.27 rad/s at the bottom, how high vertically did it start on the hill above the bottom?

A. 2.46 m   **B.** 3.57 m   **C.** 4.85 m   **D.** 6.24 m   **E.** 8.44 m

24. When Steve rides a bicycle, in what direction is the angular velocity of the wheels?

A. to his left   **C.** forward

B. to his right   **D.** backward   **E.** up

25. A rolling wheel of a diameter of 68.0 cm slows down uniformly from 8.4 m/s to rest over a distance of 115.0 m. What is the magnitude of its angular acceleration if there was no slipping?

A. 0.90 rad/s²   **C.** 4.2 rad/s²

B. 1.6 rad/s²   **D.** 7.8 rad/s²   **E.** 11.4 rad/s²

26. A uniform solid cylinder with a radius of 10.0 cm and a mass of 3.0 kg is rotating about its center axis with an angular speed of 33.4 rpm. What is the kinetic energy of the uniform solid cylinder?

A. 0.091 J   **C.** 0.66 J
B. 0.19 J   **D.** 1.14 J   **E.** 2.46 J

27. A uniform 135.0-g meter stick rotates about an axis perpendicular to the stick passing through its center with an angular speed of 3.50 rad/s. What is the magnitude of the angular momentum of the stick?

A. 0.0394 kg·m²/s   **C.** 0.286 kg·m²/s
B. 0.0848 kg·m²/s   **D.** 0.458 kg·m²/s   **E.** 0.826 kg·m²/s

28. A 23.0 kg mass is connected to a nail on a frictionless table by a massless string of length 1.3 m. If the tension in the string is 51.0 N while the mass moves in a uniform circle on the table, how long does it take for the mass to make one complete revolution?

A. 2.8 s   **C.** 4.8 s
B. 3.6 s   **D.** 5.4 s   **E.** 6.2 s

29. A machinist turns on the power to a grinding wheel at time $t = 0$ s. The wheel accelerates uniformly from rest for 10.0 s and reaches the operating angular speed of 38.0 rad/s. The wheel is run at that angular speed for 30.0 s and then power is shut off. The wheel slows down uniformly at 2.1 rad/s² until the wheel stops. What is the angular acceleration of the wheel between $t = 0$ s and $t = 10.0$ s?

A. 1.21 rad/s²   **C.** 3.80 rad/s²
B. 2.63 rad/s²   **D.** 5.40 rad/s²   **E.** 6.81 rad/s²

30. A force of 17.0 N is applied to the end of a 0.63 m long torque wrench at an angle 45° from a line joining the pivot point to the handle. What is the magnitude of the torque generated about the pivot point?

A. 4.3 N·m   **C.** 7.6 N·m
B. 8.2 N·m   **D.** 11.8 N·m   **E.** 14.0 N·m

31. A solid disk of radius 1.60 m and mass 2.30 kg rolls from rest without slipping to the bottom of an inclined plane. If the angular velocity of the disk is 4.27 rad/s at the bottom, what is the height of the inclined plane?

A. 0.57 m   **C.** 2.84 m
B. 1.08 m   **D.** 3.57 m   **E.** 5.66 m

32. A merry-go-round spins freely when Paul moves quickly to the center along a radius of the merry-go-round. As he does this, the moment of inertia of the system:

    A. increases and the angular speed increases
    B. decreases and the angular speed remains the same
    C. decreases and the angular speed decreases
    D. decreases and the angular speed increases
    E. increases and the angular speed decreases

33. What is the angular speed of a compact disc that, at a certain instant, is rotating at 210.0 rpm?

    A. 8.5 rad/s   **C.** 36.4 rad/s
    B. 22.0 rad/s   **D.** 52.6 rad/s   **E.** 68.2 rad/s

34. A solid uniform sphere is rolling without slipping along a horizontal surface with a speed of 5.5 m/s when it starts up a ramp that makes an angle of 25° with the horizontal. What is the speed of the sphere after it has rolled 3.0 m up as measured along the surface of the ramp?

    A. 0.8 m/s   **B.** 1.6 m/s   **C.** 3.5 m/s   **D.** 4.8 m/s   **E.** 6.4 m/s

35. A force of 16.88 N is applied tangentially to a wheel of radius 0.340 m and gives rise to angular acceleration of 1.20 rad/s². What is the rotational inertia of the wheel?

    A. 1.48 kg·m²   **C.** 3.48 kg·m²
    B. 2.26 kg·m²   **D.** 4.78 kg·m²   **E.** 6.42 kg·m²

36. A machine does 3.9 kJ of work on a spinning flywheel to bring it from 500.0 rpm to rest. This flywheel is in the shape of a solid uniform disk of radius 1.2 m. What is the mass of this flywheel?

    A. 2.6 kg   **B.** 4.0 kg   **C.** 5.2 kg   **D.** 6.4 kg   **E.** 8.6 kg

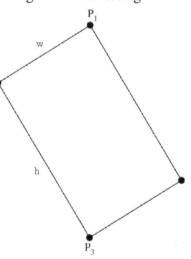

37. A rectangular billboard with h = 20.0 cm high and w = 11.0 cm wide loses three of its four support bolts and rotates into the position as shown, with P_1 directly over P_3.

It is supported by P_2, which is so tight it holds the billboard from further rotation. What is the gravitational torque about P_2, if the mass of the billboard is 5.0 kg?

    A. 1.2 Nm   **C.** 4.7 Nm
    B. 2.5 Nm   **D.** 6.8 Nm   **E.** 8.2 Nm

38. A disk, a hoop, and a solid sphere are released at the same time at the top of an inclined plane. In which order do they reach the bottom if each is uniform and rolls without slipping?

A. sphere, hoop, disk   **C.** hoop, sphere, disk

B. sphere, disk, hoop   **D.** disk, hoop, sphere   **E.** hoop, disk, sphere

39. A uniform disk is attached at the rim to a vertical shaft and is used as a cam. A side view and top view of the disk and shaft are shown.

The disk has a diameter of 80.0 cm. The moment of inertia of the disk about the axis of the shaft is 6.0×10^{-3} kg·m^2. What is the kinetic energy of the disk as the shaft rotates uniformly about its axis at 96.0 rpm?

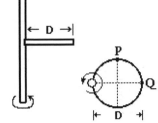

A. 0.18 J   **C.** 0.49 J

B. 0.30 J   **D.** 0.57 J   **E.** 1.0 J

40. A scooter has wheels with a diameter of 240.0 mm. What is the angular speed of the wheels when the scooter is moving forward at 6.00 m/s?

A. 128.6 rpm   **C.** 472.0 rpm

B. 248.2 rpm   **D.** 478.0 rpm   **E.** 1,260.6 rpm

41. A spinning ice skater on frictionless ice can control the rate at which she rotates by pulling in her arms. Which of the following statements are true about the skater during this process?

    I. Her kinetic energy remains constant
    II. Her moment of inertia remains constant
    III. Her angular momentum remains constant

A. I only   **C.** III only

B. II only   **D.** I and II only   **E.** I, II and III

42. Tanya is riding a merry-go-round that has an instantaneous angular speed of 1.25 rad/s and an angular acceleration of 0.745 rad/s^2. Tanya is standing 4.65 m from the center of the merry-go-round. What is the magnitude of the linear acceleration of Tanya?

A. 2.45 m/s^2 **C.** 6.82 m/s^2

B. 4.20 m/s^2 **D.** 8.05 m/s^2 **E.** 12.10 m/s^2

43. Through how many degrees does a 33.0 rpm turntable rotate in 0.32 s?

    A. 31°   **B.** 42°   **C.** 63°   **D.** 76°   **E.** 85°

44. A 50.0 kg uniform ladder, length $L = 5.00$ m long, is placed against a smooth wall at the height of $h = 3.70$ m. The base of the ladder rests on a rough horizontal surface whose coefficient of static friction $\mu = 0.750$. An 80.0 kg block is suspended from the top rung of the ladder, just at the wall. What is the approximate magnitude of the force exerted on the base of the ladder, due to contact with the rough horizontal surface?

A. 1,370 N   **C.** 1,580 N

B. 1,460 N   **D.** 1,640 N   **E.** 1,760 N

45. At time $t = 0$ s, a wheel has an angular displacement of zero radians and an angular velocity of +29.0 rad/s. The wheel has a constant acceleration of -0.52 rad/s^2. In this situation, what is the maximum value of the angular displacement?

A. +467 rad   **C.** +1,110 rad

B. +809 rad   **D.** +1,460 rad   **E.** +1,840 rad

46. A disk lies in the xz-plane with its center at the origin. When viewed from the positive y-axis (i.e., above the disk), the direction of rotation appears clockwise. In what direction does the angular velocity of the disk point?

A. to her right   **C.** down

B. to her left   **D.** up   **E.** forwards

Waves and Periodic Motion

1. A simple harmonic oscillator oscillates with frequency f when its amplitude is A. What is the new frequency if the amplitude is doubled to 2A?

A. $f / 2$ **B.** f **C.** $4f$ **D.** $2f$ **E.** $f / 4$

2. Springs A and B are attached in series with the free end of spring B attached to a wall. The free end of spring A is pulled, and both springs expand from their equilibrium lengths. The length of spring A increases by L_A, and the length of spring B increases by L_B. What is the expression for the spring constant k_B of spring B?

A. L_B/k_A **B.** k_A^2 **C.** $k_A L_B$ **D.** $(k_A L_A) / L_B$ **E.** $2k_A$

3. Particles of a material that move back and forth in the same direction the wave is moving are in what type of wave?

A. Standing   **C.** Transverse
B. Torsional   **D.** Longitudinal
                        E. Diffusion

4. If a wave has a wavelength of 25 cm and a frequency of 1.68 kHz, what is its speed?

A. 44 m/s   **B.** 160 m/s   **C.** 420 m/s   **D.** 314 m/s   **E.** 16 m/s

5. The total stored energy in a system undergoing simple harmonic motion (SHM) is proportional to the:

A. (amplitude)^2 **C.** (spring constant)^2
B. wavelength   **D.** amplitude   **E.** $\sqrt{\lambda}$

6. An 11 kg mass m is attached to a spring and allowed to hang in the Earth's gravitational field. The spring stretches 3 cm before reaching its equilibrium position. If the spring were allowed to oscillate, what would be its frequency? (Use acceleration due to gravity $g = 9.8$ m/s^2)

A. 0.7 Hz   **B.** 1.8 Hz   **C.** 4.1 Hz   **D.** 0.6×10^{-3} Hz   **E.** 2.9 Hz

7. The time required for one cycle of any repeating event is the:

A. amplitude   **C.** period
B. frequency   **D.** rotation   **E.** second

8. A pendulum of length L is suspended from the ceiling of an elevator. When the elevator is at rest, the period of the pendulum is T. How does T change when the elevator moves upward with a constant velocity?

    A. Decreases only if the upward acceleration is less than $\frac{1}{2}g$

    B. Decreases

    C. Increases

    D. Remains the same

    E. Increases only if the upward acceleration is more than $\frac{1}{2}g$

9. What is the period of a transverse wave with a frequency of 100 Hz?

    A. 0.01 s   **B.** 0.05 s   **C.** 0.2 s   **D.** 20 s   **E.** 50 s

10. Two radio antennae are located on a seacoast 10 km apart on a North-South axis. The antennas broadcast identical in-phase AM radio waves at a frequency of 4.7 MHz. 200 km offshore, a steamship travels North at 15 km/h passing East of the antennae with a radio tuned to the broadcast frequency. From the moment of the maximum reception of the radio signal on the ship, what is the time interval until the next occurrence of maximum reception? (Use the speed of radio waves equals the speed of light $c = 3 \times 10^8$ m/s and the path difference $= 1\ \lambda$)

    A. 7.7 min   **B.** 6.4 min   **C.** 3.8 min   **D.** 8.9 min   **E.** 5.1 min

11. A 2.31 kg rope is stretched between supports 10.4 m apart. If one end of the rope is tweaked, how long will it take for the resulting disturbance to reach the other end? Assume that the tension in the rope is 74.4 N.

    A. 0.33 s   **B.** 0.74 s   **C.** 0.65 s   **D.** 0.57 s   **E.** 0.42 s

12. Simple pendulum A swings back and forth at twice the frequency of simple pendulum B. Which statement is correct?

    A. Pendulum A is $\frac{1}{4}$ as long as B   **C.** Pendulum A is $\frac{1}{2}$ as long as B

    B. Pendulum A is twice as massive as B   **D.** Pendulum B is twice as massive as A

                                                       E. Pendulum B is $\frac{1}{4}$ as long as A

13. A weight attached to the free end of an anchored spring is allowed to slide back and forth in simple harmonic motion on a frictionless table. How many times greater is the spring's restoring force at $x = 5$ cm compared to $x = 1$ cm (measured from equilibrium)?

    A. 2.5   **B.** 5   **C.** 7.5   **D.** 15   **E.** $\sqrt{2.5}$

14. A massless, ideal spring projects horizontally from a wall and is connected to a 1 kg mass. The mass is oscillating in one dimension, such that it moves 0.5 m from one end of its oscillation to the other. It undergoes 10 complete oscillations in 60 s. What is the period of the oscillation?

   A. 9 s   **B.** 3 s   **C.** 6 s   **D.** 12 s   **E.** 0.6 s

15. The total mechanical energy of a simple harmonic oscillating system is:

   A. always zero, which is why it is oscillating
   B. maximum when it reaches the maximum displacement
   C. zero when it reaches the maximum displacement
   D. zero as it passes the equilibrium point
   E. a nonzero constant

16. What is the frequency of the oscillations when a vibrating spring moves from its position of maximum elongation to its position of maximum compression in 1 s?

   A. 0.75 Hz   **B.** 0.5 Hz   **C.** 1 Hz   **D.** 2.5 Hz   **E.** 4 Hz

17. Which of the following is not a transverse wave?

    I. Radio   II. Light   III. Sound

   A. I only   **B.** II only   **C.** III only   **D.** I and II only   **E.** I and III only

18. If a wave has a speed of 362 m/s and a period of 4 ms, its wavelength is closest to:

   A. 8.6 m   **B.** 5.2 m   **C.** 0.86 m   **D.** 15 m   **E.** 1.5 m

19. Simple harmonic motion is characterized by:

   A. acceleration that is proportional to the negative displacement
   B. acceleration that is proportional to the velocity
   C. constant positive acceleration
   D. acceleration that is inversely proportional to the negative displacement
   E. acceleration that is inversely proportional to the velocity

20. If the frequency of a harmonic oscillator doubles, by what factor does the maximum value of acceleration change?

   A. $2/\pi$ **B.** $\sqrt{2}$ **C.** 2   **D.** 4   **E.** ½

21. An object that hangs from the ceiling of a stationary elevator by an ideal spring oscillates with a period T. If the elevator were to accelerate upwards with an acceleration of 2*g*, what is the period of oscillation of the object?

    A. T/2   **B.** T   **C.** 2T   **D.** 4T   **E.** T/4

22. Which of the following changes made to a transverse wave must increase wavelength?

    A. An increase in frequency and a decrease in speed
    B. The wavelength is only affected by a change in amplitude
    C. An increase in frequency and an increase in speed
    D. A decrease in frequency and a decrease in speed
    E. A decrease in frequency and an increase in speed

23. If a wave travels 30 m in 1 s, making 60 vibrations per second, what are its frequency and speed, respectively?

    A. 30 Hz and 60 m/s   **C.** 30 Hz and 30 m/s
    B. 60 Hz and 30 m/s   **D.** 60 Hz and 15 m/s   **E.** 15 Hz and 30 m/s

24. Transverse waves propagate at 40 m/s in a string that is subjected to a tension of 60 N. If the string is 16 m long, what is its mass?

    A. 0.6 kg   **B.** 0.9 kg   **C.** 0.2 kg   **D.** 9 kg   **E.** 2 kg

25. Doubling only the amplitude of a vibrating mass-on-spring system, changes the system frequency by what factor?

    A. Increases by 3   **C.** Increases by 5
    B. Increases by 2   **D.** Increases by 4   **E.** Remains the same

26. A leaky faucet drips 60 times in 40 s. What is the frequency of the dripping?

    A. 0.75 Hz   **B.** 0.67 Hz   **C.** 1.5 Hz   **D.** 12 Hz   **E.** 0.3 Hz

27. Particles of a material that move up and down perpendicular to the direction that the wave is moving are in what type of wave?

    A. torsional   **C.** longitudinal
    B. mechanical   **D.** transverse   **E.** surface

28. The figure shows a graph of the velocity v as a function of time t for a system undergoing simple harmonic motion. Which one of the following graphs represents the acceleration of this system as a function of time?

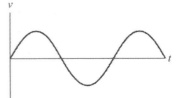

A.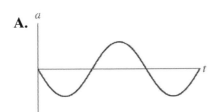

C.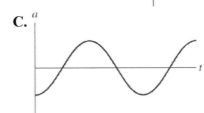

B.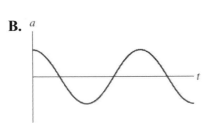

D.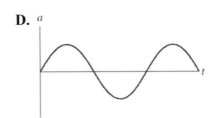

E. None of these

29. When compared, a transverse wave and a longitudinal wave are found to have amplitudes of equal magnitude. Which statement is true about their speeds?

   A. The waves have the same speeds
   B. The transverse wave has exactly twice the speed of the longitudinal wave
   C. The transverse wave has a slower speed
   D. The longitudinal wave has a slower speed
   E. The speeds of the two waves are unrelated to their amplitudes

30. What is the frequency when a weight on the end of a spring bobs up and down and completes one cycle every 2 s?

   A. 0.5 Hz   **B.** 1 Hz   **C.** 2 Hz   **D.** 2.5 Hz   **E.** Depends on the mass

31. The velocity of a given longitudinal sound wave in an ideal gas is $v = 340$ m/s at constant pressure and constant volume. Assuming an ideal gas, what is the wavelength for a 2,100 Hz sound wave?

   A. 0.08 m   **B.** 0.16 m   **C.** 1.6 m   **D.** 7.3 m   **E.** 0.73 m

32. When the mass of a simple pendulum is quadrupled, how does the time t required for one complete oscillation change?

   A. Decreases to ¼t **C.** Increases to 4t
   B. Decreases to ¾t **D.** Remains the same   **E.** Decreases to ½t

33. An object undergoing simple harmonic motion has an amplitude of 2.5 m. If the maximum velocity of the object is 15 m/s, what is the object's angular frequency (ω)?

    A. 0.17 rad/s   **B.** 3.6 rad/s   **C.** 37.5 rad/s   **D.** 8.8 rad/s   **E.** 6.0 rad/s

34. Unpolarized light is incident upon two polarization filters that do not have their transmission axes aligned. If 14% of the light passes through, what is the measure of the angle between the transmission axes of the filters?

    A. 73°   **B.** 81°   **C.** 43°   **D.** 58°   **E.** 64°

35. A mass on a spring undergoes simple harmonic motion. Which of the statements is true when the mass is at its maximum distance from the equilibrium position?

    A. KE is nonzero
    B. Acceleration is at a minimum
    C. Speed is zero
    D. Speed is maximum
    E. Total mechanical energy = KE

36. What is the frequency if the speed of a sound wave is 240 m/s and its wavelength is 10 cm?

    A. 2.4 Hz   **B.** 24 Hz   **C.** 240 Hz   **D.** 2,400 Hz   **E.** 0.24 Hz

37. Unlike a transverse wave, a longitudinal wave has no:

    A. wavelength
    B. crests or troughs
    C. amplitude
    D. frequency
    E. all of the above

38. The density of aluminum is 2,700 kg/m³. If transverse waves propagate at 36 m/s in a 9.2 mm diameter aluminum wire, what is the tension in the wire?

    A. 43 N   **B.** 68 N   **C.** 233 N   **D.** 350 N   **E.** 72 N

39. When a wave obliquely crosses a boundary into another medium, it is:

    A. always slowed down
    B. reflected
    C. diffracted
    D. refracted
    E. always sped up

40. A floating leaf oscillates up and down two complete cycles each second as a water wave passes by. What is the wave's frequency?

    A. 0.5 Hz   **B.** 1 Hz   **C.** 2 Hz   **D.** 3 Hz   **E.** 6 Hz

41. A higher pitch for a sound wave means the wave has a greater:

    A. frequency
    B. wavelength
    C. amplitude
    D. period
    E. acceleration

42. An object is attached to a vertical spring and bobs up and down between points A and B. Where is the object located when its kinetic energy is at a maximum?

A. One-fourth of the way between A and B
C. Midway between A and B
B. One-third of the way between A and B
D. At either A or B
E. At none of the above points

43. A pendulum consists of a 0.5 kg mass attached to the end of a 1 m rod of negligible mass. What is the magnitude of the torque τ about the pivot when the rod makes an angle θ of 60° with the vertical? (Use acceleration due to gravity $g = 10$ m/s^2)

A. 2.7 N·m   **B.** 4.4 N·m   **C.** 5.2 N·m   **D.** 10.6 N·m   **E.** 12.7 N·m

44. The Doppler effect is characteristic of:

   I. light waves   II. sound waves   III. water waves

A. I only   **B.** II only   **C.** III only   **D.** I and III only   **E.** I, II and III

45. A crane lifts a 2,500 kg cement block using a steel cable which has a mass per unit length of 0.65 kg/m. What is the speed of the transverse waves on this cable? (Use acceleration due to gravity $g = 10$ m/s^2)

A. 196 m/s   **B.** 1,162 m/s   **C.** 322 m/s   **D.** 558 m/s   **E.** 1,420 m/s

46. A simple pendulum consists of a mass M attached to a weightless string of length L. Which statement about the frequency f is accurate for this system when it experiences small oscillations?

A. The f is directly proportional to the period
B. The f is independent of the mass M
C. The f is inversely proportional to the amplitude
D. The f is independent of the length L
E. The f is dependent on the mass M

47. A child on a swing set swings back and forth. If the length of the supporting cables for the swing is 3.3 m, what is the period of oscillation? (Use acceleration due to gravity $g = 10$ m/s^2)

A. 3.6 s   **B.** 5.9 s   **C.** 4.3 s   **D.** 2.7 s   **E.** 5 s

48. A massless, ideal spring projects horizontally from a wall and is connected to a 0.3 kg mass. The mass is oscillating in one dimension, such that it moves 0.4 m from one end of its oscillation to the other. It undergoes 15 complete oscillations in 60 s. How does the frequency change if the spring constant is increased by a factor of 2?

A. Increases by 200%
C. Increases by 41%
B. Decreases by 59%
D. Decreases by 41%
E. Increases by 59%

49. A ball swinging at the end of a massless string undergoes simple harmonic motion. At what point(s) is the instantaneous acceleration of the ball the greatest?

A. A **C.** C

B. B **D.** A and D **E.** B and C

50. A simple pendulum, consisting of a 2 kg weight connected to a 10 m massless rod, is brought to an angle of 90° from the vertical, and then released. What is the speed of the weight at its lowest point? (Use the acceleration due to gravity $g = 10$ m/s²)

A. 14 m/s **B.** 10 m/s **C.** 20 m/s **D.** 25 m/s **E.** 7 m/s

51. A sound source of high pitch emits a wave with a high:

I. frequency II. amplitude III. speed

A. I only **B.** II only **C.** III only **D.** I, II and III **E.** I and III only

52. Find the wavelength of a train whistle that is heard by a fixed observer as the train moves toward him with a velocity of 50 m/s. Wind blows at 5 m/s from the observer to the train. The whistle has a natural frequency of 500 Hz. (Use the v of sound = 340 m/s)

A. 0.75 m **B.** 0.43 m **C.** 0.58 m **D.** 7.5 m **E.** 5.5 m

53. Considering a vibrating mass on a spring, what effect on the system's mechanical energy is caused by doubling of the amplitude only?

A. Increases by a factor of two

B. Increases by a factor of four

C. Increases by a factor of three

D. Produces no change

E. Increases by a factor of $\sqrt{2}$

54. Which of the following is an accurate statement?

A. Tensile stress is measured in N·m

B. Stress is a measure of external forces on a body

C. Stress is inversely proportional to strain

D. Tensile strain is measured in meters

E. The ratio stress/strain is called the elastic modulus

55. The efficient transfer of energy taking place at a natural frequency occurs in a phenomenon called:

A. reverberation **C.** beats

B. the Doppler effect **D.** resonance **E.** the standing wave phenomenon

Sound

1. A 20 decibel (dB) noise is heard from a cricket 30 m away. How loud would it sound if the cricket were 3 m away?

   A. 30 dB   **B.** 40 dB   **C.** $20 \times \sqrt{2}$ dB   **D.** 80 dB   **E.** 60 dB

2. A thunderclap occurs at a distance of 6 km from a stationary person. How soon does the person hear it? (Use speed of sound in air $v = 340$ m/s)

   A. 18 s   **B.** 30 s   **C.** 48 s   **D.** 56 s   **E.** 96 s

3. Enrico Caruso, a famous opera singer, is said to have made a crystal chandelier shatter with his voice. This is a demonstration of:

   A. ideal frequency   **C.** a standing wave
   B. resonance   **D.** sound refraction   **E.** interference

4. A taut 2 m string is fixed at both ends and plucked. What is the wavelength corresponding to the third harmonic?

   A. 2/3 m   **B.** 1 m   **C.** 4/3 m   **D.** 3 m   **E.** 4 m

5. High-pitched sound has a high:

   I. number of partial tones   II. frequency   III. speed

   A. I only   **B.** II only   **C.** III only   **D.** I and II only   **E.** I and III only

6. A light ray in air strikes a medium whose index of refraction is 1.5. If the angle of incidence is 60°, which of the following expressions gives the angle of refraction? (Use the $n_{air} = 1$)

   A. $\sin^{-1}(1.5 \sin 60°)$ **C.** $\sin^{-1}(1.5 \sin 30°)$
   B. $\sin^{-1}(1.5 \cos 60°)$ **D.** $\sin^{-1}(0.67 \sin 30°)$ **E.** $\sin^{-1}(0.67 \sin 60°)$

7. A string, 2 m in length, is fixed at both ends and tightened until the wave speed is 92 m/s. What is the frequency of the standing wave shown?

   A. 46 Hz   **B.** 33 Hz   **C.** 240 Hz   **D.** 138 Hz   **E.** 184 Hz

8. A 0.6 m uniform bar of metal, with a diameter of 2 cm, has a mass of 2.5 kg. A 1.5 MHz longitudinal wave is propagated along the length of the bar. A wave compression traverses the length of the bar in 0.14 ms. What is the wavelength of the longitudinal wave in the metal?

   A. 2.9 mm   **B.** 1.8 mm   **C.** 3.2 mm   **D.** 4.6 mm   **E.** 3.8 mm

Questions **9-12** are based on the following:

The velocity of a wave on a wire or string is not dependent (to a close approximation) on frequency or amplitude and is given by $v^2 = T / \rho_L$. T is the tension in the wire. The linear mass density ρ_L (rho) is the mass per unit length of wire. Therefore, ρ_L is the product of the mass density and the cross-sectional area (A).

A sine wave is traveling to the right with frequency 250 Hz. Wire A is composed of steel and has a circular cross-section diameter of 0.6 mm, and a tension of 2,000 N. Wire B is under the same tension and is made of the same material as wire A, but has a circular cross-section diameter of 0.3 mm. Wire C has the same tension as wire A and is made of a composite material. (Use the density of steel wire $\rho = 7$ g/cm^3 and the density of the composite material $\rho = 3$ g/cm^3)

9. By how much does the tension need to be increased to increase the wave velocity on a wire by 30%?

    A. 37%   **B.** 60%   **C.** 69%   **D.** 81%   **E.** 74%

10. What is the linear mass density of wire B compared to wire A?

    A. $\sqrt{2}$ times   **B.** 2 times   **C.** 1/8   **D.** 1/4   **E.** 4 times

11. What must the diameter of wire C be to have the same wave velocity as wire A?

    A. 0.41 mm   **B.** 0.92 mm   **C.** 0.83 mm   **D.** 3.2 mm   **E.** 0.2 mm

12. How does the cross-sectional area change if the diameter increases by a factor of 4?

    A. Increases by a factor of 16   **C.** Increases by a factor of 2
    B. Increases by a factor of 4   **D.** Decreases by a factor of 4
                                   E. Increases by a factor of $\sqrt{2}$

13. A bird, emitting sounds with a frequency of 60 kHz, is moving at a speed of 10 m/s toward a stationary observer. What is the frequency of the sound waves detected by the observer? (Use the speed of sound in air $v = 340$ m/s)

    A. 55 kHz   **B.** 46 kHz   **C.** 68 kHz   **D.** 76 kHz   **E.** 62 kHz

14. What is observed for a frequency heard by a stationary person when a sound source is approaching?

    A. Equal to zero   **C.** Higher than the source
    B. The same as the source   **D.** Lower than the source
                                  E. Requires more information

15. Which of the following is a false statement?

A. The transverse waves on a vibrating string are different from sound waves
B. Sound travels much slower than light
C. Sound waves are longitudinal pressure waves
D. Sound can travel through a vacuum
E. Perceived musical pitch is correlated with the frequency

16. Which of the following is a real-life example of the Doppler effect?

A. London police whistle, which uses two short pipes to produce a three-note sound
B. Radio signal transmission
C. Sound becomes quieter as the observer moves away from the source
D. Human hearing is most acute at 2,500 Hz
E. Changing pitch of the siren as an ambulance passes by the observer

17. Two sound waves have the same frequency and amplitudes of 0.4 Pa and 0.6 Pa, respectively. When they arrive at point X, what is the range of possible amplitudes for sound at point X?

A. 0 – 0.4 Pa
B. 0.4 – 0.6 Pa
C. 0.2 – 1.0 Pa
D. 0.4 – 0.8 Pa
E. 0.2 – 0.6 Pa

18. The intensity of the waves from a point source at a distance d from the source is I. What is the intensity at a distance $2d$ from the source?

A. I/2
B. I/4
C. 4I
D. 2I
E. I/$\sqrt{2}$

19. Sound would be expected to travel most slowly in a medium that exhibited:

A. low resistance to compression and high density
B. high resistance to compression and low density
C. low resistance to compression and low density
D. high resistance to compression and high density
E. equal resistance to compression and density

20. Which is true for a resonating pipe that is open at both ends?

A. Displacement node at one end and a displacement antinode at the other end
B. Displacement antinodes at each end
C. Displacement nodes at each end
D. Displacement node at one end and a one-fourth antinode at the other end
E. Displacement antinode at one end and a one-fourth node at the other end

21. In a pipe of length L that is open at both ends, the lowest tone to resonate is 200 Hz. Which of the following frequencies does not resonate in this pipe?

A. 400 Hz
B. 600 Hz
C. 1,200 Hz
D. 800 Hz
E. 500 Hz

22. In general, a sound is conducted fastest through:

A. vacuum   **B.** gases   **C.** liquids   **D.** solids   **E.** warm air

23. If an electric charge is shaken up and down:

A. electron excitation occurs   **C.** sound is emitted

B. a magnetic field is created   **D.** its charge changes   **E.** its mass decreases

24. What is the wavelength of a sound wave of frequency 620 Hz in steel, given that the speed of sound in steel is 5,000 m/s?

A. 1.8 m   **B.** 6.2 m   **C.** 8.1 m   **D.** 2.6 m   **E.** 5.7 m

25. If the sound from a constant sound source is radiating equally in all directions, as the distance doubles, by what amount is the intensity of the sound reduced?

A. 1/8   **B.** 1/16   **C.** $1/\sqrt{2}$ **D.** ½   **E.** ¼

26. Why does the intensity of waves from a sound source decrease with the square of the distance from the source?

A. The medium through which the waves travel absorbs the energy of the waves

B. The waves speed up as they travel away from the source

C. The waves lose energy as they travel

D. The waves spread out as they travel

E. The frequency of the waves decreases as they get farther from the source

---

Questions **27-30** are based on the following:

Steven is preparing a mailing tube that is 1.5 m long and 4 cm in diameter. The tube is open at one end and sealed at the other. Before he inserted his documents, the mailing tube fell to the floor and produced a note. (Use the speed of sound in air $v = 340$ m/s)

27. What is the wavelength of the fundamental?

A. 0.04 m   **B.** 6 m   **C.** 0.75 m   **D.** 1.5 m   **E.** 9 m

28. If the tube was filled with helium, in which sound travels at 960 m/s, what would be the frequency of the fundamental?

A. 160 Hz   **B.** 320 Hz   **C.** 80 Hz   **D.** 640 Hz   **E.** 590 Hz

29. What is the wavelength of the fifth harmonic?

A. 3.2 m   **B.** 0.6 m   **C.** 2.4 m   **D.** 1.5 m   **E.** 1.2 m

30. What is the frequency of the note that Steven heard?

    A. 57 Hz   **B.** 85 Hz   **C.** 30 Hz   **D.** 120 Hz   **E.** 25 Hz

31. A 4 g string, 0.34 m long, is under tension. The string vibrates in the third harmonic. What is the wavelength of the standing wave in the string? (Use the speed of sound in air = 344 m/s)

    A. 0.56 m   **B.** 0.33 m   **C.** 0.23 m   **D.** 0.61 m   **E.** 0.87 m

32. Two pure tones are sounded together, and a particular beat frequency is heard. What happens to the beat frequency if the frequency of one of the tones is increased?

    A. Increases   **C.** Remains the same

    B. Decreases   **D.** Either increase or decrease

                                    E. Increases logarithmically

33. Consider a closed pipe of length L. What are the wavelengths of the three lowest tones produced by this pipe?

    A. $4L$, $4/3L$, $4/5L$ **C.** $2L$, L, ½L

    B. $2L$, L, $2/3L$ **D.** $4L$, $2L$, L **E.** $4L$, $4/3L$, L

34. Mary hears the barely perceptible buzz of a mosquito one meter away from her ear in a quiet room. How much energy does a mosquito produce in 200 s? (Note: an almost inaudible sound has a threshold value of 9.8×10^{-12} W/m²)

    A. 6.1×10^{-8} J   **C.** 6.4×10^{-10} J

    B. 1.3×10^{-8} J   **D.** 3.6×10^{-10} J   **E.** 2.5×10^{-8} J

35. How long does it take for a light wave to travel 1 km through the water with a refractive index of 1.33? (Use the speed of light $c = 3 \times 10^8$ m/s)

    A. 4.4×10^{-6} s   **C.** 2.8×10^{-9} s

    B. 4.4×10^{-9} s   **D.** 2.8×10^{-12} s   **E.** 3.4×10^{-9} s

36. In designing a music hall, an acoustical engineer deals mainly with:

    A. beats   **C.** forced vibrations

    B. resonance   **D.** modulation   **E.** wave interference

37. Which curve in the figure represents the variation of wave speed (v) as a function of tension (T) for transverse waves on a stretched string?

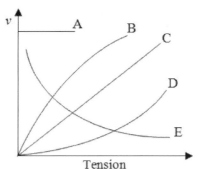

    A. A
    B. B
    C. C
    D. D
    E. E

38. A string, 4 meters in length, is fixed at both ends and tightened until the wave speed is 20 m/s. What is the frequency of the standing wave shown?

    A. 13 Hz   **B.** 8.1 Hz   **C.** 5.4 Hz   **D.** 15.4 Hz   **E.** 7.8 Hz

39. Compared to the velocity of a 600 Hz sound, the velocity of a 300 Hz sound through air is:

    A. one-half as great   **C.** twice as great
    B. one-fourth as great   **D.** four times as great   **E.** the same

40. Consider a string having a linear mass density of 0.40 g/m stretched to a length of 0.50 m by tension of 75 N, vibrating at the 6th harmonic. It excites an open pipe into the second overtone. What is the length of the pipe?

    A. 0.25 m   **B.** 0.1 m   **C.** 0.20 m   **D.** 0.6 m   **E.** 0.32 m

41. A string of length L is under tension, and the speed of a wave in the string is v. What is the speed of a wave in a string of the same mass under the same tension but twice as long?

    A. $v\sqrt{2}$ **B.** $2v$ **C.** $v/2$ **D.** $v/\sqrt{2}$ **E.** $4v$

42. If a guitar string has a fundamental frequency of 500 Hz, which one of the following frequencies can set the string into resonant vibration?

    A. 450 Hz   **B.** 760 Hz   **C.** 1,500 Hz   **D.** 2,250 Hz   **E.** 1,250 Hz

43. When a light wave is passing from a medium with a lower refractive index to a medium with a higher refractive index, some of the incident light is refracted, while some are reflected. What is the angle of refraction?

    A. Greater than the angle of incidence and less than the angle of reflection
    B. Less than the angle of incidence and greater than the angle of reflection
    C. Greater than the angles of incidence and reflection
    D. Less than the angles of incidence and reflection
    E. Equal to the angles of incidence and reflection

44. The speed of a sound wave in air depends on:

    I. the air temperature   II. its wavelength   III. its frequency

    A. I only   **B.** II only   **C.** III only   **D.** I and II only   **E.** I and III only

45. Which of the following statements is false?

    A. The speed of a wave and the speed of the vibrating particles that constitute the wave are different entities
    B. Waves transport energy and matter from one region to another
    C. In a transverse wave, the particle motion is perpendicular to the velocity vector of the wave
    D. Not all waves are mechanical in nature
    E. A wave in which particles move back and forth in the same direction that the wave is moving is referred to as a longitudinal wave

46. A 2.5 g string, 0.75 m long, is under tension. The string produces a 700 Hz tone when it vibrates in the third harmonic. What is the wavelength of the tone in the air? (Use the speed of sound in air $v = 344$ m/s)

    A. 0.65 m   **B.** 0.57 m   **C.** 0.33 m   **D.** 0.4 m   **E.** 0.5 m

47. Suppose that a source of sound is emitting waves uniformly in all directions. If an observer moves to a point twice as far away from the source, what is the frequency of the sound?

    A. $\sqrt{2}$ as large   **C.** Unchanged
    B. Twice as large   **D.** Half as large   **E.** One-fourth as large

48. A 2.5 kg rope is stretched between supports 8 m apart. If one end of the rope is tweaked, how long will it take for the resulting disturbance to reach the other end? Assume that the tension in the rope is 40 N.

    A. 0.71 s   **B.** 0.62 s   **C.** 0.58 s   **D.** 0.47 s   **E.** 0.84 s

49. An office machine is making a rattling sound with an intensity of 10^{-5} W/m² when perceived by an office worker that is sitting 3 m away. What is the sound level in decibels for the sound of the machine? (Use threshold of hearing $I_0 = 10^{-12}$ W/m²)

    A. 10 dB   **B.** 35 dB   **C.** 70 dB   **D.** 95 dB   **E.** 45 dB

50. A taut 1 m string is plucked. Point B is midway between both ends, and a finger is placed on point B such that a waveform exists with a node at B. What is the lowest frequency that can be heard? (Use the speed of waves on the string $v = 3.8 \times 10^4$ m/s)

    A. 4.8×10^5 Hz   **C.** 9.7×10^3 Hz
    B. 2.3×10^4 Hz   **D.** 7.4×10^3 Hz   **E.** 3.8×10^4 Hz

51. For a light wave traveling in a vacuum, which of the following properties is true?

A. Increased f results in an increased amplitude
B. Increased f results in a decreased speed
C. Increased f results in an increased wavelength
D. Increased f results in a decreased wavelength
E. Increased f results in a decreased amplitude

52. Which wave is a different classification than the others (i.e., does not belong to the same grouping)?

A. Pressure wave
B. Radio wave
C. Ultrasonic wave
D. Infrasonic wave
E. Acoustic wave

53. Two speakers are placed 2 m apart, and both produce a sound wave (in phase) with wavelength 0.8 m. A microphone is placed an equal distance from both speakers to determine the intensity of the sound at various points. What point is precisely halfway between the two speakers? (Use the speed of sound $v = 340$ m/s)

A. Both an antinode and a node
B. Neither an antinode nor a node
C. A node
D. An antinode
E. Need information about the frequency

54. The siren of an ambulance blares at 1,200 Hz when the ambulance is stationary. What frequency does a stationary observer hear after this ambulance passes her while traveling at 30 m/s? (Use the speed of sound $v = 342$ m/s)

A. 1,240 Hz
B. 1,128 Hz
C. 1,103 Hz
D. 1,427 Hz
E. 1,182 Hz

55. Compared to the wavelength of a 600 Hz sound, the wavelength of a 300 Hz sound in air is:

A. one-half as long
B. the same
C. one-fourth as long
D. four times as long
E. twice as long

Fluids

Questions **1-3** are based on the following:

A container has a vertical tube with an inner radius of 20 mm that is connected to the container at its side. An unknown liquid reaches level A in the container and level B in the tube. Level A is 5 cm higher than level B. The liquid supports a 20 cm high column of oil between levels B and C that has a density of 850 kg/m^3. (Use the acceleration due to gravity $g = 9.8$ m/s^2)

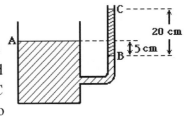

1. What is the density of the unknown liquid?

   A. 2,800 kg/m^3 **C.** 3,400 kg/m^3
   B. 2,100 kg/m^3 **D.** 3,850 kg/m^3 **E.** 1,800 kg/m^3

2. The gauge pressure at level B is closest to:

   A. 1,250 Pa   **B.** 1,830 Pa   **C.** 340 Pa   **D.** 1,666 Pa   **E.** 920 Pa

3. What is the mass of the oil?

   A. 210 g   **B.** 453 g   **C.** 620 g   **D.** 847 g   **E.** 344 g

4. A cubical block of stone is lowered at a steady rate into the ocean by a crane, always keeping the top and bottom faces horizontal. Which of the following graphs best describes the gauge pressure P on the bottom of this block as a function of time *t* if the block just enters the water at time $t = 0$ s?

A. *p*

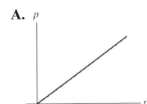

C. *p*

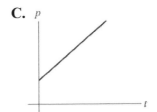

B. *p*

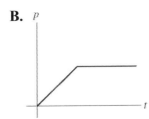

D. *p*

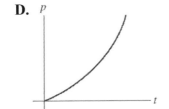

E. *p*

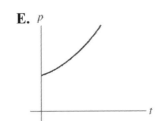

5. Consider a very small hole in the bottom of a tank that is 19 cm in diameter and is filled with water to a height of 80 cm. What is the speed at which the water exits the tank through the hole? (Use the acceleration due to gravity $g = 9.8$ m/s^2)

  A. 8.6 m/s   **B.** 12 m/s   **C.** 14.8 m/s   **D.** 8.4 m/s   **E.** 4 m/s

6. An ideal gas at standard temperature and pressure is compressed until its volume is half the initial volume, and then it is allowed to expand until its pressure is half the initial pressure. This is achieved while holding the temperature constant. If the initial internal energy of the gas is U, the final internal energy of the gas is:

  A. U/2   **B.** U/3   **C.** U   **D.** 2U   **E.** U/4

7. An object is sinking in a fluid. What is the weight of the fluid displaced by the sinking object when the object is completely submerged?

  A. Dependent on the viscosity of the liquid   **C.** Greater than the weight of the object
  B. Equal to the weight of the object   **D.** Zero
                                                     E. Less than the weight of the object

8. A submarine in neutral buoyancy is 100 m below the surface of the water. For the submarine to surface, how much air pressure must be supplied to remove water from the ballast tanks? (Use the acceleration due to gravity $g = 9.8$ m/s^2 and the density of water $\rho = 10^3$ kg/m^3)

  A. 9.8×10^5 N/m^2 **C.** 7.6×10^5 N/m^2
  B. 4.7×10^5 N/m^2 **D.** 5.6×10^5 N/m^2
                                           E. Requires the cross-sectional area of the tank

9. When atmospheric pressure increases, what happens to the absolute pressure at the bottom of a pool?

  A. It does not change   **C.** It increases by the same amount
  B. It increases by double the amount **D.** It increases by half the amount
                                            E. It depends on the depth of the pool

10. When soup gets cold, it often tastes greasy because oil spreads out on the surface of the soup, instead of staying in small globules. This is explained in terms of the:

  A. increase in the surface tension of water with a decreasing temperature
  B. Archimedes' principle
  C. decrease in the surface tension of water with a decreasing temperature
  D. Joule-Thomson effect
  E. Braggs' law

11. An object whose weight is 60 N is floating at the surface of a container of water. How much of the object's volume is submerged? (Use acceleration due to gravity $g = 10$ m/s^2)

　　A. 0.006 m^3　　　　**B.** 0.06 m^3　　　　**C.** 0.6 m^3　　　　**D.** 6%　　　　**E.** 60%

12. What is the volume flow rate of a fluid, if it flows at 2.5 m/s through a pipe of diameter 3 cm?

　　A. 0.9 m^3/s　　　　　　**C.** 5.7×10^{-4} m^3/s

　　B. 4.7 m^3/s　　　　　　**D.** 5.7×10^{-3} m^3/s　　　　　　**E.** 1.8×10^{-3} m^3/s

13. What is the specific gravity of a cork that floats with three-quarters of its volume in and one-quarter of its volume out of the water?

　　A. 0.25　　　　**B.** 0.5　　　　**C.** 0.75　　　　**D.** 2　　　　**E.** 1

14. What volume does 600 g of cottonseed oil occupy, if the density of cottonseed oil is 0.93 g/cm^3?

　　A. 255 cm^3　　　**B.** 360 cm^3　　　**C.** 470 cm^3　　　**D.** 645 cm^3　　　**E.** 690 cm^3

15. The kinetic theory of a monatomic gas suggests the average kinetic energy per molecule is:

　　A. $1/3 \; k_B$T　　　**B.** $2 \; k_B$T　　　**C.** $3/2 \; k_B$T　　　**D.** $2/3 \; k_B$T　　　**E.** $\sqrt{2}k_B$T

16. An object is weighed in air, and it is also weighed while totally submerged in water. If it weighs 150 N less when submerged, find the volume of the object. (Use the acceleration due to gravity $g = 10$ m/s^2 and the density of water $\rho = 1{,}000$ kg/m^3)

　　A. 0.0015 m^3　　　**B.** 0.015 m^3　　　**C.** 0.15 m^3　　　**D.** 1 m^3　　　**E.** 1.5 m^3

17. When a container of water is placed on a laboratory scale, the scale reads 140 g. Now a 30 g piece of copper is suspended from a thread and lowered into the water without making contact with the bottom of the container. What does the scale read? (Use the acceleration due to gravity $g = 9.8$ m/s^2, density of water $\rho = 1$ g/cm^3 and density of copper $\rho = 8.9$ g/cm^3)

　　A. 122 g　　　**B.** 168 g　　　**C.** 143 g　　　**D.** 110 g　　　**E.** 94 g

18. An ideal, incompressible fluid flows through a 6 cm diameter pipe at 1 m/s. There is a 3 cm decrease in diameter within the pipe. What is the speed of the fluid in this constriction?

　　A. 3 m/s　　　**B.** 1.5 m/s　　　**C.** 8 m/s　　　**D.** 4 m/s　　　**E.** 2.5 m/s

19. Two blocks are submerged in a fluid. Block A has dimensions 2 cm high × 3 cm wide × 4 cm long and Block B is 2 cm × 3 cm × 8 cm. Both blocks are submerged with their large faces pointing up and down (i.e., the blocks are horizontal), and they are submerged to the same depth. Compared to the fluid pressure on the bottom of Block A, the bottom of Block B experiences:

    A. pressure that depends on the density of the objects
    B. greater fluid pressure
    C. exactly double the fluid pressure
    D. less fluid pressure
    E. equal fluid pressure

20. A piece of thread of diameter d is in the shape of a rectangle (length l, width w) and is lying on the surface of the water in a beaker. If A is the surface tension of the water, what is the maximum weight that the thread can have without sinking?

    A. $Ad(l + w) / \pi$ **C.** $4A(l + w)$
    B. $A(l + w)$ **D.** $A(l + w) / 2$ **E.** $Ad(l + w)$

21. What is the difference between the pressure inside and outside a tire called?

    A. Absolute pressure   **C.** Atmospheric pressure
    B. Fluid pressure   **D.** Gauge pressure   **E.** N/m^2

22. Which of the following is NOT a unit of pressure?

    A. atm   **B.** psi   **C.** inches of mercury   **D.** Pascal   **E.** $N{\cdot}m^2$

23. Which of the following is a dimensionless number?

    I. Reynolds number   II. specific gravity   III. shear stress

    A. I only   **B.** II only   **C.** III only   **D.** I and II only   **E.** I and III only

24. Water flows out of a large reservoir through a 5 cm diameter pipe. The pipe connects to a 3 cm diameter pipe that is open to the atmosphere, as shown. What is the speed of the water in the 5 cm pipe? Treat the water as an ideal incompressible fluid. (Use the acceleration due to gravity $g = 9.8$ m/s^2)

    A. 2.6 m/s   **C.** 4.8 m/s
    B. 3.2 m/s   **D.** 8.9 m/s   **E.** 6.7 m/s

25. If the pressure acting on an ideal gas at constant temperature is tripled, what is the resulting volume of the ideal gas?

    A. Increased by a factor of two   **C.** Reduced to one-half

    B. Remains the same   **D.** Increased by a factor of three

        E. Reduced to one-third

26. A circular plate with an area of 1 m^2 covers a drain-hole at the bottom of a tank of water that is 1 m deep. Approximately how much force is required to lift the cover if it weighs 1,500 N? (Use the acceleration due to gravity $g = 10$ m/s^2)

    A. 4,250 N   **B.** 9,550 N   **C.** 16,000 N   **D.** 11,500 N   **E.** 14,000 N

27. A bowling ball that weighs 80 N is dropped into a swimming pool filled with water. If the buoyant force on the bowling ball is 20 N when the ball is 1 m below the surface (and sinking), what is the normal force exerted by the bottom of the pool on the ball when it comes to rest there, 4 m below the surface?

    A. 0 N   **B.** 60 N   **C.** 50 N   **D.** 70 N   **E.** 40 N

28. A block of an unknown material is floating in a fluid, half-submerged. If the specific gravity of the fluid is 1.6, what is the block's density? (Use the specific gravity $= \rho_{fluid} / \rho_{water}$ and the density of water $\rho = 1,000$ kg/m^3)

    A. 350 kg/m^3 **C.** 900 kg/m^3

    B. 800 kg/m^3 **D.** 1,250 kg/m^3 **E.** 1,600 kg/m^3

29. In a closed container of fluid, object A is submerged at 6 m from the bottom, and object B is submerged at 12 m from the bottom. Compared to object A, object B experiences:

    A. less fluid pressure   **C.** equal fluid pressure

    B. double the fluid pressure   **D.** triple the fluid pressure

        E. one fifth the fluid pressure

30. Ideal, incompressible water flows at 14 m/s in a horizontal pipe with a pressure of 3.5×10^4 Pa. If the pipe widens to twice its original radius, what is the pressure in the wider section? (Use the density of water $\rho = 1,000$ kg/m^3)

    A. 7.6×10^4 Pa   **C.** 2×10^5 Pa

    B. 12.7×10^4 Pa   **D.** 11.1×10^3 Pa   **E.** 6.3×10^4 Pa

31. Two kilometers above the surface of the Earth, the atmospheric pressure is:

A. unrelated to the atmospheric pressure at the surface
B. twice the atmospheric pressure at the surface
C. triple the atmospheric pressure at the surface
D. less than the atmospheric pressure at the surface
E. requires more information

32. An 80 kg man would weigh 784 N if there were no atmosphere. By how much does the buoyancy due to air reduce the man's weight? (Use the density of the man = 1 g/cm^3, the density of the air = 1.2×10^{-3} g/cm^3, m = 80 kg and the acceleration due to gravity g = 9.8 m/s^2)

A. 0.58 N   B. 0.32 N   C. 0.94 N   D. 2.8 N   E. 1.2 N

33. Diffusion is described by which law?

A. Dulong's   C. Kepler's
B. Faraday's   D. Graham's   E. Archimedes'

34. A pump uses a piston 12 cm in diameter that moves 3 cm/s. What is the fluid velocity in a tube that is 2 mm in diameter?

A. 218 cm/s   B. 88 cm/s   C. 136 cm/s   D. 108 m/s   E. 52 m/s

35. What is its specific gravity of an object floating with one-tenth of its volume out of the water?

A. 0.3   B. 0.9   C. 1.3   D. 2.1   E. 2.9

36. If each of the factors listed below was changed by 15%, which would have the greatest effect on the flow rate?

A. Fluid density   C. Length of the pipe
B. Pressure difference   D. Fluid viscosity   E. Radius of the pipe

37. A 680 g steel hammer (m_h) is tied to a string that is hung from a force meter. A 5 kg container of water (m_w) sits on a scale. The hammer is lowered completely into the water but above the bottom. What does the force meter read? (Use the density of steel ρ = 7.9 g/cm^3, density of water ρ = 1 g/cm^3 and acceleration due to gravity g = 10 m/s^2)

A. 5.9 N   C. 10.7 N
B. 8.4 N   D. 5.2 N   E. 11.2 N

38. An external pressure applied to an enclosed fluid that is transmitted unchanged to every point within the fluid is known as:

A. Torricelli's law

B. Bernoulli's principle

C. Archimedes' principle

D. Pascal's principle

E. Fermat's principle

39. A submarine rests on the bottom of the sea. What is the normal force exerted upon the submarine by the sea floor equal to?

A. weight of the submarine

B. weight of the submarine minus the weight of the displaced water

C. buoyant force minus the atmospheric pressure acting on the submarine

D. weight of the submarine plus the weight of the displaced water

E. buoyant force plus the atmospheric pressure acting on the submarine

40. Consider a brick that is totally immersed in water, with the long edge of the brick vertical. Which statement describes the pressure on the brick?

A. Greatest on the sides of the brick

B. Greatest on the top of the brick

C. Smallest on the sides with largest area

D. Same on all surfaces of the brick

E. Greatest on the bottom of the brick

41. Water is flowing in a drainage channel of a rectangular cross-section. The width of the channel is 14 m, the depth of water is 7 m, and the speed of the flow is 3 m/s. What is the mass flow rate of the water? (Use the density of water $\rho = 1,000$ kg/m^3)

A. 2.9×10^5 kg/s

B. 4.8×10^4 kg/s

C. 6.2×10^5 kg/s

D. 9.3×10^4 kg/s

E. 4.3×10^2 kg/s

42. What is the magnitude of the buoyant force if a 3 kg object floats motionlessly in a fluid of specific gravity 0.8? (Use the acceleration due to gravity $g = 10$ m/s^2)

A. 15 N   B. 7.5 N   C. 30 N   D. 45 N   E. 0 N

43. What is the pressure 6 m below the surface of the ocean? (Use the density of water $\rho = 10^3$ kg/m^3, the atmospheric pressure $P_{atm} = 1.01 \times 10^5$ Pa and the acceleration due to gravity $g = 10$ m/s^2)

A. 1.6×10^5 Pa

B. 0.8×10^5 Pa

C. 2.7×10^4 Pa

D. 3.3×10^4 Pa

E. 4.8×10^4 Pa

44. Density is:

    A. inversely proportional to both mass and volume

    B. proportional to mass and inversely proportional to the volume

    C. inversely proportional to mass and proportional to the volume

    D. proportional to both mass and volume

    E. inversely proportional to mass and independent of volume

45. Which of the following would be expected to have the smallest bulk modulus?

    A. Solid plutonium   **C.** Solid lead

    B. Liquid water   **D.** Liquid mercury   **E.** Helium vapor

46. If atmospheric pressure increases by an amount ΔP, which of the following statements about the pressure in a large pond is true?

    A. The gauge pressure increases by ΔP

    B. The absolute pressure increases by ΔP

    C. The absolute pressure increases, but by an amount less than ΔP

    D. The absolute pressure does not change

    E. The gauge pressure decreases by ΔP

47. Fluid is flowing through a 19 cm long tube with a radius of 2.1 mm at an average speed of 1.8 m/s. What is the viscosity of the fluid, if the drop in pressure is 970 Pa?

    A. 0.036 N·s/m^2 **C.** 0.0044 N·s/m^2

    B. 0.013 N·s/m^2 **D.** 0.0016 N·s/m^2 **E.** 0.0022 N·s/m^2

48. The pressure differential across the cross-section of a condor's wing due to the difference in air flow is explained by:

    A. Torricelli's law   **C.** Bernoulli's equation

    B. Poiseuille's law   **D.** Newton's First Law   **E.** Pascal's principle

Electrostatics

1. How many excess electrons are present for an object that has a charge of -1 Coulomb? (Use Coulomb's constant $k = 9 \times 10^9$ N·m^2/C^2 and charge of an electron $e = -1.6 \times 10^{-19}$ C)

    A. 3.1×10^{19} electrons   **C.** 6.3×10^{18} electrons

    B. 6.3×10^{19} electrons   **D.** 1.6×10^{19} electrons   **E.** 6.5×10^{17} electrons

2. Two charges $Q_1 = 2.4 \times 10^{-10}$ C and $Q_2 = 9.2 \times 10^{-10}$ C are near each other, and charge Q_1 exerts a force F_1 on Q_2. How does F_1 change if the distance between Q_1 and Q_2 is increased by a factor of 4?

    A. Decreases by a factor of 4   **C.** Decreases by a factor of 16

    B. Increases by a factor of 16   **D.** Increases by a factor of 4

    E. Remains the same

3. A 54,000 kg asteroid carrying a negative charge of 15 µC is 180 m from another 51,000 kg asteroid carrying a negative charge of 11 µC. What is the net force the asteroids exert upon each other? (Use the gravitational constant $G = 6.673 \times 10^{-11}$ N·m^2/kg^2 and Coulomb's constant $k = 9 \times 10^9$ N·m^2/C^2)

    A. 400,000 N   **C.** -4.0×10^{-5} N

    B. 5,700 N   **D.** 4.0×10^{-5} N   **E.** 5.7×10^{-5} N

4. Two small beads are 30 cm apart with no other charges or fields present. Bead A has 20 µC of charge, and bead B has 5 µC. Which of the following statements is true about the electric forces on these beads?

    A. The force on A is 120 times the force on B

    B. The force on A is exactly equal to the force on B

    C. The force on B is 4 times the force on A

    D. The force on A is 20 times the force on B

    E. The force on B is 120 times the force on A

5. A point charge $Q = -10$ µC. What is the number of excess electrons on charge Q? (Use the charge of an electron $e = -1.6 \times 10^{-19}$ C)

    A. 4.5×10^{13} electrons   **C.** 9.0×10^{13} electrons

    B. 1.6×10^{13} electrons   **D.** 8.5×10^{13} electrons   **E.** 6.3×10^{13} electrons

6. A distance of 3 m separates an electron and a proton. What happens to the magnitude of the force on the proton if the electron is moved 1.5 m closer to the proton?

    A. It increases to twice its original value

    B. It decreases to one-fourth its original value

    C. It increases to four times its original value

    D. It decreases to one-half its original value

    E. It remains the same

7. How will the magnitude of the electrostatic force between two objects be affected, if the distance between them and both of their charges are doubled?

    A. It will increase by a factor of 4   **C.** It will decrease by a factor of 2

    B. It will increase by a factor of 2   **D.** It will increase by a factor of $\sqrt{2}$

                                       E. It will be unchanged

8. Two oppositely charged particles are slowly separated from each other. What happens to the force as the particles are slowly moved apart?

    A. attractive and decreasing   **C.** attractive and increasing

    B. repulsive and decreasing   **D.** repulsive and increasing

                                       E. none of the above

9. Two charges $Q_1 = 3 \times 10^{-8}$ C and $Q_2 = 9 \times 10^{-8}$ C are near each other, and charge Q_1 exerts a force F_1 on Q_2. What is F_2, the force that charge Q_2 exerts on charge Q_1?

    A. $F_1 / 3$ **B.** F_1 **C.** $3F_1$ **D.** $2F_1$ **E.** $F_1 / 2$

10. Two electrons are passing 30 mm apart. What is the electric repulsive force that they exert on each other? (Use Coulomb's constant $k = 9 \times 10^9$ N·m^2/C^2 and the charge of an electron $= -1.6 \times 10^{-19}$ C)

    A. 1.3×10^{-25} N   **C.** 1.3×10^{27} N

    B. 3.4×10^{-27} N   **D.** 3.4×10^{10} N   **E.** 2.56×10^{-25} N

11. Suppose a van de Graaff generator builds a negative static charge, and a grounded conductor is placed near enough to it so that an 8 μC of negative charge arcs to the conductor. What is the number of electrons that are transferred? (Use the charge of an electron $e = -1.6 \times 10^{-19}$ C)

    A. 1.8×10^{14} electrons   **C.** 5×10^{13} electrons

    B. 48 electrons   **D.** 74 electrons   **E.** 5×10^{20} electrons

12. Which statement must be true if two objects are electrically attracted to each other?

A. One of the objects could be electrically neutral
B. One object must be negatively charged, and the other must be positively charged
C. At least one of the objects must be positively charged
D. At least one of the objects must be negatively charged
E. None of the above statements are true

13. Two charges ($Q_1 = 2.3 \times 10^{-8}$ C and $Q_2 = 2.5 \times 10^{-9}$ C) are a distance 0.1 m apart. How much energy is required to bring them to a distance 0.01 m apart? (Use Coulomb's constant $k = 9 \times 10^9$ N·m²/C²)

A. 2.2×10^{-4} J   **C.** 1.7×10^{-5} J
B. 8.9×10^{-5} J   **D.** 4.7×10^{-5} J   **E.** 6.2×10^{-5} J

14. In the figure below, the charge in the middle is fixed and $Q = -7.5$ nC. For what fixed, positive charge q_1 will non-stationary, negative charge q_2 be in static equilibrium?

A. 53 nC   **C.** 15 nC
B. 7.5 nC   **D.** 30 nC   **E.** 12.8 nC

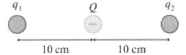

15. All of the following affect the electrostatic field strength at a point at a distance from a source charge, EXCEPT:

A. the sign of the source charge
B. the distance from the source charge
C. the magnitude of the source charge
D. the nature of the medium surrounding the source charge
E. the presence of nearby conducting objects

16. Two charges separated by 1 m exert a 1 N force on each other. If the magnitude of each charge is doubled, the force on each charge is:

A. 1 N   **B.** 2 N   **C.** 4 N   **D.** 6 N   **E.** 10 N

17. In a water solution of NaCl, the NaCl dissociates into ions surrounded by water molecules. Consider a water molecule near a Na^+ ion. What tends to be the orientation of the water molecule?

A. The hydrogen atoms are nearer the Na^+ ion because of their positive charge
B. The hydrogen atoms are nearer the Na^+ ion because of their negative charge
C. The oxygen atom is nearer the Na^+ ion because of the oxygen's positive charge
D. The oxygen atom is nearer the Na^+ ion because of the oxygen's negative charge
E. The hydrogen and oxygen atom center themselves on either side of the Na^+ ion because an atom itself has no charge

18. A metal sphere is insulated electrically and is given a charge. If 30 electrons are added to the sphere in giving a charge, how many Coulombs are added to the sphere? (Use Coulomb's constant $k = 9 \times 10^9$ N·m^2/C^2 and the charge of an electron $e = -1.6 \times 10^{-19}$ C)

    A. -2.4 C   **B.** -30 C   **C.** -4.8×10^{-18} C   **D.** -4.8×10^{-16} C   **E.** -13 C

19. A positive test charge q is released near a positive fixed charge Q. As q moves away from Q, it experiences:

    A. increasing acceleration   **C.** constant velocity

    B. decreasing acceleration   **D.** decreasing velocity   **E.** constant momentum

20. A Coulomb is a unit of electrical:

    A. capacity   **C.** charge

    B. resistance   **D.** potential difference   **E.** pressure

21. To say that electric charge is conserved means that no case has ever been found where:

    A. charge has been created or destroyed

    B. the total charge on an object has increased

    C. the net negative charge on an object is unbalanced by a positive charge on another object

    D. the total charge on an object has changed by a significant amount

    E. the total charge on an object has decreased

22. Two charges $Q_1 = 1.7 \times 10^{-10}$ C and $Q_2 = 6.8 \times 10^{-10}$ C are near each other. How would F change if the charges were both doubled, but the distance between them remained the same?

    A. F increases by a factor of 2

    B. F increases by a factor of 4

    C. F decreases by a factor of $\sqrt{2}$

    D. F decreases by a factor of 4

    E. F increases by a factor of $\sqrt{2}$

23. Two like charges of the same magnitude are 10 mm apart. If the force of repulsion they exert upon each other is 4 N, what is the magnitude of each charge? (Use Coulomb's constant $k = 9 \times 10^9$ N·m^2/C^2)

    A. 6×10^{-5} C   **C.** 2×10^{-7} C

    B. 6×10^{5} C   **D.** 1.5×10^{-7} C   **E.** 6×10^{-7} C

24. Two identical small charged spheres are a certain distance apart, and each initially experiences an electrostatic force of magnitude F due to the other. With time, charge gradually diminishes on both spheres. What is the magnitude of the electrostatic force when each of the spheres has lost half its initial charge?

    A. $1/16\ F$ **B.** $1/8\ F$ **C.** $1/4\ F$ **D.** $2\ F$ **E.** F

25. A charge $Q = 3.1 \times 10^{-5}$ C is fixed in space while another charge $q = -10^{-6}$ C is 6 m away. Charge q is slowly moved 4 m in a straight line directly toward the charge Q. How much work is required to move charge q? (Use Coulomb's constant $k = 9 \times 10^9$ N·m^2/C^2)

    A. -0.09 J   **B.** -0.03 J   **C.** 0.16 J   **D.** 0.08 J   **E.** 0.8 J

26. A point charge $Q = -600$ nC. What is the number of excess electrons in charge Q? (Use the charge of an electron $e = -1.6 \times 10^{-19}$ C)

    A. 5.6×10^{12} electrons   **C.** 2.8×10^{11} electrons
    B. 2.1×10^{10} electrons   **D.** 3.8×10^{12} electrons   **E.** 4.3×10^{8} electrons

27. If an object is characterized as electrically polarized:

    A. its internal electric field is zero   **C.** it is electrically charged
    B. it is a strong insulator   **D.** its charges have been rearranged
                                      E. it is a weak insulator

Electric Circuits

1. What is the new resistance of wire if the length of a certain wire is doubled and its radius is also doubled?

    A. It is $\sqrt{2}$ times as large   **C.** It stays the same

    B. It is ½ as large   **D.** It is 2 times as large   **E.** It is ¼ as large

2. A 6 Ω resistor is connected across the terminals of a 12 V battery. If 0.6 A of current flows, what is the internal resistance of the battery?

    A. 2 Ω   **B.** 26 Ω   **C.** 20 Ω   **D.** 14 Ω   **E.** 3.6 Ω

3. Three 8 V batteries are connected in series to power light bulbs A and B. The resistance of light bulb A is 60 Ω and the resistance of light bulb B is 30 Ω. How does the current through light bulb A compare with the current through light bulb B?

    A. The current through light bulb A is less

    B. The current through light bulb A is greater

    C. The current through light bulb A is the same

    D. The current through light bulb A is exactly doubled that through light bulb B

    E. None are true

4. A sphere with radius 2 mm carries a 1 µC charge. What is the potential difference, $V_B - V_A$, between point B 3.5 m from the center of the sphere and point A 8 m from the center of the sphere? (Use Coulomb's constant $k = 9 \times 10^9$ N·m²/C²)

    A. –485 V   **B.** 1,140 V   **C.** –140 V   **D.** 1,446 V   **E.** 2,457 V

5. Which of the following effect (s) capacitance of capacitors?

        I. material between the conductors

        II. distance between the conductors

        III. geometry of the conductors

    A. I only   **B.** II only   **C.** III only   **D.** I and III only   **E.** I, II and III

6. A proton with an initial speed of 1.5×10^5 m/s falls through a potential difference of 100 volts, gaining speed. What is the speed reached? (Use the mass of a proton = 1.67×10^{-27} kg and the charge of a proton = 1.6×10^{-19} C)

    A. 2×10^5 m/s   **C.** 8.6×10^5 m/s

    B. 4×10^5 m/s   **D.** 7.6×10^5 m/s   **E.** 6.6×10^5 m/s

7. The current flowing through a circuit of constant resistance is doubled. What is the effect on the power dissipated by that circuit?

   A. Decreases to one-half its original value   **C.** Quadruples its original value

   B. Decreases to one-fourth its original value   **D.** Doubles its original value

   E. Decreases to one-eighth its original value

8. A positively-charged particle is at rest in an unknown medium. What is the magnitude of the magnetic field generated by this particle?

   A. Constant everywhere and dependent only on the mass of the medium

   B. Less at points near to the particle compared to a distant point

   C. Greater at points near to the particle compared to a distant point

   D. Equal to zero

   E. Constant everywhere and dependent only on the density of the medium

9. The heating element of a toaster is a long wire of some metal, often a metal alloy, which heats up when a 120 V potential difference is applied across it. Consider a 300 W toaster connected to a wall outlet. Which statement would result in an increase in the rate by which heat is produced?

   A. Use a longer wire   **C.** Use a thicker and longer wire

   B. Use a thicker wire   **D.** Use a thinner and longer wire

   E. Use a thinner wire of the same length

10. A 4 μC point charge and an 8 μC point charge are initially infinitely far apart. How much work is required to bring the 4 μC point charge to ($x = 2$ mm, $y = 0$ mm), and the 8 μC point charge to ($x = -2$ mm, $y = 0$ mm)? (Use Coulomb's constant $k = 9 \times 10^9$ N·m^2/C^2)

   A. 32.6 J   **B.** 9.8 J   **C.** 47 J   **D.** 81 J   **E.** 72 J

11. What current flows when a 400 Ω resistor is connected across a 220 V circuit?

   A. 0.55 A   **B.** 1.8 A   **C.** 5.5 A   **D.** 0.18 A   **E.** 18 A

12. Which statement is accurate for when different resistors are connected in parallel across an ideal battery?

   A. Power dissipated in each is the same

   B. Their equivalent resistance is greater than the resistance of any one of the individual resistors

   C. Current flowing in each is the same

   D. Their equivalent resistance is equal to the average of the individual resistances

   E. Potential difference across each is the same

13. An electron was accelerated from rest through a potential difference of 990 V. What is its speed? (Use the mass of an electron $= 9.11 \times 10^{-31}$ kg, the mass of a proton $= 1.67 \times 10^{-27}$ kg and the charge of a proton $= 1.6 \times 10^{-19}$ C)

A. 0.8×10^7 m/s   **C.** 7.4×10^7 m/s

B. 3.7×10^7 m/s   **D.** 1.9×10^7 m/s   **E.** 6.9×10^7 m/s

14. A circular conducting loop with a radius of 0.5 m and a small gap filled with a 12 Ω resistor is oriented in the *xy*-plane. If a magnetic field of 1 T, making an angle of 30° with the *z*-axis, increases to 12 T, in 5 s, what is the magnitude of the current flowing in the conductor?

A. 0.33 A   **B.** 0.13 A   **C.** 0.88 A   **D.** 1.5 A   **E.** 4.5 A

15. For an electric motor with a resistance of 35 Ω that draws 10 A of current, what is the voltage drop?

A. 3.5 V   **B.** 25 V   **C.** 350 V   **D.** 3,500 V   **E.** 0.3 V

16. A charged parallel-plate capacitor has an electric field E_0 between its plates. The bare nuclei of a stationary ^{1}H and ^{4}He are between the plates. Ignoring the force of gravity, how does the magnitude of the acceleration of the hydrogen nucleus a_H compare with the magnitude of the acceleration of the helium nucleus a_{He}? (Use the mass of an electron $= 9 \times 10^{-31}$ kg, the mass of a proton $= 1.67 \times 10^{-27}$ kg, the mass of a neutron $= 1.67 \times 10^{-27}$ kg and the charge of a proton $= 1.6 \times 10^{-19}$ C)

A. $a_H = 2a_{He}$ **B.** $a_H = 4a_{He}$ **C.** $a_H = \frac{1}{4}a_{He}$ **D.** $a_H = a_{He}$ **E.** $a_H = \frac{1}{2}a_{He}$

17. Identical light bulbs are attached to identical batteries in three different ways (A, B, or C), as shown in the figure. What is the ranking (from lowest to highest) of the total power produced by the battery?

A. C, B, A   **C.** A, C, B

B. B, A, C   **D.** A, B, C

E. C, A, B

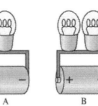

18. A parallel-plate capacitor consists of two parallel, square plates that have dimensions 1 cm by 1 cm. If the plates are separated by 1 mm, and the space between them is filled with Teflon, what is the capacitance? (Use the dielectric constant *k* for Teflon $= 2.1$ and the electric permittivity $\varepsilon_0 = 8.854 \times 10^{-12}$ F/m)

A. 0.83 pF   **B.** 2.2 pF   **C.** 0.46 pF   **D.** 1.9 pF   **E.** 0.11 pF

19. The resistor R has a variable resistance. Which statement is true when R is decreased? (Neglect the very small internal resistance r of the battery)

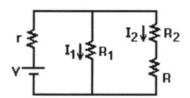

A. I_1 decreases, I_2 increases

B. I_1 increases, I_2 remains the same

C. I_1 remains the same, I_2 increases

D. I_1 remains the same, I_2 decreases

E. I_1 increases, I_2 increases

20. What physical quantity does the slope of the graph represent?

A. 1 / Current

B. Voltage

C. Current

D. Resistivity

E. 1 / Voltage

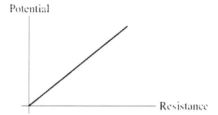

21. An alternating current is supplied to an electronic component with a rating that it be used only for voltages below 12 V. What is the highest V_{rms} that can be supplied to this component while staying below the voltage limit?

A. 6 V   B. 12 V   C. $3\sqrt{2}$ V   D. $12\sqrt{2}$ V   E. $6\sqrt{2}$ V

22. A generator produces alternating current electricity with a frequency of 40 cycles per second. What is the maximum potential difference created by the generator, if the RMS voltage is 150 V?

A. 54 V   B. 91 V   C. 212 V   D. 141 V   E. 223 V

23. Kirchhoff's junction rule is a statement of:

A. Law of conservation of energy   C. Law of conservation of momentum

B. Law of conservation of angular momentum   D. Law of conservation of charge

                                                  E. Newton's Second Law

24. Four identical capacitors are connected in parallel to a battery. If a total charge of Q flows from the battery, how much charge does each capacitor carry?

A. $Q/4$ B. Q C. $4Q$ D. $16Q$ E. $Q/16$

25. Which statement is correct for two conductors that are joined by a long copper wire?

    A. The electric field at the surface of each conductor is the same
    B. Each conductor must be at the same potential
    C. Each conductor must have the same resistivity
    D. A free charge must be present on either conductor
    E. The potential of the wire is the average of the potential of each conductor

26. Electromagnetic induction occurs in a coil when there is a change in the:

    A. coil's charge
    B. current in the coil
    C. magnetic field intensity in the coil
    D. electric field intensity in the coil
    E. electromagnetic polarity

27. When unequal resistors are connected in series across an ideal battery, the:

    A. current flowing in each is the same
    B. equivalent resistance of the circuit is less than that of the greatest resistor
    C. power dissipated in each turn is the same
    D. potential difference across each is the same
    E. current is still unequal in the two resistors

28. Electric current flows only from the point of:

    A. equal potential
    B. high pressure to the point of lower pressure
    C. low pressure to the point of higher pressure
    D. high potential to the point of lower potential
    E. low potential to the point of higher potential

29. Consider the group of charges in this figure. All three charges have $Q = 3.8$ nC. What is their electric potential energy? (Use Coulomb's constant $k = 9.0 \times 10^9$ N·m^2/C^2)

    A. 1.9×10^{-6} J
    B. 7.4×10^{-5} J
    C. 8.8×10^{-6} J
    D. 9.7×10^{-6} J
    E. 1.0×10^{-5} J

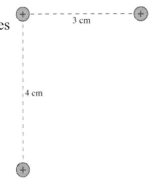

30. A positively-charged and negatively-charged particle are traveling on the same path perpendicular to a constant magnetic field. How do the forces experienced by the two particles differ, if the magnitudes of the charges are equal?

    A. Differ in direction, but not in the magnitude
    B. Differ in magnitude, but not in the direction
    C. No difference in magnitude or the direction
    D. Differ in both magnitude and the direction
    E. Cannot be predicted

31. An electron moves in a direction opposite to an electric field. The potential energy of the system:

    A. decreases, and the electron moves toward a region of a lower potential
    B. increases, and the electron moves toward a region of a higher potential
    C. decreases, and the electron moves toward a region of a higher potential
    D. remains constant, and the electron moves toward a region of a higher potential
    E. remains constant, and the electron moves toward a region of a lower potential

32. What is the name of a device that transforms electrical energy into mechanical energy?

    A. Magnet   **B.** Transformer   **C.** Turbine   **D.** Generator   **E.** Motor

33. A hydrogen atom consists of a proton and an electron. If the orbital radius of the electron increases, the absolute magnitude of the potential energy of the electron:

    A. remains the same   **C.** increases
    B. decreases   **D.** depends on the potential of the electron
                          E. is independent of the orbital radius

34. Copper wire A has a length L and a radius r. Copper wire B has a length $2L$ and a radius $2r$. Which of the following is true regarding the resistances across the ends of the wires?

    A. The resistance of wire A is one-half that of wire B
    B. The resistance of wire A is four times higher than that of wire B
    C. The resistance of wire A is twice as high as that of wire B
    D. The resistance of wire A is equal to that of wire B
    E. The resistance of wire A is one-fourth that of wire B

35. When a negative charge is free, it tries to move:

    A. toward infinity   **C.** from high potential to low potential
    B. away from infinity   **D.** from low potential to high potential
                             E. in the direction of the electric field

36. Four 6 V batteries (in a linear sequence of A → B → C → D) are connected in series to power lights A and B. The resistance of light A is 50 Ω and the resistance of light B is 25 Ω. What is the potential difference at a point between battery C and battery D? (Assume that the potential at the start of the sequence is zero)

 A. 4 volts   **B.** 12 volts   **C.** 18 volts   **D.** 26 volts   **E.** 30 volts

37. By what factor does the dielectric constant change when a material is introduced between the plates of a parallel-plate capacitor if the capacitance increases by a factor of 4?

 A. ½   **B.** 4   **C.** 0.4   **D.** ¼   **E.** 2

38. Two isolated copper plates, each of area 0.4 m^2, carry opposite charges of magnitude 6.8×10^{-10} C. They are placed opposite each other in parallel alignment. What is the potential difference between the plates when their spacing is 4 cm? (Use the dielectric constant $k = 1$ in air and the electric permittivity $\mathcal{E}_0 = 8.854 \times 10^{-12}$ F/m)

 A. 1.4 V   **B.** 4.1 V   **C.** 5.8 V   **D.** 3.2 V   **E.** 7.7 V

39. The force on an electron moving in a magnetic field is largest when its direction is:

 A. perpendicular to the magnetic field direction
 B. at an angle greater than 90° to the magnetic field direction
 C. at an angle less than 90° to the magnetic field direction
 D. exactly opposite to the magnetic field direction
 E. parallel to the magnetic field direction

40. What is the quantity that is calculated in units of A·s?

 A. Passivity   **B.** Capacitance   **C.** Potential   **D.** Current   **E.** Charge

41. A proton with a speed of 1.7×10^5 m/s falls through a potential difference V and thereby increases its speed to 3.2×10^5 m/s. Through what potential difference did the proton fall? (Use the mass of a proton = 1.67×10^{-27} kg and the charge of a proton = 1.6×10^{-19} C)

 A. 880 V   **B.** 1,020 V   **C.** 384 V   **D.** 430 V   **E.** 130 V

42. Three capacitors are connected to a battery as shown. The capacitances are: $C_1 = 2C_2$ and $C_1 = 3C_3$. Which of the three capacitors stores the smallest amount of charge?

 A. C_1 **C.** C_2
 B. C_1 or C_3 **D.** C_3
 E. Amount of charge is the same in all three capacitors

43. Two isolated copper plates, each of area 0.6 m^2, carry opposite charges of magnitude 7.08×10^{-10} C. They are placed opposite each other in parallel alignment, with a spacing of 2 mm. What will be the potential difference between the plates when their spacing is increased to 6 cm? (Use the dielectric constant $k = 1$ in air and the electric permittivity $\varepsilon_0 = 8.854 \times 10^{-12}$ F/m)

    A. 8.0 V   **B.** 3.1 V   **C.** 4.3 V   **D.** 7.2 V   **E.** 0.9 V

44. Electric current can only flow:

    A. in a region of negligible resistance   **C.** in a perfect conductor
    B. through a potential difference   **D.** in the absence of resistance
                                                       E. in a semi-perfect conductor

45. The metal detectors used to screen passengers at airports operate via:

    A. Newton's Laws   **C.** Faraday's Law
    B. Bragg's Law   **D.** Ohm's Law   **E.** Ampere's Law

46. A 7 µC negative charge is attracted to a large, well-anchored, positive charge. How much kinetic energy does the negatively-charged object gain if the potential difference through which it moves is 3.5 mV?

    A. 0.86 J   **B.** 6.7 µJ   **C.** 36.7 µJ   **D.** 0.5 kJ   **E.** 24.5 nJ

47. A wire of resistivity ρ is replaced in a circuit by a wire of the same material but four times as long. If the total resistance remains the same, the diameter of the new wire must be:

    A. one-fourth the original diameter   **C.** the same as the original diameter
    B. two times the original diameter   **D.** one-half the original diameter
                                                       E. four times the original diameter

48. The addition of resistors in series to a resistor in an existing circuit, while voltage remains constant, would result in [   ] in the original resistor.

    A. an increase in current   **C.** an increase in resistance
    B. a decrease in resistance   **D.** a decrease in current   **E.** no change

49. In an experiment, a battery is connected to a variable resistor R, where resistance can be adjusted by turning a knob. The potential difference across the resistor and the current through it are recorded for different settings of the resistor knob. The battery is an ideal potential source in series with an internal resistor. The emf of the potential source is 9 V, and the internal resistance is 0.1 Ω. What is the current if the variable resistor is set at 0.5 Ω?

    A. 15 A   **B.** 0.9 A   **C.** 4.5 A   **D.** 45 A   **E.** 9 A

50. Two parallel plates that are initially uncharged are separated by 1.6 mm. What charge must be transferred from one plate to the other if 10 kJ of energy is to be stored in the plates? The area of each plate is 24 mm^2. (Use the dielectric constant $k = 1$ in air and the electric permittivity $\varepsilon_0 = 8.854 \times 10^{-12}$ F/m)

    A. 78 μC   **B.** 15 mC   **C.** 52 μC   **D.** 29 μC   **E.** 66 mC

51. When a proton is moving in the direction of the electric field, the potential energy of the system [ ] and t moves toward [ ] electric potential. (Use the dielectric constant $k = 1$ in air and the electric permittivity $\varepsilon_0 = 8.854 \times 10^{-12}$ F/m)

    A. increases ... increasing   **C.** increases ... decreasing
    B. decreases ... decreasing   **D.** decreases ... increasing
                                          E. remains the same ... decreasing

52. Each plate of a parallel-plate air capacitor has an area of 0.004 m^2, and the separation of the plates is 0.02 mm. An electric field of 8.6×10^6 V/m is present between the plates. What is the energy density between the plates? (Use the electric permittivity $\varepsilon_0 = 8.854 \times 10^{-12}$ F/m)

    A. 100 J/m^3 **B.** 400 J/m^3 **C.** 220 J/m^3 **D.** 330 J/m^3 **E.** 510 J/m^3

53. What is the quantity that is calculated with units of kg·m^2/(s·C^2)?

    A. Resistance   **C.** Potential
    B. Capacitance   **D.** Resistivity   **E.** Current

54. At a constant voltage, an increase in the resistance of a circuit results in:

    A. no change in *I* or V   **C.** an increase in power
    B. an increase in *I*   **D.** constant power   **E.** a decrease in *I*

55. A charge $+Q$ is located at one of the corners of a square. The absolute potential at the center of a square is 3 V. If a second charge $-Q$ is placed at one of the other three corners, what is the absolute potential at the square's center?

    A. −6 V   **B.** 12 V   **C.** 6 V   **D.** 0 V   **E.** −12 V

Light and Optics

1. What is the minimum thickness of a soap film that reflects a given wavelength of light?

A. ¼ the wavelength
B. ½ the wavelength
C. One wavelength
D. Two wavelengths
E. There is no minimum thickness

2. As the angle of an incident ray of light increases, the angle of the reflected ray:

A. increases
B. decreases
C. stays the same
D. increases or decreases
E. requires more information

3. At what distance from a concave spherical mirror (with a focal length of 100 cm) must a woman stand to see an upright image of herself that is twice her actual height?

A. 100 cm   **B.** 50 cm   **C.** 300 cm   **D.** 25 cm   **E.** 150 cm

4. If a person's eyeball is too long from front to back, what is the name of the condition that the person likely suffers?

A. Hyperopia
B. Astigmatism
C. Presbyopia
D. Myopia
E. Diplopia

5. According to the relationship between frequency and energy of light ($E = hf$), which color of light has more energy?

A. Red   **B.** Yellow   **C.** Green   **D.** Orange   **E.** Blue

6. A candle 18 cm tall sits 4 m away from a diverging lens with a focal length of 3 m. What is the size of the image?

A. 6.3 cm   **B.** 7.7 cm   **C.** 2.9 cm   **D.** 13.5 cm   **E.** 18 cm

> Questions **7-8** are based on the following:

A tank holds a layer of oil 1.58 m thick that floats on a layer of syrup that is 0.66 m thick. Both liquids are clear and do not intermix. A ray, which originates at the bottom of the tank on a vertical axis (see figure), crosses the oil-syrup interface at a point 0.9 m to the right of the vertical axis. The ray continues and arrives at the oil-air interface, 2 m from the axis and at the critical angle. (Use the refractive index $n = 1$ for air)

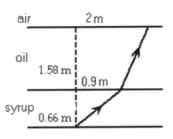

7. The index of refraction of the oil is closest to:

    A. 1.39   **B.** 1.56   **C.** 1.75   **D.** 1.82   **E.** 1.94

8. What is the index of refraction of the syrup?

    A. 1.53   **B.** 1.46   **C.** 1.17   **D.** 1.24   **E.** 1.33

9. Which of the following cannot be explained with the wave theory of light?

    A. Photoelectric effect   **C.** Polarization

    B. Interference   **D.** Diffusion   **E.** All of the above

10. The use of wavefronts and rays to describe optical phenomena is known as:

    A. dispersive optics   **C.** wave optics

    B. reflector optics   **D.** geometrical optics   **E.** array optics

11. In the investigation of a new type of optical fiber (index of refraction $n = 1.26$), a laser beam is incident on the flat end of a straight fiber in air, as shown in the figure below. What is the maximum angle of incidence (θ_1) if the beam is not to escape from the fiber?

    A. 36°   **B.** 43°   **C.** 58°   **D.** 50°   **E.** 28°

12. An object is placed at a distance of 0.5 m from a converging lens with a power of 10 diopters. At what distance from the lens does the image appear?

    A. 0.13 m   **B.** 0.47 m   **C.** 0.7 m   **D.** 1.5 m   **E.** 1.8 m

13. A virtual image is:

    I. produced by light rays
    II. the brain's interpretations of light rays
    III. found only on a concave mirror

    A. I only   **B.** II only   **C.** III only   **D.** I and II only   **E.** I and III only

14. If Karen stands in front of a convex mirror, at the same distance from it as its radius of curvature:

    A. Karen does not see her image because it's focused at a different distance
    B. Karen sees her image, and she appears the same size
    C. Karen does not see her image, and she is not within its range
    D. Karen sees her image, and she appears larger
    E. Karen sees her image, and she appears smaller

15. An object is viewed at various distances using a mirror with a focal length of 10 m. If the object is 20 m away from the mirror, what best characterizes the image?

    A. Inverted and real
    B. Inverted and virtual
    C. Upright and real
    D. Upright and virtual
    E. Real, but it cannot be determined if it is inverted or upright

16. If an object is placed at a position beyond $2f$ of the focal point of a converging lens, the image is:

    A. real, upright and enlarged
    C. virtual, upright and reduced
    B. virtual, inverted and enlarged
    D. real, inverted and enlarged
    E. real, inverted and reduced

17. Which form of electromagnetic radiation has photons with the lowest energy?

    A. X-rays
    C. Radio waves
    B. Ultraviolet radiation
    D. Microwaves
    E. Infrared radiation

18. If the index of refraction of diamond is 2.43, a given wavelength of light travels:

    A. 2.43 times faster in diamond than it does in air
    B. 2.43 times faster in a vacuum than it does in diamond
    C. 2.43 times faster in diamond than it does in a vacuum
    D. 2.43 times faster in a vacuum than it does in air
    E. 2.43 times faster in the air than it does in a vacuum

19. An object is placed 15 cm to the left of a double-convex lens of focal length 20 cm. Where is the image of this object located?

    A. 15 cm to the left of the lens
    C. 60 cm to the right of the lens
    B. 30 cm to the left of the lens
    D. 60 cm to the left of the lens
    E. 30 cm to the right of the lens

20. A sheet of red paper appears black when it is illuminated with:

    A. orange light
    C. red light
    B. cyan light
    D. yellow light
    E. violet light

21. Where is an object if the image produced by a lens appears very close to its focal point?

    A. near the center of curvature of the lens
    C. near the lens
    B. far from the lens
    D. near the focal point
    E. requires more information

22. A light with the frequency 4.9×10^{14} Hz is produced by a source located 6 m from a converging lens with a focal length of 3 m. For a different frequency of light, the focal length of the lens is different than 3 m. This phenomenon is called:

A. Diffusion   **C.** Interference

B. Incidence   **D.** Refraction   **E.** Dispersion

23. If an image appears at the same distance from a mirror as the object, the size of the image is:

A. exactly quadruple the size of the object   **C.** the same size as the object

B. exactly ¼ the size of the object   **D.** exactly twice the size of the object

     E. exactly ½ the size of the object

24. When viewed straight down (90° to the surface), an incident light ray moving from water to air is refracted:

A. 37° away from the normal   **C.** 28° toward the normal

B. 37° toward the normal   **D.** 28° away from the normal   **E.** 0°

25. Suppose that a beachgoer uses two lenses from a pair of disassembled polarized sunglasses and places one on top of the other. What would he observe if he rotates one lens 90° with respect to the normal position of the other lens and looks directly at the sun overhead?

A. Light with an intensity reduced to about 50% of what it would be with one lens

B. Light with an intensity that is the same of what it would be with one lens

C. Complete darkness, since no light would be transmitted

D. Light with an intensity reduced to about 25% of what it would be with one lens

E. Light with an intensity increased to about 150% of what it would be with one lens

26. A glass plate with an index of refraction of 1.45 is immersed in a liquid. The liquid is an oil with an index of refraction of 1.35. The surface of the glass is inclined at an angle of 54° with the vertical. A horizontal ray in the glass is incident on the interface of glass and liquid. The horizontal incident ray refracts at the interface. The angle that the refracted ray in the oil makes with the horizontal is closest to:

A. 8.3°   **B.** 14°   **C.** 6°   **D.** 12°   **E.** 17°

27. Two plane mirrors make an angle of 30°. A light ray enters the system and is reflected once off each mirror. Through what angle is the ray turned?

A. 60°   **B.** 90°   **C.** 120°   **D.** 160°   **E.** 180°

28. Which of the following statements about light is TRUE?

  A. A packet of light energy is known as a photon
  B. Color can be used to determine the approximate energy of visible light
  C. Light travels through space at a speed of 3.0×10^8 m/s
  D. Ultraviolet light cannot be seen with the unaided eye
  E. All of the above

29. The angle of incidence:

  A. may be greater than, less than, or equal to the angle of refraction
  B. is always less than the angle of refraction
  C. must equal the angle of refraction
  D. is always greater than the angle of refraction
  E. is independent of the angle of refraction

30. As a person walks away from a plane mirror on a wall, her image:

  A. is always a real image, no matter how far she is from the mirror
  B. changes from being upright to being inverted as she passes the focal point
  C. gets smaller
  D. may or may not get smaller, depending on where she is positioned
  E. is always the same size

31. If a spherical concave mirror has a radius of curvature R, its focal length is:

  A. $2R$ **B.** R **C.** $R/2$ **D.** $R/4$ **E.** $4R$

32. Let n_1 be the index of refraction of the incident medium and let n_2 be the index of refraction of the refracting medium. Which of the following must be true if the angle that the refracted ray makes with the boundary (not with the normal) is less than the angle that the incident ray makes with the boundary?

  A. $n_1 < n_2$ **B.** $n_1 > n_2$ **C.** $n_1 < 1$ **D.** $n_2 < 1$ **E.** $n_1 = n_2$

33. If a person's eyeball is too short from front to back, the person is likely to suffer from:

  A. nearsightedness   **C.** presbyopia
  B. farsightedness   **D.** astigmatism   **E.** diplopia

34. The shimmering that is observed over a hot surface is:

  A. changing refraction from the mixing of warm and cool air
  B. a mirage
  C. heat rays
  D. reflections from evaporating water vapor
  E. reflections from condensing water vapor

35. When two parallel white rays pass through the outer edges of a converging glass lens, chromatic aberrations cause colors to appear on the screen in what order, from the top down?

A. blue, blue, red, red   C. blue, red, blue, red

B. red, blue, blue, red   D. red, red, blue, blue   E. blue, red, red, blue

36. Two thin converging lenses are near each other so that the lens on the left has a focal length of 2 m and the one on the right has a focal length of 4 m. What is the focal length of the combination?

A. 1/4 m   B. 4/3 m   C. 3/4 m   D. 4 m   E. 8 m

37. A cylindrical tank is 50 ft. deep, 37.5 ft. in diameter, and filled to the top with water. A flashlight shines into the tank from above. What is the minimum angle θ that its beam can make with the water surface if the beam is to illuminate part of the bottom? (Use the index of refraction $n = 1.33$ for water)

A. 25°   B. 31°   C. 37°   D. 53°   E. 18°

38. Which color of the visible spectrum has the shortest wavelength (400 nm)?

A. Violet   B. Green   C. Orange   D. Blue   E. Yellow

39. An object is placed at a distance d in front of a plane mirror. The size of the image is:

A. dependent on where the observer is positioned when looking at the image
B. twice the size of the object
C. half the size of the object
D. dependent on the distance d
E. the same as the object, independent of the position of the observer or distance d

40. If a single lens forms a virtual image of an object, then the:

     I. image must be upright
     II. lens must be a converging lens
     III. lens could be either diverging or converging

A. I only   B. I and III only   C. III only   D. I and II only   E. II only

41. When neon light passes through a prism, what is observed?

A. White light   C. The same neon light

B. Bright spots or lines   D. Continuous spectrum   E. Both A and B

42. The law of reflection holds for:

     I. plane mirrors   II. curved mirrors   III. spherical mirrors

A. I only   B. II only   C. III only   D. I and III only   E. I, II and III

43. The image formed by a single concave lens:

A. can be real or virtual but is always real when the object is placed at the focal point
B. can be real or virtual, depending on the object's distance compared to the focal length
C. is always virtual
D. is always real
E. is always inverted

44. A lens forms a virtual image of an object. Which of the following must be true of the image?

A. It is inverted
B. It is upright

C. It is larger than the object and upright
D. It is smaller than the object and inverted
E. It is the same size as the object and upright

45. Light with the lowest frequency (longest wavelength) detected by your eyes is perceived as:

A. violet   B. green   C. yellow   D. orange   E. red

46. A 0.1 m tall candle is observed through a converging lens that is 3 m away and has a focal length of 6 m. The resulting image is:

A. 3 m from the lens on the opposite side of the object
B. 6 m from the lens on the opposite side of the object
C. 3 m from the lens on the same side as the object
D. 6 m from the lens on the same side as the object
E. 0.5 m from the lens on the opposite side of the object

47. Which statement about thin lenses is correct when considering only a single lens?

A. A diverging lens always produces a virtual, erect image
B. A diverging lens always produces a real, erect image
C. A diverging lens always produces a virtual, inverted image
D. A diverging lens always produces a real, inverted image
E. A converging lens always produces a real, inverted image

48. A double-concave lens has equal radii of curvature of 15 cm. An object placed 14 cm from the lens forms a virtual image 5 cm from the lens. What is the index of refraction of the lens material?

A. 0.8   B. 1.4   C. 2   D. 2.6   E. 2.8

49. The magnification m for an object reflected from a mirror is the ratio of what characteristic of the image to the object?

A. Center of curvature
B. Focal distances

C. Orientation
D. Angular size   E. Distance

50. Suppose Mike places his face in front of a concave mirror. Which of the following statements is correct?

    A. Mike's image is diminished in size
    B. Mike's image is always inverted
    C. No matter where Mike places himself, a virtual image is formed
    D. If Mike positions himself between the center of curvature and the focal point of the mirror, he will not be able to see his image
    E. Mike's image is enlarged in size

51. Single-concave spherical mirrors produce images that:

    A. are always smaller than the actual object
    B. are always the same size as the actual object
    C. are always larger than the actual object
    D. could be smaller than, larger than, or the same size as the actual object, depending on the placement of the object
    E. are always upright

52. When two converging lenses of equal focal lengths are used together, the effective combined focal length is less than the focal length of either one of the individual lens. The combined power of the two lenses used together is:

    A. greater than the power of either individual lens
    B. the same as the power of either individual lens
    C. less than the power of either individual lens
    D. greater than the sum of the powers of both individual lens
    E. exactly the sum of the powers of both individual lens

53. The index of refraction is based on the ratio of the speed of light in:

    A. water to the speed of light in the transparent material
    B. a vacuum to the speed of light in the transparent material
    C. two different transparent materials
    D. air to the speed of light in the transparent material
    E. a solid to the speed of light in the transparent material

54. An object is located 2.2 m in front of a plane mirror. The image formed by the mirror appears:

    A. 4.4 m behind the mirror's surface   **C.** 4.4 m in front of the mirror's surface
    B. 2.2 m in front of the mirror's surface   **D.** on the mirror's surface
                                      E. 2.2 m behind the mirror's surface

55. An upright object is 40 cm from a concave mirror with a radius of 50 cm. The image is:

    A. virtual and inverted   **C.** real and inverted
    B. virtual and upright   **D.** real and upright   **E.** real or virtual

Heat and Thermodynamics

1. Compared to the initial value, what is the resulting pressure for an ideal gas that is compressed isothermally to one-third of its initial volume?

A. Equal
B. Three times larger

C. Larger, but less than three times larger
D. More than three times larger
E. Requires more information

2. A uniform hole in a brass plate has a diameter of 1.2 cm at 25 °C. What is the diameter of the hole when the plate is heated to 225 °C? (Use the coefficient of linear thermal expansion for brass = 19×10^{-6} K^{-1})

A. 2.2 cm   B. 2.8 cm   C. 1.2 cm   D. 1.6 cm   E. 0.8 cm

3. A student heats 90 g of water using 50 W of power, with 100% efficiency. How long does it take to raise the temperature of the water from 10 °C to 30 °C? (Use specific heat of water $c = 4.186$ J/g·°C)

A. 232 s   B. 81 s   C. 59 s   D. 151 s   E. 102 s

4. A runner generates 1,260 W of thermal energy. If her heat is to be dissipated only by evaporation, how much water does she shed in 15 minutes of running? (Use the latent heat of vaporization of water $L_v = 22.6 \times 10^5$ J/kg)

A. 500 g   B. 35 g   C. 350 g   D. 50 g   E. 40 g

5. Phase changes occur as temperature:

        I. decreases   II. increases   III. remains the same

A. I only   B. II only   C. III only   D. I and II only   E. I and III only

6. How much heat is needed to melt a 55 kg sample of ice that is at 0 °C? (Use the latent heat of fusion for water $L_f = 334$ kJ/kg and the latent heat of vaporization $L_v = 2,257$ kJ/kg)

A. 0 kJ
B. 2.6×10^5 kJ

C. 3×10^5 kJ
D. 4.6×10^6 kJ

E. 1.8×10^4 kJ

7. Metals are both good heat conductors and good electrical conductors because of the:

A. relatively high densities of metals
B. high elasticity of metals
C. ductility of metals
D. looseness of outer electrons in metal atoms
E. crystal structure of metals

8. Solar houses are designed to retain the heat absorbed during the day so that the stored heat can be released during the night. A botanist produces steam at 100 °C during the day, and then allows the steam to cool to 0 °C and freeze during the night. How many kilograms of water are needed to store 200 kJ of energy for this process? (Use the latent heat of vaporization of water $L_v = 22.6 \times 10^5$ J/kg, the latent heat of fusion of water $L_f = 33.5 \times 10^4$ J/kg, and the specific heat capacity of water $c = 4,186$ J/kg·K)

    A. 0.066 kg   **B.** 0.103 kg   **C.** 0.482 kg   **D.** 1.18 kg   **E.** 3.66 kg

9. The heat required to change a substance from the solid to the liquid state is referred to as the heat of:

    A. condensation   **B.** freezing   **C.** fusion   **D.** vaporization   **E.** sublimation

10. A rigid container holds 0.2 kg of hydrogen gas. How much heat is needed to change the temperature of the gas from 250 K to 280 K? (Use specific heat of hydrogen gas = 14.3 J/g·K)

    A. 46 kJ   **B.** 72 kJ   **C.** 56 kJ   **D.** 35 kJ   **E.** 86 kJ

11. An aluminum electric tea kettle with a mass of 500 g is heated with a 500 W heating coil. How many minutes are required to heat 1 kg of water from 18 °C to 98 °C in the tea kettle? (Use the specific heat of aluminum = 900 J/kg·K and the specific heat of water = 4,186 J/kg·K)

    A. 16 min   **B.** 12 min   **C.** 8 min   **D.** 4 min   **E.** 10 min

12. Heat is added at a constant rate to a pure substance in a closed container. The temperature of the substance as a function of time is shown in the graph. If $L_f =$ latent heat of fusion and $L_v =$ latent heat of vaporization, what is the value of the ratio L_v / L_f for this substance?

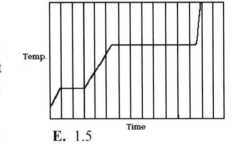

    A. 3.5   **B.** 7.2   **C.** 4.5   **D.** 5.0   **E.** 1.5

13. The moderate temperatures of islands throughout the world have much to do with water's:

    A. high evaporation rate   **C.** vast supply of thermal energy
    B. high specific heat capacity   **D.** poor conductivity
    E. absorption of solar energy

14. A 4.5 g lead BB moving at 46 m/s penetrates a wood block and comes to rest inside the block. If the BB absorbs half of the kinetic energy, what is the change in the temperature of the BB? (Use the specific heat of lead = 128 J/kg·K)

    A. 2.8 K   **B.** 3.6 K   **C.** 1.6 K   **D.** 0.8 K   **E.** 4.1 K

15. The heat required to change a substance from the liquid to the vapor state is referred to as the heat of:

    A. melting   **B.** condensation   **C.** vaporization   **D.** fusion   **E.** sublimation

16. A Carnot engine operating between a reservoir of liquid mercury at its melting point and a colder reservoir extracts 18 J of heat from the mercury and does 5 J of work during each cycle. What is the temperature of the colder reservoir? (Use the melting temperature of mercury = 233 K)

    A. 168 K   **B.** 66 K   **C.** 57 K   **D.** 82 K   **E.** 94 K

17. A 920 g empty iron pan is put on a stove. How much heat in joules must the iron pan absorb to raise its temperature from 18 °C to 96 °C? (Use specific heat for iron = 113 cal/kg·°C and 1 cal = 4.186 J)

    A. 50,180 J   **B.** 81,010 J   **C.** 63,420 J   **D.** 33,940 J   **E.** 26,500 J

18. When a solid melts, what change occurs in the substance?

    A. Heat energy dissipates   **C.** Temperature increases
    B. Heat energy enters   **D.** Temperature decreases   **E.** Kinetic energy increases

19. Which of the following is an accurate statement about the work done for a cyclic process carried out in a gas? (Use P for pressure and V for volume on the graph)

    A. It is equal to the area under *ab* minus the area under *dc*
    B. It is equal to the area under the curve *adc*
    C. It is equal to the area under the curve *abc*
    D. It equals zero
    E. It is equal to the area enclosed by the cyclic process

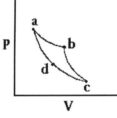

20. Substance A has a higher specific heat than substance B. With all other factors equal, which substance requires more energy to be heated to the same temperature?

    A. Substance A   **C.** Both require the same amount of heat
    B. Substance B   **D.** Depends on the density of each substance
                       E. Depends on the volume of each substance

21. A 6.5 g meteor hits the Earth at a speed of 300 m/s. If the meteor's kinetic energy is entirely converted to heat, by how much does its temperature rise? (Use the specific heat of the meteor = 120 cal/kg·°C and the conversion of 1 cal = 4.186 J)

    A. 134 °C   **B.** 68 °C   **C.** 120 °C   **D.** 90 °C   **E.** 44 °C

22. When a liquid freezes, what change occurs in the substance?

    A. Heat energy dissipates   **C.** Temperature increases
    B. Heat energy enters   **D.** Temperature decreases
                                        E. Kinetic energy increases

23. A monatomic ideal gas ($C_v = 3/2$ R) undergoes an isothermal expansion at 300 K, as the volume increases from 0.05 m^3 to 0.2 m^3. The final pressure is 130 kPa. What is the heat transfer of the gas? (Use the ideal gas constant R = 8.314 J/mol·K)

    A. −14 kJ   **B.** 36 kJ   **C.** 14 kJ   **D.** −21 kJ   **E.** 0 kJ

24. What is the maximum temperature rise expected for 1 kg of water falling from a waterfall with a vertical drop of 30 m? (Use the acceleration due to gravity $g = 9.8$ m/s^2 and the specific heat of water = 4,186 J/kg·K)

    A. 0.1 °C   **B.** 0.06 °C   **C.** 0.15 °C   **D.** 0.07 °C   **E.** 0.03 °C

25. When 0.75 kg of water at 0 °C freezes, what is the change in entropy of the water? (Use the latent heat of fusion of water $L_f = 33{,}400$ J/kg)

    A. −92 J/K   **B.** −18 J/K   **C.** 44 J/K   **D.** 80 J/K   **E.** −60 J/K

26. When a bimetallic bar made of a copper and iron strip is heated, the copper part of the bar bends toward the iron strip. The reason for this is:

    A. copper expands more than iron   **C.** iron gets hotter before copper
    B. iron expands more than copper   **D.** copper gets hotter before iron
                                         E. both copper and iron expand at the same rate

27. In a flask, 110 g of water is heated using 60 W of power, with perfect efficiency. How long does it take to raise the temperature of the water from 20 °C to 30 °C? (Use the specific heat of water $c = 4{,}186$ J/kg·K)

    A. 132 s   **B.** 57 s   **C.** 9.6 s   **D.** 77 s   **E.** 41 s

28. When a liquid evaporates, what change occurs in the substance?

    A. Heat energy dissipates   **C.** Temperature increases
    B. Heat energy enters   **D.** Temperature decreases
                                         E. Kinetic energy increases

29. A flask of liquid nitrogen is at a temperature of −243 °C. If the nitrogen is heated until the average energy of the particles is doubled, what is the new temperature?

    A. 356 °C   **B.** −356 °C   **C.** −134 °C   **D.** 134 °C   **E.** −213 °C

30. If a researcher is attempting to determine how much the temperature of a particular piece of material would rise when a known amount of heat is added to it, knowing which of the following quantities would be most helpful?

A. density
B. coefficient of linear expansion
C. initial temperature
D. specific heat
E. thermal conductivity

31. A substance has a density of 1,800 kg/m^3 in the liquid state. At atmospheric pressure, the substance has a boiling point of 170 °C. The vapor has a density of 6 kg/m^3 at the boiling point at atmospheric pressure. What is the change in the internal energy of 1 kg of the substance, as it vaporizes at atmospheric pressure? (Use the heat of vaporization $L_v = 1.7 \times 10^5$ J/kg)

A. 180 kJ
B. 170 kJ
C. 6 kJ
D. 12 kJ
E. 200 kJ

32. If an aluminum rod that is at 5 °C is heated until it has twice the thermal energy, its temperature is:

A. 108 °C
B. 56 °C
C. 278 °C
D. 283 °C
E. 556 °C

33. A thermally isolated system is made up of a hot piece of aluminum and a cold piece of copper, with the aluminum and the copper in thermal contact. The specific heat capacity of aluminum is more than double that of copper. Which object experiences the greater temperature change during the time the system takes to reach thermal equilibrium?

A. Both experience the same magnitude of temperature change
B. The volume of each is required
C. The copper
D. The aluminum
E. The mass of each is required

34. In liquid water of a given temperature, the water molecules are moving randomly at different speeds. Electrostatic forces of cohesion tend to hold them together. However, occasionally one molecule gains enough energy through multiple collisions to pull away from the others and escape from the liquid. Which of the following is an illustration of this phenomenon?

A. When a large steel suspension bridge is built, gaps are left between the girders
B. When a body gets too warm, it produces sweat to cool itself down
C. Increasing the atmospheric pressure over a liquid causes the boiling temperature to decrease
D. If snow begins to fall when Mary is skiing, she feels colder than before it started to snow
E. A hot water bottle is more effective in keeping a person warm than would a rock of the same mass heated to the same temperature

35. A 2,200 kg sample of water at 0 °C is cooled to –30 °C, and freezes in the process. Approximately how much heat is liberated during this process? (Use heat of fusion for water L_f = 334 kJ/kg, heat of vaporization L_v = 2,257 kJ/kg and specific heat for ice = 2,050 J/kg·K)

A. 328,600 kJ   **C.** 637,200 kJ

B. 190,040 kJ   **D.** 870,100 kJ   **E.** 768,200 kJ

36. Object 1 has three times the specific heat capacity and four times the mass of Object 2. The same amount of heat is transferred to the two objects. If the temperature of Object 1 changes by an amount of ΔT, what is the change in temperature of Object 2?

A. (4/3)ΔT   **B.** 3ΔT   **C.** ΔT   **D.** (3/4)ΔT   **E.** 12ΔT

37. The process whereby heat flows using molecular collisions is known as:

A. radiation   **B.** inversion   **C.** conduction   **D.** convection   **E.** evaporation

38. The graph shows a PV diagram for 5.1 g of oxygen gas in a sealed container. The temperature of T_1 is 20 °C. What are the values for temperatures of T_3 and T_4, respectively? (Use the gas constant R= 8.314 J/mol·K)

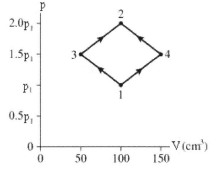

A. –53 °C and 387 °C   **C.** 210 °C and 640 °C

B. –14 °C and 34 °C   **D.** 12 °C and 58 °C

                              E. 29 °C and 171 °C

39. On a cold day, a piece of steel feels much colder to the touch than a piece of plastic. This is due to the difference in which one of the following physical properties of these materials?

A. Emissivity   **C.** Density

B. Thermal conductivity   **D.** Specific heat   **E.** Mass

40. What is the term for a process when a gas is allowed to expand as heat is added to it at constant pressure?

A. Isochoric   **B.** Isobaric   **C.** Adiabatic   **D.** Isothermal   **E.** Isentropic

41. A Carnot engine is used as an air conditioner to cool a house in the summer. The air conditioner removes 20 kJ of heat per second from the house, and maintains the inside temperature at 293 K, while the outside temperature is 307 K. What is the power required for the air conditioner?

A. 2.3 kW   **B.** 3.22 kW   **C.** 1.6 kW   **D.** 4.88 kW   **E.** 0.96 kW

42. Heat energy is measured in units of:

    I. Joules   II. calories   III. work

A. I only   **B.** II only   **C.** I and II only   **D.** III only   **E.** I, II and III

43. The process in which heat flows by the mass movement of molecules from one place to another is known as:

       I. conduction   II. convection   III. radiation

A. I only   **B.** II only   **C.** III only   **D.** I and II only   **E.** I and III only

44. The process whereby heat flows in the absence of any medium is known as:

A. radiation   **C.** conduction

B. inversion   **D.** convection   **E.** evaporation

45. The figure shows 0.008 mol of gas that undergoes the process $1 \rightarrow 2 \rightarrow 3$. What is the volume of V_3?

(Use the ideal gas constant R = 8.314 J/mol·K and the conversion of 1 atm = 101,325 Pa)

A. 435 cm^3 **C.** 656 cm^3

B. 568 cm^3 **D.** 800 cm^3 **E.** 940 cm^3

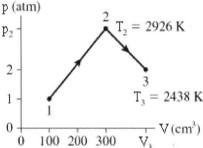

46. When a gas expands adiabatically:

A. it does no work   **C.** the internal (thermal) energy of the gas decreases

B. work is done on the gas   **D.** the internal (thermal) energy of the gas increases

                                  E. the temperature of the gas remains constant

47. Why is it that when a swimmer gets out of a swimming pool and stands in a breeze dripping wet, he feels much colder compared to when he dries off?

A. This is a physiological effect resulting from the skin's sensory nerves

B. The water on his skin is colder than the surrounding air

C. The moisture on his skin has good thermal conductivity

D. Water has a relatively small specific heat

E. To evaporate a gram of water from his skin requires heat and most of this heat flows out of his body

48. Which method of heat flow requires the movement of energy through solid matter to a new location?

       I. Conduction   II. Convection   III. Radiation

A. I only   **B.** II only   **C.** III only   **D.** I and II only   **E.** I and III only

49. An ideal gas is compressed via an isobaric process to one-third of its initial volume. Compared to the initial pressure, the resulting pressure is:

A. more than three times greater   **C.** three times greater

B. nine times greater   **D.** the same   **E.** requires more information

50. Which of the following would be the best radiator of thermal energy?

A. A metallic surface   **C.** A white surface

B. A black surface   **D.** A shiny surface   **E.** Styrofoam

51. A brass rod is 59.1 cm long, and an aluminum rod is 39.3 cm long when both rods are at an initial temperature of 0 °C. The rods are placed with a distance of 1.1 cm between them. The distance between the far ends of the rods is maintained at 99.5 cm. The temperature is raised until the two rods are barely in contact. In the figure, what is the temperature at which contact of the rods barely occurs? (Use a coefficient of linear expansion of brass = 2×10^{-5} K^{-1} and coefficient of linear expansion of aluminum = 2.4×10^{-5} K^{-1})

$\longleftarrow$ 99.5 cm $\longrightarrow$

A. 424 °C   **C.** 483 °C

B. 588 °C   **D.** 363 °C   **E.** 518 °C

brass   aluminum
59.1 cm   39.3 cm

52. At room temperature, a person loses energy to the surroundings at the rate of 60 W. If an equivalent food intake compensates this energy loss, how many kilocalories does he need to consume every 24 hours? (Use the conversion of 1 cal = 4.186 J)

A. 1,240 kcal   **B.** 1,660 kcal   **C.** 600 kcal   **D.** 880 kcal   **E.** 1,920 kcal

53. By what primary heat transfer mechanism does one end of an iron bar become hot when the other end is placed in a flame?

A. Convection   **C.** Radiation

B. Forced convection   **D.** Conduction   **E.** Diffusion

Questions **54-55** are based on the following:

Two experiments are performed to determine the calorimetric properties of an alcohol which has a melting point of –10 °C. In the first trial, a 220 g cube of frozen alcohol, at the melting point, is added to 350 g of water at 26 °C in a Styrofoam container. When thermal equilibrium is reached, the alcohol-water solution is at a temperature of 5 °C. In the second trial, an identical cube of alcohol is added to 400 g of water at 30 °C, and the temperature at thermal equilibrium is 10 °C. (Use the specific heat of water = 4,190 J/kg·K and assume no heat exchange between the Styrofoam container and the surroundings).

54. What is the specific heat capacity of the alcohol?

A. 2,150 J/kg·K   **C.** 1,175 J/kg·K

B. 2,475 J/kg·K   **D.** 1,820 J/kg·K   **E.** 2,730 J/kg·K

55. What is the heat of fusion of the alcohol?

A. 7.2×10^3 J/kg   **C.** 5.2×10^4 J/kg

B. 1.9×10^5 J/kg   **D.** 10.3×10^4 J/kg   **E.** 3.3×10^4 J/kg

Diagnostic Tests

Answer Keys &
Detailed Explanations

Diagnostic test #1

1	B	Kinematics & dynamics	31	B	Equilibrium & momentum
2	C	Force, motion, gravitation	32	C	Work & energy
3	E	Heat & thermodynamics	33	E	Waves & periodic motion
4	A	Work & energy	34	A	Heat & thermodynamics
5	B	Waves & periodic motion	35	A	Light & optics
6	C	Sound	36	B	Electric circuits
7	A	Waves & periodic motion	37	D	Electrostatics
8	B	Electrostatics	38	E	Fluids
9	E	Electric circuits	39	C	Sound
10	D	Light & optics	40	E	Waves & periodic motion
11	B	Rotational motion	41	D	Work & energy
12	D	Equilibrium & momentum	42	C	Equilibrium & momentum
13	C	Work & energy	43	B	Force, motion, gravitation
14	A	Waves & periodic motion	44	A	Kinematics & dynamics
15	C	Sound	45	C	Heat & thermodynamics
16	E	Fluids	46	E	Work & energy
17	C	Electrostatics	47	B	Sound
18	B	Electric circuits	48	B	Electrostatics
19	C	Light & optics	49	D	Light & optics
20	E	Rotational motion	50	E	Kinematics & dynamics
21	D	Heat & thermodynamics	51	A	Equilibrium & momentum
22	A	Force, motion, gravitation	52	B	Waves & periodic motion
23	B	Sound	53	E	Fluids
24	A	Fluids	54	D	Electric circuits
25	E	Electrostatics	55	B	Rotational motion
26	B	Electric circuits	56	D	Heat & thermodynamics
27	C	Light & optics	57	C	Kinematics & dynamics
28	E	Waves & periodic motion	58	C	Force, motion, gravitation
29	A	Kinematics & dynamics	59	B	Equilibrium & momentum
30	D	Force, motion, gravitation	60	E	Light & optics

Diagnostic test #2

1	D	Kinematics & dynamics	31	D	Equilibrium & momentum
2	C	Force, motion, gravitation	32	B	Work & energy
3	D	Heat & thermodynamics	33	A	Waves & periodic motion
4	A	Work & energy	34	E	Heat & thermodynamics
5	C	Waves & periodic motion	35	C	Light & optics
6	B	Sound	36	C	Electric circuits
7	A	Fluids	37	C	Electrostatics
8	C	Electrostatics	38	C	Fluids
9	E	Electric circuits	39	E	Sound
10	C	Light & optics	40	C	Waves & periodic motion
11	D	Rotational motion	41	A	Work & energy
12	D	Equilibrium & momentum	42	E	Equilibrium & momentum
13	B	Work & energy	43	E	Force, motion, gravitation
14	A	Waves & periodic motion	44	D	Kinematics & dynamics
15	B	Sound	45	C	Heat & thermodynamics
16	D	Fluids	46	E	Work & energy
17	A	Electrostatics	47	D	Sound
18	C	Electric circuits	48	D	Electrostatics
19	E	Light & optics	49	A	Light & optics
20	D	Rotational motion	50	D	Kinematics & dynamics
21	A	Heat & thermodynamics	51	C	Equilibrium & momentum
22	E	Force, motion, gravitation	52	B	Waves & periodic motion
23	C	Sound	53	D	Fluids
24	A	Fluids	54	E	Electric circuits
25	B	Electrostatics	55	B	Rotational motion
26	D	Electric circuits	56	C	Heat & thermodynamics
27	B	Light & optics	57	A	Kinematics & dynamics
28	C	Waves & periodic motion	58	E	Force, motion, gravitation
29	B	Kinematics & dynamics	59	A	Equilibrium & momentum
30	E	Force, motion, gravitation	60	C	Light & optics

Diagnostic test #3

1	E	Kinematics & dynamics	31	C	Equilibrium & momentum
2	D	Force, motion, gravitation	32	D	Work & energy
3	A	Heat & thermodynamics	33	E	Waves & periodic motion
4	C	Work & energy	34	A	Heat & thermodynamics
5	A	Waves & periodic motion	35	C	Light & optics
6	C	Sound	36	E	Electric circuits
7	D	Fluids	37	D	Electrostatics
8	C	Electrostatics	38	D	Fluids
9	B	Electric circuits	39	A	Sound
10	E	Light & optics	40	A	Waves & periodic motion
11	D	Rotational motion	41	E	Work & energy
12	B	Equilibrium & momentum	42	D	Equilibrium & momentum
13	A	Work & energy	43	A	Force, motion, gravitation
14	D	Waves & periodic motion	44	B	Kinematics & dynamics
15	B	Sound	45	B	Heat & thermodynamics
16	E	Fluids	46	B	Work & energy
17	C	Electrostatics	47	C	Sound
18	A	Electric circuits	48	B	Electrostatics
19	A	Light & optics	49	B	Light & optics
20	E	Rotational motion	50	E	Kinematics & dynamics
21	B	Heat & thermodynamics	51	C	Equilibrium & momentum
22	A	Force, motion, gravitation	52	E	Waves & periodic motion
23	C	Sound	53	B	Fluids
24	A	Fluids	54	D	Electric circuits
25	A	Electrostatics	55	A	Rotational motion
26	D	Electric circuits	56	D	Heat & thermodynamics
27	B	Light & optics	57	B	Kinematics & dynamics
28	E	Waves & periodic motion	58	E	Force, motion, gravitation
29	E	Kinematics & dynamics	59	D	Equilibrium & momentum
30	B	Force, motion, gravitation	60	B	Light & optics

Diagnostic test #4

1	D	Kinematics & dynamics	31	A	Equilibrium & momentum
2	C	Force, motion, gravitation	32	D	Work & energy
3	E	Heat & thermodynamics	33	A	Waves & periodic motion
4	C	Work & energy	34	C	Heat & thermodynamics
5	A	Waves & periodic motion	35	E	Light & optics
6	B	Sound	36	B	Electric circuits
7	E	Fluids	37	C	Electrostatics
8	B	Electrostatics	38	A	Fluids
9	A	Electric circuits	39	A	Sound
10	E	Light & optics	40	C	Waves & periodic motion
11	B	Rotational motion	41	B	Work & energy
12	D	Equilibrium & momentum	42	E	Equilibrium & momentum
13	B	Work & energy	43	B	Force, motion, gravitation
14	E	Waves & periodic motion	44	B	Kinematics & dynamics
15	B	Sound	45	A	Heat & thermodynamics
16	B	Fluids	46	E	Work & energy
17	D	Electrostatics	47	E	Sound
18	C	Electric circuits	48	D	Electrostatics
19	D	Light & optics	49	B	Light & optics
20	B	Rotational motion	50	C	Kinematics & dynamics
21	D	Heat & thermodynamics	51	D	Equilibrium & momentum
22	C	Force, motion, gravitation	52	E	Waves & periodic motion
23	E	Sound	53	C	Fluids
24	A	Fluids	54	C	Electric circuits
25	B	Electrostatics	55	C	Rotational motion
26	D	Electric circuits	56	C	Heat & thermodynamics
27	D	Light & optics	57	D	Kinematics & dynamics
28	E	Waves & periodic motion	58	A	Force, motion, gravitation
29	A	Kinematics & dynamics	59	D	Equilibrium & momentum
30	B	Force, motion, gravitation	60	B	Light & optics

Explanations: Diagnostic Test #1

1. B is correct.

The equation for displacement given an initial velocity and constant acceleration is:

$$d = v_i t + \tfrac{1}{2}at^2$$

$$a = (v_f - v_i) / t$$

$$a = (1.8 \text{ m/s} - 0.4 \text{ m/s}) / 4 \text{ s}$$

$$a = 0.35 \text{ m/s}^2$$

Substituting $a = 0.35$ m/s^2 into the equation for displacement,

$$d = v_i t + \tfrac{1}{2}at^2$$

$$d = (0.4 \text{ m/s}) \cdot (4 \text{ s}) + \tfrac{1}{2}(0.35 \text{ m/s}^2) \cdot (4 \text{ s})^2$$

$$d = 4.4 \text{ m}$$

2. C is correct.

The object experiencing the force increases in speed due to the acceleration from the force:

$$F = ma$$

However, because the force is decreasing, *the rate of increase of its speed* (not the speed itself) will decrease.

3. E is correct.

$$Q = mc\Delta T$$

$$c = Q / m\Delta T$$

$$c = (150 \text{ kcal}) / [(3 \text{ kg}) \cdot (200 \text{ °C})]$$

$$c = 0.25 \text{ kcal/kg·°C}$$

4. A is correct.

$$W = F \times d \cos \theta$$

$$F = W / d$$

$$F = 40 \text{ J} / 4 \text{ m}$$

$$F = 10 \text{ N}$$

5. B is correct.

Equation for the period T of a simple pendulum:

$$T = 2\pi\sqrt{(L / g)}$$

Rearranging the equation for g,

$$g = (2\pi / T)^2 L$$
$$g = (4\pi^2)L / T^2$$
$$g = 4\pi^2(0.58 \text{ m}) / (2.5 \text{ s})^2$$
$$g = 3.7 \text{ m/s}^2$$

6. C is correct.

Electromagnetic waves are created by accelerating electric charges (change in velocity or speed).

7. A is correct.

Speed of the wave = wavelength × frequency

$$v = \lambda f$$
$$v = (0.5 \text{ m}) \cdot (800 \text{ Hz})$$
$$v = 400 \text{ m/s}$$

Distance = velocity × time, the distance covered in one second is:

$$d = vt$$
$$d = (400 \text{ m/s}) \cdot (1 \text{ s})$$
$$d = 400 \text{ m}$$

8. B is correct.

$$V = IR$$
$$R = V / I$$
$$R = 12 \text{ V} / 2 \text{ A}$$
$$R = 6 \text{ ohms}$$

9. E is correct.

Connecting two identical batteries in parallel yields the same voltage but twice the total available charge.

10. D is correct.

The power of the combination of the lenses is the sum of the powers.

$$5 \text{ D} + 3 \text{ D} = 8 \text{ D}$$

11. B is correct.

Consider this formula for rotational kinematics:

$\omega_f = \omega_i + \alpha \Delta t$

Solve for Δt:

$\Delta t = (\omega_f - \omega_i) / \alpha$

$\Delta t = (33.3 \text{ rad/s} - 15.0 \text{ rad/s}) / 3.45 \text{ rad/s}^2$

$\Delta t = 5.30 \text{ s}$

12. D is correct.

$m_1 v_1 = m_2 v_2$

$(1{,}450 \text{ kg})v_1 = (90 \text{ kg}) \cdot (30 \text{ m/s})$

$v_1 = (90 \text{ kg}) \cdot (30 \text{ m/s}) / (1{,}450 \text{ kg})$

$v_1 = 1.9 \text{ m/s}$

13. C is correct.

work = force × distance

$W = Fd$

Machines reduce the amount of force required, but the distance through which the force acts increases. They do not reduce the amount of work required.

If 900 J of energy is expended to lift the block to a certain height, then, even if a perfectly efficient pulley were used, the engineer expends a total of 900 J of work to lift the block to the same height using the pulley.

14. A is correct.

amplitude = ½(total displacement)

amplitude = ½(0.4 m)

amplitude = 0.2 m

The amplitude is the displacement from the position of equilibrium.

The amplitude is 0.2 m because the mass travels 0.2 m to the left of equilibrium and 0.2 m to the right of equilibrium in one oscillation.

15. C is correct.

One wave is completed at the 3rd node.

From the figure, the given wave has 1.5 λ:

$L = 1.5 \lambda$

$\lambda = 2/3\ L$

$\lambda = (2/3)\cdot(\text{total length})$

$\lambda = (2/3)\cdot(0.6\ \text{m})$

$\lambda = 0.4\ \text{m}$

$v = f\lambda$

$1\ \text{Hz} = 1\ \text{s}^{-1}$

$v = (900\ \text{s}^{-1})\cdot(0.4\ \text{m})$

$v = 360\ \text{m/s}$

16. E is correct.

density = mass / volume

$\rho = m\ /\ V$

$\rho = \text{kg/m}^3$

17. C is correct.

The charge q is equally attracted to both Qs because q is equidistant from each.

$q_{net} = 0$

$F_{1\rightarrow2} = kq_1q_2\ /\ r^2$

$F_{2\rightarrow1} = -kq_1q_2\ /\ r^2$

One force is attractive to the first Q, but the other force is attractive to the second Q and therefore points in the opposite direction.

The sign of the second force is reversed.

$F_{net} = 0$

18. B is correct.

A simple LC circuit with 0 resistance acts as an oscillator with charge flowing back and forth across the capacitor and inductor.

19. C is correct.

Light passing through a prism will be dispersed according to wavelength and display a continuous spectrum of colors (wavelengths).

20. E is correct.

Use the conservation of energy.

Note that in the initial state, the ball is at rest, so the initial kinetic energy is zero. Take the zero of gravitational potential energy to be the height of the ball at its final position.

The final kinetic energy has a translational part and a rotational part:

$$E_f = E_i$$

$$KE_f = PE_i$$

$$KE_{\text{translation}} + KE_{\text{rotation}} = PE_i$$

$$\tfrac{1}{2}mv^2 + \tfrac{1}{2}I\omega^2 = mgh$$

The ball is rolling without slipping, so the relationship between translational velocity and rotational velocity is:

$$v = r\omega$$

Then, the above expression becomes:

$$\tfrac{1}{2}mr^2\omega^2 + \tfrac{1}{2}(2/5)mr^2\omega^2 = mgh$$

$$(7/10)mr^2\omega^2 = mgh$$

Solving for the angular speed:

$$\omega = \sqrt{(10gh\,/\,7r^2)}$$

$$\omega = \sqrt{\{[10 \cdot (9.8\ \text{m/s}^2) \cdot (5.3\ \text{m})]\,/\,[7 \cdot (1.7\ \text{m})^2]\}}$$

$$\omega = 5.1\ \text{rad/s}$$

21. D is correct.

Because the path *ca* is adiabatic, no heat is added or lost by the system during this process.

Adiabatic process:

$$Q = 0\ \text{kJ}$$

22. A is correct.

$$\Sigma F_x = 0$$

$$0 = F_{Ax} + F_{Bx} + F_{Cx} + F_x$$

$$0 = (30\ \text{N}) \cdot (\sin 35°) - (40\ \text{N}) \cdot (\cos 25°) + (50\ \text{N}) \cdot (\cos 40°) + F_x$$

$$0 = (30\ \text{N}) \cdot (0.57) - (40\ \text{N}) \cdot (0.91) + (50\ \text{N}) \cdot (0.77) + F_x$$

$$0 = (17\ \text{N} - 36\ \text{N} + 39\ \text{N}) + F_x$$

$$F_x = -20\ \text{N}$$

23. B is correct.

The 4th harmonic has four nodes (i.e., three nodes more than the fundamental), and the ends are antinodes.

The harmonic to wavelength relationship for an organ pipe is calculated by:

$$\lambda_n = 2L\,/\,n$$

where L is the length of the pipe and n is the harmonic number (1, 2, 3,…)

For n = 4:

$\lambda_4 = (2) \cdot (0.2 \text{ m}) / 4$

$\lambda_4 = 0.1 \text{ m}$

24. A is correct.

Volumetric flow rate = velocity × area

$V = vA$

Water is incompressible, so volumetric flow rate is constant.

$(vA)_{in} = (vA)_{out}$

$(0.02 \text{ m/s})(\pi/4)(0.15 \text{ m})^2 = v_{out}(\pi/4)(0.003 \text{ m})^2$

$v_{out} = [(0.02 \text{ m/s})(0.15 \text{ m})^2] / (0.003 \text{ m})^2$

$v_{out} = 50 \text{ m/s}$

25. E is correct.

Both microwaves and blue light are electromagnetic radiation.

The difference between them is with respect to their frequency, wavelength and corresponding energy.

$c = \lambda f$

$E = hf$

26. B is correct.

The internal resistance is added to the external resistance of the circuit.

If the external resistance is large, then the current is small, and the internal resistance can be ignored.

27. C is correct.

A plane mirror does not magnify the image and always produces an erect, virtual image.

$m = 1$

$1 = d_i / d_o$

$1 = h_i / h_o$

28. E is correct.

Constructive interference occurs when two or more waves of equal frequency and phase produce a single amplitude wave that is the sum of amplitudes of the individual waves.

If there is any phase difference, the interference will not be the total of the amplitude of each wave.

If the phase difference is 180°, there will be total destructive interference.

29. A is correct.

Average acceleration is a change in velocity over change in time:

average acceleration $= \Delta v \, / \, \Delta t$

30. D is correct.

Equilibrium occurs when the sum of the forces equals zero.

$0 = F_1 + F_2 + F_3$

Set down as the negative direction:

$0 = 80 \text{ N} - 24 \text{ N} + F_3$

$F_3 = -56 \text{ N}$

A negative value corresponds to the downward direction, so 56 N points down.

31. B is correct. Impulse:

$J = F \Delta t$

Increase in Δt = decrease in F

Decreased force means that it is less likely to break.

Impulse and change in momentum are directly related.

$F \Delta t = m \Delta v$

Because the wine glass always goes from terminal velocity to zero in both cases, and the mass is constant, the impulse is constant and equal in both cases.

Thus, the only way to decrease force is to increase Δt which is the stopping time.

32. C is correct.

$W = Fd \cos \theta$

θ is perpendicular to the direction of the velocity

$\cos 90° = 0$

$Fd \cos \theta = 0$ J, no work is done against the force of gravity.

Since the velocity is constant, there is no net horizontal force, so no net work is done by horizontal forces.

33. E is correct.

velocity = wavelength × frequency

$v = \lambda f$

For velocity to remain constant, as frequency decreases, wavelength must increase.

34. A is correct.

$\Delta L / L_i = \alpha_L \Delta T$

$\alpha_L = \Delta L / L_i \Delta T$

$\alpha_L = (2.0005 \text{ m} - 2.0000 \text{ m}) / (2.0000 \text{ m}){\cdot}(40 \text{ °C} - 20 \text{ °C})$

$\alpha_L = 0.0005 \text{ m} / 40 \text{ m}{\cdot}\text{°C}$

$\alpha_L = 1.25 \times 10^{-5} \text{ K}^{-1}$

35. A is correct.

$1 / f = 1 / d_i + 1 / d_o$

$1 / 12 \text{ m} = 1 / d_i + 1 / 6 \text{ m}$

$1 / 12 \text{ m} - 2 / 12 \text{ m} = 1 / d_i$

$-1 / 12 \text{ m} = 1 / d_i$

$d_i = -12 \text{ m}$

A negative sign indicates that the image is behind the mirror.

36. B is correct.

The total resistance for a circuit with parallel resistors decreases as more resistors are added.

A decrease in the total resistance increases the total current in the circuit.

37. D is correct.

$E = kQ / r^2$

E is directly proportional to Q and inversely proportional to r^2:

$2Q = 2E$

The only solution that doubles the magnitude of E is to double Q.

38. E is correct.

If an object's entire volume is suspended in a liquid, the object's density is equal to that of the liquid.

If 20% of the floating buoy is above the surface of the liquid, 80% of its volume is suspended in the liquid.

Since 80% of the buoy's volume is in the liquid, it is only 80% as dense as the liquid.

39. C is correct.

The wave of the fundamental frequency for an open pipe is shown in the figure.

Therefore:

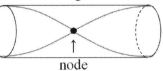

$\lambda = 2L$

The two endpoints are antinodes, and the midpoint is a node.

node

40. E is correct.

Wave interference occurs for all types of waves, both mechanical and electromagnetic.

41. D is correct.

$F = -kx$

$-k = F / x$

$-k = 30 \text{ N} / -0.75 \text{ m}$

$k = 40 \text{ N/m}$

42. C is correct.

Since the two objects come to rest immediately, they must have equal but opposite momenta before the collision:

$p_A = p_B$

$p = mv$

$m_A v_A = m_B v_B$

$v_A / v_B = m_B / m_A$

v_A is 5 times greater than v_B

$v_A / v_B = 5$

$5 = m_B / m_A,$ take the reciprocal of each side

$m_A / m_B = 1 / 5$

The ratio of the mass of A to the mass of B is 1: 5

43. B is correct.

If mass and force are constant:

$F = ma$

$a = F / m$

$a = $ constant

Therefore, acceleration is constant.

44. A is correct.

$$v_{Parallel} = v \sin \theta$$

The component of velocity in the direction of the slope is:

$$v_P = v \sin \theta, \text{ where } \theta = 20°$$

The velocity parallel to the slope:

$$v_P = v \sin \theta$$

$$v_P = v \sin 20°$$

$$v_P = (16 \text{ m/s}) \cdot (0.34)$$

$$v_P = 5.47 \approx 5.5 \text{ m/s}$$

45. C is correct.

In isothermal compression, all heat is released to the surroundings and is equal to the work needed to compress the gas.

$$Q_{released} = W$$

$$W = nRT \ln (V_2 / V_1)$$

46. E is correct.

All three answer choices are correct because they all describe PE:

$$PE = mgh$$

PE equals the work done by the pile driver:

$$PE = W$$

$$PE = Fd$$

$$PE / d = F$$

The force is directly proportional to PE, so all three choices are correct because they relate to the PE of the piledriver.

47. B is correct.

An organ pipe is either open at both ends or closed at one end.

Open pipe:

$$f_n = nv / 2L$$

where n = 1, 2, 3…

Closed pipe:

$$f_n = nv / 4L$$

where n = 1, 3, 5…

Observing the equation for frequencies produced by an open or closed pipe, there is an infinite number of frequencies possible depending on the value of n.

48. B is correct.

Ohms is the unit used to measure electrical resistance.

49. D is correct.

A diopter is a unit of measurement of the optical power of a lens or a curved mirror.

The power equals the reciprocal of the focal length (i.e., $1 / f$). Therefore, the diopter is a unit of reciprocal length.

For example, a 3 diopter lens brings parallel rays of light to focus at 1/3 m.

$1 / d_o + 1 / d_i = 1 / f$

Setting object at infinity (∞):

$1 / \infty + 1 / d_i = 1 / f$

$0 + 1 / d_i = 1 / f$

$1 / d_i = 1 / f$

Power of the lens:

$P = 1 / f$

$3 = 1 / d_i$

$d_i = 1 / 3 \text{ m} = 0.33 \text{ m}$

50. E is correct.

Accelerating uniformly for 8 s:

$\Delta v = a \Delta t$

$v_2 - v_1 = a \Delta t$

$v_2 = v_1 + a \Delta t$

$v_2 = 0 \text{ m/s} + (2.5 \text{ m/s}^2) \cdot (8 \text{ s})$

$v_2 = 20 \text{ m/s}$

51. A is correct.

Set North as the positive direction.

Conservation of momentum:

$(m_1 + m_2)v = m_1 v_1 + m_2 v_2$

$(m_1 + m_2)v = (2,500 \text{ kg}) \cdot (7 \text{ m/s}) + (2,000 \text{ kg}) \cdot (-14 \text{ m/s})$

$(m_1 + m_2)v = 17,500 \text{ kg·m/s} + (-28,000 \text{ kg·m/s})$

$(m_1 + m_2)v = -10,500 \text{ kg·m/s}$

$-10,500 \text{ kg·m/s} = (4,500 \text{ kg})v$

Velocity immediately after the inelastic collision:

$v = (-10{,}500 \text{ kg·m/s}) / (4{,}500 \text{ kg})$

$v = -2.3$ m/s, the minus sign indicates v points South.

52. B is correct.

$T = 2\pi\sqrt{(L / g)}$

If the clock is too slow, that means the period (T) is too large.

Decrease T by raising the weight which effectively decreases L.

53. E is correct.

When the air above the paper is blown the air moves faster, and the decrease in pressure causes the air below the paper to attempt to fill that void, pushing the paper upward in the process.

54. D is correct.

voltage = current × resistance

$V = IR$

$4 \text{ V} = I(20 \text{ } \Omega)$

$I = 4 \text{ V} / 20 \text{ } \Omega$

$I = 0.2$ A

55. B is correct.

We have three rotating bodies.

The total angular momentum is the sum of their angular momenta.

$L_{\text{total}} = L_1 + L_2 + L_3$

The angular momentum of a rotating object is:

$L = I\omega$

The flywheels are identical, so they each have the same rotational inertia I, so:

$L = I(\omega_1 + \omega_2 + \omega_3)$

The moment of inertia of the flywheels is:

$I = \frac{1}{2}mr^2$

$I = 0.5(65.0 \text{ kg})(1.47 \text{ m})^2$

$I = 70.23$ kg m^2

Thus:

$L = (70.23 \text{ kg m}^2) \cdot (3.83 \text{ rad/s} + 3.83 \text{ rad/s} - 3.42 \text{ rad/s})$

$L = 298$ kg m^2/s

56. D is correct.

As the temperature rises both the mercury and glass will expand by:

$\Delta V = \alpha V_i \Delta T$

Thus, to reach 450 m,l the expansion of both the glass and the mercury must be taken into account:

$V_G + \Delta V_G = V_M + \Delta V_M$

$450 \text{ ml} + \Delta V_G = 442 \text{ ml} + \Delta V_M$

$8 \text{ ml} = \Delta V_M - \Delta V_G$

$8 \text{ ml} = \alpha_M V_{iM} \Delta T - \alpha_G V_{iG} \Delta T$

$8 \text{ ml} = \Delta T(\alpha_M V_{iM} - \alpha V_{iG})$

$8 \text{ ml} = \Delta T[(18 \times 10^{-5} \text{ K}^{-1}) \cdot (442 \text{ ml}) - (2 \times 10^{-5} \text{ K}^{-1}) \cdot (450 \text{ ml})]$

$8 \text{ ml} = \Delta T(0.0706 \text{ K}^{-1} \text{ ml})$

$\Delta T = 113.4 \text{ °C}$

$T_f = T_i + \Delta T$

$T_f = 22 \text{ °C} + 113.4 \text{ °C}$

$T_f = 135 \text{ °C}$

57. C is correct.

A constant positive acceleration increases the velocity linearly upwards over time.

The velocity vs. time graph with a positive slope represents a constant positive acceleration.

58. C is correct.

First convert the final velocity from km/h to m/s:

$v_f = (100 \text{ km/1 h}) \cdot (1,000 \text{ m/1 km}) \cdot (1 \text{ h/3,600 s})$

$v_f = 100,000 \text{ m} / 3,600 \text{ s}$

$v_f = 27.8 \text{ m/s}$

$a = \Delta v / \Delta t$

$a = (27.8 \text{ m/s}) / (4.8 \text{ s})$

$a = 5.8 \text{ m/s}^2$

$F = ma$

$F = (68 \text{ kg}) \cdot (5.8 \text{ m/s}^2)$

$F = 394 \text{ N}$

59. B is correct.

Torque can be written as:

$\tau = I\alpha$

where τ = torque, I = moment of inertia and α = angular acceleration

Thus, if torque is constant, then the angular acceleration must be constant as well because the moment of inertia does not change

60. E is correct.

Calculate the focal length:

$1 / f = 1 / d_i + 1 / d_o$

where f is focal length d_o is distance to the object and d_i is distance to the image

$1 / f = 1 / 2 \text{ m} + 1 / 4 \text{ m}$

$1 / f = 2 / 4 \text{ m} + 1 / 4 \text{ m}$

$1 / f = 3 / 4 \text{ m}$

$f = 4 / 3 \text{ m}$

Explanations: Diagnostic Test #2

1. D is correct.

Let $y = 0$ be the ground, which is also the final position of the package.

Then:

$$y_f = y_i + v_i\Delta t - \tfrac{1}{2}g(\Delta t)^2$$

$$0 = d + v_i\Delta t - \tfrac{1}{2}g(\Delta t)^2$$

$$d = v_i\Delta t + \tfrac{1}{2}g\Delta t^2$$

$$d = (-15 \text{ m/s})\cdot(16 \text{ s}) + \tfrac{1}{2}(10 \text{ m/s}^2)\cdot(16 \text{ s})^2$$

$$d = (-240 \text{ m} + 1{,}280 \text{ m})$$

$$d = 1{,}040 \text{ m}$$

2. C is correct.

$$F = ma$$

$$m = F / a$$

$$m = 3{,}000 \text{ N} / (2 \text{ m/s}^2)$$

$$m = 1{,}500 \text{ kg}$$

3. D is correct.

If metal A has a larger coefficient of thermal expansion, it will elongate more than metal B when the strip is heated. Because the two strips are bound together, the bimetallic strip will curve downward when heated as the configuration gives strip A more room for expansion.

4. A is correct.

$$F = -kx$$

The negative sign is only by convention. It indicates that the spring resting force is opposite the stretch direction.

$$x = F / k$$

$$x = mg / k$$

$$x = [(30 \text{ kg})\cdot(10 \text{ m/s}^2)] / 4{,}600 \text{ N/m}$$

$$x = 0.0652 \text{ m}$$

$$PE = \tfrac{1}{2}kx^2$$

$$PE = \tfrac{1}{2}(4{,}600 \text{ N/m})\cdot(0.0652 \text{ m})^2$$

$$PE = 9.8 \text{ J}$$

An increase in PE due to the addition of the weight.

5. C is correct. Frequency = # of cycles / time

f = 2 cycles / 1 s

$f = 2$ s^{-1}

$v = \lambda f$

v = (6 m)·(2 s^{-1})

v = 12 m/s

6. B is correct. The decibel rating for sound is based on a logarithmic scale:

Sound intensity equation:

I (dB) = 10 log$_{10}$(I / I$_0$)

where I$_0$ = 10^{-12} W/m^2 and is the threshold of human hearing.

Example:

sound intensity decreases from 10 W/m^2 to 1 W/m^2

I$_1$ (dB) = 10 log$_{10}$(10 W/m^2 / 10^{-12} W/m^2)

I$_1$ = 130 dB

I$_2$ (dB) = 10 log$_{10}$(1 W/m^2 / 10^{-12} W/m^2)

I$_1$ = 120 dB

I$_1$ − I$_2$ = 130 dB − 120 dB

I$_1$ − I$_2$ = 10 dB

Thus, the sound intensity decreases by 10 dB if the intensity decreases by a factor of 10.

7. A is correct.

Buoyancy force:

$F_B = \rho g$V, where V is the volume of water displaced.

When the two blocks are stacked on each other:

$F_B = \rho g$V$_0$ = F_1 + F_2

When the two blocks are both in the water:

$F_{B1} = \rho g$V$_1$ = F_1

$F_{B2} = \rho g$V$_2$ = F_2

Total volume displaced in both cases:

V$_0$ = (1/ρg)·(F_1 + F_2)

V$_1$ + V$_2$ = (1/ρg)·(F_1 + F_2)

V$_0$ = V$_1$ + V$_2$

Same displacement of water in both cases so the water level does not change.

8. C is correct.

To find # excess electrons, divide Q_1 by the charge of a single electron:

excess electrons = Q_1 / e

excess electrons = $(-1 \times 10^{-6}\,C) / (-1.60 \times 10^{-19}\,C)$

excess electrons = 6.3×10^{12}

9. E is correct.

Capacitance only depends on the geometry (i.e., surface area) of a conductor and the permittivity of the dielectric used.

10. C is correct.

A flat plane mirror has no curvature, so the radius is considered to be infinite.

11. D is correct.

It seems that there is not enough information because neither the masses nor the radii of the sphere and cylinder are known. However, various parameters often cancel out.

Try to find the acceleration of the two objects. The object with the larger acceleration will reach the bottom first.

An object is rolling down an incline experiences three forces, and hence three torques.

The forces are the force of gravity acting on the center of mass of the object, the normal force between the incline and the object, and the force of friction between the incline and the object.

If the origin is taken to be the center of the object, the force of gravity provides zero torque.

This can be seen by noting that the distance between the origin and the point of application of the force is zero.

$$\tau_{gravity} = F_{gravity}r = mg(0) = 0$$

Similarly, the normal force contributes zero torque because the direction of the force is directed through the origin (pivot point).

$$\tau_{normal} = F_{normal}\,r \sin \theta = F_{normal}(R){\cdot}(\sin 180°) = F_{normal}(R){\cdot}(0) = 0$$

Use a coordinate system in which the x-axis is parallel to the incline and the y-axis is perpendicular. The object is rolling in the positive x-direction.

The dynamical equation for linear motion along the x-direction is:

$F_{net} = ma$

$(mg \sin \theta - f) = ma$

Note that the normal force is only in the *y*-direction, and thus does not directly contribute to the acceleration in the *x*-direction.

The dynamical equation for rotational motion is:

$$\tau_{net} = I\alpha$$

$$fR = I\alpha$$

(Note that the frictional force is perpendicular to the *r* vector, and sin 90° = 1)

where *R* is the radius of the object, *f* is the force of friction, and *I* is the moment of inertia.

A relation is needed to couple these two dynamical equations.

The equation of constraint imposed by the restriction that object rolls without slipping:

$$\alpha = a / R$$

To find the linear acceleration, use the equation of constraint to eliminate α from the rotational equation by replacing it with a / R:

$$fR = I(a / R)$$

The force of friction is of no interest, so rearrange this last expression:

$$f = Ia / R^2$$

Substitute this into the linear dynamic equation from above in place of *f*:

$$mg \sin \theta - (Ia / R^2) = ma$$

Solving this for *a*:

$$a = mg \sin \theta / [(m + (I / R^2)]$$

$$a = g \sin \theta / [1 + (I / mR^2)]$$

For a sphere, $I = (2/5)mR^2$, so:

$$a_{sphere} = g \sin \theta / (1 + 2/5)$$

$$a_{sphere} = (5/7)g \sin \theta$$

For the cylinder,

$$I = \frac{1}{2}mR^2$$

So:

$$a_{cylinder} = g \sin \theta / (1 + \frac{1}{2})$$

$$a_{cylinder} = (2/3)g \sin \theta$$

Since 5/7 > 2/3, the acceleration of the sphere is greater than the acceleration of the cylinder so that the sphere will reach the bottom first.

Interestingly, neither the mass nor the size of the sphere or cylinder enters into the result.

Indeed, both the mass and radius cancel out.

Since neither the masses nor the radii were given in the statement of the problem, it would not be possible to solve this problem by brute force numerical calculation.

12. D is correct.

The moment of inertia:

I = mass × the square of the distance from the rotational axis

$I = mr^2$

Since,

$r_1 = r_2$

I_1 / I_2 is simply the ratio of the masses.

Therefore, a moment of inertia I is directly proportional to the mass *m*.

Doubling the mass doubles the moment of inertia, giving a ratio of 2 : 1 comparing the more massive to the less massive sphere.

13. B is correct.

power = work / time

$P = W / t$

$P = (1{,}000 \text{ J}) / (40 \text{ s})$

$P = 25 \text{ W}$

14. A is correct.

A spring mass oscillator has a frequency:

$\omega = \sqrt{(k / m_0)}$

$f = \omega / 2\pi$

$f = \sqrt{(k / m_0)} / 2\pi$

Period:

$T = 1 / f$

$T_0 = 2\pi / \sqrt{(k / m_0)}$

If mass is doubled:

$T = 2\pi / \sqrt{(k / 2\, m_0)}$

$T = 2\pi / \sqrt{(k / m_0)} \times \sqrt{2}$

$T = \sqrt{2}\, T_0$

The period increases by a factor of $\sqrt{2}$.

15. B is correct.

For a pipe or tube that is closed at one end and open at the other end:

harmonic wavelengths λ_n have values of n which are only odd (n = 1, 3, 5, …).

After the fundamental wavelength (n = 1), the next consecutive harmonic wavelength is the third harmonic (n = 3).

The harmonic wavelength can be determined from the equation:

$$\lambda = 4L \: / \: n$$

$$\lambda = 4(1.5 \text{ m}) \: / \: 3$$

$$\lambda = 2 \text{ m}$$

16. D is correct.

$$\rho = m \: / \: V$$

$$V = (4/3)\pi r^3$$

$$\rho = m \: / \: (4/3)\pi r^3$$

$$\rho = (115 \text{ kg}) \: / \: (4/3)\pi \times (0.6 \text{ m})^3$$

$$\rho = 127 \text{ kg/m}^3$$

17. A is correct.

When a potential difference exists across a wire (for example connecting a battery to both ends of the wire) electrons flow in order to move from high potential to low potential.

In the case of a battery, the electrons flow along the wire towards the positive terminal to lower their potential.

18. C is correct.

$$1 \text{ A} = 1 \text{ C/s}$$

19. E is correct.

For a concave spherical mirror:

$$r = 2f$$

If the object is located at the radius of curvature:

$$r = d_o$$

$$d_o = 2f$$

Use the mirror equation:

$$1 \: / \: f = 1 \: / \: d_o + 1 \: / \: d_i$$

$$1 \: / \: f = 1 \: / \: 2f + 1 \: / \: d_i$$

$$1 \: / \: 2f = 1 \: / \: d_i$$

$$d_i = 2f = d_o, \text{ the image and object are located at the same point.}$$

Use the magnification equation:

$$m = -d_i / d_o$$

$$m = h_i / h_o$$

$$-(2f) / 2f = h_i / h_o$$

$$-1 = h_i / h_o$$

$$-h_i = h_o$$

If the object is located at the radius of curvature, then the image distance is equal to the object distance and the image is inverted because the height is the negative of the object height.

20. D is correct.

$$813.0 \text{ rpm} \cdot (1 \text{ min} / 60 \text{ s}) \cdot (2\pi \text{ rad/rev}) = 85.14 \text{ rad/s}$$

21. A is correct.

An isobaric process is a process in which the pressure remains constant throughout.

From the diagram, the volume changes but the pressure is constant, consistent with an isobaric process.

22. E is correct.

$$F = ma, \text{ on Earth}$$

$$20 \text{ N} = m(4 \text{ m/s}^2)$$

$$m = 20 \text{ N} / (4 \text{ m/s}^2)$$

$$m = 5 \text{ kg}$$

$$W = ma, \text{ on Moon}$$

$$W = (5 \text{ kg}) \cdot (1.62 \text{ m/s}^2)$$

$$W = 8.1 \text{ N}$$

23. C is correct.

Frequency is the amount of cycles that a wave makes in a certain amount of time.

$$f = \# \text{ cycles} / \text{time}$$

The figure shows the wave making 2 cycles in 4 seconds.

$$f = 2 \text{ cycles} / 4 \text{ s}$$

$$f = 0.5 \text{ s}^{-1} = 0.5 \text{ Hz}$$

24. A is correct.

$½\rho v^2 = \rho gh$, cancel ρ from both sides of the expression

$½v^2 = gh$

$v^2 = 2gh$

$v^2 = 2(9.8 \text{ m/s}^2)\cdot(0.8 \text{ m})$

$v^2 = 15.68 \text{ m}^2/\text{s}^2$

$v = 3.95 \text{ m/s} \approx 4 \text{ m/s}$

25. B is correct.

By Newton's Third Law, F_1 and F_2 form an *action-reaction* pair.

The ratio of their magnitudes equals 1.

26. D is correct.

$P = I^2 R$

$I^2 = P / R$

$I^2 = 16 \text{ W} / 18 \text{ } \Omega$

$I^2 = 0.89 \text{ A}^2$

$I = 0.94 \text{ A}$

27. B is correct.

$c = \lambda f$

$f = c / \lambda$

. Wavelength and frequency are inversely proportional.

28. C is correct.

velocity = frequency × wavelength

$v = f\lambda$

$\lambda = v / f$

$f = 1 / \text{T}$

$\lambda = v \times \text{T}$

$\lambda = 360 \text{ m/s} \times 4.2 \text{ s}$

$\lambda \approx 1,512 \text{ m}$

29. B is correct.

Given the angular velocity, the linear velocity at a given radius is calculated by:

$v = \omega r$

where v is the linear velocity and ω is the angular velocity

Convert from revolutions/minute to radians/second to arrive at an answer in m/s.

1 revolution = 2π radians and 1 min = 60 sec, angular velocity in radians/s is given by:

$\omega = (8.3 \text{ rev/min}){\cdot}(2\pi \text{ rad/rev}){\cdot}(1 \text{ min/60 s})$

$\omega = 0.87 \text{ rad/s}$

Calculate linear velocity. The problem gives the diameter, but the formula requires radius:

$v = (0.87 \text{ rad/s}){\cdot}(9 \text{ m})$

$v = 7.8 \text{ m/s}$

30. E is correct.

1,700 N is the magnitude of the instantaneous force with which a ball hits a bat if a batter hits a ball pitched with a 1,700 N instantaneous force.

31. D is correct.

In an elastic collision, KE and momentum are conserved:

KE before collision = KE after collision

Block$_1$ + Block$_2$ = Block$_1$ + Block$_2$

$\frac{1}{2}m_1v_1^2 + \frac{1}{2}m_2v_2^2 = \frac{1}{2}m_1u_1^2 + \frac{1}{2}m_2u_2^2$

Initially,

$v_2 = 0$

$\frac{1}{2}m_1v_1^2 = \frac{1}{2}m_1u_1^2 + \frac{1}{2}m_2u_2^2$

Solve for u_2:

$[m_1(v_1^2 - u_1^2) / m_2]^{\frac{1}{2}} = u_2$

Momentum:

$m_1v_1 = m_1u_1 + m_2u_2$

Solve for u_2:

$m_1(v_1 - u_1) / m_2 = u_2$

Set equal and isolate m_2:

$[m_1(v_1^2 - u_1^2) / m_2]^{\frac{1}{2}} = m_1(v_1 - u_1) / m_2$

$m_2 = m_1(v_1 - u_1)^2 / (v_1^2 - u_1^2)$

Solve for m_2:

$$m_2 = [(2.8 \text{ kg}) \cdot (8.5 \text{ m/s} - (-1.1 \text{ m/s}))^2] / [(8.5 \text{ m/s})^2 - (-1.1 \text{ m/s})^2]$$

$$m_2 = [(2.8 \text{ kg}) \cdot (92 \text{ m}^2/\text{s}^2)] / (71 \text{ m}^2/\text{s}^2)$$

$$m_2 = 3.6 \text{ kg}$$

32. B is correct.

Work is defined as:

$$W = Fd,$$

where d is the displacement in the direction of the force; in this case, it is $-h$, where the minus sign indicates that the direction of the displacement is down.

The force is the force of gravity:

$$F = -mg,$$

where again the minus sign indicates that the force is directed downward.

Therefore:

$$W = Fd$$

$$W = (-mg) \cdot (-h)$$

$$W = mgh$$

33. A is correct.

Frequency = 1 / period

$$f = 1 / T$$

$$f = 1.6 \text{ kHz}$$

$$v = \lambda f$$

$$v = (0.25 \text{ m}) \cdot (1.6 \text{ kHz})$$

$$v = (0.25 \text{ m}) \cdot (1{,}600 \text{ s}^{-1})$$

$$v = 400 \text{ m/s}$$

34. E is correct.

60 mL = 60 g water

$$Q = (mc\Delta T)_{\text{beaker}} + (mc\Delta T)_{\text{water}}$$

Change in temperature is the same.

$$Q = \Delta T[(m_{\text{beaker}}) \cdot (c_{\text{beaker}}) + (m_{\text{water}}) \cdot (c_{\text{water}})]$$

$$2{,}200 \text{ cal} = (25 \text{ °C}) \cdot [(m_{\text{beaker}})(0.18 \text{ cal/g·°C}) + (60 \text{ g}) \cdot (1 \text{ cal/g·°C})]$$

$$2{,}200 \text{ cal} / 25 \text{ °C} = (m_{\text{beaker}}) \cdot (0.18 \text{ cal/g·°C}) + 60 \text{ cal/°C}$$

$$88 \text{ cal/°C} = (m_{beaker}) \cdot (0.18 \text{ cal/g·°C}) + 60 \text{ cal/°C}$$

$$m_{beaker} = (88 \text{ cal/°C} - 60 \text{ cal/°C}) / (0.18 \text{ cal/g·°C})$$

$$m_{beaker} = (28 \text{ cal/°C}) / (0.18 \text{ cal/g·°C})$$

$$m_{beaker} = 156 \text{ g}$$

35. C is correct.

Spherical mirror equation:

$$f = -r / 2$$

The negative is only included to imply convergence of the lens.

$$f = r / 2$$

$$r = 2f$$

$$r = (2) \cdot (20 \text{ cm})$$

$$r = 40 \text{ cm}$$

36. C is correct.

Find R_{eq} for entire circuit:

R_1: in series:

$$R_1 = 2 \ \Omega + 1 \ \Omega$$

$$R_1 = 3 \ \Omega$$

R_2: in series:

$$R_2 = 5 \ \Omega + 1 \ \Omega$$

$$R_2 = 6 \ \Omega$$

R_1 and R_2 are in parallel:

$$1 / R_3 = 1 / R_1 + 1 / R_2$$

$$1 / R_3 = 1 / 3 \ \Omega + 1 / 6 \ \Omega$$

$$1 / R_3 = 2 / 6 \ \Omega + 1 / 6 \ \Omega$$

$$1 / R_3 = 1 / 2 \ \Omega$$

$$R_3 = 2 \ \Omega$$

R_3 is in series with the 4 Ω resistor:

$$R_{total} = 2 \ \Omega + 4 \ \Omega$$

$$R_{total} = 6 \ \Omega$$

Calculate the current around the entire circuit:

$V = IR$

$12 \text{ V} = I(6 \text{ }\Omega)$

$I = 2 \text{ A}$

Calculate voltage drop across parallel section using R_3 as equivalent resistor:

$V = IR$

$V = (2 \text{ A}) \cdot (2 \text{ }\Omega)$

$V = 4 \text{ V}$

*Note: voltage drop is equal across parallel branches.

Calculate current running through the branch the 2 Ω is on:

$V = IR$

$4 \text{ V} = I(3 \text{ }\Omega)$

$I = 1.33 \text{ A}$

Calculate power dissipated by the 2 Ω resistor:

$P = I^2 R$

$P = (1.33 \text{ A})^2 (2 \text{ }\Omega)$

$P = 3.5 \text{ W}$

37. C is correct.

An object becomes electrostatically charged when a charge imbalance exists.

Charge can only be transferred by electrons because protons are not mobile.

Thus, electron transfer creates an electrostatic charge.

38. C is correct.

gauge pressure $= P_{absolute} - P_{atm}$

$\rho g h = P_{absolute} - P_{atm}$

gauge pressure $= \rho g h$

gauge pressure $= (10^3 \text{ kg/m}^3) \cdot (9.8 \text{ m/s}^2) \cdot (10 \text{ m})$

gauge pressure $= 9.8 \times 10^4 \text{ Pa}$

39. E is correct.

The distance between any two adjacent nodes is $= \frac{1}{2}\lambda$.

$\frac{1}{2}\lambda = 75 \text{ cm}$

$\lambda = 150 \text{ cm}$

40. C is correct.

$$v = \lambda f$$

$$\lambda = v \, / f$$

$$\text{Hz} = \text{s}^{-1}$$

$$\lambda = (4{,}900 \text{ m/s}) \, / \, (640 \text{ s}^{-1})$$

$$\lambda = 7.7 \text{ m}$$

41. A is correct.

There is no force acting in the direction of motion (constant velocity), so there is no work done.

$$W = Fd \cos \theta$$

Assuming there is no friction, Stacey performed no work because the mass experienced no acceleration due to its constant velocity.

$$F = ma$$

$$F = (15 \text{ kg}) \cdot (0 \text{ m/s}^2)$$

$$F = 0 \text{ N}$$

$$W = (0 \text{ N}) \cdot (100 \text{ m})$$

$$W = 0 \text{ J}$$

42. E is correct.

The force delivered by the block to her hand and her hand to the block are equal by Newton's Third Law. The time of impact is the same for the block and the hand.

Impulse is calculated by:

$$J = F \Delta t$$

Thus, if the force and time are equal for the block and the hand, then they experience the same impulse.

43. E is correct.

The textbooks are following a straight path. By turning the car's steering wheel, Karen pulls her car door into the path of the textbooks, giving the illusion that the textbooks have a force acting on them.

44. D is correct. $d = (v_f^2 - v_i^2) \, / \, 2a$

$$d = [(21 \text{ m/s})^2 - (5 \text{ m/s})^2] \, / \, 2(4 \text{ m/s}^2)$$

$$d = [(441 \text{ m}^2/\text{s}^2) - (25 \text{ m}^2/\text{s}^2)] \, / \, (8 \text{ m/s}^2)$$

$$d = (416 \text{ m}^2/\text{s}^2) \, / \, (8 \text{ m/s}^2)$$

$$d = 52 \text{ m}$$

45. C is correct.

$$\Delta L / L_0 = \alpha \Delta T$$

$$\Delta T = \Delta L / \alpha L_0$$

$$\Delta T = 3 \times 10^{-3} \, m / (30 \times 10^{-6} \, K^{-1}) \cdot (10 \, m)$$

$$\Delta T = 10 \, K$$

46. E is correct.

$$F = ma$$

$$a = F / m$$

$$a = 10 \, N / 2 \, kg$$

$$a = 5 \, m/s^2$$

$$v_f = v_i + at$$

$$v_f = 0 \, m/s + (5 \, m/s) \cdot (15 \, s)$$

$$v_f = 75 \, m/s$$

$$KE = \tfrac{1}{2}mv^2$$

$$KE = \tfrac{1}{2}(2 \, kg) \cdot (75 \, m/s)^2$$

$$KE = 5{,}625 \, J$$

47. D is correct.

The beat frequency is twice per second, or 2 Hz.

$$f_{beat} = |f_1 - f_2|$$

$$2 \, Hz = |680 \, Hz - f_2|$$

$$f_2 = 678 \, Hz \text{ or } 682 \, Hz$$

48. D is correct.

$$F = ma$$

$$a = F / m$$

The force is an inverse-square with respect to distance.

$$F = (kqQ) / r^2$$

F decreases as q moves away from Q, and F decreases asymptotically (never reaching zero).

The charges move away from each other because both are positive.

49. A is correct.

For a diverging lens, regardless of the object position, the image is:

- virtual
- upright
- reduced

50. D is correct.

The magnitude and direction of the combined vectors A and B if vector A has a length of 5 units and is directed to the North (N) while vector B has a length of 11 units and is directed to the South (S) is 6 units, S

$$5N + (-11S) = -6S.$$

51. C is correct.

Newton's First Law: an object either remains at rest or continues to move at a constant velocity unless acted upon by an external force.

Newton's Second Law: $F = ma$

Newton's Third Law: when one body exerts a force on a second body, the second body simultaneously exerts a force equal in magnitude and opposite in direction on the first body.

While the conservation of momentum is related to all three Newton's laws, Newton's Third Law is the closest to the concept that momentum can be transferred from one object to another, and the total momentum does not change during this process.

52. B is correct.

Ignoring the dissipative forces due to friction, the total mechanical energy of a pendulum is conserved. Gravitational PE is constantly being converted into KE, and vice versa.

The total mechanical energy (i.e., KE + PE) remains constant.

53. D is correct.

Volumetric flow rate is constant:

$$v_1 A_1 = v_2 A_2$$

$$v_1 / v_2 = A_2 / A_1$$

$$v_1 / v_2 = (\pi / 4\, D_2{}^2) / (\pi / 4\, D_1{}^2)$$

$$v_1 / v_2 = (8\text{ cm})^2 / (3\text{ cm})^2$$

$$v_1 / v_2 = 7$$

$$v_1 = 7v_2$$

If the diameter increases, then the speed decreases by a factor of 7.

54. E is correct.

Changing the current in a nearby wire changes the magnetic field around it and induces a voltage in the wire close to it by Faraday's Law.

Moving a magnet close to the wire or moving the wire close to a magnetic field changes the magnetic field around the wire and induces a voltage by Faraday's Law.

55. B is correct.

The angular speed changes according to the kinematic relation:

$\Delta \omega = \alpha \Delta t$

$\Delta t = \Delta \omega / \alpha$

$\Delta t = (0 \text{ rad/s} - 96.0 \text{ rad/s}) / (-1.5 \text{ rad/s}^2)$

The angular acceleration is negative because the wheel is slowing down and the initial ω is in the positive direction.

$\Delta t = 64.0 \text{ s}$

56. C is correct.

Isothermal process experiences a change in entropy:

$\Delta s = Q / T$

An isothermal process has work equal to the heat added.

$Q = W$

$\Delta s = W / T$

$W = T \Delta s$

$W = (273 \text{ K}) \cdot (2.6 \text{ J/K})$

$W = 710 \text{ J}$

$W = 7.1 \times 10^2 \text{ J}$

57. A is correct.

The rock starts at the velocity Jack throws it, which is downward and therefore negative.

The velocity continues to increase negatively due to acceleration from gravity which is constant.

Thus, the velocity is linear with a downward slope.

$v_f = v_i + at$

$y = mx + b$

58. E is correct.

By the definition of impulse:

$$F\Delta t = m\Delta v$$

Therefore:

$$F = m\Delta v / \Delta t$$

The problem is asking to find the force on the block.

Proceed by focusing on the block, first finding Δv, and then using the relation above to find the force.

To determine Δv, calculate velocity after the collision using conservation of momentum:

$$m_i v_i = (m_i + m_f)v_f$$

$$v_f = m_i v_i / (m_i + m_f)$$

$$v_f = (0.1 \text{ kg}) \cdot (50 \text{ m/s}) / (0.1 \text{ kg} + 0.9 \text{ kg})$$

$$v_f = (5 \text{ kg·m/s}) / 1 \text{ kg}$$

$$v_f = 5 \text{ m/s}$$

$$F\Delta t = m(v_f - v_i)$$

$$F = m(v_f - v_i) / \Delta t$$

$$F = (0.9 \text{ kg})(5 \text{ m/s} - 0 \text{ m/s}) / 0.01 \text{ s}$$

$$F = (4.5 \text{ kg m/s}) / (0.01 \text{ s})$$

$$F = 450 \text{ N}$$

59. A is correct.

Use conservation of momentum:

$$m_A v_{Ai} + m_B v_{Bi} = m_A v_{Af} + m_B v_{Bf}$$

$$(2 \text{ kg}) \cdot (0.6 \text{ m/s}) + 0 = 0 + (2.5 \text{ kg})v_{Bf}$$

$$v_{Bf} = (1.2 \text{ kg·m/s}) / (2.5 \text{ kg})$$

$$v_{Bf} = 0.48 \text{ m/s}$$

60. C is correct. The plane mirror is double the distance from an object, so ½h is required for the minimum length.

Law of reflection:

$$\theta_1 = \theta_2$$

$$h = 2x$$

$$x = \tfrac{1}{2}h$$

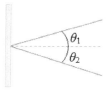
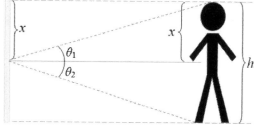

Explanations: Diagnostic Test #3

1. E is correct.

$$d_y = v_{0y}t + \frac{1}{2}at^2$$

where a is equal to g

In projectile motion, the only acceleration is due to gravity and is always equal to -10 m/s^2.

2. D is correct. Find acceleration of system:

$$\Delta x = v_0 t + \frac{1}{2}at^2$$

$$1\ \text{m} = 0 + \frac{1}{2}(a)\cdot(0.95\ \text{s})^2$$

$$a = 2.2\ \text{m/s}^2$$

Balance forces and solve for m:

$$F_{net} = F_1 - F_2$$

$$(m + 110\ \text{kg})\cdot(2.2\ \text{m/s}^2) = (110\ \text{kg})\cdot(9.8\ \text{m/s}^2) - m(9.8\ \text{m/s}^2)$$

$$(12\ \text{m/s}^2)m = 836\ \text{kg}\cdot\text{m/s}^2$$

$$m = 70\ \text{kg}$$

3. A is correct. An isothermal process does more work than an adiabatic process, and thus there is more area under the curve of the isothermal process than the adiabatic.

4. C is correct. Conservation of Energy:

$$PE_i + KE_i = PE_f + KE_f$$

At beginning, energy is entirely potential, and at the end, energy is entirely kinetic.

$mgh = \frac{1}{2}mv^2$, cancel m from both sides of the equation

$$v^2 = 2gh$$

$$v^2 = 2(10\ \text{m/s}^2)\cdot(4\ \text{m})$$

$$v^2 = 80\ \text{m}^2/\text{s}^2$$

$$v = 9\ \text{m/s}$$

5. A is correct.

$$f = 1 / T$$

Period $= (60\ \text{s}) / (10\ \text{oscillations})$

$$T = 6\ \text{s}$$

$$f = 1 / 6\ \text{s}$$

$$f = 0.17\ \text{Hz}$$

6. C is correct.

$$f = nv / 2L$$

n = 1 for the frequency of the fundamental

$$f = v / 2L$$

$$f = (340 \text{ m/s}) / 2(0.1 \text{ m})$$

$$f = 1{,}700 \text{ Hz}$$

7. D is correct.

Volume strain:

$$\Delta V / V$$

$$B = -\Delta P / (\Delta V / V)$$

$$\Delta P = -B(\Delta V / V)$$

$$\Delta P = (-6.3 \times 10^9 \text{ Pa}) \cdot (-3 \times 10^{-4})$$

$$\Delta P = 19 \times 10^5 \text{ Pa}$$

$$\Delta P = (19 \times 10^5 \text{ Pa} / 1) \cdot (1 \text{ atm} / 10^5 \text{ Pa})$$

$$\Delta P = 19 \text{ atm}$$

The negative sign indicates that the final volume is lower than the initial volume.

Since the volume has decreased, the pressure increased.

8. C is correct.

Each ion has a net charge of –1.

Because gravity is ignored the mass of each ion is irrelevant, and only the electric force is taken into account.

$$F = qE_0$$

From the overall charge, the forces are equal:

$$F_{Cl} = F_F$$

9. B is correct.

$$P = IV$$

$$P = (0.004 \text{ A}) \cdot (4 \text{ V})$$

$$P = 0.016 \text{ W} = 1.6 \times 10^{-2} \text{ W}$$

10. E is correct.

Snell's Law:

$$n_1 \sin \theta_1 = n_2 \sin \theta_2$$

$$n_1 = n_2 (\sin \theta_2 / \sin \theta_1)$$

$$n_1 = (1.33) \cdot [\sin (72°) / \sin (48°)]$$

$$n_1 = 1.7$$

$$(1.7) \sin (37°) = (1.33) \sin \theta_2$$

$$\sin \theta_2 = 0.769$$

$$\theta_2 = 50°$$

11. D is correct.

Apply the law of conservation of energy.

There is no potential energy in this situation – all of the energy is kinetic (rotational kinetic energy in the initial state, translational kinetic energy in the final state).

$$E_f = E_i$$

$$K_f = K_i$$

$$\tfrac{1}{2}m_{car}v^2 = \tfrac{1}{2}I\omega^2$$

The moment of inertia of a disk is:

$$\tfrac{1}{2}mR^2,$$

where m is the mass of the disk, and R is its radius.

Then:

$$\tfrac{1}{2}m_{car}v^2 = \tfrac{1}{2}(\tfrac{1}{2}m_{wheel}R^2)\omega^2$$

Solving for velocity:

$$v = R\omega\sqrt{(m_{wheel} / 2m_{car})}$$

The angular speed in rev/s must be converted to rad/s:

$$200.0 \text{ rev/s} \cdot (2\pi \text{ rad/rev}) = 1{,}256.6 \text{ rad/s}$$

Finally:

$$v = (0.50 \text{ m}) \cdot (1{,}256.6 \text{ rad/s}) \cdot \sqrt{[370.0 \text{ kg} / (2 \cdot 1{,}500.0 \text{ kg})]}$$

$$v = 221 \text{ m/s}$$

12. B is correct.

Determine how fast the 2 kg object is moving as it makes contact with the stationary object:

$$v_1 = at$$
$$v_1 = (3 \text{ m/s}^2){\cdot}(4 \text{ s})$$
$$v_1 = 12 \text{ m/s}$$

Conservation of momentum:

$$p_{\text{before}} = p_{\text{after}}$$
$$m_1v_1 + m_2v_2 = (m_1 + m_2)v$$
$$(2 \text{ kg}){\cdot}(12 \text{ m/s}) + (1 \text{ kg}){\cdot}(0 \text{ m/s}) = (2 \text{ kg} + 1 \text{ kg})v$$
$$24 \text{ kg}{\cdot}\text{m/s} = (3 \text{ kg})v$$
$$v = 8 \text{ m/s}$$

13. A is correct.

$$F_1 = -kx_1$$

Solve for the spring constant k:

$$k = F_1 / x_1$$
$$k = (120 \text{ N}) / (0.20 \text{ m})$$
$$k = 600 \text{ N/m}$$

What is the force needed to stretch the spring 44 cm?

$$F_2 = -kx_2$$
$$F_2 = (600 \text{ N/m}){\cdot}(0.44 \text{ m})$$
$$F_2 = 264 \text{ N}$$

14. D is correct.

$$PE = \tfrac{1}{2}kx^2$$

PE is maximized at maximum x.

15. B is correct.

Since D and E give beats of 3 Hz, D is either 3 Hz less or 3 Hz more than E.

Similarly, F is either 3 Hz more or 3 Hz less than E.

Therefore, D differs from F by either:

$$(3 \text{ Hz} - 3 \text{ Hz}) = 0 \text{ Hz or}$$
$$(3 \text{ Hz} + 3 \text{ Hz}) = 6 \text{ Hz}$$

16. E is correct.

$$v_1 A_1 = v_2 A_2$$

$$v_2 = v_1 A_1 / A_2$$

$$v_2 = [v_1(\pi / 4)d_1^2] / (\pi / 4)d_2^2$$

$$v_2 = v_1(d_1^2 / d_2^2)$$

$$v_2 = (1.5 \text{ m/s}) \cdot [(9 \text{ cm})^2 / (3 \text{ cm})^2]$$

$$v_2 = 13.5 \text{ m/s}$$

17. C is correct. charge = (# electrons)·(electron charge)

$$Q = n(e^-)$$

$$n = Q / e^-$$

$$n = (-9 \times 10^{-6} \text{ C}) / (-1.6 \times 10^{-19} \text{ C})$$

$$n = 5.6 \times 10^{13} \text{ electrons}$$

18. A is correct. Ohm's law: $\Delta V_i = IR_i$, since I is constant.

The light bulb with the higher resistance has a proportionally greater voltage drop.

Find current through circuit:

$$R_{eq} = 60 \ \Omega + 30 \ \Omega$$

$$R_{eq} = 90 \ \Omega$$

$$V_{eq} = 4(6 \text{ V})$$

$$V_{eq} = 24 \text{ V}$$

$$V_{eq} = IR_{eq}$$

$$I = V_{eq} / R_{eq}$$

$$I = 24 \text{ V} / 90 \ \Omega$$

$$I = 0.27 \text{ A}$$

Voltage drop for light bulb A:

$$V_A = IR$$

$$V_A = (0.27 \text{ A}) \cdot (60 \ \Omega)$$

$$V_A = 16.2 \text{ V}$$

Voltage drop for light bulb B:

$$V_B = IR$$

$$V_B = (0.27 \text{ A}) \cdot (30 \ \Omega)$$

$$V_B = 8.1 \text{ V}$$

$$V_A = 2V_B$$

19. A is correct.

It is possible to see virtual images but not possible to capture them on a screen.

The images seen in a convex mirror and converging lens are virtual images.

20. E is correct.

Since the motor spins at constant speed, there is no tangential component for the linear acceleration.

The linear acceleration is just the centripetal acceleration:

$$a = r\omega^2$$

Angular speed is in rpm, but needs to be in rad/s:

$$2695.0 \text{ rpm} \cdot (1 \text{ min}/60 \text{ s}) \cdot (2\pi \text{ rad/rev}) = 282.22 \text{ rad/s}$$

$$a = (0.07165 \text{ m}) \cdot (282.22 \text{ rad/s})^2$$

$$a = 5,707 \text{ m/s}^2$$

21. B is correct.

Equation for volume is given as:

$$V = m / \rho$$

$$\Delta V = m / \rho_1 - m / \rho_2$$

$$\Delta V = 2 \text{ kg} / \rho_1 - (2 \text{ kg}) / \rho_2$$

$$\Delta V = [(2 \text{ kg}) / (4 \text{ kg/m}^3)] - [(2 \text{ kg}) / (1,800 \text{ kg/m}^3)]$$

$$\Delta V = (0.5 \text{ m}^3) - (0.0011 \text{ m}^3)$$

$$\Delta V = 0.499 \text{ m}^3$$

Use $1 \times 10^5 \text{ Pa} = 1 \times 10^5 \text{ N/m}^2$:

$$W = P\Delta V$$

$$W = (1 \times 10^5 \text{ N/m}^2) \cdot (0.499 \text{ m}^3)$$

$$W = 4.99 \times 10^4 \text{ J} \approx 50 \text{ kJ}$$

22. A is correct.

When an object reaches terminal velocity the force of air resistance balances the force of gravity:

$$F_{air} = F_{gravity}$$

Thus, the net force on the object is zero.

23. C is correct.

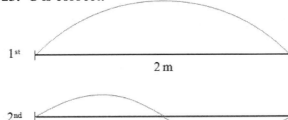

1st — 2 m

$\lambda_1 = 4$ m (fundamental)

$\lambda_2 = 2$ m (second harmonic)

2nd

Harmonic wavelength:

$$\lambda_n = (2L) / n$$
$$\lambda_1 = (2L) / 1$$
$$\lambda_1 = 2(2 \text{ m})$$
$$\lambda_1 = 4 \text{ m}$$
$$\lambda_2 = (2L) / 2$$
$$\lambda_2 = 2(2 \text{ m}) / 2$$
$$\lambda_2 = 2 \text{ m}$$
$$\lambda_1 / \lambda_2 = 4 \text{ m} / 2 \text{ m}$$
$$\lambda_1 / \lambda_2 = 2$$

24. A is correct.

Volume flow rate (Q) is how much water is flowing per second.

Find the cross-sectional area of the pipe and multiply the area with the velocity of the water.

$$Q = A_{pipe}v$$
$$Q = \pi(0.03 \text{ m})^2 \times (4 \text{ m/s})$$
$$Q = 0.0113 \text{ m}^3/\text{s}$$
$$Q = 1.1 \times 10^{-2} \text{ m}^3/\text{s}$$

25. A is correct.

Coulomb's Law:

$$F = kQ_1Q_2 / r^2$$

When charges are doubled:

$$F_2 = k(2Q_1)(2Q_2) / r^2$$
$$F_2 = 4kQ_1Q_2 / r^2$$
$$F_2 = 4F$$

F increases by a factor of 4 (quadruples).

26. D is correct.

$$KE_{before} + W = KE_{after}$$

$$W = \Delta KE$$

$$W = \Delta Vq$$

$$\Delta Vq = \Delta KE$$

$$qV = \tfrac{1}{2}m(v_f^2 - v_i^2)$$

$$v_f^2 = (2qV / m) + v_i^2$$

$$v_f^2 = [2(1.6 \times 10^{-19}\,C)\cdot(110\,V) / (1.67 \times 10^{-27}\,kg)] + (2.5 \times 10^5\,m/s)^2$$

$$v_f^2 = (2.1 \times 10^{10}\,m^2/s^2) + (6.3 \times 10^{10}\,m^2/s^2)$$

$$v_f^2 = (8.4 \times 10^{10}\,m^2/s^2)$$

$$v_f = 2.9 \times 10^5\,m/s$$

27. B is correct.

When light enters a different medium only the speed and wavelength change.

The frequency does not change.

28. E is correct.

The displacement of the tines of a tuning fork from their resting positions is a measure of the amplitude of the resulting sound wave.

29. E is correct.

In projectile motion, the maximum height corresponds to a zero vertical velocity component.

If this were not true, the projectile would continue to rise.

The projectile momentarily pauses when it reaches the highest point, thus making the velocity = 0.

30. B is correct.

$$T = ma_{centripetal}$$

$$a_c = v^2 / r$$

$$T = m(v^2 / r)$$

$$v = \sqrt{(Tr / m)}$$

$$v = \sqrt{[(55\,N)\cdot(1.3\,m) / (81\,kg)]}$$

$$v = 0.94\,m/s$$

Distance traveled in 1 revolution:

$C = 2\pi r$

$C = 2\pi(1.3 \text{ m})$

$C = 8.17 \text{ m}$

Time for one revolution:

$t = d / v$

$t = (8.17 \text{ m}) / (0.94 \text{ m/s})$

$t = 8.7 \text{ s}$

31. C is correct.

Momentum is conserved

$m_1v_1 + m_2v_2 = (m_1 + m_2)v_3$

$m_1v_1 = (m_1 + m_2)v_3$

$v_1 = [(m_1 + m_2)v_3] / m_1$

$v_1 = [(5,000 \text{ kg} + 10,000 \text{ kg}) \cdot (3.5 \text{ m/s})] / (5,000 \text{ kg})$

$v_1 = 10.5 \text{ m/s}$

32. D is correct.

$W = Fd \cos \theta$

$F = W / d \cos \theta$

$F = (880 \text{ J}) / [(14 \text{ m}) \cdot (\cos 32°)]$

$F = 74 \text{ N}$

$F_T = F$

$F_T = 74 \text{ N}$

33. E is correct.

$T = 2\pi\sqrt{(L / g)}$

$T = 2\pi\sqrt{[(12 \text{ m}) / (9.8 \text{ m/s}^2)]}$

$T = 6.9 \text{ s}$

34. A is correct. $Q = mc\Delta T$

$c = Q / m\Delta T$

$c = (200 \text{ kcal}) / [(3 \text{ kg}) \cdot (90 °C)]$

$c = 0.74 \text{ kcal/kg} \cdot °C$

35. C is correct.

For a convex (converging) lens, an object located beyond $2f$ has an image distance between f and $2f$.

$$1/f = 1/d_o + 1/d_i$$

Use $d_o = 3f$:

$$1/f = 1/3f + 1/d_i$$

$$(1/f - 1/3f) = 1/d_i$$

$$2/3f = 1/d_i$$

$$d_i = 1.5f$$

36. E is correct.

Power is given by:

$$P = I\Delta V$$

$$I = P/\Delta V$$

$$I = (360 \text{ W})/(120 \text{ V})$$

$$I = 3 \text{ A}$$

$$V = IR$$

$$R = V/I$$

$$R = (120 \text{ V})/(3 \text{ A})$$

$$R = 40 \text{ } \Omega$$

Another method to solve this question:

$$P = (\Delta V)^2/R$$

$$R = (\Delta V)^2/P$$

$$R = (120 \text{ V})^2/(360 \text{ W})$$

$$R = 40 \text{ } \Omega$$

37. D is correct.

From Coulomb's Law, the electrostatic force is *inversely proportional* to the square of the distance between the charges.

$$F = kq_1q_2/r^2$$

If the distance increases by a factor of 2, then the force decreases by a factor of $2^2 = 4$.

38. D is correct.

Increasing the viscosity will decrease the Reynolds number, decreasing the likelihood of turbulence occurring.

Increasing the flow rate or increasing the radius of the pipe increases the likelihood of turbulence.

Reynold's number does not include a term for temperature (i.e., it has no bearing on the value of Reynold's number).

39. A is correct.

By the definition of the sequence of harmonics, the second harmonic has twice the frequency of the fundamental,

Therefore,

$f_1 / f_2 = 0.5.$

Mathematically, this can be solved as follows:

$v = \lambda f$

$\lambda = (2L) / n$

$v = (2Lf) / n$

$f = (vn) / (2L)$

$f_1 = v / (2L)$

$f_1 = (3 \times 10^4 \, \text{m/s}) / (2 \times 3 \, \text{m})$

$f_1 = 5{,}000 \, \text{Hz}$

$f_2 = 2v / (2L)$, cancel 2 from the expression

$f_2 = v / L$

$f_2 = (3 \times 10^4 \, \text{m/s}) / (3 \, \text{m})$

$f_2 = 10{,}000 \, \text{Hz}$

$f_1 / f_2 = (5{,}000 \, \text{Hz}) / (10{,}000 \, \text{Hz})$

$f_1 / f_2 = 0.5$

Since the frequency is inversely related to the wavelength, the ratio f_1 / f_2 equals 0.5.

40. A is correct. A period is how long it would take the float to return to the original point.

$\frac{1}{2}T = 2.4 \, \text{s}$

$T = 4.8 \, \text{s}$

$V = \lambda / T$

$V = 48 \, \text{m} / 4.8 \, \text{s}$

$V = 10 \, \text{m/s}$

41. E is correct.

The direction of travel is in the opposite direction of the road's force.

$W = F \times d$

$W = \Delta KE$

$F \times d = \frac{1}{2}mv^2$

$F = (\frac{1}{2}mv^2) / d$

$F = [\frac{1}{2}(1{,}500 \text{ kg}){\cdot}(25 \text{ m/s})^2] / 30 \text{ m}$

$F = 15{,}625 \text{ N}$

42. D is correct.

$\Delta p = F\Delta t$

$\Delta t = \Delta p / F$

$\Delta p = m\Delta v$

$\Delta p = m[-35 \text{ m/s} - 30 \text{ m/s}]$

Note that v_f is negative because the ball is travelling in the negative direction after the impact (since the problem states the ball changed direction).

$\Delta p = 0.10 \text{ kg} \times (-65\text{m/s})$

$\Delta p = -6.5 \text{ kg{\cdot}m/s}$

$\Delta t = \Delta p / F$

$\Delta t = (-6.5 \text{ kg{\cdot}m/s}) / (-5{,}000 \text{ N})$

F is negative because the force the bat exerts on the ball is in the negative direction.

$\Delta t = 0.0013 \text{ s} = 1.3 \times 10^{-3} \text{ s}$

43. A is correct.

$a = \Delta v / \Delta t$

$a = (v_f - v_i) / \Delta t$

$a = (4 \text{ m/s} - 1.5 \text{ m/s}) / 4 \text{ s}$

$a = (2.5 \text{ m/s}) / 4 \text{ s}$

$a = 0.625 \text{ m/s}^2$

$F_{net} = ma$

$F_{net} = (50 \text{ kg}){\cdot}(0.625 \text{ m/s}^2)$

$F_{net} = 31.3 \text{ N}$

44. B is correct.

Within a vacuum there is no air resistance, therefore both objects, regardless of their mass, will reach the ground at the same time.

This is because both objects experience the same acceleration due to gravity.

45. B is correct.

Efficiency of a heat engine:

$$n = Q_H - Q_C / Q_H$$

$$n = (8{,}500 \text{ J} - 4{,}500 \text{ J}) / (8{,}500 \text{ J})$$

$$n = 0.47$$

$$n = 47\%$$

46. B is correct. Hooke's Law:

$F = -kx$, so force and distance stretched are inversely proportional.

The negative sign indicates that the force is in a direction opposite to the direction of the displacement.

47. C is correct.

$$\lambda_n = (2L) / n$$

$$\lambda_3 = (2){\cdot}(0.380 \text{ m}) / 3$$

$$\lambda_3 = 0.253 \text{ m}$$

$$v = \lambda f$$

$$v = (0.253 \text{ m}){\cdot}(600.0 \text{ Hz})$$

$$v = 151.8 \text{ m/s}$$

$$T = (mv^2) / L$$

$$T = [(0.00420 \text{ kg}){\cdot}(151.8 \text{ m/s})^2] / 0.380 \text{ m}$$

$$T = 254.7 \approx 255 \text{ N}$$

48. B is correct. The work is path-independent.

$$W = q\Delta V$$

$$W = q(V_D - V_A)$$

$$W = (10^{-14} \text{ C}){\cdot}(750 \text{ V} - 750 \text{ V})$$

$$W = 0 \text{ J}$$

The force does positive work during the first part of the motion and negative work in the final part. The total work is zero.

49. B is correct.

For a concave mirror with the object located at a distance equal to the focal length:

$$d_o = f$$

An object located at the focal point of a concave mirror will form no image.

50. E is correct.

$$t = d / v$$

$$t = (460 \text{ mi}) / (65 \text{ mi/h})$$

$$t = 7.1 \text{ h}$$

The time she can stop is the difference between her total allowed time and the time t that it takes to make the trip:

$$t_{stop} = 9.4 \text{ h} - 7.1 \text{ h}$$

$$t_{stop} = 2.3 \text{ h}$$

51. C is correct.

The centripetal force is the net force required to maintain an object in uniform circular motion.

$$F_{centripetal} = mv^2/r$$

where m is the object's mass, v is velocity, and r is the radius of the circular path.

Since m is constant and v remains unchanged, the centripetal force is inversely proportional to r.

Thus, if r is doubled, then $F_{centripetal}$ is halved.

52. E is correct.

In a pipe closed at one end:

$$f_n = (nv / 4L) \text{ for } n = 1, 3, 5 \ldots$$

The fundamental frequency is $n = 1$:

$$f_1 = v / 4L$$

Thus, longer pipes resonate at lower frequencies than shorter pipes.

$$\lambda = v / f$$

Longer pipes have higher wavelengths (longer waves) because f and λ are inversely proportional and a lower frequency gives a longer wavelength.

53. B is correct. Buoyancy force:

$$F_B = \rho g h A$$

$$F_B = \rho g V$$

Because the cube is lowered at a constant rate the volume of the cube underwater increases linearly and thus the F_B increases linearly.

Once cube is submerged, F_B is constant because the volume of displaced water is constant.

A linearly increasing line, then steady flat (zero) slope of zero for buoyant force vs. time.

54. D is correct. The magnitude of the acceleration is given by:

$$F = ma$$

$$a = F / m$$

$$F = qE_0$$

$$a = qE_0 / m$$

$$|\, a_p / a_e \,| = |\, (q_p E_0 / m_p) \, / \, (q_e E_0 / m_e) \,|$$

$$a_p / a_e = (m_e / m_p)$$

$$a_p = (m_e / m_p) a_e$$

$$a_p = (9 \times 10^{-31} \text{ kg} / 1.67 \times 10^{-27} \text{ kg}) a_e$$

$$a_p \approx (1 / 1{,}850) a_e$$

The electric field is constant.

The charges of the proton and the electron are equal in magnitude and are opposite in sign.

$$1.67 \times 10^{-27} \text{ kg divided by } 9 \times 10^{-31} \text{ kg} \approx 1{,}850.$$

The proton is about 1,850 times more massive, so its acceleration is 1,850 times smaller.

55. A is correct. The kinetic energy stored in a rotating object is:

$$K = \tfrac{1}{2} I \omega^2$$

With this, the angular speed as a function of energy is:

$$\omega^2 = 2K / I$$

The moment of inertia of a disk is:

$$I = \tfrac{1}{2} m r^2$$

Giving:

$$\omega^2 = 4K / m r^2$$

$$\omega = \sqrt{(4K / m r^2)}$$

$$\omega = \sqrt{[4 \cdot (3.2 \times 10^7 \text{ J})] / [(400.0 \text{ kg}) \cdot (0.60 \text{ m})^2]}$$

$$\omega = 943 \text{ rad/s}$$

56. D is correct. Break into three parts: heating the ice, melting the ice, heating the water.

Heating ice:

$$\Delta Q_1 = mc\Delta T$$

$$\Delta Q_1 = (10 \text{ kg}) \cdot (0.5 \text{ kcal/kg·°C}) \cdot [0 \text{ °C} - (-8 \text{ °C})]$$

$$\Delta Q_1 = 40 \text{ kcal}$$

Melting ice:

$$\Delta Q_2 = mL_f$$

$$\Delta Q_2 = (10 \text{ kg}) \cdot (80 \text{ kcal/kg})$$

$$\Delta Q_2 = 800 \text{ kcal}$$

Heating water:

$$\Delta Q_3 = mc\Delta T$$

$$\Delta Q_3 = (10 \text{ kg}) \cdot (1 \text{ kcal/kg·°C}) \cdot (14 \text{ °C} - 0 \text{ °C})$$

$$\Delta Q_3 = 140 \text{ kcal}$$

Combine:

$$\Delta Q_{total} = (40 \text{ kcal} + 800 \text{ kcal} + 140 \text{ kcal})$$

$$\Delta Q_{total} = 980 \text{ kcal}$$

57. B is correct.

$$v_f^2 = v_i^2 + 2a\Delta x$$

$$v_f^2 = 0 + 2(10 \text{ m/s}^2) \cdot (10 \text{ m})$$

$$v_f^2 = 200 \text{ m}^2/\text{s}^2$$

$$v_f \approx 14 \text{ m/s}$$

58. E is correct.

Consider the blocks separately. Identify all of the forces on each block and apply Newton's Second Law to each of the blocks individually.

Since there is no motion in the vertical direction, all vertical forces are balanced and can be ignored.

The lower block has four contacts with other objects, so there are four forces: tension in the rope (T), friction between the block and the floor, friction between the block and the upper block, and the applied force

$$F_a = 18 \text{ N}.$$

Impose a coordinate system where the positive direction is to the right.

The applied force (to the right) is positive, and the two friction forces and the tension force are to the left and negative.

Applying Newton's Second Law to the lower block:

$$m_l a_l = F_a - T - \mu m_u g - \mu(m_u + m_l)g$$

where the subscripts *l* and *u* represent the lower and upper block respectively.

Considering the upper object, there are two points of contact (the rope and the lower block) and two forces: tension and friction against the lower block.

Again, choose a coordinate system where the positive direction is to the right: tension is negative and friction positive. (The sign that results at the end of the calculation will determine the direction of the acceleration.)

Applying Newton's Second Law to the upper block:

$$m_u a_u = -T + \mu m_u g$$

The two accelerations above are not independent.

When the lower block moves to the right (positive), the upper block moves to the left (negative) by the same amount.

Therefore:

$$a_l = -a_u$$

Using this, the equation for the upper block can be expressed as:

$$m_u a_l = T - \mu m_u g$$

Adding this to the equation for the lower block:

$$(m_u + m_l)a_l = F_a - 2\mu m_u g - \mu(m_u + m_l)g$$

$$(m_u + m_l)a_l = F_a - \mu g(3m_u + m_l)$$

Solve for the acceleration of the lower block:

$$a_l = [F_a - \mu g(3m_u + m_l)] / (m_u + m_l)$$

$$a_l = [18 \text{ N} - (0.17)\cdot(9.8 \text{ m/s}^2)\cdot(3 \text{ kg} + 2 \text{ kg})] / (1 \text{ kg} + 2 \text{ kg})$$

$$a_l = [18 \text{ N} - (0.17)\cdot(9.8 \text{ m/s}^2)\cdot(5 \text{ kg})] / 3 \text{ kg}$$

$$a_l = (18 \text{ N} - 8.33 \text{ m/s}^2 \cdot \text{kg}) / (3 \text{ kg})$$

$$a_l = (9.67 \text{ m/s}^2 \cdot \text{kg}) / (3 \text{ kg})$$

$$a_l = 3.2 \text{ m/s}^2$$

59. D is correct.

If the skater's arms are thought of as a uniform rod with an axis of rotation about the center, then the moment of inertia is:

$$I = 1/12 mL^2$$

When she pulls in her arms, *L* is reduced and the moment of inertia decreases.

60. B is correct.

A blue object illuminated with yellow light appears black because it absorbs the yellow light and reflects none.

Explanations: Diagnostic Test #4

1. D is correct.

$$a = \Delta v / \Delta t$$

$$a = (v_f - v_i) / \Delta t$$

$$a = (0 \text{ m/s} - 28 \text{ m/s}) / 0.14 \text{ s}$$

$$a = -28 \text{ m/s} / 0.14 \text{ s}$$

$$a = -200 \text{ m/s}^2$$

When acceleration is expressed in terms of g, it is the magnitude of the acceleration:

$$a = | (-200 \text{ m/s}^2) / (9.8 \text{ m/s}^2) |$$

$$a = 20.4 \ g \approx 20 \ g$$

2. C is correct. According to Newton's Third Law, when two objects interact, the force on the first due to the second is equal in magnitude and opposite in direction from the force on the second due to the first.

3. E is correct. Find heat for -8 °C to 0 °C temperature change:

$$Q_1 = mc\Delta T$$

$$Q_1 = (12 \text{ kg}) \cdot (2{,}050 \text{ J/kg·°C}) \cdot [0 \text{ °C} - (-8 \text{ °C})]$$

$$Q_1 = 196{,}800 \text{ J}$$

Find heat for phase change:

$$Q_2 = mL_f$$

$$Q_2 = (12 \text{ kg}) \cdot (334{,}000 \text{ J/kg})$$

$$Q_2 = 4{,}008{,}000 \text{ J}$$

Find heat for 0 °C to 16 °C temperature change:

$$Q_3 = mc\Delta T$$

$$Q_3 = (12 \text{ kg}) \cdot (4{,}186 \text{ J/kg·K}) \cdot (16 \text{ °C} - 0 \text{ °C})$$

$$Q_3 = 803{,}712 \text{ J}$$

Find total heat:

$$Q_{net} = Q_1 + Q_2 + Q_3$$

$$Q_{net} = (196{,}800 \text{ J} + 4{,}008{,}000 \text{ J} + 803{,}712 \text{ J})$$

$$Q_{net} = 5{,}008{,}512 \text{ J}$$

Convert to kilocalories:

$$Q_{net} = (5{,}008{,}512 \text{ J/1}) \cdot (1 \text{ cal}/4.186 \text{ J}) \cdot (1 \text{ kcal}/10^3 \text{ cal})$$

$$Q_{net} = 1{,}196 \text{ kcal}$$

4. C is correct.

The work done by the crane is:

$W = F_c \times d$

where F_c = the force of the crane on the beam, and d = the distance it was lifted.

Find F_c by applying Newton's Second Law. Let F_g be the force of gravity on the beam, and a is the acceleration of the beam.

$F_{net} = F_c - F_g$

$F_{net} = F_c - mg$

$F_{net} = ma$

Solving for F_c:

$F_c = ma + mg$

$F_c = m(a + g)$

Therefore:

$W = F_c \times d$

$W = m(a + g)d$

$W = (450 \text{ kg}) \cdot (1.8 \text{ m/s}^2 + 9.8 \text{ m/s}^2) \cdot (110 \text{ m})$

$W = 5.7 \times 10^5 \text{ J}$

5. A is correct.

In an oscillating system, the energy is going back and forth between two or more forms.

When the spring reaches its maximum amplitude, its velocity is zero, and therefore its kinetic energy is zero, and its potential energy is maximum.

When the spring passes through its equilibrium position, its velocity is maximum and therefore its kinetic energy is maximum and potential energy is zero.

Gravitational PE is not applicable.

6. B is correct.

Higher harmonics have shorter wavelengths.

The harmonic number n gives the 2.5 m wave, and the harmonic number n + 1 (i.e., next consecutive value) produces the 2 m wave:

$L = (n / 2)\lambda$

where L = length of the pipe, λ = harmonic wavelength and n = 1, 2, 3....

$n = 2L / \lambda$

$n = 2L / (2.5 \text{ m})$

$n = 0.8L$

and

$$(n + 1) = 2L / (2 \text{ m})$$

$$L = n + 1$$

Combine and solve for L:

$$L = 0.8L + 1$$

$$0.2L = 1$$

$$L = 5 \text{ m}$$

7. E is correct.

Volume strain = Δ Volume / Volume

$$\Delta\text{Volume} = \text{Volume strain} \times \text{Volume}$$

$$\Delta V = (-3 \times 10^{-4}){\cdot}(12 \text{ L})$$

$$\Delta V = -3.6 \times 10^{-3} \text{ L}$$

$$\Delta V = -3.6 \text{ mL}$$

The value of ΔV is negative, meaning the final volume is smaller than the initial volume, confirming that it is a reduction.

8. B is correct.

Force exerted on a particle of charge q:

$$F = qE$$

The acceleration of the proton is to the right, so the force is also to the right.

Therefore, the electric field must be to the right.

9. A is correct.

Batteries in series add voltage:

$$V_{eq} = 4(8 \text{ V})$$

$$V_{eq} = 32 \text{ V}$$

Resistors in series add resistance:

$$R_{eq} = 45 \text{ }\Omega + 25 \text{ }\Omega$$

$$R_{eq} = 70 \text{ }\Omega$$

Ohm's law:

$$V = IR$$

$$I = V / R$$

Current through series circuit is constant:

$I = 32$ V $/ 70$ Ω

$I = 0.46$ A

The point at which the current is measured does not matter because the circuit is connected in series.

10. E is correct.

An image seen in a plane mirror remains the same size as the viewer moves away.

11. B is correct.

An object having moment of inertia I rotating with an angular speed of ω has angular momentum:

$L = I\omega$

The moment of inertia of a solid right circular cylinder about the axis indicated is $\frac{1}{2}mR^2$:

$L = (\frac{1}{2}mR^2)\omega$

$L = 0.5(15.0$ kg$)\cdot(1.4$ m$)^2\cdot(2.7$ rad/s$)$

$L = 39.69$ kg m^2/s

$L = 40$ kg m^2/s

12. D is correct. When the string is cut, there are no unbalanced external forces.

Set the momentum before the string is cut equal to the momentum after the string is cut.

$p_{before} = p_{after}$

$(m_A + m_B)v_i = m_A v_{Af} + m_B v_{Bf}$

$0 = (3.5$ kg$)\cdot(-0.3$ m/s$) + (2.5$ kg$)v_{Bf}$

$0 = (-1.05$ kg·m/s$) + (2.5$ kg$)v_{Bf}$

$v_{Bf}(-2.5$ kg$) = -1.05$ kg·m/s

$v_{Bf} = (-1.05$ kg·m/s$) / (-2.5$ kg$)$

$v_{Bf} = 0.42$ m/s

13. B is correct.

PE $= mgh$

$h = $ PE $/ mg$

$h = 40$ J $/ (2$ kg$)\cdot(9.8$ m/s$^2)$

$h = 2$ m

14. E is correct.

There is no relationship between amplitude and the spring constant.

15. B is correct.

If a mosquito were 10 m away (instead of 1 m), then the sound intensity is $10^2 = 100$ times less. Thus, there would have to be 100 mosquitoes to be barely perceptible.

16. B is correct.

$$PV = n\text{RT}$$

$$T_0 = PV / n\text{R}$$

$$T_1 = (2P) \cdot (2V) / (n\text{R})$$

$$T_1 = 4(PV / n\text{R})$$

17. D is correct.

Electric field lines go from positive charge to negative charge.

The electron will go against the field lines due to attraction to the positive charge emitting the field lines.

They do not follow path X because momentum in the horizontal direction must be conserved.

18. C is correct.

$$PE_c = PE_1 + PE_2 + PE_3$$

$$PE_c = (kQ_1Q_2) / r_1 + (kQ_2Q_3) / r_2 + (kQ_1Q_3) / r_3$$

The distance between the bottom charge and the right charge can be found using the Pythagorean Theorem.

$$d^2 = (0.06 \text{ m})^2 + (0.04 \text{ m})^2$$

$$d^2 = 0.0036 \text{ m}^2 + 0.0016 \text{ m}^2$$

$$d^2 = 0.0052 \text{ m}^2$$

$$d = 0.072 \text{ m}$$

$Q_1 = Q_2 = Q_3$, so:

$$PE_c = kQ^2[(1 / 0.06 \text{ m}) + (1 / 0.04 \text{ m}) + (1 / 0.072 \text{ m})]$$

$$PE_c = (9 \times 10^9 \text{ Nm}^2/\text{C}^2) \cdot (6.2 \times 10^{-9} \text{ C})^2 \cdot [(1 / 0.06 \text{ m}) + (1 / 0.04 \text{ m}) + (1 / 0.072 \text{ m})]$$

$$PE_c = (9 \times 10^9 \text{ Nm}^2/\text{C}^2) \cdot (6.2 \times 10^{-9} \text{ C})^2 \times (16.7 \text{ m}^{-1} + 25 \text{ m}^{-1} + 13.9 \text{ m}^{-1})$$

$$PE_c = 1.9 \times 10^{-5} \text{ J}$$

19. D is correct.

$1 / f = 1 / d_o + 1 / d_i$

$1 / 6\ m = 1 / 3\ m + 1 / d_i$

$1 / d_i = 1 / 6\ m - 2 / 6\ m$

$1 / d_i = -1 / 6\ m$

$d_i = -6\ m$

$m = -(d_i / d_o)$

$m = -(-6\ m / 3\ m)$

$m = 2$

20. B is correct.

The angular speed changes according to the kinematic relation:

$\Delta \omega = \alpha \Delta t$

$\Delta t = \Delta \omega / \alpha$

The torque is given and the moment of inertia of a right circular cylinder is:

$\frac{1}{2} m R^2$

Find the angular acceleration from the dynamic relation:

$\tau = I \alpha$

$\alpha = \tau / I = \tau / (\frac{1}{2} m R^2) = 2\tau / m R^2$

Combining the two results:

$\Delta t = m R^2 \Delta \omega / 2\tau$

$\Delta t = (10.0\ kg) \cdot (3.00\ m)^2 \cdot (8.13\ rad/s) / [2(110.0\ N\ m)]$

$\Delta t = 3.33\ s$

21. D is correct.

Heat liberated during temperature drop:

$Q_1 = mc\Delta T$

Heat liberated during phase change:

$Q_2 = mL_f$

Total heat liberated in process:

$Q_{net} = Q_1 + Q_2$

$Q_{net} = mc\Delta T + mL_f$

$Q_{net} - mL_f = mc\Delta T$

$\Delta T = (Q_{net} - mL_f) / (mc)$

$\Delta T = [(135 \text{ kJ}) - (9 \text{ kg}) \cdot (11.3 \text{ kJ/kg})] / (9 \text{ kg}) \cdot (0.14 \text{ kJ/kg·K})$

$\Delta T = 26 \text{ K}$

$T_{initial} = T_{melt} + \Delta T$

$T_{initial} = 234 \text{ K} + 26 \text{ K}$

$T_i = 260 \text{ K}$

22. C is correct.

$a = (v_f - v_i) / t$

$a = (22 \text{ m/s} - 0 \text{ m/s}) / (10 \text{ s})$

$a = 2.2 \text{ m/s}^2$

$F_{net} = ma$

$F_{net} = (100 \text{ kg}) \cdot (2.2 \text{ m/s}^2)$

$F_{net} = 220 \text{ N}$

23. E is correct.

$v = \lambda f$

$f = v / \lambda$

Distance from sound source is not part of the equation for frequency.

24. A is correct.

Archimedes' principle: the buoyant force acting on an object of volume V that is completely submerged in a liquid of a specific density has a magnitude that is expressed as:

$F_B = \rho(V_{displaced})g$

A change in the density of the liquid and thus, the volume affects the buoyant force.

density = mass / volume

F_B does not include the density of the object.

Differences in the density of a liquid that results from depth can be ignored.

25. B is correct. Power lost in transmission line:

$P = I^2 R$

$P = IV$

If a high current were used, then too much power would be lost in the lines due to the square of the current term.

If a high voltage is used then the current is reduced, and less power is dissipated.

26. D is correct.

$E = qV$

$E = \frac{1}{2}mv^2$

$qV = \frac{1}{2}mv^2$

$v^2 = 2qV \ / \ m$

$v^2 = [2(1.6 \times 10^{-19} \text{ C}) \cdot (1,200 \text{ V})] \ / \ (9.11 \times 10^{-31} \text{ kg})$

$v^2 = 4.2 \times 10^{14} \text{ m}^2/\text{s}^2$

$v = 2.1 \times 10^7 \text{ m/s}$

27. D is correct.

$E = hf$, where h is Planck's constant.

$f = c \ / \ \lambda$

$E = h(c \ / \ \lambda)$

The energy and wavelength of light are inversely related.

28. E is correct.

The period of a pendulum:

$T = 2\pi\sqrt{(L \ / \ g)}$

where L is the length of the pendulum and g is acceleration due to gravity.

Use $g \ / \ 6$ for g.

$T = 2\pi\sqrt{(L \ / \ (g \ / \ 6))}$

$T = 2\pi\sqrt{(6L \ / \ g)}$

$T = 2\pi\sqrt{(L \ / \ g)} \times \sqrt{6}$

New period $= T\sqrt{6}$

29. A is correct.

Convert the final velocity from km/h to m/s:

$v_f = (230 \text{ km/h}) \times [(1,000 \text{ m}) \ / \ (1 \text{ km})] \times [(1 \text{ h}) \ / \ (3,600 \text{ s})]$

$v_f = 63.9 \text{ m/s}$

$a = (v_i^2 + v_f^2) \ / \ 2d$

$a = [(0 \text{ m/s})^2 + (63.9 \text{ m/s})^2] \ / \ 2(2,300 \text{ m})$

$a = (4,083 \text{ m}^2/\text{s}^2) \ / \ 4,600 \text{ m}$

$a = 0.89 \text{ m/s}^2$

30. B is correct. $F_N = mg \cos \theta$

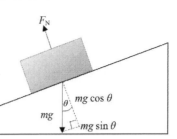

Velocity is not present in the above equation.

The normal force is perpendicular to the inclined plane and does not depend on the coefficient of kinetic friction between the plane and the block or depend on the block's velocity.

31. A is correct.

The total momentum before the collision is determined by adding the individual momenta as vectors.

$$p = mv$$

From the Pythagorean Theorem:

$$p_1{}^2 + p_2{}^2 = p_f{}^2$$
$$p_i = \sqrt{(p_1{}^2 + p_2{}^2)}$$
$$p_i = \sqrt{[(m_1v_1)^2 + (m_2v_2)^2]}$$
$$p_i = \sqrt{[(1.5 \text{ kg}) \cdot (4 \text{ m/s})^2 + (3 \text{ kg}) \cdot (2.5 \text{ m/s})^2]}$$
$$p_i = 9.6 \text{ kg·m/s}$$
$$p_i = p_f$$
$$p_i = (m_1 + m_2)v_f$$
$$(9.6 \text{ kg·m/s}) = (1.5 \text{ kg} + 3 \text{ kg})v_f$$
$$v_f = 2.1 \text{ m/s}$$

32. D is correct.

Energy transferred by a spring is given as:

$$PE = \tfrac{1}{2}kx^2$$

If x (the distance the spring is compressed) remains constant in both experiments, the energy is the same.

Mass is not a component of the expression and therefore is irrelevant.

$$PE = KE_1$$
$$PE = KE_2$$
$$KE_1 = KE_2$$

33. A is correct.

$$f = \text{\# cycles / second}$$
$$f = 1 / 2 \text{ s}$$
$$f = \tfrac{1}{2} \text{ Hz} = 0.5 \text{ Hz}$$

34. C is correct.

Isothermal means that temperature is constant.

Therefore, if there is no temperature change, U (internal energy) experiences no change.

$\Delta U = 0$

35. E is correct.

Snell's Law:

$n_1 \sin \theta_1 = n_2 \sin \theta_2$

$1.43 \sin \theta_1 = 1.33 \sin 90°$

$\sin \theta_c = 1.33 / 1.43$

Find critical angle (note: ratio of refractive index must be < 1):

$\theta_c = \sin^{-1}(n_w / n_g)$

$\theta_c = \sin^{-1}(1.33 / 1.43)$

$\theta_c = 68°$

$\theta_c / 2 = 68 / 2 = 34°$

Snell's Law:

$n_1 \sin \theta_1 = n_2 \sin \theta_2$

$(1.43) \sin (34°) = (1.33) \sin \theta_2$

$\sin \theta_2 = 0.6$

$\sin^{-1} (0.6) = \theta_2$

$\theta_2 = 37°$

36. B is correct.

In a circuit with capacitors connected in parallel, the charge in each branch of the circuit is not constant (like the current in different branches is different).

The equivalent capacitance of the two capacitors in series, C_2 and C_3, is lower than the capacitance of each capacitor ($1 / C_{eq} = 1 / C_2 + 1 / C_3$).

The charge across these capacitors is lower than across C_1 due to the relation $V = Q / C$ and the fact that voltage across C_1 and the voltage across the branch containing C_2 and C_3 is the same.

For a capacitor:

$U = (1/2) C V^2$

Note: U is the symbol for potential energy.

Since C is the same for each capacitor, but V is higher in C_1 than in C_2 or C_3, the PE is higher.

37. C is correct.

$$E = kQ / r^2$$
$$E_2 = k(2Q) / r^2$$
$$E_2 = 2E$$

38. A is correct.

Poiseuille's law:

$$Q = \pi\Delta Pr^4 / 8\eta L$$
$$2L_A = L_B$$
$$Q_A = \pi\Delta Pr^4 / 8\eta L_A$$
$$Q_B = \pi\Delta Pr^4 / 8\eta(2L_A)$$
$$Q_B = \tfrac{1}{2}(\pi\Delta Pr^4 / 8\eta L_A)$$
$$Q_B = \tfrac{1}{2}Q_A$$
$$Q_A = 2Q_B$$

39. A is correct.

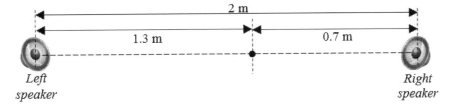

The distance from the point to the left speaker is 1.3 m.

The distance from the point to the right speaker is 0.7 m.

For a given λ, antinodes exist at distances:

$$L_A = (n / 4)\lambda, \text{ where } n = 1, 3, 5 \dots$$

For a given λ, nodes exist at distances:

$$L_N = (n / 2)\lambda, \text{ where } n = 1, 2, 3 \dots$$

Because the speakers are in phase, use a distance of either 1.3 m or 0.7 m.

For an antinode:

$$(1.3 \text{ m}) = (n / 4)\cdot(0.8 \text{ m})$$
$$n = 6.5$$

The calculated value for n is not a whole number so n does not equal 1, 3, 5 ….

Thus, the point is not at an antinode.

For a node:

$$(1.3 \text{ m}) = (n/2) \cdot (0.8 \text{ m})$$

$$n = 3.25$$

The calculated value for n is not a whole number, so n does not equal 1, 2, 3 ….

Thus, the point is not at a node.

Therefore, the point is neither an antinode nor a node.

40. C is correct.

$v = \sqrt{(T / \mu)}$, where μ is the linear density of the wire.

$$\mu = m / L$$

$$v = \sqrt{[T / (m / L)]}$$

$$m = TL / v^2$$

$$m = (50 \text{ N}) \cdot (18 \text{ m}) / (45 \text{ m/s})^2$$

$$m = 0.44 \text{ kg}$$

41. B is correct.

Work = Force × displacement × cos θ

$$W_g = Fd \cos \theta$$

The gravitational force is perpendicular to the direction of movement.

$$W_g = ma \times d \cos 90$$

$$W_g = ma \times 0 \text{ m}$$

$$W_g = 0 \text{ J}$$

Since the force of gravity acts perpendicular to the distance traveled, the force due to gravity does no work.

42. E is correct. An external force of 3 N provides Cart I momentum.

The change of momentum = $F\Delta t$

$$\Delta p_I = F\Delta t$$

$$\Delta p_I = (3 \text{ N}) \cdot (2 \text{ s})$$

$$\Delta p_I = 6 \text{ N·s}$$

$$\Delta p_I = 6 \text{ kg·m/s}$$

$$p_I = 6 \text{ kg·m/s} - 0 \text{ kg·m/s}$$

$$p_I = 6 \text{ kg·m/s}$$

Cart I starts with zero momentum, momentum after force, but before the collision is 6 kg·m/s.

43. B is correct.

Use a rotated coordinate system in which the normal force points along the positive *y*-axis and "up the incline" is in the negative *x*-direction.

In this coordinate system, there is no motion or acceleration in the *y*-direction; this means the normal force F_N must be equal to $mg \cos \theta$, so the *y*-forces balance.

Next, consider forces and components of forces in the *x*-direction.

There is the frictional force to the right ("down the incline," since friction opposes the motion and is stopping the car) and there is a component of the gravitational force to the right $mg \sin \theta$.

$$F_{net} = F_{net,x} = F_{friction} + F_{gravity,x}$$

$$F_{friction} = \mu_k F_N = \mu_k \, (mg \cos \theta)$$

$$F_{net,x} = \mu_k \, (mg \cos \theta) + mg \sin \theta$$

$$F_{net,x} = mg \, (\mu_k \cos \theta + \sin \theta),$$

where downhill is positive.

Note: use μ_k because the tires locked up, meaning the tires are sliding over the road surface.

If the tires were gripping the surface (a condition called "smooth rolling"), the static friction would be used because in that case, the tires are *not* sliding against the surface in that case.

44. B is correct.

Two objects thrown with the same initial speed (one up and the other down) are traveling at the same speed when they hit the ground.

45. A is correct.

Change in entropy:

$$\Delta S = Q \, / \, T$$

where Q = (power)·(time)

Temperature outside:

$$T = (-10 \; ^\circ C + 273 \; K)$$

$$T = 263 \; K$$

Calculate:

$$\Delta S = [(30 \times 10^3 \; J/s)·(15 \; s)] \, / \, 263 \; K$$

$$\Delta S = 7.6 \; J/K$$

46. E is correct.

KE is a type of energy of a system, and work is energy transferred to the system.

If negative work is being done upon an object with KE, then the work is simply decreasing the energy of the object and thus its kinetic energy.

If positive work is performed, then the energy of the object increases and kinetic energy increases (if energy is transformed into kinetic energy).

47. E is correct.

Waves are repeating patterns.

Waves are cyclic, with one λ corresponding to one cycle of 360°.

Since the two waves are offset by ¼ of a wavelength at $t = 0$, wave A has an antinode (i.e., maximal displacement), and wave B has a node (i.e., no displacement).

There is a phase difference of ¼ of a cycle:

¼(360°) = 90°

48. D is correct.

Acceleration is always positive and away from charge Q.

Therefore, velocity increases (no opposing force of friction).

The energy of the system starts as electrical PE.

$PE_{elec} = (kQq) / r$

where r is the initial distance between the point charges.

Electrical PE is the energy required to bring a system together from the charges starting at infinity.

After charge Q has moved very far away, the energy of the system is only KE = $\frac{1}{2}mv^2$

v has a limit because KE cannot exceed kQq / r

49. B is correct.

Total magnification = magnification of eyepiece × magnification of objective

Total magnification = (near point/focal length of eyepiece) × magnification of objective

Total magnification = 25 cm / 2.5 cm × 30

Total magnification = 10 × 30 = 300

50. C is correct.

$t = d_x / v_x$

$t = (1{,}000 \text{ m}) / (50 \text{ m/s})$

$t = 20$ s

$d_y = v_{iy}t + \frac{1}{2}at^2$

$d_y = (240 \text{ m/s})\cdot(20 \text{ s}) + \frac{1}{2}(-9.8 \text{ m/s}^2)\cdot(20 \text{ s})^2$

$d_y = (4{,}800 \text{ m}) + \frac{1}{2}(-9.8 \text{ m/s}^2)\cdot(400 \text{ s}^2)$

$d_y = (4{,}800 \text{ m}) - (1{,}960 \text{ m})$

$d_y = 2{,}840$ m

51. D is correct. Choose the positive direction to be to the right with the ball thrown in the positive direction:

$F = ma$

$a = \Delta v \,/\, t$

$a = (v_f - v_i) \,/\, t$

$a = (-25 \text{ m/s} - 25 \text{ m/s}) \,/\, 0.05 \text{ s}^*$

$a = -1{,}000 \text{ m/s}^2$

$F = (0.8 \text{ kg})\cdot(-1{,}000 \text{ m/s}^2)$

$F = -800$ N, to the left

* use negative velocity for v_f because the ball bounces

52. E is correct.

Maximum acceleration in simple harmonic motion is:

$a_{max} = \omega^2 y$

where $\omega =$ frequency and $y =$ position

If frequency doubles:

$a_{max} = (2\omega)^2 y$

$a_{max} = 4\omega^2 y$

The maximum acceleration increases by a factor of 4.

53. C is correct.

Hydrostatic equilibrium:

$P_{bottom} = P_{atm} + \rho g(h_3 - h_1)$

Absolute pressure:

$P = P_{atm} + \rho g(h_3 - h_1)$

Gauge pressure:

$P = \rho g(h_3 - h_1)$

54. C is correct. Ohm's law is:

$I = V / R$

The current I depends on the voltage V and the resistance R (i.e., V and R are the *inputs*, and I is the result). So, for an ohmic resistor, R stays the same regardless of the voltage.

The current that runs through the resistor will change.

55. C is correct.

The gravitational force is the only influence making the satellite move in a circular path, so the centripetal acceleration in orbit is the gravitational acceleration at that orbital radius.

$v^2 / r = g'$

$v = \sqrt{(g'r)}$

$v = \sqrt{[(2.3 \text{ m/s}^2) \cdot (34,000 \text{ m})]}$

$v = 280 \text{ m/s}$

56. C is correct.

Work during an isothermal process:

$W = nRT \times \ln(V_f / V_i)$

$W = (4 \text{ mol}) \cdot (8.134 \text{ J/mol} \cdot \text{K}) \cdot (650 \text{ K}) \times \ln(0.33 \text{ m}^3 / 0.025 \text{ m}^3)$

$W = 56 \text{ kJ}$

57. D is correct.

Use energy equals work done by friction, assuming F is the same:

$KE = W$

$\frac{1}{2}mv^2 = Fd$

$mv^2 / 2d = F$

F is the same because $F = ma$.

The mass and acceleration of the car are equal in both cases.

$F_1 = F_2$

$\frac{1}{2}mv_1^2 / d_1 = \frac{1}{2}mv_2^2 / d_2$

$(v_1^2 / d_1) = (v_2^2 / d_2)$

$(v_1^2 / v_2^2) = (d_1 / d_2)$

$(58 \text{ mi/h})^2 / (26 \text{ mi/h})^2 = (d_1 / d_2)$

$(d_1 / d_2) = 5$

58. A is correct.

Total mass of A + B

$$M_{total} = M_A + M_B$$

$$M_B = 2M_A$$

$$M_{total} = M_A + 2M_A$$

$$M_{total} = 3M_A$$

Fraction of box B mass to total mass:

$$M_B \,/\, M_{total} = M_B \,/\, 3M_A$$

$$M_B \,/\, M_{total} = 2M_A \,/\, 3M_A$$

$$M_B \,/\, M_{total} = 2 \,/\, 3$$

$$M_B = 2/3 \; M_{total}$$

If box B is 2/3 the total mass and the force is:

$$F_{total} = (M_{total})a$$

Then box B experiences 2/3 total force.

$$F_B = 2/3 \; F_{total}$$

59. D is correct.

Moment of inertia for solid disk:

$$I = \tfrac{1}{2}mr^2$$

$$I = \tfrac{1}{2}(12 \text{ kg}) \cdot (1.8 \text{ m})^2$$

$$I = 19.44 \text{ kg·m}^2$$

Angular momentum:

$$L = I \times \omega$$

$$L = (19.44 \text{ kg·m}^2) \cdot (2.9 \text{ rad/s})$$

$$L = 56.4 \text{ kg·m}^2/\text{s}$$

60. B is correct.

For the critical angle, the refracted angle is 90°

$$n_{water} \sin \theta_{crit} = n_{air} \sin 90^\circ$$

$$\sin \theta_{crit} = (n_{air} \,/\, n_{water}) \sin 90^\circ$$

$$\theta_{crit} = \sin^{-1} [(1 \,/\, 1.33) \cdot (1)]$$

$$\theta_{crit} = \sin^{-1} (3/4)$$

Topical
Practice Questions

Answer Keys &
Detailed Explanations

Kinematics & Dynamics

1: D	11: C	21: E	31: B	41: C	51: A
2: B	12: B	22: A	32: C	42: A	52: A
3: B	13: A	23: B	33: D	43: E	53: E
4: A	14: C	24: D	34: E	44: B	54: D
5: C	15: B	25: B	35: C	45: A	55: A
6: E	16: D	26: E	36: E	46: D	
7: D	17: E	27: C	37: D	47: E	
8: B	18: B	28: D	38: B	48: C	
9: A	19: D	29: D	39: E	49: D	
10: B	20: C	30: E	40: E	50: E	

Force, Motion, Gravitation

1: B	11: A	21: B	31: C	41: A	51: C
2: E	12: E	22: A	32: E	42: C	52: B
3: A	13: B	23: C	33: D	43: B	53: D
4: C	14: C	24: E	34: A	44: C	54: E
5: E	15: E	25: D	35: D	45: A	55: B
6: D	16: A	26: A	36: A	46: C	
7: A	17: D	27: E	37: D	47: E	
8: E	18: C	28: D	38: B	48: E	
9: A	19: E	29: A	39: B	49: C	
10: C	20: B	30: D	40: C	50: A	

Equilibrium & Momentum

1: A	11: E	21: D	31: C	41: B	51: D
2: D	12: C	22: B	32: E	42: A	52: D
3: E	13: D	23: A	33: C	43: C	53: A
4: C	14: B	24: E	34: B	44: B	54: E
5: E	15: E	25: D	35: E	45: D	55: B
6: B	16: D	26: A	36: C	46: C	
7: D	17: B	27: E	37: B	47: B	
8: A	18: E	28: C	38: C	48: A	
9: B	19: B	29: A	39: E	49: D	
10: C	20: C	30: B	40: A	50: C	

Work & Energy

1: D	11: D	21: B	31: B	41: A	51: D
2: B	12: B	22: D	32: C	42: A	52: C
3: A	13: A	23: B	33: D	43: C	53: C
4: B	14: C	24: C	34: E	44: E	54: B
5: E	15: B	25: E	35: B	45: D	55: C
6: A	16: D	26: A	36: B	46: E	
7: D	17: E	27: D	37: C	47: A	
8: C	18: A	28: E	38: D	48: A	
9: A	19: D	29: B	39: E	49: E	
10: B	20: A	30: C	40: B	50: B	

Rotational Motion

1: D	11: A	21: B	31: D	41: C
2: B	12: E	22: D	32: D	42: D
3: A	13: C	23: B	33: B	43: C
4: D	14: B	24: A	34: C	44: C
5: C	15: D	25: A	35: D	45: B
6: C	16: D	26: A	36: B	46: C
7: E	17: E	27: A	37: C	
8: A	18: A	28: C	38: B	
9: C	19: D	29: C	39: B	
10: B	20: D	30: C	40: D	

Waves & Periodic Motion

1: B	11: D	21: B	31: B	41: A	51: A
2: D	12: A	22: E	32: D	42: C	52: C
3: D	13: B	23: B	33: E	43: B	53: B
4: C	14: C	24: A	34: D	44: E	54: E
5: A	15: E	25: E	35: C	45: A	55: D
6: E	16: B	26: C	36: D	46: B	
7: C	17: C	27: D	37: B	47: A	
8: D	18: E	28: B	38: C	48: C	
9: A	19: A	29: E	39: D	49: D	
10: E	20: D	30: A	40: C	50: A	

Sound

1: B	11: B	21: E	31: C	41: A	51: D
2: A	12: A	22: D	32: D	42: C	52: B
3: B	13: E	23: B	33: A	43: D	53: D
4: C	14: C	24: C	34: E	44: A	54: C
5: B	15: D	25: E	35: A	45: B	55: E
6: E	16: E	26: D	36: E	46: E	
7: D	17: C	27: B	37: B	47: C	
8: A	18: B	28: A	38: D	48: A	
9: C	19: A	29: E	39: E	49: C	
10: D	20: B	30: A	40: C	50: E	

Fluids

1: C	11: A	21: D	31: D	41: A
2: D	12: E	22: E	32: C	42: C
3: A	13: C	23: D	33: D	43: A
4: A	14: D	24: B	34: D	44: B
5: E	15: C	25: E	35: B	45: E
6: C	16: B	26: D	36: E	46: B
7: E	17: C	27: B	37: A	47: D
8: A	18: D	28: B	38: D	48: C
9: C	19: E	29: A	39: B	
10: A	20: C	30: B	40: E	

Electrostatics

1: C	11: C	21: A
2: C	12: A	22: B
3: D	13: D	23: C
4: B	14: D	24: C
5: E	15: A	25: A
6: C	16: C	26: D
7: E	17: D	27: D
8: A	18: C	
9: B	19: B	
10: E	20: C	

Electric Circuits

1: B	11: A	21: E	31: C	41: C	51: B
2: D	12: E	22: C	32: E	42: E	52: D
3: C	13: D	23: D	33: B	43: A	53: A
4: D	14: B	24: A	34: C	44: B	54: E
5: E	15: C	25: B	35: D	45: C	55: D
6: A	16: A	26: C	36: C	46: E	
7: C	17: B	27: A	37: B	47: B	
8: D	18: D	28: D	38: E	48: D	
9: B	19: C	29: E	39: A	49: A	
10: E	20: C	30: A	40: E	50: C	

Light & Optics

1: A	11: D	21: B	31: C	41: B	51: D
2: A	12: A	22: E	32: B	42: E	52: A
3: B	13: D	23: C	33: B	43: C	53: B
4: D	14: E	24: E	34: A	44: B	54: E
5: E	15: A	25: C	35: E	45: E	55: C
6: B	16: E	26: C	36: B	46: D	
7: C	17: C	27: A	37: C	47: A	
8: D	18: B	28: E	38: A	48: C	
9: A	19: D	29: A	39: E	49: E	
10: D	20: B	30: E	40: B	50: D	

Heat & Thermodynamics

1: B	11: B	21: D	31: B	41: E	51: E
2: C	12: A	22: A	32: D	42: C	52: A
3: D	13: B	23: B	33: E	43: B	53: D
4: A	14: E	24: D	34: B	44: A	54: B
5: C	15: C	25: A	35: D	45: D	55: D
6: E	16: A	26: A	36: E	46: C	
7: D	17: D	27: D	37: C	47: E	
8: A	18: B	28: B	38: A	48: A	
9: C	19: E	29: E	39: B	49: D	
10: E	20: A	30: D	40: B	50: B	

Kinematics and Dynamics – Explanations

1. D is correct.

$$t = (v_f - v_i) / a$$

$$t = (60 \text{ mi/h} - 0 \text{ mi/h}) / (13.1 \text{ mi/h·s})$$

$$t = 4.6 \text{ s}$$

Acceleration is in mi/h·s, so miles and hours cancel and the answer is in units of seconds.

2. B is correct. At the top of the parabolic trajectory, the vertical velocity $v_{yf} = 0$

The initial upward velocity is the vertical component of the initial velocity:

$$v_{yi} = v \sin \theta$$

$$v_{yi} = (20 \text{ m/s}) \sin 30°$$

$$v_{yi} = (20 \text{ m/s}) \cdot (0.5)$$

$$v_{yi} = 10 \text{ m/s}$$

$$t = (v_{yf} - v_{yi}) / a$$

$$t = (0 - 10 \text{ m/s}) / (-10 \text{ m/s}^2)$$

$$t = (-10 \text{ m/s}) / (-10 \text{ m/s}^2)$$

$$t = 1 \text{ s}$$

3. B is correct.

$$\Delta d = 31.5 \text{ km} = 31,500 \text{ m}$$

$$1.25 \text{ hr} \times 60 \text{ min/hr} = 75 \text{ min}$$

$$\Delta t = 75 \text{ min} \times 60 \text{ s/min} = 4,500 \text{ s}$$

$$v_{avg} = \Delta d / \Delta t$$

$$v_{avg} = 31,500 \text{ m} / 4,500 \text{ s}$$

$$v_{avg} = 7 \text{ m/s}$$

4. A is correct. Instantaneous speed is the scalar magnitude of the velocity. It can only be positive or zero (because magnitudes cannot be negative).

5. C is correct.

$$d = (v_f^2 - v_i^2) / 2a$$

$$d = [(21 \text{ m/s})^2 - (5 \text{ m/s})^2] / [2(3 \text{ m/s}^2)]$$

$$d = (441 \text{ m}^2/\text{s}^2 - 25 \text{ m}^2/\text{s}^2) / 6 \text{ m/s}^2$$

$$d = (416 \text{ m}^2/\text{s}^2) / 6 \text{ m/s}^2$$

$$d = 69 \text{ m}$$

6. E is correct.

$$a = (v_f - v_i) / t$$

$$a = [0 - (-30 \text{ m/s})] / 0.15 \text{ s}$$

$$a = (30 \text{ m/s}) / 0.15 \text{ s}$$

$$a = 200 \text{ m/s}^2$$

To represent the acceleration in terms of g, divide a by 9.8 m/s^2:

$$\# \text{ of } g = (200 \text{ m/s}^2) / 9.8 \text{ m/s}^2$$

$$\# \text{ of } g = 20 \, g$$

The initial velocity (v_i) is negative due to the acceleration of the car being a positive value.

Since the car is decelerating, its acceleration is opposite of its initial velocity.

7. D is correct.

When a bullet is fired, it is in projectile motion.

The only force in projectile motion (if air resistance is ignored) is the force of gravity.

8. B is correct.

When a car is slowing down, it is decelerating, which is equivalent to acceleration in the opposite direction.

9. A is correct

Uniform acceleration:

$$a = \text{change in velocity} / \text{change in time}$$

$$a = \Delta v / \Delta t$$

$$\Delta v = a \Delta t$$

$$\Delta v = (20 \text{ m/s}^2) \cdot (1 \text{ s})$$

$$\Delta v = 20 \text{ m/s}$$

10. B is correct.

Uniform acceleration:

$$a = \text{change in velocity} / \text{change in time}$$

$$a = \Delta v / \Delta t$$

$$a = (40 \text{ m/s} - 15 \text{ m/s}) / 10 \text{ s}$$

$$a = (25 \text{ m/s}) / 10 \text{ s}$$

$$a = 2.5 \text{ m/s}^2$$

11. C is correct.

$$t = d / v$$

$$t = (540 \text{ mi}) / (65 \text{ mi/h})$$

$$t = 8.3 \text{ h}$$

The time she can stop is the difference between her total allowed time and the time t that it takes to make the trip:

$$t_{\text{stop}} = 9.8 \text{ h} - 8.3 \text{ h}$$

$$t_{\text{stop}} = 1.5 \text{ h}$$

12. B is correct. Average velocity is the change in position with respect to time:

$$v = \Delta x / \Delta t$$

After one lap, the racecar's final position is the same as its initial position.

Thus, $x = 0$, which implies the average velocity of 0 m/s.

13. A is correct.

$$d = v_i\Delta t + \tfrac{1}{2}a\Delta t^2$$

$$d = (0.2 \text{ m/s})\cdot(5 \text{ s}) + \tfrac{1}{2}(-0.05 \text{ m/s}^2)\cdot(5 \text{ s})^2$$

$$d = 1 \text{ m} + \tfrac{1}{2}(-0.05 \text{ m/s}^2)\cdot(25 \text{ s}^2)$$

$$d = 1 \text{ m} + (-0.625 \text{ m})$$

$$d = 0.375 \text{ m} \approx 0.38 \text{ m}$$

Decelerating is set to negative.

The net displacement is the difference between the final and initial positions after 5 s.

14. C is correct.

$$a = \text{change in velocity} / \text{change in time}$$

$$a = \Delta v / \Delta t$$

15. B is correct. Convert the final speed from km/h to m/s:

$$v_f = (210 \text{ km/h}) \times [(1{,}000 \text{ m}/1 \text{ km})] \times [(1 \text{ h}/3{,}600 \text{ s})]$$

$$v_f = 58.33 \text{ m/s}$$

Calculate the acceleration necessary to reach this speed:

$$a = (v_f^2 - v_i^2) / 2d$$

$$a = [(58.33 \text{ m/s})^2 - (0 \text{ m/s})^2] / 2(1{,}800 \text{ m})$$

$$a = (3{,}402.39 \text{ m}^2/\text{s}^2) / (3{,}600 \text{ m})$$

$$a = 0.95 \text{ m/s}^2$$

16. D is correct.

The distance the rocket travels during its acceleration upward is calculated by:

$d_1 = \frac{1}{2}at^2$

$d_1 = \frac{1}{2}(22 \text{ m/s}^2) \cdot (4 \text{ s})^2$

$d_1 = 176 \text{ m}$

The distance from when the motor shuts off to when the rocket reaches maximum height can be calculated using the conservation of energy:

$mgd_2 = \frac{1}{2}mv^2$, cancel m from both sides of the expression

$gd_2 = \frac{1}{2}v^2$

where $v = at$

$gd_2 = \frac{1}{2}(at)^2$

$d_2 = \frac{1}{2}(at)^2 / g$

$d_2 = \frac{1}{2}[(22 \text{ m/s}^2) \cdot (4 \text{ s})]^2 / (10 \text{ m/s}^2)$

Magnitudes are not vectors but scalars, so no direction is needed

$d_2 = 387 \text{ m}$

For the maximum elevation, add the two distances:

$h = d_1 + d_2$

$h = 176 \text{ m} + 387 \text{ m}$

$h = 563 \text{ m}$

17. E is correct.

Speed is a scalar (i.e., one-dimensional physical property), while velocity is a vector (i.e., has both magnitude and direction).

18. B is correct.

Acceleration due to gravity is constant and independent of mass.

19. D is correct.

As an object falls, its acceleration is constant due to gravity. However, the magnitude of the velocity increases due to the acceleration of gravity and the displacement increases because the object is going further away from its starting point.

20. C is correct.

The man is moving at constant velocity (no acceleration), so it's known immediately that the net force is zero. The only objects interacting with the man directly are Earth and the floor of the elevator. The cable is not touching the man; it pulls the elevator car up and the floor of the elevator is what pushes on the man.

21. E is correct. Horizontal velocity (v_x):

$v_x = d_x / t$

$v_x = (44 \text{ m}) / (2.9 \text{ s})$

$v_x = 15.2 \text{ m/s}$

The x component of a vector is calculated by:

$v_x = v \cos \theta$

Rearrange the equation to determine the initial velocity of the ball:

$v = v_x / \cos \theta$

$v = (15.2 \text{ m/s}) / (\cos 45°)$

$v = (15.2 \text{ m/s}) / 0.7$

$v = 21.4 \text{ m/s}$

22. A is correct. Conservation of energy:

$mgh = \frac{1}{2}mv_f^2$, cancel m from both sides of the expression

$gh = \frac{1}{2}v_f^2$

$(10 \text{ m/s}^2)h = \frac{1}{2}(14 \text{ m/s})^2$

$(10 \text{ m/s}^2)h = \frac{1}{2}(196 \text{ m}^2/\text{s}^2)$

$h = (98 \text{ m}^2/\text{s}^2) / (10 \text{ m/s}^2)$

$h = 9.8 \text{ m} \approx 10 \text{ m}$

23. B is correct.

$d = v_i t + \frac{1}{2}at^2$

$d = (20 \text{ m/s}) \cdot (7 \text{ s}) + \frac{1}{2}(1.4 \text{ m/s}^2) \cdot (7 \text{ s})^2$

$d = (140 \text{ m}) + \frac{1}{2}(1.4 \text{ m/s}^2) \cdot (49 \text{ s}^2)$

$d = 174.3 \text{ m} \approx 174 \text{ m}$

24. D is correct. Force is not a scalar because it has a magnitude and direction.

25. B is correct.

$d = \frac{1}{2}at^2$

$d_A = \frac{1}{2}at^2$

$d_B = \frac{1}{2}a(2t)^2$

$d_B = \frac{1}{2}a(4t^2)$

$d_B = 4 \times \frac{1}{2}at^2$

$d_B = 4d_A$

26. E is correct.

$$d = v_{\text{average}} \times \Delta t$$
$$d = \frac{1}{2}(v_i + v_f)\Delta t$$
$$d = \frac{1}{2}(5 \text{ m/s} + 30 \text{ m/s})\cdot(10 \text{ s})$$
$$d = 175 \text{ m}$$

27. C is correct.

If there is no acceleration, then velocity is constant.

28. D is correct.

The gravitational force between two objects in space, each having masses of m_1 and m_2, is:

$$F_G = Gm_1m_2 / r^2$$

where G is the gravitational constant and r is the distance between the two objects.

Doubling the distance between the two objects:

$$F_{G2} = Gm_1m_2 / (2r)^2$$
$$F_{G2} = Gm_1m_2 / (4r^2)$$
$$F_{G2} = \frac{1}{4}Gm_1m_2 / r^2$$
$$F_{G2} = \frac{1}{4}Gm_1m_2 / r^2$$
$$F_{G2} = \frac{1}{4}F_G$$

Therefore, when distance between objects is doubled, the force (F_G) is one fourth as much.

29. D is correct.

I: If the velocity is constant, the instantaneous velocity is always equal to the average velocity.

II and III: If the velocity is increasing, the average value of velocity over an interval must lie between the initial velocity and the final velocity. In going from its initial value to its final value, the instantaneous velocity must cross the average value at one point, regardless of whether or not the velocity is changing at a constant rate, or changing irregularly.

30. E is correct.

$$\text{velocity} = \text{acceleration} \times \text{time}$$
$$v = at$$
$$v = (10 \text{ m/s}^2)\cdot(10 \text{ s})$$
$$v = 100 \text{ m/s}$$

31. B is correct.

velocity = distance / time

$v = d / t$

d is constant, while t decreases by a factor of 3

32. C is correct. The equation for distance, given a constant acceleration and both the initial and final velocity, is:

$d = (v_i^2 + v_f^2) / 2a$

Since the car is coming to rest, $v_f = 0$

$d = v_i^2 / 2a$

If the initial velocity is doubled while acceleration and final velocity remain unchanged, the new distance traveled is:

$d_2 = (2v_i)^2 / 2a$

$d_2 = 4(v_i^2 / 2a)$

$d_2 = 4d_1$

Another method to solve this problem:

$d_1 = (29 \text{ mi/h})^2 / 2a$

$d_2 = (59 \text{ mi/h})^2 / 2a$

$d_2 / d_1 = [(59 \text{ mi/h})^2 / 2a] / [(29 \text{ mi/h})^2 / 2a]$

$d_2 / d_1 = (59 \text{ mi/h})^2 / (29 \text{ mi/h})^2$

$d_2 / d_1 = (3{,}481 \text{ mi/h}) / (841 \text{ mi/h})$

$d_2 / d_1 = 4$

33. D is correct.

speed$_{average}$ = total distance / time

speed = (400 m) / (20 s) = 20 m/s

If this were velocity, it would be 0.

34. E is correct.

$\Delta v = a\Delta t$

$(v_f - v_i) = a\Delta t$, where $v_f = 0$ m/s (when the car stops)

$a = -0.1$ m/s^2 (negative because deceleration), $\Delta t = 5$ s

$v_i = v_f - a\Delta t$

$v_i = [(0 \text{ m/s}) - (-0.1 \text{ m/s}^2)] \cdot (5 \text{ s})$

$v_i = (0.1 \text{ m/s}^2) \cdot (5 \text{ s}) = 0.5$ m/s

35. C is correct.

If acceleration is constant, then the velocity vs. time graph is linear, and the average velocity is the average of the final and initial velocity.

$$v_{average} = v_f - v_i \,/\, \Delta t$$

If acceleration is not constant, then the velocity vs. time graph is nonlinear.

$$v_{average} \neq v_f - v_i \,/\, \Delta t$$

36. E is correct.

Find velocity of thrown rock:

$$v_{f1}^2 - v_i^2 = 2ad$$

$$v_{f1}^2 = v_i^2 + 2ad$$

$$v_{f1}^2 = (10 \text{ m/s})^2 + [2(9.8 \text{ m/s}^2)\cdot(300 \text{ m})]$$

$$v_{f1}^2 = 100 \text{ m}^2/\text{s}^2 + 5{,}880 \text{ m}^2/\text{s}^2$$

$$v_{f1}^2 = 5{,}980 \text{ m}^2/\text{s}^2$$

$$v_{f1} = 77.33 \text{ m/s}$$

$$t_1 = (v_f - v_i) \,/\, a$$

$$t_1 = (77.33 \text{ m/s} - 10 \text{ m/s}) \,/\, 9.8 \text{ m/s}^2$$

$$t_1 = (67.33 \text{ m/s}) \,/\, (9.8 \text{ m/s}^2)$$

$$t_1 = 6.87 \text{ s}$$

Find velocity of dropped rock:

$$v_{f2} = \sqrt{2ad}$$

$$v_{f2} = \sqrt{[(2)\cdot(9.8 \text{ m/s}^2)\cdot(300 \text{ m})]}$$

$$v_{f2} = 76.7 \text{ m/s}$$

$$t_2 = (76.7 \text{ m/s}) \,/\, (9.8 \text{ m/s}^2)$$

$$t_2 = 7.82 \text{ s}$$

$$\Delta t = (7.82 \text{ s} - 6.87 \text{ s})$$

$$\Delta t = 0.95 \text{ s}$$

37. D is correct.

$$F = ma$$

Force and acceleration are directly proportional so doubling force doubles acceleration.

38. B is correct.

Velocity is defined as having speed and direction.

If either, or both, of these change then the object is experiencing acceleration.

39. E is correct.

The acceleration is negative because it acts to slow the car down against the $+y$ direction.

It is unclear if the acceleration decreases in magnitude from the data provided.

40. E is correct.

Total distance is represented by area under the velocity-time curve.

This graph can be broken up into sections; calculate the area under the curve.

$$d_{total} = d_A + d_B + d_C + d_D$$

$$d_A = \tfrac{1}{2}(4 \text{ m/s}){\cdot}(2 \text{ s}) = 4 \text{ m}$$

$$d_B = \tfrac{1}{2}(4 \text{ m/s} + 2 \text{ m/s}){\cdot}(2 \text{ s}) = 6 \text{ m}$$

$$d_C = (2 \text{ m/s}){\cdot}(4 \text{ s}) = 8 \text{ m}$$

Since the total distance traveled needs to be calculated, the area under the curve when the velocity is negative is calculated as a positive value.

Distance is a scalar quantity and therefore has no direction.

$$d_D = \tfrac{1}{2}(2 \text{ m/s}){\cdot}(1 \text{ s}) + \tfrac{1}{2}(2 \text{ m/s}){\cdot}(1 \text{ s}) = 2 \text{ m}$$

$$d_{total} = 4 \text{ m} + 6 \text{ m} + 8 \text{ m} + 2 \text{ m}$$

$$d_{total} = 20 \text{ m}$$

If the question was asking to find the displacement, the area under the curve would be calculated as negative and the answer would be 18 m.

41. C is correct.

The two bullets have different velocities when hitting the water, but they both only experience the force due to gravity.

Thus, the acceleration due to gravity is the same for each bullet.

42. A is correct.

$$v_f = v_i + at$$

$$v_f = 0 + (2.5 \text{ m/s}^2){\cdot}(9 \text{ s})$$

$$v_f = 22.5 \text{ m/s}$$

43. E is correct.

The equation for impulse is used for contact between two objects over a specified time period:

$$F\Delta t = m\Delta v$$

$$ma\Delta t = m(v_f - v_i), \text{ cancel } m \text{ from both sides of the expression}$$

$a\Delta t = (v_f - v_i)$

$a = (v_f - v_i) / \Delta t$

$a = (-2v - v) / (0.45 \text{ s})$

$a = (-3v) / (0.45 \text{ s})$

$a = (-6.7 \text{ s}^{-1})v$

Ratio $a : v = -6.7 \text{ s}^{-1} : 1$

44. B is correct.

The time for the round trip is 4 s.

The weight reaches the top of its path in ½ time:

$\frac{1}{2}(4 \text{ s}) = 2 \text{ s}$, where $v = 0$

$a = \Delta v / t$ for the first half of the trip

$a = (v_f - v_i) / t$

$a = (0 - 3.2 \text{ m/s}) / 2 \text{ s}$

$a = -1.6 \text{ m/s}^2$

$|a| = 1.6 \text{ m/s}^2$

Acceleration is a vector and the negative direction only indicates direction.

45. A is correct.

$\Delta v = a\Delta t$

$\Delta v = (0.3 \text{ m/s}^2) \cdot (3 \text{ s})$

$\Delta v = 0.9 \text{ m/s}$

46. D is correct.

Velocity, displacement, acceleration and force are all vectors. Mass is not a vector quantity.

47. E is correct.

$d = d_0 + (v_i^2 + v_f^2) / 2a$

$d = 64 \text{ m} + (0 \text{ m/s} + 60 \text{ m/s})^2 / 2(9.8 \text{ m/s}^2)$

$d = 64 \text{ m} + (3{,}600 \text{ m}^2/\text{s}^2) / (19.6 \text{ m/s}^2)$

$d = 64 \text{ m} + 184 \text{ m}$

$d = 248 \text{ m}$

48. C is correct.

$$a = (v_f^2 + v_i^2) / 2d$$
$$a = [(60 \text{ m/s})^2 + (0 \text{ m/s})^2] / [2(64 \text{ m})]$$
$$a = (3,600 \text{ m}^2/\text{s}^2) / 128 \text{ m}$$
$$a = 28 \text{ m/s}^2$$

49. D is correct.

Expression for the time interval during constant acceleration upward:

$$d = \tfrac{1}{2}at^2$$

Solving for acceleration:

$$a = (v_f^2 + v_i^2) / 2d$$
$$a = [(60 \text{ m/s})^2 + (0 \text{ m/s})^2] / [2(64 \text{ m})]$$
$$a = (3,600 \text{ m}^2/\text{s}^2) / (128 \text{ m})$$
$$a = 28.1 \text{ m/s}^2$$

Solving for time:

$$t^2 = 2d / a$$
$$t^2 = 2(64 \text{ m}) / 28.1 \text{ m/s}^2$$
$$t^2 = 4.5 \text{ s}^2$$
$$t = 2.1 \text{ s}$$

50. E is correct.

$$d = (v_i^2 + v_f^2) / 2a, \text{ where } v_i = 0$$
$$d = v_f^2 / 2a$$

For half the final velocity:

$$d_2 = (v_f / 2)^2 / 2a$$
$$d_2 = \tfrac{1}{4}v_f^2 / 2a$$
$$d_2 = \tfrac{1}{4}d$$

51. A is correct. $v_{\text{average}} = \Delta d / \Delta t$

52. A is correct. Use an equation that relates v, d and t:

$$d = vt$$
$$v = d / t$$

If v increases by a factor of 3, then t decreases by a factor of 3.

Another method to solve this problem:

$d = vt$, t = original time and t_N = new time

$d = 3vt_N$

$vt = d = 3vt_N$

$vt = 3vt_N$

$t = 3t_N$

$t / 3 = t_N$

Thus, if v increases by a factor of 3, then the original time decreases by a factor of 3.

53. E is correct.

$v_f = v_i + at$

$t = (v_f - v_i) / a$

Since the ball is thrown straight up, its initial speed upward equals its final speed downward (just before hitting the ground): $v_f = -v_i$

$t = [39 \text{ m/s} - (-39 \text{ m/s})] / 9.8 \text{ m/s}^2$

$t = (78 \text{ m/s}) / 9.8 \text{ m/s}^2$

$t = 8 \text{ s}$

54. D is correct. Since the speed is changing, the velocity is changing, and therefore there *is* an acceleration.

Since the speed is *decreasing*, the acceleration must be *in the reverse direction* (i.e., opposite to the direction of travel).

Since the particle is moving to the right, the acceleration vector points to the left.

If the speed were increasing, the acceleration is in the *same* direction as the direction of travel, and the acceleration vector points to the right.

55. A is correct. The only force that Larry applies to the package is the normal force due to his hand (there is no horizontal force as the package moves with constant velocity.) The normal force due to his hand points upward.

The displacement of the package is horizontal:

$W = Fd \cos \theta$

where θ is the angle between the force and the displacement.

$\theta = 90°$

Since $\cos 90° = 0$

$W = 0 \text{ J}$

Force, Motion, Gravitation – Explanations

1. B is correct. The tension of the string keeps the weight traveling in a circular path; otherwise it would move linearly on a tangent path to the circle. Without the string, there are no horizontal forces on the weight and no horizontal acceleration. The horizontal motion of the weight is in a straight line at constant speed.

2. E is correct. The vertical force on the garment bag from the left side of the clothesline is:

$$T_{y,\text{left}} = T \cos \theta$$

Similarly, for the right side:

$$T_{y,\text{right}} = T \cos \theta$$

where $T = 10$ N (tension) and $\theta = 60°$

Since the garment bag is at rest, its acceleration is zero. Therefore, according to Newton's second law:

$$T_{y,\text{left}} + T_{y,\text{right}} - mg = 0 = 2T (\cos \theta) - mg$$

Or: $2T (\cos \theta) = mg$

$m = 2T (\cos \theta) / g$

$m = 2(10 \text{ N}) \cdot (\cos 60°) / (10.0 \text{ m/s}^2)$

$m = 2(10 \text{ N}) \cdot (0.5) / (10.0 \text{ m/s}^2)$

$m = 1$ kg

3. A is correct. An object's inertia is its resistance to change in motion. The milk carton has enough inertia to overcome the force of static friction.

4. C is correct.

$$(F_{\text{net}})_y = (F_N)_y - (F_g)_y$$

The car is not moving up or down, so $a_y = 0$:

$(F_{\text{net}})_y = 0$

$0 = (F_N)_y - (F_g)_y$

$F_N = (F_g)_y$

$F_N = F_g \cos \theta$

$F_N = mg \cos \theta$

The normal force is a force that is perpendicular to the plane of contact (the slope).

5. E is correct.

$F = ma$

$F = (27 \text{ kg}) \cdot (1.7 \text{ m/s}^2)$

$F = 46 \text{ N}$

6. D is correct. The mass on the table causes a tension force in the string that acts against the force of gravity.

7. A is correct. Although the net force acting on the object is decreasing with time and the magnitude of the object's acceleration is decreasing there exists a positive acceleration. Therefore, the object's speed continues to increase.

8. E is correct. An object moving at constant velocity experiences zero net force.

9. A is correct. The sine of an angle is equal to the opposite side over the hypotenuse:

$\sin \theta = \text{opposite} / \text{hypotenuse}$

$\sin \theta = h / L$

$h = L \sin \theta$

10. C is correct. A car accelerating horizontally does not rely on the force of gravity to move it. Since mass does not depend on gravity, a car on Earth and a car on the Moon that experience the same horizontal acceleration also experience the same force.

11. A is correct.

$a = (v_f - v_i) / t$

$a = (3.5 \text{ m/s} - 1.5 \text{ m/s}) / (3 \text{ s})$

$a = (2 \text{ m/s}) / (3 \text{ s})$

$a = 0.67 \text{ m/s}^2$

12. E is correct. An object with a uniform circular motion (i.e., constant angular velocity) only experiences centripetal acceleration directed toward the center of the circle.

13. B is correct. $F = ma$, so zero force means zero acceleration in any direction.

14. C is correct.

$F = ma$

$a = F / m$

$a = 9 \text{ N} / 9 \text{ kg}$

$a = 1 \text{ m/s}^2$

15. E is correct. The only force acting on a projectile in motion is the force due to gravity. Since that force always acts downward, there is always only a downward acceleration.

16. A is correct.

$F_{net} = ma$

If an object moves with constant v, its $a = 0$, so:

$F_{net} = 0$

Since gravity pulls down on the can with a force of mg:

$F_g = mg$

$F_g = (10 \text{ kg}) \cdot (10 \text{ m/s}^2)$

$F_g = 100 \text{ N}$

The rope pulls *up* on the can with the same magnitude of force, so the tension is 100 N, for a net force = 0.

17. D is correct.

$F = ma$

$F = (1,000 \text{ kg}) \cdot (2 \text{ m/s}^2)$

$F = 2,000 \text{ N}$

18. C is correct.

$a_{cent} = v^2 / r$

$a_{cent} = (4 \text{ m/s})^2 / (4 \text{ m})$

$a_{cent} = (16 \text{ m}^2/\text{s}^2) / (4 \text{ m})$

$a_{cent} = 4 \text{ m/s}^2$

19. E is correct.

Solve for m_1:

$F_{net} = 0$

$m_2 g = F_T$

$m_1 g \sin \theta + F_f = F_T$

$m_1 g \sin \theta + \mu_s m_1 g \cos \theta = m_2 g$

cancel g from both sides

$m_1 (\sin \theta + \mu_s \cos \theta) = m_2$

$m_1 = m_2 / (\sin \theta + \mu_s \cos \theta)$

$m_1 = 2 \text{ kg} / [\sin 20° + (0.55) \cos 20°]$

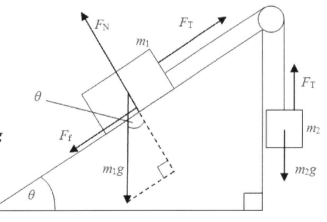

$$m_1 = 2 \text{ kg} / 0.86$$

$$m_1 = 2.3 \text{ kg}$$

Kinetic friction is only used when the mass is in motion.

20. B is correct. Since the masses are identical, the force of gravity on each is the same.

The force of gravity on one of the masses produces the tension force in the string, which in turn pulls on the other mass.

Since this tension force is equal to the force of gravity, there is no net force, and the objects remain at rest.

21. B is correct.

Newton's Third Law states that for every action there is an equal and opposite reaction.

22. A is correct.

Newton's Third Law states that for every action there is an equal and opposite reaction.

23. C is correct. If w denotes the magnitude of the box's weight, then the component of this force that is parallel to the inclined plane is $w \sin \theta$, where θ is the incline angle.

If θ is less than $90°$, then $\sin \theta$ is less than 1.

The component of w parallel to the inclined plane is less than w.

24. E is correct.

The package experiences projectile motion upon leaving the truck, so it experiences no horizontal forces, and its initial velocity of 30 m/s remains unchanged.

25. D is correct.

$$f = \text{revolutions} / \text{unit of time}$$

The time (period) for one complete revolution is:

$$T = 1 / f$$

Each revolution represents a length of $2\pi r$.

Velocity is the distance traveled in one revolution over duration of one revolution (circumference over period):

$$v = 2\pi r / t$$

$$v = 2\pi r f$$

If f doubles, then v doubles.

26. A is correct.

$$F = ma$$
$$m = F / a$$
$$m = 4{,}500 \text{ N} / 5 \text{ m/s}^2$$
$$m = 900 \text{ kg}$$

27. E is correct.

Newton's First Law states that every object will remain at rest or in uniform motion unless acted upon by an outside force.

In this case, Steve and the bus are in uniform constant motion until the bus stops due to sudden deceleration (the ground exerts no frictional force on Steve). There is no force acting upon Steve.

However, his inertia carries him forward because he is still in uniform motion while the bus comes to a stop.

28. D is correct.

The ball is in a state of rest, so $F_{net} = 0$

$$F_{down} = F_{up}$$
$$F_{external} + F_w = F_{buoyant}$$
$$F_{external} = F_{buoyant} - F_w$$
$$F_{external} = 8.4 \text{ N} - 4.4 \text{ N}$$
$$F_{external} = 4 \text{ N, in the same direction as the weight}$$

29. A is correct.

The luggage and the train move at the same speed, so when the luggage moves forward with respect to the train, it means the train has slowed down while the luggage is continuing to move at the train's original speed.

30. D is correct. The mass does not change by changing the object's location.

Since the object is outside of Earth's atmosphere, the object's weight is represented by the equation:

$$F_g = GmM_{Earth} / R^2$$

If the altitude is $2R_{Earth}$, then the distance from the center of the Earth is $3R_{Earth}$.

The gravitational acceleration decreases by a factor of $3^2 = 9$ ($g = GmM / R^2$).

Weight decreases by a factor of 9.

$$\text{New weight} = 360 \text{ N} / 9 = 40 \text{ N}$$

31. C is correct.

The velocity of the rock just after its release is the same as the truck's.

Once in free fall, there are no horizontal forces on the rock.

The rock's velocity remains unchanged and is equal to that of the truck.

32. E is correct.

The acceleration of Jason due to thrust is:

$F_{net} = ma_1$

$ma_1 = F_{ski} - \mu_k mg$

$a_1 = (F_{ski} - \mu_k mg) \, / \, m$

$a_1 = [200 \text{ N} - (0.1) \cdot (75 \text{ kg}) \cdot (9.8 \text{ m/s}^2)] \, / \, 75 \text{ kg}$

$a_1 = (126.5 \text{ N}) \, / \, 75 \text{ kg}$

$a_1 = 1.69 \text{ m/s}^2$

The distance traveled during the acceleration stage is:

$d_1 = \frac{1}{2} a_1 t^2$

$d_1 = \frac{1}{2} (1.69 \text{ m/s}^2) \cdot (67 \text{ s})^2$

$d_1 = 3{,}793 \text{ m}$

The distance traveled after the skis run out of fuel is:

$d_2 = (v_f^2 - v_i^2) \, / \, 2a_2$

a_2 is Jason's acceleration after the fuel runs out:

$F_{net} = ma_2$

$ma_2 = -\mu_k mg$, cancel m from both sides of the expression

$a_2 = -\mu_k g$

$a_2 = -(0.1) \cdot (9.8 \text{ m/s}^2)$

$a_2 = -0.98 \text{ m/s}^2$

The acceleration is negative since the frictional force opposes the direction of motion.

v_i is the velocity at the moment when the fuel runs out:

$v_i = a_1 t$

$v_i = (1.69 \text{ m/s}^2) \cdot (67 \text{ s})$

$v_i = 113.2 \text{ m/s}$

Substitute a_2 and v_i into the equation for d_2:

$d_2 = [(0 \text{ m/s})^2 - (113.2 \text{ m/s})^2] \, / \, 2(-0.98 \text{ m/s}^2)$

$d_2 = (-12{,}814.2 \text{ m}^2/\text{s}^2) \, / -1.96 \text{ m/s}^2$

$d_2 = 6{,}538 \text{ m}$

The total distance Jason traveled is:

$$d_{total} = d_1 + d_2$$

$$d_{total} = 3{,}793 \text{ m} + 6{,}538 \text{ m}$$

$$d_{total} = 10{,}331 \text{ m}$$

33. D is correct.

Using the force analysis:

$$F_{net} = F_g + F_{fk}$$

$$F_g = mg \sin \theta$$

$$F_g = (0.2 \text{ kg}) \cdot (-9.8 \text{ m/s}^2) \sin 30°$$

$$F_g = (0.2 \text{ kg}) \cdot (-9.8 \text{ m/s}^2) \cdot (1/2)$$

$$F_g = -1 \text{ N}$$

$$F_{fk} = \mu_k F_N$$

$$F_{fk} = \mu_k mg \cos \theta$$

$$F_{fk} = (0.3) \cdot (0.2 \text{ kg}) \cdot (-9.8 \text{ m/s}^2) \cos 30°$$

$$F_{fk} = (0.3) \cdot (0.2 \text{ kg}) \cdot (-9.8 \text{ m/s}^2) \cdot (0.866)$$

$$F_{fk} = -0.5 \text{ N}$$

$$F_{net} = -1 \text{ N} + (-0.5 \text{ N})$$

$$F_{net} = -1.5 \text{ N}$$

$$a = F_{net} / m$$

$$a = -1.5 \text{ N} / 0.2 \text{ kg}$$

$$a = -7.5 \text{ m/s}^2$$

The distance it travels until it reaches a velocity of 0 at its maximum height:

$$d = (v_f^2 - v_i^2) / 2a$$

$$d = [(0 \text{ m/s})^2 - (63 \text{ m/s})^2] / 2(-7.5 \text{ m/s}^2)$$

$$d = (-4{,}000 \text{ m}^2/\text{s}^2) / (-15 \text{ m/s}^2)$$

$$d = 267 \text{ m}$$

The vertical height is:

$$h = d \sin \theta$$

$$h = (267 \text{ m}) \sin 30°$$

$$h = (267 \text{ m}) \cdot (0.5)$$

$$h = 130 \text{ m}$$

Using energy to solve the problem:

$$KE = PE + W_f$$

$$\tfrac{1}{2}mv^2 = mgd \sin \theta + \mu_k mgd \cos \theta, \text{ cancel } m \text{ from the expression}$$

$$\tfrac{1}{2}v^2 = gd \sin \theta + \mu_k gd \cos \theta$$

$$\tfrac{1}{2}v^2 = d(g \sin \theta + \mu_k g \cos \theta)$$

$$d = v^2 / [2g(\sin \theta + \mu_k \cos \theta)]$$

$$d = (63 \text{ m/s})^2 / [(2) \cdot (9.8 \text{ m/s}^2) \cdot (\sin 30° + 0.3 \times \cos 30°)]$$

$$d = 267 \text{ m}$$

$$h = d \sin \theta$$

$$h = (267 \text{ m}) \sin 30°$$

$$h = 130 \text{ m}$$

34. A is correct.

$$F = ma$$

$$a = F / m$$

$$a_1 = F / 4 \text{ kg}$$

$$a_2 = F / 10 \text{ kg}$$

$$4a_1 = 10a_2$$

$$a_1 = 2.5a_2$$

35. D is correct.

Mass is independent of gravity. However weight is not; as a person moves farther away from any stars or planets, the gravitational pull decreases and, therefore, her weight decreases.

36. A is correct.

Newton's Third Law describes that any time one object pushes on another, the second object pushes right back with the same force. Mathematically, it can be expressed as:

$$F_{\text{AonB}} = -F_{\text{BonA}}$$

In the described scenario, the force that the truck exerts on the car is in the opposite direction to the force that the car exerts on the truck (since they push on each other) and, crucially, the *magnitudes* of the two forces are the same.

This may seem counterintuitive since it is known that the car will get far more damaged than the truck. To understand this apparent contradiction, remember Newton's Second Law which states that the car will *accelerate* at a much higher rate (since it is less massive than the truck). It is this extreme acceleration that causes the car to be completely destroyed.

Therefore, to understand this situation fully, two Newton's laws must be applied:

The Third Law, which states that each vehicle experiences a force of the same magnitude

The Second Law, which describes why the car *responds* to that force more violently due to its smaller mass.

37. D is correct.

$$m = F / a_{Earth}$$

$$m = 20 \text{ N} / 3 \text{ m/s}^2$$

$$m = 6.67 \text{ kg}$$

$$F_{Moon} = mg_{Moon}$$

$$F_{Moon} = (6.67 \text{ kg}) \cdot (1.62 \text{ m/s}^2)$$

$$F_{Moon} = 11 \text{ N} \backslash$$

38. B is correct.

weight = mass × gravity

$$w = (0.4 \text{ kg}) \cdot (9.8 \text{ m/s}^2)$$

$$w \approx 4 \text{ N}$$

39. B is correct. Need an expression which connects time and mass.

Given information for F, v_1, and d:

$$a = F / m$$

$$d = v_1 t + \tfrac{1}{2} a t^2$$

Combine the expressions and set $v_i = 0$ m/s because initial velocity is zero:

$$d = \tfrac{1}{2} a t^2$$

$$a = F / m$$

$$d = \tfrac{1}{2}(F / m) t^2$$

$$t^2 = 2dm / F$$

$$t = \sqrt{(2dm / F)}$$

If m increases by a factor of 4, t increases by a factor of $\sqrt{4} = 2$

40. C is correct.

$$a = (v_f^2 - v_i^2) / 2d$$

$$a = [(0 \text{ m/s})^2 - (27 \text{ m/s})^2] / 2(578 \text{ m})$$

$$a = (-729 \text{ m}^2/\text{s}^2) / 1{,}056 \text{ m}$$

$$a = -0.63 \text{ m/s}^2$$

$$F = ma$$

$$F = (1{,}100 \text{ kg}) \cdot (-0.63 \text{ m/s}^2)$$

$$F = -690 \text{ N}$$

The car is decelerating, so the acceleration (and therefore the force) is negative.

41. A is correct.

Constant speed upward means no net force.

Tension = weight (equals Mg)

42. C is correct.

$$\text{Weight} = mg$$
$$75 \text{ N} = mg$$
$$m = 75 \text{ N} / 9.8 \text{ m/s}^2$$
$$m = 7.65 \text{ kg}$$
$$F_{net} = F_{right} - F_{left}$$
$$F_{net} = 50 \text{ N} - 30 \text{ N}$$
$$F_{net} = 20 \text{ N}$$
$$F_{net} = ma$$
$$a = F_{net} / m$$
$$a = 20 \text{ N} / 7.65 \text{ kg}$$
$$a = 2.6 \text{ m/s}^2$$

43. B is correct.

The string was traveling at the same velocity as the plane with respect to the ground outside.

When the plane began accelerating backward (decelerating), the string continued to move forward at its original velocity and appeared to go towards the front of the plane.

Since the string is attached to the ceiling at one end, only the bottom of the string moved.

44. C is correct.

If the object slides down the ramp with a constant speed, velocity is constant.

Acceleration and the net force = 0

$$F_{net} = F_{grav \; down \; ramp} - F_{friction}$$
$$F_{net} = mg \sin \theta - \mu_k mg \cos \theta$$
$$F_{net} = 0$$
$$mg \sin \theta - \mu_k mg \cos \theta = 0$$
$$mg \sin \theta = \mu_k mg \cos \theta$$
$$\mu_k = \sin \theta / \cos \theta$$

45. A is correct.

The net force on an object in free fall is equal to its weight.

46. C is correct.

$$a = \Delta v / \Delta t$$

$$a = (v_f - v_i) / t$$

$$a = (20 \text{ m/s} - 0 \text{ m/s}) / (10 \text{ s})$$

$$a = (20 \text{ m/s}) / (10 \text{ s})$$

$$a = 2 \text{ m/s}^2$$

47. E is correct.

Since the object does not move, it is in a state of equilibrium, so forces are acting on it that equal and oppose the force *F* that Yana applies to the object.

48. E is correct.

Newton's Third Law describes that any time one object pushes on another, the second object pushes back with the same force. Mathematically, it can be expressed as:

$$F_{AonB} = -F_{BonA}$$

In this situation, this means if one pushes on an object with force *F*, the object must push back on them equally strongly (magnitude is *F*) and in the opposite direction (hence the negative sign); therefore, the force vector of the object is just –*F*.

49. C is correct. $F = mg$

$$m = F / g$$

$$m = 685 \text{ N} / 9.8 \text{ m/s}^2$$

$$m = 69.9 \text{ kg} \approx 70 \text{ kg}$$

50. A is correct. $m_{Bob} = 4m_{Sarah}$

Conservation of momentum, since the system (Bob and Sarah combined) initially, had a total momentum of 0, in the final state Sarah's momentum and Bob's momentum must add to 0 (i.e., they will be the same magnitude, but opposite directions):

$$m_{Bob}v_{Bob} = m_{Sarah}v_{Sarah}$$

$$4m_{Sarah}\, v_{Bob} = m_{Sarah}v_{Sarah}$$

$$4v_{Bob} = v_{Sarah}$$

51. C is correct. For most surfaces, the coefficient of static friction is greater than the coefficient of kinetic friction.

Thus, the force needed to overcome static friction and start the object's motion is greater than the amount of force needed to overcome kinetic friction and keep the object moving at a constant velocity.

52. B is correct.

Weight on Jupiter:

$$W = mg$$
$$W = m(3g)$$
$$W = (100 \text{ kg}) \cdot (3 \times 10 \text{ m/s}^2)$$
$$W = 3{,}000 \text{ N}$$

53. D is correct.

Neither Joe nor Bill is moving, so the net force is zero:

$$F_{net} = F_{Joe} - F_{T}$$
$$0 = F_{Joe} - F_{T}$$
$$F_{Joe} = F_{T}$$
$$F_{T} = 200 \text{ N}$$

54. E is correct.

Tension in the rope is always equal to F_T.

The net force on block A to the right is:

$$F_{right} = m_A a_A = 2F_T$$

The net force of block B downward is:

$$F_{down} = m_B a_B = m_B g - F_T$$

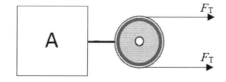

Since block A is connected to both the pulley at the end of the table and the wall, it uses twice the amount of rope length to travel the same distance as block B.

Therefore, the distance block A moves is half that of block B, the velocity of block A is half the velocity of block B, and the acceleration of block A is half the acceleration of block B:

$$a_A = a_B / 2$$
$$F_{right} = m_A (a_B / 2)$$
$$m_A (a_B / 2) = 2F_T$$
$$m_A a_B = 4F_T$$
$$F_T = \tfrac{1}{4} m_A a_B$$
$$m_B a_B = m_B g - \tfrac{1}{4} m_A a_B$$
$$m_B a_B + \tfrac{1}{4} m_A a_B = m_B g$$
$$a_B [m_B + \tfrac{1}{4} m_A] = m_B g$$
$$a_B = m_B g / [m_B + \tfrac{1}{4} m_A]$$

$a_B = (5 \text{ kg}) \cdot (9.8 \text{ m/s}^2) / [5 \text{ kg} + \frac{1}{4}(4 \text{ kg})]$

$a_B = 49 \text{ N} / 6 \text{ kg}$

$a_B = 8.2 \text{ m/s}^2$

$a_A = a_B / 2$

$a_A = (8.2 \text{ m/s}^2) / 2$

$a_A = 4.1 \text{ m/s}^2$

55. B is correct.

The force exerted by one surface on another has a perpendicular component (i.e., normal force) and a parallel component (i.e., friction force).

The force of kinetic friction on an object acts opposite to the direction of its velocity relative to the surface.

Equilibrium and Momentum – Explanations

1. A is correct.

The rate of change of angular momentum of a system is equal to the net external torque:

$$\tau_{net} = \Delta L / \Delta t$$

If the angular momentum is constant, then the net external torque must be zero.

2. D is correct.

If the velocity is 7 m/s down the mountain, the horizontal component v_x is:

$$v_x = v \cos \theta$$
$$1.8 \text{ m/s} = (7 \text{ m/s}) \cos \theta$$
$$\cos \theta = 0.26$$
$$\theta \approx 75°$$

3. E is correct.

The hill exerts a normal force on the sled. However, this force is *perpendicular* to the surface of the hill.

There is no parallel force that the hill exerts because it is frictionless.

4. C is correct.

Assuming that the water flow is tangent to the wheel, it is perpendicular to the radius vector at the point of contact.

The torque around the center of the wheel is:

$$\tau = rF$$
$$\tau = (10 \text{ m}) \cdot (300 \text{ N})$$
$$\tau = 3,000 \text{ N·m}$$

5. E is correct.

$$1 \text{ revolution} = 360°, \ 1 \text{ min} = 60 \text{ s}$$
$$33 \text{ rpm} = 33 \text{ revs/min}$$
$$(33 \text{ revs/min}) \cdot (360°/\text{rev}) = 11,880°/\text{min}$$
$$(11,880°/\text{min}) \cdot (1 \text{ min}/60 \text{ s}) = 198°/\text{s}$$

Degrees per second is a *rate*:

$$\text{rate} \times \text{time} = \text{total degrees}$$
$$(198°/\text{s}) \cdot (0.32 \text{ s}) \approx 63°$$

6. B is correct.

momentum = mass × velocity

$p = mv$

Since momentum is directly proportional to mass, doubling the mass doubles the momentum.

7. D is correct.

The total momentum before the collision is:

$p_{total} = m_Iv_I + m_{II}v_{II} + m_{III}v_{III}$

$p_{before} = (1 \text{ kg}) \cdot (0.5 \text{ m/s}) + (1.5 \text{ kg}) \cdot (-0.3 \text{ m/s}) + (3.5 \text{ kg}) \cdot (-0.5 \text{ m/s})$

$p_{before} = (0.5 \text{ kg·m/s}) + (-0.45 \text{ kg·m/s}) + (-1.75 \text{ kg·m/s})$

$p_{before} = -1.7 \text{ kg·m/s}$

8. A is correct.

The collision of I and II does not affect the momentum of the system:

$p_{before} = p_{after}$

$p_{I \& II} = (1 \text{ kg}) \cdot (0.5 \text{ m/s}) + (1.5 \text{ kg}) \cdot (-0.3 \text{ m/s})$

$p_{I \& II} = (0.5 \text{ kg·m/s}) - (0.45 \text{ kg·m/s})$

$p_{I \& II} = 0.05 \text{ kg·m/s}$

$p_{III} = (3.5 \text{ kg}) \cdot (-0.5 \text{ m/s})$

$p_{III} = -1.75 \text{ kg·m/s}$

$p_{net} = p_{I \text{ and } II} + p_{III}$

$p_{net} = (0.05 \text{ kg·m/s}) + (-1.75 \text{ kg·m/s})$

$p_{net} = -1.7 \text{ kg·m/s}$

Momentum is conserved at all times.

9. B is correct.

Set the initial momentum equal to the final momentum after all the collisions have occurred.

$p_{before} = p_{after}$

$p_{before} = (m_I + m_{II} + m_{III})v_f$

$-1.7 \text{ kg·m/s} = (1 \text{ kg} + 1.5 \text{ kg} + 3.5 \text{ kg})v_f$

$v_f = (-1.7 \text{ kg·m/s}) / (6 \text{ kg})$

$v_f = -0.28 \text{ m/s}$

10. C is correct.

Momentum is conserved in this system. The momentum of each car is given by mv, and the sum of the momenta before the collision must equal the sum of the momenta after the collision:

$$p_{before} = p_{after}$$

Solve for the velocity of the first car after the collision. Each car is traveling in the same direction before and after the collision, so each velocity value has the same sign.

$$m_1 v_{i1} + m_2 v_{i2} = m_1 v_{f1} + m_2 v_{f2}$$

$$(480 \text{ kg}){\cdot}(14.4 \text{ m/s}) + (570 \text{ kg}){\cdot}(13.3 \text{ m/s}) = (480 \text{ kg}){\cdot}(v_{f2}) + (570 \text{ kg}){\cdot}(17.9 \text{ m/s})$$

$$(480 \text{ kg}){\cdot}(v_{f2}) = (480 \text{ kg}){\cdot}(14.4 \text{ m/s}) + (570 \text{ kg}){\cdot}(13.3 \text{ m/s}) - (570 \text{ kg}){\cdot}(17.9 \text{ m/s})$$

$$v_{f2} = [(480 \text{ kg}){\cdot}(14.4 \text{ m/s}) + (570 \text{ kg}){\cdot}(13.3 \text{ m/s}) - (570 \text{ kg}){\cdot}(17.9 \text{ m/s})] / (480 \text{ kg})$$

$$v_{f2} = 8.9 \text{ m/s} \approx 9 \text{ m/s}$$

11. E is correct.

Impulse is a force acting over some time:

$$J = F\Delta t$$

An impulse changes a system's momentum, so:

$$F\Delta t = \Delta p_{system}$$

The moving block with the lodged bullet comes to a stop when it compresses the spring, losing all momentum.

The initial velocity of the block and bullet separately can be determined by conservation of energy. The two values of interest are the KE of the block and bullet and the PE of the spring.

$$(KE + PE)_{before} = (KE + PE)_{after}$$

$$\tfrac{1}{2}mv^2 + 0 = 0 + \tfrac{1}{2}kx^2$$

$x =$ distance of compression of the spring

$k =$ spring constant

$$\tfrac{1}{2}(4 \text{ kg} + 0.008 \text{ kg})v^2 = \tfrac{1}{2}(1{,}400 \text{ N/m}){\cdot}(0.089 \text{ m})^2$$

$$v^2 = (1{,}400 \text{ N/m}){\cdot}(0.089 \text{ m})^2 / (4.008 \text{ kg})$$

$$v^2 = 2.76 \text{ m}^2/\text{s}^2$$

$$v = 1.66 \text{ m/s}$$

Thus, the block with the lodged bullet hits the spring with an initial velocity of 1.66 m/s.

Since there is no friction, the block is sent in the opposite direction with the same speed of 1.66 m/s when the spring decompresses.

Calculate the momentum, with initial momentum toward the spring and final momentum away from the spring.

$\Delta p = p_{final} - p_{initial}$

$\Delta p = (4.008 \text{ kg}) \cdot (-1.66 \text{ m/s}) - (4.008 \text{ kg}) \cdot (1.66 \text{ m/s})$

$\Delta p = (-6.65 \text{ kg·m/s}) - (6.65 \text{ kg·m/s})$

$\Delta p \approx -13 \text{ kg·m/s}$

$\Delta p \approx -13 \text{ N·s}$

Since $F\Delta t = \Delta p$, the impulse is also -13 kg·m/s $= -13$ N·s

The negative sign signifies the coordinate system chosen in this calculation: toward the spring is the positive direction, and away from the spring is the negative direction.

12. C is correct.

For a rotating body, kinetic energy is:

$K = \frac{1}{2} I \omega^2$

Angular momentum is:

$L = I \omega$

Therefore:

$I = L / \omega$

Replacing this for I in the expression for kinetic energy:

$K = L^2 / 2I$

Taking the ice to be frictionless, there is no external torque on the skater. Thus, angular momentum is conserved and does not change as she brings in her arms. The moment of inertia of a body of a given mass is smaller if its mass is more concentrated toward the rotation axis (e.g., when she draws her arms in close).

Therefore, the moment of inertia of the skater decreases.

Consequently, the skater's kinetic energy increases.

13. D is correct.

The centripetal force is the net force required to maintain an object in uniform circular motion.

$F_{centripetal} = mv^2/r$

where r is the radius of the circular path

Since m is constant and r remains unchanged, the centripetal force is proportional to v^2.

$2^2 = 4$

Thus, if v is doubled, then $F_{centripetal}$ is quadrupled.

14. B is correct.

$$1 \text{ J} = \text{kg·m}^2/\text{s}^2$$

$$p = mv = \text{kg·m/s}$$

$$\text{J·s/m} = (\text{kg·m}^2/\text{s}^2)\cdot(\text{s/m})$$

$$\text{J·s/m} = \text{kg·m/s}$$

$$\text{kg·m/s} = p$$

$$\text{J·s/m} = p$$

15. E is correct.

Impulse is a change in momentum.

$$J = \Delta p$$

$$J = m\Delta v$$

Impulse is also the product of average force and time.

$$J = F\Delta t$$

$$F\Delta t = m\Delta v$$

$ma\Delta t = m\Delta v$, cancel m from both sides of the expression

$$a\Delta t = \Delta v$$

Because acceleration g is constant impulse depends only upon time and velocity.

The speed of the apple affects the impulse as this is included in the Δv term.

Bouncing results in a change in direction. This means a greater change in velocity (the Δv term), so the impulse is greater.

The time of impulse changes the impulse as it is included in the Δt term.

16. D is correct.

$$F\Delta t = m\Delta v$$

$$F = m\Delta v \, / \, \Delta t$$

Choosing toward the wall as the positive direction, the initial velocity is 25 m/s, and the final velocity is –25 m/s:

$$F = m(v_\text{f} - v_\text{i}) \, / \, \Delta t$$

$$F = (0.8 \text{ kg})\cdot(-25 \text{ m/s} - 25 \text{ m/s}) \, / \, (0.05 \text{ s})$$

$$F = -800 \text{ N}$$

Thus, the wall exerts an average force of 800 N on the ball in the negative direction.

From Newton's Third Law, the ball exerts a force of 800 N on the wall in the opposite direction.

17. B is correct.

$$p = mv$$

Sum momentum:

$$p_{total} = m_1 v_1 + m_2 v_2 + m_3 v_3$$

All objects moving to the left have negative velocity.

$$p_{total} = (7 \text{ kg})\cdot(6 \text{ m/s}) + (12 \text{ kg})\cdot(3 \text{ m/s}) + (4 \text{ kg})\cdot(-2 \text{ m/s})$$

$$p_{total} = (42 \text{ kg·m/s}) + (36 \text{ kg·m/s}) + (-8 \text{ kg·m/s})$$

$$p_{total} = 70 \text{ kg·m/s}$$

18. E is correct.

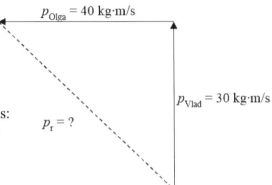

Use conservation of momentum to determine the momentum after the collision. Since they stick together, treat it as a perfectly inelastic collision.

Before the collision, Vladimir's momentum is:
(60 kg)·(0.5 m/s) = 30 kg·m/s pointing North

Before the collision, Olga's momentum is:

(40 kg)·(1 m/s) = 40 kg·m/s pointing West

Write two expressions: one for the conservation of momentum on the *y*-axis (North-South) and one for the conservation of momentum on the *x*-axis (East-West). They do not interact since they are perpendicular to each other.

Since Olga and Vladimir stick together, the final mass is the sum of their masses.

Simply use the Pythagorean Theorem:

$$a^2 + b^2 = c^2$$

$$(30 \text{ kg·m/s})^2 + (40 \text{ kg·m/s})^2 = p^2$$

$$900 \text{ (kg·m/s)}^2 + 1{,}600 \text{ (kg·m/s)}^2 = p^2$$

$$2{,}500 \text{(kg·m/s)}^2 = p^2$$

$$p = 50 \text{ kg·m/s}$$

Use this to solve for velocity:

$$p = mv$$

$$50 \text{ kg·m/s} = (100 \text{ kg})v$$

$$v = 50 \text{ kg·m/s} / 100 \text{ kg}$$

$$v = 0.5 \text{ m/s}$$

Also, this problem can be solved algebraically:

$$p_{before} = p_{after}$$

$$p = mv$$

On the *y* coordinate:

$$(60 \text{ kg}) \cdot (0.5 \text{ m/s}) = (60 \text{ kg} + 40 \text{ kg})v_y$$

$$v_y = (30 \text{ kg·m/s}) / (100 \text{ kg})$$

$$v_y = 0.3 \text{ m/s}$$

On the *x* coordinate:

$$(40 \text{ kg}) \cdot (1 \text{ m/s}) = (60 \text{ kg} + 40 \text{ kg})v_x$$

$$v_x = (40 \text{ kg·m/s}) / (100 \text{ kg})$$

$$v_x = 0.4 \text{ m/s}$$

Combine these final velocity components using the Pythagorean Theorem since they are perpendicular.

$$v^2 = v_x{}^2 + v_y{}^2$$

$$v^2 = (0.4 \text{ m/s})^2 + (0.3 \text{ m/s})^2$$

$$v = 0.5 \text{ m/s}$$

19. B is correct.

Use conservation of momentum to determine the momentum after the collision. Since they stick together, treat it as a perfectly inelastic collision.

Before collision, Vladimir's momentum is:

$$(60 \text{ kg}) \cdot (0.5 \text{ m/s}) = 30 \text{ kg·m/s pointing North}$$

Before collision, Olga's momentum is:

$$(40 \text{ kg}) \cdot (1 \text{ m/s}) = 40 \text{ kg·m/s pointing West}$$

Write two expressions: one for the conservation of momentum on the *y* coordinate (North-South) and one for the conservation of momentum on the *x* coordinate (East-West).

They do not interact since they are perpendicular to each other.

Since they stick together, the final mass is the sum of their masses.

Simply use the Pythagorean Theorem:

$$a^2 + b^2 = c^2$$

$$(30 \text{ kg·m/s})^2 + (40 \text{ kg·m/s})^2 = p^2$$

$$900(\text{kg·m/s})^2 + 1{,}600(\text{kg·m/s})^2 = p^2$$

$$2{,}500(\text{kg·m/s})^2 = p^2$$

$$p = 50 \text{ kg·m/s}$$

This problem can also be solved algebraically:

$$p_{\text{before}} = p_{\text{after}}$$

$$p = mv$$

On the y coordinate:

$$(60 \text{ kg}) \cdot (0.5 \text{ m/s}) = (60 \text{ kg} + 40 \text{ kg})v_y$$

$$v_y = (30 \text{ kg·m/s}) / (100 \text{ kg})$$

$$v_y = 0.3 \text{ m/s}$$

On the x coordinate:

$$(40 \text{ kg}) \cdot (1 \text{ m/s}) = (60 \text{ kg} + 40 \text{ kg})v_x$$

$$v_x = (40 \text{ kg·m/s}) / (100 \text{ kg})$$

$$v_x = 0.4 \text{ m/s}$$

Combine these final velocity components using the Pythagorean Theorem since they are perpendicular:

$$v^2 = v_x{}^2 + v_y{}^2$$

$$v^2 = (0.4 \text{ m/s})^2 + (0.3 \text{ m/s})^2$$

$$v = 0.5 \text{ m/s}$$

Use the final weight and final velocity to find the final momentum directly after the collision:

$$p = mv$$

$$p = (60 \text{ kg} + 40 \text{ kg}) \cdot (0.5 \text{ m/s})$$

$$p = 50 \text{ kg·m/s}$$

20. C is correct.

$$p_0 = mv$$

If m and v are doubled:

$$p = (2m) \cdot (2v)$$

$$p = 4mv$$

$$p = 4p_0$$

The momentum increases by a factor of 4.

21. D is correct.

Balance forces on box Q to solve for tension on box P cable:

$$m_Q a = F - T_P$$

$$T_P = F - m_Q a$$

$$0 < T_P < F$$

Thus, the tension on the cable connected to box P is less than F because it is equal to the difference between F and $m_Q a$ but is not equal because the boxes are accelerating.

22. B is correct.

At all points on a rotating body, the angular velocity is equal.

The speed at different points along a rotating body is directly proportional to the radius.

$v = \omega r$

where v = speed, ω = angular velocity and r = radius

Thus, Melissa and her friend have different speeds due to their different radial locations.

23. A is correct.

Impulse is directly proportional to force and change in time:

$J = F\Delta t$

Increasing the change in time lowers the impact force while decreasing the change in time increases the force.

24. E is correct.

Angular momentum is always conserved unless a system experiences a net torque greater than zero.

Angular momentum is the rotational equivalent of Newton's First Law of motion.

25. D is correct.

$F\Delta t = m\Delta v$

$F = (m\Delta v) / (\Delta t)$

$F = (6.8 \text{ kg}) \cdot (-3.2 \text{ m/s} - 5.4 \text{ m/s}) / (2 \text{ s})$

$F = (-58.48 \text{ kg·m/s}) / (2 \text{ s})$

$F = -29.2 \text{ N}$

$|F| = 29.2 \text{ N}$

26. A is correct.

Before collision, the total momentum of the system:

0 kg·m/s

Momentum is conserved in the explosion.

The momentum of the moving rifle and bullet are in opposite directions:

Therefore, $p = 0$

The total momentum after the explosion:

0 kg·m/s

27. E is correct.

$p = mv$

Conservation of momentum:

$p_{initial} = p_{final}$

$0 \text{ kg·m/s} = (0.01 \text{ kg})·(300 \text{ m/s}) + (4 \text{ kg})v_{recoil}$

$0 \text{ kg·m/s} = 3 \text{ kg·m/s} + (4 \text{ kg})v_{recoil}$

$-3 \text{ kg·m/s} = (4 \text{ kg})v_{recoil}$

$(-3 \text{ kg·m/s}) / (4 \text{ kg}) = v_{recoil}$

$v_{recoil} = -0.75 \text{ m/s}$

Velocity is negative since the gun recoils in the opposite direction of the bullet.

28. C is correct.

Since the initial velocity only has a horizontal component, the y component of the initial velocity = 0.

Use 24 m to calculate the time the ball is in the air:

$d_y = \frac{1}{2}at^2$

$t^2 = 2d_y / a$

$t^2 = 2(24 \text{ m}) / (9.8 \text{ m/s}^2)$

$t^2 = 4.89 \text{ s}^2$

$t = 2.21 \text{ s}$

Use the time in the air and the horizontal distance to calculate the horizontal speed of the ball:

$v_x = d_x / t$

$v_x = (18 \text{ m}) / (2.21 \text{ s})$

$v_x = 8.1 \text{ m/s}$

29. A is correct.

An object moving in a circle at constant speed is undergoing uniform circular motion. In uniform circular motion, the acceleration is due to centripetal acceleration and points inward towards the center of a circle.

30. B is correct.

Impulse:

$J = F\Delta t$

$J = \Delta p$

where p is momentum

31. C is correct.

Conservation of energy:

$$KE_i + PE_i = KE_f + PE_f$$

$$KE_i + PE_i = KE_f + 0$$

$$KE_f = \tfrac{1}{2}mv_i^2 + mgh_i$$

$$KE_f = \tfrac{1}{2}(4 \text{ kg}) \cdot (20 \text{ m/s})^2 + (4 \text{ kg}) \cdot (10 \text{ m/s}^2) \cdot (10 \text{ m})$$

$$KE_f = 800 \text{ J} + 400 \text{ J}$$

$$KE_f = 1{,}200 \text{ J}$$

32. E is correct.

The force needed to stop a car can be related to KE and work:

$$KE = W$$

$$\tfrac{1}{2}mv^2 = Fd$$

$$F = \tfrac{1}{2}mv^2 / d$$

Momentum is included in the KE term.

$$p = mv$$

$$F = \tfrac{1}{2}(mv)v / d$$

$$F = \tfrac{1}{2}(p)v / d$$

If there is less stopping distance the force increases as they are inversely proportional.

If the momentum or mass increase the force increases as they are directly proportional.

33. C is correct.

Impulse:

$$J = F\Delta t$$

Based on Newton's Third Law, the force experienced by these two objects is equal and opposite.

Therefore, the magnitudes of impulse are the same.

34. B is correct.

Balance the counterclockwise (CCW) torque with the clockwise (CW) torque.

Let the axis of rotation be at the point where the rope attaches to the bar.

This placement causes the torque from the rope to be zero since the lever arm is zero.

$$\Sigma \tau : \tau_1 - \tau_2 = 0$$

$$\tau_1 = \tau_2$$

The CCW torque due to the weight of the 6 kg mass:

$\tau = r_1 F_1$

$r_1 F_1 = (x) \cdot (6 \text{ kg}) \cdot (9.8 \text{ m/s}^2)$

The CW torque due to the weight of the 30 kg mass:

$r_2 F_2 = (5 \text{ m} - x) \cdot (30 \text{ kg}) \cdot (9.8 \text{ m/s}^2)$

Set the two expressions equal to each other

$(9.8 \text{ m/s}^2) \cdot (x) \cdot (6 \text{ kg}) = (5 \text{ m} - x) \cdot (30 \text{ kg}) \cdot (9.8 \text{ m/s}^2)$

Cancel *g* and kg from each side of the equation:

$6x = 30(5 \text{ m} - x)$

$6x = 150 \text{ m} - 30x$

$36x = 150 \text{ m}$

$x = 4.2 \text{ m}$

35. E is correct.

If the block is at rest, then the force of static friction is equal to the force of gravity at angle θ.

$F_f = mg \sin \theta$

36. C is correct.

$F_{net} = 0$ is necessary to maintain a constant velocity.

If 45 N must be exerted on the block to maintain a constant velocity, the force due to kinetic friction against the block equals 45 N.

For a horizontal surface and no other vertical forces acting, the normal force on the block equals its weight.

$N = mg$

$F_{friction} = \mu_k N$

$F_{friction} = \mu_k mg$

$\mu_k = (F_{friction}) / mg$

$\mu_k = (45 \text{ N}) / [(30 \text{ kg}) \cdot (10 \text{ m/s}^2)]$

$\mu_k = 0.15$

37. B is correct. Newton's Second Law: $F = ma$

The impulse-momentum relationship can be derived by multiplying Δt on both sides:

$F\Delta t = ma\Delta t$

$F\Delta t = m\Delta v$

$J = m\Delta v$

Thus, the impulse is equal to the change in momentum.

38. C is correct.

Force X acts perpendicular to the short arm of the rectangle; this is the lever arm.

$\tau = rF$

$\tau = (0.5 \text{ m}) \cdot (15 \text{ N})$

$\tau = 7.5 \text{ N·m}$

Since the torque causes the plate to rotate clockwise its sign is negative.

$\tau = -7.5 \text{ N·m}$

39. E is correct.

$\tau = rF$

Force Z acts directly at the pivot, so the lever arm equals zero.

$\tau = (0 \text{ m}) \cdot (30 \text{ N})$

$\tau = 0 \text{ N·m}$

40. A is correct.

$\tau = rF$

Force Y acts perpendicular to the long arm of the rectangle; this is the lever arm.

$\tau = (0.6 \text{ m}) \cdot (25 \text{ N})$

$\tau = 15 \text{ N·m}$

The torque is clockwise, so its sign is negative.

$\tau = -15 \text{ N·m}$

41. B is correct.

The tension in the string provides the centripetal force.

$T = mv^2 / r$

$m = 50 \text{ g} = 0.05 \text{ kg}$

$T = [(0.05 \text{ kg}) \cdot (20 \text{ m/s})^2] / (2 \text{ m})$

$T = [(0.05 \text{ kg}) \cdot (400 \text{ m}^2/\text{s}^2)] / (2 \text{ m})$

$T = (20 \text{ kg·m}^2/\text{s}^2) / (2 \text{ m})$

$T = 10 \text{ N}$

42. A is correct.

Newton's Third Law states that each force is paired with an equal and opposite reaction force. Therefore, the small car and the truck each receive the same force.

43. C is correct.

Choose the axis of rotation at the point where the bar attaches to the wall.

Since the lever arm of the force that the wall exerts is zero, the torque at that point is zero and can be ignored.

The two other torques present arise from the weight of the bar exerting a force downward and the cable exerting force upward. The weight of the bar acts at the center of mass, so its lever arm is 1 m.

The lever arm for the cable is 2 m since it acts the full 2 m away from the wall at the end of the bar.

Torque is the product of the length of the lever arm and the component of force perpendicular to the arm.

The torque applied by the wire is:

$F_T l \sin \theta$

The sum of torques = 0, since the bar is in rotational equilibrium.

Let the torque of the cable be positive and the torque of the weight be negative.

$(F_T \sin 30°) \cdot (2 \text{ m}) - (10 \text{ kg}) \cdot (10 \text{ m/s}^2) \cdot (1 \text{ m}) = 0$

$F_T = [(10 \text{ kg}) \cdot (10 \text{ m/s}^2) \cdot (1 \text{ m})] / [(2 \text{ m}) \cdot (\sin 30°)]$

$F_T = [(10 \text{ kg}) \cdot (10 \text{ m/s}^2) \cdot (1 \text{ m})] / [(2 \text{ m}) \cdot (0.5)]$

$F_T = 100 \text{ N}$

44. B is correct.

Momentum is defined as:

$p = mv$

$m_A = 2m_B$

$p_A = 2m_B v$

$p_B = m_B v$

$p_A = 2p_B$

If both objects reach the ground at the same time they have equal velocities.

However, because A is twice the mass, it has twice the momentum as object B.

45. D is correct.

Use conservation of momentum to make equations for momenta along the *x*-axis and the *y*-axis. Since the mass ratio is 1 : 4, one car has a mass of *m,* and the other has a mass of 4*m.*

The entangled cars after the collision have a combined mass of 5*m.*

Let the car of mass *m* be traveling in the positive *x* direction and the car of mass 4*m* be traveling in the positive *y* direction. The choice of directions here is arbitrary, but the angle of impact is important.

$p_{initial} = p_{final}$ for both the *x*- and *y*-axes

$p = mv$

For the *x*-axis:

$m_i v_i = m_f v_{fx}$

$m(12 \text{ m/s}) = 5mv_x$, cancel *m*

$12 \text{ m/s} = 5v_x$

$v_x = 2.4 \text{ m/s}$

For the *y*-axis:

$m_i v_i = m_f v_{fy}$

$4m(12 \text{ m/s}) = 5mv_y$, cancel *m*

$4(12 \text{ m/s}) = 5v_y$

$v_y = 9.6 \text{ m/s}$

The question asks for the magnitude of the final velocity, so combine the *x* and *y* components of the final velocity using the Pythagorean Theorem.

$v^2 = (2.4 \text{ m/s})^2 + (9.6 \text{ m/s})^2$

$v^2 = 5.76 \text{ m}^2/\text{s}^2 + 92.16 \text{ m}^2/\text{s}^2$

$v = 9.9 \text{ m/s}$

46. C is correct.

Use conservation of momentum on the horizontal plane.

Before the throw, the total momentum of the skater-ball system is zero.

Thus, after the throw, the total horizontal momentum must sum to zero: the horizontal component of the ball's momentum equals the momentum of the skater moving the opposite way.

Use m_s for the skater's mass and $m_s/3$ for the ball's mass.

$p = mv$

$p_{skater} = p_{ball}$

$m_s v_s = m_b v_b$

$m_s(2.9 \text{ m/s}) = (1/3)m_s v \cos 5°$, cancel *m*

$$v = (2.9 \text{ m/s})\cdot(3) / (\cos 5°)$$

$$v = (2.9 \text{ m/s})\cdot(3) / (0.996)$$

$$v = 8.73 \text{ m/s}$$

47. B is correct.

weight = mass × gravity

$$W = mg$$

$$m = W / g$$

$$m = (98 \text{ N}) / (9.8 \text{ m/s}^2)$$

$$m = 10 \text{ kg}$$

Newton's Second Law:

$$F = ma$$

$$F = (10 \text{ kg})\cdot(10 \text{ m/s}^2)$$

$$F = 100 \text{ N}$$

48. A is correct.

KE is constant because speed is constant.

PE increases because the cart is at a greater height at point B.

The cart as a system is not isolated since the winch does work on it and so its energy is not conserved.

Conservation of energy: PE increase of the cart = work done by the winch

49. D is correct.

The vertical component of the initial velocity:

$$v_{iy} = (140 \text{ m/s}) \sin 35°$$

$$v_{iy} = (140 \text{ m/s})\cdot(0.57)$$

$$v_{iy} = 79.8 \text{ m/s}$$

The initial velocity upward, time elapsed, and acceleration due to gravity is known.

Determine the final velocity after 4 s.

$$v_y = v_{iy} + at$$

$$v_y = 79.8 \text{ m/s} + (-9.8 \text{ m/s}^2)\cdot(4 \text{ s})$$

$$v_y = 41 \text{ m/s}$$

50. C is correct.

impulse = force × time

$J = F\Delta t$

51. D is correct.

Conservation of momentum: the momentum of the fired bullet is equal and opposite to that of the rifle.

$p = mv$

$p_{\text{before}} = p_{\text{after}}$

$0 = p_{\text{rifle}} + p_{\text{bullet}}$

$-p_{\text{rifle}} = p_{\text{bullet}}$

$-(2 \text{ kg})v = (0.01 \text{ kg}) \cdot (220 \text{ m/s})$

$v = (0.01 \text{ kg}) \cdot (220 \text{ m/s}) / (-2 \text{ kg})$

$v = -1.1 \text{ m/s}$

Thus, the velocity of the rifle is 1.1 m/s in the opposite direction as the bullet.

52. D is correct.

Airbags reduce the force by increasing the time of contact between the passenger and surface.

In a collision, an impulse is experienced by a passenger:

$J = F\Delta t$

$F = J / \Delta t$

The impulse is a constant but the force experienced by the passenger is inversely related to the time of contact.

Airbags increase the time of impact and thus reduce the forces experienced by the person.

53. A is correct.

Since Force I is perpendicular to the beam, the entire force acts to produce torque without any horizontal force component.

$\tau = rF$

$\tau = (0.5 \text{ m}) \cdot (10 \text{ N})$

$\tau = 5 \text{ N·m}$

Because the force causes the beam to rotate clockwise against the positive counterclockwise direction, the torque sign should be negative:

$\tau = -5 \text{ N·m}$

54. E is correct.

To calculate torque, use the 35° angle.

For torque:

$\tau = rF \sin \theta$

$\tau = (1 \text{ m}) \cdot (5 \text{ N}) \sin 35°$

$\tau = 2.9 \text{ N·m}$

The torque is counterclockwise, so the sign is positive.

55. B is correct.

Force III acts purely in tension with the beam and has no component acting vertically against the beam.

Torque can only be calculated using a force with some component perpendicular to the length vector.

Because Force III has no perpendicular component to the length vector, torque is zero.

$\tau = rF$

$\tau = (1 \text{ m}) \cdot (0 \text{ N})$

$\tau = 0 \text{ N·m}$

Work and Energy – Explanations

1. D is correct. The final velocity in projectile motion is related to the maximum height of the projectile through conservation of energy:

$$KE = PE$$

$$\tfrac{1}{2}mv^2 = mgh$$

When the stone thrown straight up passes its starting point on its way back down, its downward speed is equal to its initial upward velocity (2D motion). The stone thrown straight downward contains the same magnitude of initial velocity as the stone thrown upward, and thus both the stone thrown upward and the stone thrown downward have the same final speed.

A stone thrown horizontally (or for example, a stone thrown at 45°) does not achieve the same height *h* as a stone thrown straight up, so it has a smaller final vertical velocity.

2. B is correct.

$$\text{Work} = \text{force} \times \text{displacement} \times \cos\theta$$

$$W = Fd\cos\theta, \text{ where } \theta \text{ is the angle between the vectors } F \text{ and } d$$

$$W = (5\text{ N}){\cdot}(10\text{ m})\cos 45°$$

$$W = (50\text{ J}){\cdot}(0.7)$$

$$W = 35\text{ J}$$

3. A is correct.

$$KE = \tfrac{1}{2}mv^2$$

KE is influenced by mass and velocity.

However, since velocity is squared, its influence on KE is greater than the influence of mass.

4. B is correct. Work = force × displacement × cos θ

$$W = Fd\cos\theta$$

$$\cos 90° = 0$$

$$W = 0$$

Since the force of gravity acts perpendicular to the distance traveled by the ball, the force due to gravity does no work in moving the ball.

5. E is correct.

$$KE = \tfrac{1}{2}mv^2$$

$$KE = \tfrac{1}{2}(5\text{ kg}){\cdot}(2\text{ m/s})^2$$

$$KE = 10\text{ J}$$

6. A is correct.

$W = Fd \cos \theta$

$\cos \theta = 1$

$F = W / d$

$F = (360 \text{ J}) / (8 \text{ m})$

$F = 45 \text{ N}$

$F = ma$

$m = F / a$

$m = (45 \text{ N}) / (10 \text{ m/s}^2)$

$m = 4.5 \text{ kg}$

7. D is correct. On a displacement (x) vs. force (F) graph, the displacement is the y-axis, and the force is the x-axis.

The slope is x / F, (in units of m/N) which is the reciprocal of the spring constant k, which is measured in N/m.

8. C is correct.

Work done by a spring equation:

$W = \frac{1}{2}kx^2$

$W = \frac{1}{2}(22 \text{ N/m}) \cdot (3 \text{ m})^2$

$W = 99 \text{ J}$

9. A is correct.

The force of gravity always points down. When the ball is moving upwards, the direction of its displacement is opposite of that of the force of gravity, and therefore the work done by gravity is negative.

On the way down, the direction of displacement is the same as that of the force of gravity, and therefore the work done by gravity is positive.

10. B is correct. Work done by gravity is an object's change in gravitational PE.

$W = -PE$

$A_1 = 400 \text{ J}$

By the work-energy theorem,

$W = KE$

$B_1 = 400 \text{ J}$

11. D is correct.

Work is calculated as the product of force and displacement parallel to the direction of the applied force:

$$W = Fd \cos \theta$$

where some component of d is in the direction of the force.

12. B is correct.

Work only depends on force and distance:

$$W = Fd \cos \theta$$

Power $= W / t$ is the amount of work done in a unit of time.

13. A is correct.

The area under the curve on a graph is the product of the values of $y \times x$.

Here, the y value is a force, and the x value is distance:

$$Fd = W$$

14. C is correct.

This is the conservation of energy. The only force acting on the cat is gravity.

$$KE = PE_g$$

$$KE = mgh$$

$$KE = (3 \text{ kg}) \cdot (10 \text{ m/s}^2) \cdot (4 \text{ m})$$

$$KE = 120 \text{ J}$$

15. B is correct.

Although the book is stationary with respect to the plank, the plank is applying a force to the book causing it to accelerate in the direction of the force.

Since the displacement of the point of application of the force is in the same direction as the force, the work done is positive.

Choices D and E are not correct because work is a scalar and has no direction.

16. D is correct.

$$W = Fd$$

$$d = W / F$$

$$d = (350 \text{ J}) / (900 \text{ N})$$

$$d = 0.39 \text{ m}$$

17. E is correct. Conservation of energy between kinetic energy and potential energy:

KE = PE

KE = $\frac{1}{2}mv^2$ and PE = mgh

Set the equations equal to each other:

$\frac{1}{2}mv^2 = mgh$, cancel m from both sides

$\frac{1}{2}v^2 = gh$

h is only dependent on the initial v, which is equal between both objects, so the two objects rise to the same height.

18. A is correct.

Work = Power × time

$P_1 = W / t$

$P_2 = (3\ W) / (1/3\ t)$

$P_2 = 3(3/1){\cdot}(W / t)$

$P_2 = 9(W / t)$

$P_2 = 9(P_1)$

19. D is correct.

Conservation of energy:

KE = PE

KE = mgh

W = mg

KE = Wh

KE = (450 N)·(9 m)

KE = 4,050 J

20. A is correct.

$F_1 = -kx_1$

Solve for the spring constant k:

$k = F / x_1$

$k = (160\text{ N}) / (0.23\text{ m})$

$k = 696$ N/m

$F_2 = -kx_2$

$F_2 = (696\text{ N/m}){\cdot}(0.34\text{ m})$

$F_2 = 237$ N

21. B is correct. There is a frictional force since the net force = 0

The mule pulls in the same direction as the direction of travel so $\cos \theta = 1$

$$W = Fd \cos \theta$$
$$d = v \Delta t$$
$$W = Fv \Delta t$$

22. D is correct.

$$W = Fd \cos \theta$$
$$F_T = W / (d \times \cos \theta)$$
$$F_T = (540 \text{ J}) / (18 \text{ m} \times \cos 32°)$$
$$F_T = (540 \text{ J}) / (18 \text{ m} \times 0.848)$$
$$F_T = 35 \text{ N}$$

23. B is correct.

The spring force balances the gravitational force on the mass. Therefore:

$$Fg = -kx$$
$$mg = -kx$$

By adding an extra 120 grams, the mass is doubled:

$$(2m)g = -kx$$

Since the weight mg and the spring constant k are constant, only x changes.

Thus, after the addition of 120 g, x doubles:

$$PE_1 = \tfrac{1}{2}kx^2$$
$$PE_2 = \tfrac{1}{2}k(2x)^2$$
$$PE_2 = \tfrac{1}{2}k(4x^2)$$
$$PE_2 = 4(\tfrac{1}{2}kx^2)$$

The potential energy increases by a factor of 4.

24. C is correct.

In each case the car's energy is reduced to zero by the work done by the frictional force, or in other words:

$$KE + (-W) = 0$$
$$KE = W$$

Each car starts with kinetic energy $KE = (\tfrac{1}{2})mv^2$. The initial speed is the same for each car, so due to the differences in mass, the Ferrari has the most KE.

Thus, to reduce the Ferrari's energy to zero requires the most work.

25. E is correct.

The hammer does work on the nail as it drives it into the wood. The amount of work done is equal to the amount of kinetic energy lost by the hammer:

$\Delta KE = \Delta W$

26. A is correct.

The only force doing work is the road's friction, so the work done by the road's friction is the total work. This work equals the change in KE.

$W = \Delta KE$

$W = KE_f - KE_i$

$W = \frac{1}{2}mv_2^2 - \frac{1}{2}mv_1^2$

$W = 0 - [\frac{1}{2}(1,500 \text{ kg}) \cdot (25 \text{ m/s})^2]$

$W = -4.7 \times 10^5 \text{ J}$

27. D is correct.

$KE = \frac{1}{2}mv^2$

$KE_{car} = \frac{1}{2}(1,000 \text{ kg}) \cdot (4.72 \text{ m/s})^2$

$KE_{car} = 11,139 \text{ J}$

Calculate the KE of the 2,000 kg truck with 20 times the KE:

$KE_{truck} = KE_{car} \times 20$

$KE_{truck} = (11,139 \text{ J}) \times 20$

$KE_{truck} = 222.7 \text{ kJ}$

Calculate the speed of the 2,000 kg truck:

$KE = \frac{1}{2}mv^2$

$v^2 = 2KE / m$

$v^2 = 2(222.7 \text{ kJ}) / (2,000 \text{ kg})$

$v_{truck} = \sqrt{[2(222.7 \text{ kJ}) / (2,000 \text{ kg})]}$

$v_{truck} = 14.9 \text{ m/s}$

28. E is correct.

Gravity and the normal force are balanced, vertical forces.

Since the car is slowing (i.e., accelerating backward) there is a net force backwards, due to friction (i.e., braking).

Newton's First Law of Motion states that in the absence of any forces, the car would keep moving forward.

29. B is correct.

Energy is always conserved so the work needed to lift the piano is 0.15 m is equal to the work needed to pull the rope 1 m:

$W_1 = W_2$

$F_1 d_1 = F_2 d_2$

$F_1 d_1 / d_2 = F_2$

$F_2 = (6{,}000 \text{ N}) \cdot (0.15 \text{ m}) / 1 \text{ m}$

$F_2 = 900 \text{ N}$

30. C is correct.

The area under the curve on a graph is the product of the values of $y \times x$.

Here, the y value is a force, and the x value is distance:

$Fd = W$

31. B is correct. The vast majority of the Earth's energy comes from the sun, which produces radiation that penetrates the Earth's atmosphere. Likewise, radiation is emitted from the Earth's atmosphere.

32. C is correct.

$W = Fd$

$W = \Delta KE$

$F \times d = \frac{1}{2}mv^2$

If v is doubled:

$F \times d_2 = \frac{1}{2}m(2v)^2$

$F \times d_2 = \frac{1}{2}m(4v^2)$

$F \times d_2 = 4(\frac{1}{2}mv^2)$

For equations to remain equal to each other, d_2 must be 4 times d.

33. D is correct.

Work = Power × time

$P = W / t$

$W = Fd$

$P = (Fd) / t$

$P = [(2{,}000 \text{ N}) \cdot (320 \text{ m})] / (60 \text{ s})$

$P = 10{,}667 \text{ W} = 10.7 \text{ kW}$

34. E is correct.

Solution using the principle of conservation of energy.

Assuming the system to consist of the barbell alone, the force of gravity and the force of the hands raising the barbell are both external forces.

Since the system contains only a single object, potential energy is not defined.

The net power expended is:

$P_{net} = W_{ext} / \Delta t$

Conservation of energy requires:

$W_{ext} = \Delta KE$

$W_{ext} = \frac{1}{2}m(v_f^2 - v_i^2)$

For constant acceleration situations:

$(v_f + v_i) / 2 = v_{average} = \Delta y / \Delta t$

$(v_f + 0.0 \text{ m/s}) / 2 = 3.0 \text{ m} / 3.0 \text{ s}$

$v_f = 2.0 \text{ m/s}$

Therefore:

$W_{ext} = \frac{1}{2}(25 \text{ kg}) \cdot (2.0 \text{ m/s})^2$

$W_{ext} = 50.0 \text{ J}$

The net power expended is:

$P_{net} = 50.0 \text{ J} / 3.0 \text{ s} = 17 \text{ W}$

$P_{net} = 17 \text{ W}$

Solution using work.

The power expended in raising the barbell is:

$P_{net} = W_{net} / \Delta t$

The net work is defined as:

$W_{net} = F_{net}\Delta y$

By Newton's Second law:

$F_{net} = ma$

Find the acceleration:

$\Delta y = \frac{1}{2}a\Delta t^2$

$a = (2) \cdot (3.0 \text{ m}) / (3.0 \text{ s})^2$

$a = 0.67 \text{ m/s}^2$

The net force on the barbell is:

$F_{net} = (25 \text{ kg}) \cdot (0.67 \text{ m/s}^2)$

$F_{net} = (50 / 3) \text{ N}$

The net work is:

$$W_{net} = F_{net}\Delta y$$

$$W_{net} = [(50 / 3) \text{ N}] \cdot (3.0 \text{ m})$$

$$W_{net} = 50.0 \text{ J}$$

The net power expended:

$$P_{net} = 50.0 \text{ J} / 3.0 \text{ s}$$

$$P_{net} = 17 \text{ W}$$

35. B is correct.

The bag was never lifted off the ground and moved horizontally at a constant velocity.

$$F = 0$$

$$W = Fd$$

$$W = 0 \text{ J}$$

Because there is no acceleration, the force is zero, and thus the work is zero.

36. B is correct. Using energy conservation to solve the problem:

$$W = |\Delta KE|$$

$$Fd = |\tfrac{1}{2}m(v_f^2 - v_0^2)|$$

$$d = |m(v_f^2 - v_0^2) / 2F|$$

$$d = |(1,000 \text{ kg}) \cdot [(22 \text{ m/s})^2 - (30 \text{ m/s})^2] / (2) \cdot (9,600 \text{ N})|$$

$$d = |(1,000 \text{ kg}) \cdot (484 \text{ m}^2/\text{s}^2 - 900 \text{ m}^2/\text{s}^2) / 19,200 \text{ N}|$$

$$d = 22 \text{ m}$$

Kinematic approach:

$$F = ma$$

$$a = F / m$$

$$a = (9,600 \text{ N}) / (1,000 \text{ kg})$$

$$a = 9.6 \text{ m/s}^2$$

$$v_f^2 = v_0^2 + 2a\Delta d$$

$$(v_f^2 - v_0^2) / 2a = \Delta d$$

Note that acceleration is negative due to it acting opposite the velocity.

$$\Delta d = [(22 \text{ m/s})^2 - (30 \text{ m/s})^2] / 2(-9.6 \text{ m/s}^2)$$

$$\Delta d = (484 \text{ m}^2/\text{s}^2 - 900 \text{ m}^2/\text{s}^2) / (-19.2 \text{ m/s}^2)$$

$$\Delta d = (-416 \text{ m}^2/\text{s}^2) / (-19.2 \text{ m/s}^2)$$

$$\Delta d = 21.7 \text{ m} \approx 22 \text{ m}$$

37. C is correct.

$W = 100$ J

Work = Power × time

$P = W / t$

$P = 100$ J $/ 50$ s

$P = 2$ W

38. D is correct.
All of the original potential energy (with respect to the bottom of the cliff) is converted into kinetic energy.

$mgh = \frac{1}{2} m v_f^2$

Therefore:

$v_f = \sqrt{2gh}$

$v_f = \sqrt{(2) \cdot (10 \text{ m/s}^2) \cdot (58 \text{ m})}$

$v_f = 34$ m/s

Kinematic approach:

$v_f^2 = v_0^2 + 2a\Delta x$

$v_f^2 = 0 + 2a\Delta x$

$v_f = \sqrt{2a\Delta x}$

$v_f = \sqrt{[2(10 \text{ m/s}^2) \cdot (58 \text{ m})]}$

$v_f = \sqrt{(1{,}160 \text{ m}^2/\text{s}^2)}$

$v_f = 34$ m/s

39. E is correct.
$PE = mgh$

If height and gravity are constant, then potential energy is directly proportional to mass.

As such, if the second stone has four times the mass of the first, then it must have four times the potential energy of the first stone.

$m_2 = 4m_1$

$PE_2 = 4PE_1$

Therefore, the second stone has four times the potential energy.

40. B is correct.

$W = Fd$

$W = mgh$, work done by gravity

$W = (1.3 \text{ kg}) \cdot (10 \text{ m/s}^2) \cdot (6 \text{ m})$

$W = 78$ J

---

41. A is correct.

Potential energy is the energy associated with the relative positions of pairs of objects, regardless of their state of motion.

Kinetic energy is the energy associated with the motion of single particles, regardless of their location.

42. A is correct.

$F_{spring} = F_{centripetal}$

$F_{spring} = kx$

$kx = 15$ N

$x = (15$ N$) / (65$ N/m$)$

$x = 0.23$ m

$PE_{spring} = \frac{1}{2}kx^2$

$PE_{spring} = \frac{1}{2}(65$ N/m$) \cdot (0.23$ m$)^2$

$PE_{spring} = 1.7$ J

43. C is correct.

total time $= (3.5$ h/day$) \cdot (7$ days$) \cdot (5$ weeks$)$

total time $= 122.5$ h

cost $= (8.16$ cents/kW·h$) \cdot (122.5$ h$) \cdot (0.12$ kW$)$

cost $= 120$ cents $= \$1.20$

44. E is correct.

$x = 5.1$ m $\times (\cos 32°)$

$x = 4.33$ m

$h = 5.1$ m $- 4.33$ m

$h = 0.775$ m

$W = Fd$

$W = mg \times h$

$m = W / gh$

$m = (120$ J$) / (9.8$ m/s$^2) \cdot (0.775$ m$)$

$m = 15.8$ kg

45. D is correct.

Potential energy of spring:

$$PE_i + W = PE_f$$

$$\tfrac{1}{2} k x_i^2 + 111J = \tfrac{1}{2} k x_f^2$$

$$111J = \tfrac{1}{2} k (x_f^2 - x_i^2)$$

$$111J = \tfrac{1}{2} k [(2.9m)^2 - (1.4m)^2]$$

$$111J = \tfrac{1}{2} k [(8.41m^2) - (1.96m^2)]$$

$$111J = \tfrac{1}{2} k (6.45m^2)$$

$$k = 2(111 \text{ J}) / (6.45 \text{ m}^2)$$

$$k = 34 \text{ N/m}$$

Unit check:

$$J = kg \cdot m^2/s^2$$

$$J/m^2 = (kg \cdot m^2/s^2) \cdot (1/m^2)$$

$$J/m^2 = (kg/s^2)$$

$$N/m = (kg \cdot m/s^2) \cdot (1/m)$$

$$N/m = (kg/s^2)$$

46. E is correct.

Potential energy, kinetic energy and work are all measured in joules:

$$J = kg \cdot m^2/s^2$$

$$KE = \tfrac{1}{2}mv^2 = kg(m/s)^2 = J$$

$$PE = mgh$$

$$PE = kg(m/s^2) \cdot (m) = J$$

$$W = Fd = J$$

47. A is correct.

Potential energy of spring:

$$PE = \tfrac{1}{2}kx^2$$

Kinetic energy of mass:

$$KE = \tfrac{1}{2}mv^2$$

Set equal to each other and rearrange:

$$\tfrac{1}{2}kx^2 = \tfrac{1}{2}mv^2, \text{ cancel } \tfrac{1}{2} \text{ from both sides of the expression}$$

$$kx^2 = mv^2$$

$$x^2 = (mv^2) / k$$

$$x^2 = (m / k)v^2$$

Since m / k is provided:

$$x^2 = (0.038 \text{ kg·m/N})·(18 \text{ m/s})^2$$

$$x^2 = 12.3 \text{ m}^2$$

$$x = \sqrt{12.3} \text{ m}$$

$$x = 3.5 \text{ m}$$

48. A is correct.

$$m_t = 2m_c$$

$$v_t = 2v_c$$

KE of the truck:

$$KE_t = \tfrac{1}{2}m_t v_t^2$$

Replace mass and velocity of the truck with the equivalent mass and velocity of the car:

$$KE_t = \tfrac{1}{2}(2m_c)·(2v_c)^2$$

$$KE_t = \tfrac{1}{2}(2m_c)·(4v_c^2)$$

$$KE_t = \tfrac{1}{2}(8m_c v_c^2)$$

The truck has 8 times the kinetic energy of the car.

49. E is correct.

When a car stops, the KE is equal to the work done by the force of friction from the brakes.

Through friction, the KE is transformed into heat.

50. B is correct.

When the block comes to rest at the end of the spring, the upward force of the spring balances the downward force of gravity.

$$F = kx$$

$$mg = kx$$

$$x = mg / k$$

$$x = (30 \text{ kg})·(10 \text{ m/s}^2) / 900 \text{ N/m}$$

$$x = 0.33 \text{ m}$$

51. D is correct.

$$KE = \tfrac{1}{2}mv^2$$

$$KE = \tfrac{1}{2}(0.33 \text{ kg})·(40 \text{ m/s})^2$$

$$KE = 264 \text{ J}$$

52. C is correct.

Work is the area under a force vs. position graph.

area $= Fd = W$

The area of the triangle as the object moves from 0 to 4 m:

$A = \frac{1}{2}bh$

$A = \frac{1}{2}(4 \text{ m}\cdot)(10 \text{ N})$

$A = 20 \text{ J}$

$W = 20 \text{ J}$

53. C is correct.

$KE = PE$

$\frac{1}{2}mv^2 = mgh$

$v^2 / 2g = h$

If v is doubled:

$h_B = v_B^2 / 2g$

$v_J = 2v_B$

$(2v_B)^2 / 2g = h_J$

$4(v_B^2 / 2g) = h_J$

$4h_B = h_J$

James's ball travels 4 times higher than Bob's ball.

54. B is correct.

Hooke's Law is given as:

$F = -kx$

The negative is only by convention to demonstrate that the spring force is a restoring force.

Graph B is correct because the force is linearly increasing with increasing distance.

All other graphs are either constant or exponential.

55. C is correct.

A decrease in the KE for the rocket causes either a gain in its gravitational PE, or the transfer of heat, or a combination.

The rocket loses some KE due to air resistance (friction).

Thus, some of the rocket's KE is converted to heat that causes the temperature of the air surrounding the rocket to increase.

Therefore, the average KE of the air molecules increases.

Rotational Motion – Explanations

1. D is correct.

An object is rolling down an incline experiences three forces, and hence three torques. The forces are the force of gravity acting on the center of mass of the object, the normal force between the incline and the object, and the force of friction between the incline and the object.

If the origin is taken to be the center of the object, the force of gravity provides zero torque. This can be seen by noting that the distance between the origin and the point of application of the force is zero.

$$\tau_{\text{gravity}} = F_{\text{gravity}}r = mg(0) = 0$$

Similarly, the normal force contributes zero torque because the direction of the force is directed through the origin (pivot point).

$$\tau_{normal} = F_{normal}\,\text{r}\,\sin\theta = F_{normal}(R)\cdot(\sin 180°)$$

$$\tau_{normal} = F_{normal}(R)\cdot(0) = 0$$

Use a coordinate system in which the *x*-axis is parallel to the incline and the *y*-axis is perpendicular. The object is rolling in the positive *x*-direction.

The dynamical equation for linear motion along the *x*-direction is:

$$F_{\text{net}} = ma$$

$$(mg\sin\theta - f) = ma$$

Note that the normal force is only in the *y*-direction, and thus does not directly contribute to the acceleration in the *x*-direction.

The dynamical equation for rotational motion is:

$$\tau_{\text{net}} = I\alpha$$

$$fR = I\alpha \text{ (Note that the frictional force is perpendicular to the } r \text{ vector; } \sin 90° = 1)$$

where *R* is the radius of the object, *f* is the force of friction, and *I* is the moment of inertia.

A relation coupling these two dynamical equations is needed.

The equation of constraint imposed by the restriction that the object rolls without slipping:

$$\alpha = a / R$$

To find the linear acceleration, use the equation of constraint to eliminate α from the rotational equation by replacing it with a / R:

$$fR = I(a / R)$$

The force of friction is of no interest, so rearrange this last expression:

$$f = Ia / R^2$$

Substitute this into the linear dynamic equation from above in place of *f*:

$$(mg\sin\theta - Ia / R^2) = ma$$

Solving this for a:

$$a = mg \sin \theta \,/\, [m + (I\,/\,R^2)]$$

$$a = g \sin \theta \,/\, [1 + (I\,/\,mR^2)$$

The moment of inertia of any circular object can be written as NmR^2, where N is some real number that is different for different shapes.

For example, for a sphere,

$$I = (2/5)mR^2, \text{ so for a sphere } N = 2/5.$$

So, for any rolling object, the linear acceleration is:

$$a = g \sin \theta \,/\, (1 + N), \text{ which depends on neither the radius nor the mass of the object.}$$

Only the shape of the object is important.

2. B is correct.

Use conservation of energy.

The initial and final states are the sphere at the top and bottom of the ramp, respectively.

Take the zero of gravitational potential energy to be the configuration in which the sphere is at the bottom. The potential energy at the bottom is zero.

The sphere starts from rest, so the kinetic energy at the top is zero. With that:

$$mgh = K_{linear} + K_{rotation}$$

$$mgh = \tfrac{1}{2}mv^2 + \tfrac{1}{2}I\omega^2$$

For a sphere,

$$I = (2/5)mr^2$$

Because the sphere rolls without slipping,

$$v = r\omega$$

Substituting these into the conservation of energy equation:

$$mgh = \tfrac{1}{2}mr^2\omega^2 + \tfrac{1}{2}(2/5)mr^2\omega^2$$

$$mgh = \tfrac{1}{2}mr^2\omega^2 + (2/10)mr^2\omega^2$$

$$mgh = (7/10)mr^2\omega^2$$

Isolating ω:

$$\omega = \sqrt{(10gh\,/\,7r^2)}$$

$$\omega = \sqrt{[10\cdot(9.8 \text{ m/s}^2)\cdot(5.3 \text{ m})]\,/\,[7\cdot(1.7 \text{ m})^2]}$$

$$\omega = 5.1 \text{ rad/s}$$

3. A is correct.

There is no torque on the ball during the fall; therefore, its rotational speed does not change during the fall.

Therefore, the rotational kinetic energy just before the ball hits the floor is the same as it was when it was rolling on the horizontal surface.

The rotational kinetic energy when it was rolling on the surface can be calculated directly.

Recall that the moment of inertia of a solid sphere is:

$$I = 2/5\, mR^2$$

$$K_{rot} = \frac{1}{2} I \omega^2$$

$$K_{rot} = \frac{1}{2}(2/5)mR^2 \omega^2$$

Since the ball is rolling without slipping,

$$\omega = v / R$$

$$K_{rot} = \frac{1}{2}(2/5)mR^2(v / R)^2$$

$$K_{rot} = (2/10)mv^2$$

$$K_{rot} = (2/10)mv^2$$

$$K_{rot} = (2/10) \cdot (0.125 \text{ kg}) \cdot (4.5 \text{ m/s})^2$$

$$K_{rot} = 0.51 \text{ J}$$

4. D is correct.

The angular momentum of an object in circular motion is:

$$L = I\omega$$

where I is the moment of inertia with respect to the center of motion and ω is the angular speed.

The moment of inertia of a point mass is:

$$I = mr^2$$

The angular momentum is then:

$$L = mr^2 \omega$$

Angular speed is in rev/s.

Express in rad/s:

$$1.2 \text{ rev/s} \cdot (2\pi \text{ rad/rev}) = 7.540 \text{ rad/s}$$

Finally:

$$L = (0.38 \text{ kg}) \cdot (1.3 \text{ m})^2 \cdot (7.540 \text{ rad/s})$$

$$L = 4.8 \text{ kg m}^2/\text{s}$$

5. C is correct.

Conservation of angular momentum requires:

$L_f = L_i$

$I_f \omega_f = I_i \omega_i$

The final angular speed is:

$\omega_f = \omega_i (I_i / I_f)$

$\omega_f = (3.0 \text{ rev/s}) \cdot (5.0 \text{ kg} \cdot \text{m}^2) / (2.0 \text{ kg m}^2)$

$\omega_f = 7.5 \text{ rev/s}$

6. C is correct.

An external torque changes the angular velocity of a system:

$\alpha = \sum \tau / I$

Hence its angular momentum.

To maintain a constant angular momentum, the sum of external torques must be zero.

7. E is correct.

For a rotating circular object:

$\omega = v / r$

$\omega = v / (d / 2)$

$\omega = (4.0 \text{ m/s}) / [(0.60 \text{ m}) / 2]$

$\omega = 13.3 \text{ rad/s}$

8. A is correct.

$K = \frac{1}{2} I \omega^2$

The moment of inertia of a rod with respect to its "short axis" is:

$I = (1/12)ml^2$

$K = (1/24)ml^2\omega^2$

$K = (1/24) \cdot (0.4500 \text{ kg}) \cdot (1.20 \text{ m})^2 \cdot (3.60 \text{ rad/s})^2$

$K = 0.350 \text{ J}$

9. C is correct.

The moment of inertia can be found from the dynamic relation:

$\tau = I\alpha$

$I = \tau / \alpha$

where τ is the torque applied to the pulley, and α is the pulley's angular acceleration.

The torque is defined as:

$$FR \sin \theta$$

The force F is the tension force from the rope, R is the radius of the wheel, and $\theta = 90°$.

Thus, the torque is just the product of the tension of the rope and the radius of the pulley:

$$\tau = TR$$

Angular acceleration is related to acceleration of a point on the circumference of the pulley:

$$\alpha = a / R$$

where a is the linear acceleration at the circumference, and R is the pulley's radius.

Combining these two results, the moment of inertia is:

$$I = TR^2 / a$$

If the rope does not slip on the pulley, then the rope, and hence the hanging mass, also has an acceleration a.

To continue, find the acceleration and the tension.

The tension is found by applying Newton's Second Law to the hanging mass.

There are two forces on the hanging mass, the force of gravity pointing down, and the tension of the rope pointing up.

From Newton's Second Law (with down as the positive direction):

$$(mg - T) = ma$$

$$T = m(g - a)$$

With that, the moment of inertia becomes:

$$I = mR^2[(g - a) / a]$$

The acceleration can be found from the kinematic information given about the movement of the hanging mass.

The relation needed is:

$$\Delta y = \tfrac{1}{2}a(\Delta t)^2 + v_0(\Delta t)$$

$$a = 2\Delta y / (\Delta t)^2 = 2 \cdot (10 \text{ m}) / (2 \text{ s})^2$$

$$a = 5.000 \text{ m/s}^2$$

Calculate the moment of inertia:

$$I = (14 \text{ kg}) \cdot (2.0 \text{ m})^2 \cdot [(9.8 \text{ m/s}^2 - 5.000 \text{ m/s}^2) / (5.000 \text{ m/s}^2)]$$

$$I = 53.76 \text{ kg·m}^2$$

$$I = 53.8 \text{ kg·m}^2$$

10. B is correct.

The final speed of the string can be found if the acceleration is known:

$$v_f^2 = v_i^2 + 2ad = 0 + 2ad$$

$$v_f = \sqrt{(2ad)}$$

where d is the distance over which the acceleration occurs.

The acceleration of the string is related to the acceleration of the pulley:

$$a = r\alpha$$

The angular acceleration follows from the dynamical equation for the rotational motion:

$$\tau = I\alpha$$

The torque is the force applied times the radius of the pulley:

$$Fr = I\alpha$$

Combining these equations gives:

$$a = r^2 F / I$$

The final velocity of the string is:

$$v_f = \sqrt{(2r^2 Fd / I)}$$

$$v_f = \sqrt{[2 \cdot (0.125 \text{ m})^2 \cdot (5.00 \text{ N}) \cdot (1.25 \text{ m}) / (0.0352 \text{ kg} \cdot \text{m}^2)]}$$

$$v_f = 2.36 \text{ m/s}$$

11. A is correct.

The angle of every point remains fixed relative to all other points.

The tangential acceleration increases as one moves away from the center:

$$a_t = \alpha r$$

The radial (or centripetal) acceleration also depends on the distance r from the center:

$$a_c = \omega^2 r$$

The only choice that does not depend on r (i.e., the same for all the points in the object) is I.

12. E is correct.

Linear velocity is related to angular velocity by:

$$v = r\omega$$

13. C is correct.

For a rotating object:

$$K = \frac{1}{2}I\omega^2$$

The moment of inertia of a cylinder is:

$$I = \frac{1}{2}mr^2$$

Combining these:

$$K = \frac{1}{4}mr^2\omega^2$$

Solving for the angular speed:

$$\omega = \sqrt{(4K / mr^2)}$$

$$\omega = \sqrt{\{4\cdot(3.2 \times 10^7 \text{ J}) / [(400.0 \text{ kg}) (0.60 \text{ m})^2]\}}$$

$$\omega = 940 \text{ rad/s}$$

14. B is correct.

For a rotating object subject to a constant torque which has undergone a total angular displacement of $\Delta\theta$, the work done on the wheel is:

$$W = \tau\Delta\theta$$

Since work is the change in energy of the wheel from external forces, and since the wheel started with $E = 0$ ("from rest"), the final kinetic energy can be written as:

$$K = \tau\Delta\theta$$

By rotational kinematics:

$$\Delta\theta = \frac{1}{2}\alpha t^2$$

The equation of rotational dynamics is:

$$\tau = I\alpha, \text{ or } \alpha = \tau / I$$

So: $\Delta\theta = t^2\tau / 2I$

and $K = t^2\tau^2 / 2I$

(Note that this expression can be developed by finding the final angular velocity and using the definition of rotational kinetic energy.)

$$K = [(8.0 \text{ s})^2\cdot(3.0 \text{ N·m})^2] / [2\cdot(5.0 \text{ kg·m}^2)]$$

$$K = 58 \text{ J}$$

15. D is correct.

Tangential speed depends on the distance of the point from the fixed axis, so points at different radii have different tangential speeds.

Angular speed and acceleration of a rigid object does not depend on radius and is the same for all points (since each point on the object must rotate through the same angle in the same time interval, or else it would not be rigid).

16. D is correct.

The angular momentum of a rotating object is:

$$L = I\omega$$

For a cylinder:

$$I = \frac{1}{2}mr^2$$

Thus:

$$L = \frac{1}{2}mr^2\omega$$
$$L = (0.5)\cdot(15.0 \text{ kg})\cdot(1.4 \text{ m})^2\cdot(2.4 \text{ rad/s})$$
$$L = 35 \text{ kg m}^2/\text{s}$$

17. E is correct.

The speed of an accelerating object is related to the distance covered by the kinematic relation:

$$v_f^2 - v_i^2 = 2ad$$

In this case, the initial speed is zero.

So:

$$v_f = \sqrt{2ad}$$

Thus, find the linear acceleration of the disk.

An object is rolling down an incline experiences three forces, and hence three torques.

The forces are the force of gravity acting on the center of mass of the object, the normal force between the incline and the object, and the force of friction between the incline and the object.

If the origin is taken to be the center of the object, the force of gravity provides zero torque. This can be seen by noting that the distance between the origin and the point of application of the force is zero.

$$\tau_{gravity} = F_{gravity}r = mg(0) = 0$$

Similarly, the normal force contributes zero torque because the direction of the force is directed through the origin (pivot point).

$$\tau_{normal} = F_{normal}\, r \sin\theta = F_{normal}(R)\cdot(\sin 180°)$$

$$\tau_{normal} = F_{normal}(R)\cdot(0) = 0$$

Use a coordinate system in which the x-axis is parallel to the incline and the y-axis is perpendicular. The object is rolling in the positive x-direction.

The dynamical equation for linear motion along the x-direction is:

$F_{net} = ma$

$(mg \sin \theta - f) = ma$

Note that the normal force is only in the y-direction, and thus does not directly contribute to the acceleration in the x-direction.

The dynamical equation for rotational motion is:

$\tau_{net} = I\alpha$

$fR = I\alpha$ (Note that the frictional force is perpendicular to the r vector; $\sin 90° = 1$)

where R is the radius of the object, f is the force of friction, and I is the moment of inertia.

A relation coupling these two dynamical equations is needed.

The equation of constraint imposed by the restriction that the object rolls without slipping:

$\alpha = a / R$

To find the linear acceleration, use the equation of constraint to eliminate α from the rotational equation by replacing it with a / R:

$fR = I(a / R)$

The force of friction is of no interest, so rearrange this last expression:

$f = Ia / R^2$

Substitute this into the linear dynamic equation from above in place of f:

$(mg \sin \theta - Ia / R^2) = ma$

Solving this for a:

$a = mg \sin \theta / [m + (I / R^2)]$

$a = g \sin \theta / [1 + (I / mR^2)]$

For a disk, $I = \frac{1}{2}mR^2$, so:

$a = g \sin \theta / (1 + \frac{1}{2}) = (2/3)g \sin \theta$

Using this in the kinematic equation above:

$v_f = \sqrt{(4gd \sin \theta / 3)}$

$v_f = \sqrt{[(4/3) \cdot (9.8 \text{ m/s}^2) \cdot (3.0 \text{ m}) \cdot \sin (25°)]}$

$v_f = \sqrt{[(4/3) \cdot (9.8 \text{ m/s}^2) \cdot (3.0 \text{ m}) \cdot (0.4226)]}$

$v_f = 4.1$ m/s

18. A is correct.

The center of the tire is moving at velocity v, but the bottom of the tire is in contact with the ground without slipping, so the speed at the bottom of the tire is 0 m/s.

Thus, with respect to the ground, the tire is *instantaneously* rotating about the point of contact with the ground, and all points in the tire have the same instantaneous angular speed.

The top of the tire is twice the distance from the ground as the center.

For the center of the tire:

$v = r\omega$

At the top:

$v_{top} = (2r)\omega = 2(r\omega) = 2v$

19. D is correct.

The string does not slip. This means that the speed of the string is the same as the speed of a point on the circumference of the pulley.

The angular speed of the pulley (radius R) and the speed of a point on its circumference are related by:

$\omega = v / R$

$\omega = (5.0 \text{ m/s}) / (0.050 \text{ m})$

$\omega = 100 \text{ rad/s}$

20. D is correct.

One way of expressing the magnitude of angular momentum is:

$L = rp \sin \theta$

where r is the magnitude of the object's absolute position vector, p is the magnitude of the object's linear momentum and θ is the angle between the position vector and the momentum vector.

The magnitude of the position vector is:

$r = \sqrt{(r_x^2 + r_y^2)}$

$r = \sqrt{[(2.00 \text{ m})^2 + (3.10 \text{ m})^2]}$

$r = 3.689 \text{ m}$

Its angle with respect to the positive x axis is:

$\theta_r = \text{atan}(r_y / r_x)$

$\theta_r = \text{atan}(3.10 / 2.00)$

$\theta_r = 0.99783 \text{ rad} = 57.17°$

The magnitude of the momentum vector is:

$p = mv$

$p = (1.4 \text{ kg})(4.62 \text{ m/s})$

$p = 6.468 \text{ kg·m/s}$

The angle of the momentum vector is given in the problem:

$\theta_p = 45°$

Thus, the angle between the two vectors is:

$\theta = \theta_r - \theta_p$

$\theta = 57.17° - 45°$

$\theta = 12.17°$

The angular momentum is then:

$L = (3.689 \text{ m})\cdot(6.468 \text{ kg m/s})\cdot\sin (12.17°)$

$L = 5.0 \text{ kg}\cdot\text{m}^2/\text{s}$

21. B is correct.

Average angular acceleration is defined by:

$\alpha_{avg} = \Delta\omega / \Delta t$

$\alpha_{avg} = |(6.3 \text{ rad/s} - 10.0 \text{ rad/s}) / (5.0 \text{ s})|$

$\alpha_{avg} = 0.74 \text{ rad/s}$

22. D is correct.

The kinematic equation for angular velocity is:

$\omega_f = \omega_i + \alpha\Delta t$

Note that the sign of angular velocity is opposite from the sign of angular acceleration. That means that the wheel is slowing down.

For the final kinetic energy to be larger than the initial kinetic energy, the wheel must slow and continue beyond zero speed so that it gains speed in the opposite direction.

That is, the final angular velocity must be negative.

The kinetic energy of a rotating wheel is:

$K = ½I\omega^2$

The kinetic energy scales as the square of the angular speed.

To double the kinetic energy, the angular speed must increase by a factor of $\sqrt{2}$.

Thus: $\omega_f = -\omega_i\sqrt{2}$

Putting the result in the kinematic equation:

$-\omega_i\sqrt{2} = \omega_i + \alpha\Delta t$

Solving for Δt:

$\Delta t = -(1 + \sqrt{2})\omega_i / \alpha)$

$\Delta t = -(1 + \sqrt{2})\cdot(26.0 \text{ rad/s}) / (-0.43 \text{ rad/s}^2)$

$\Delta t = 146 \text{ s}$

23. B is correct.

Apply conservation of energy. Take the zero of gravitational potential energy to be the configuration when the disk is at the bottom of the ramp.

Conservation of energy demands:

$$E_{top} = E_{bottom}$$

At the top of the ramp, the disk is at rest, so the kinetic energy is zero.

The total energy at the top is:

$$E_{top} = K_{top} + U_{top}$$

$$E_{top} = 0 + mgh$$

At the bottom of the ramp, the gravitational potential energy is zero, and the kinetic energy is the sum of the linear and rotational kinetic energies:

$$E_{bottom} = K_{bottom} + U_{bottom}$$

$$E_{bottom} = K_{linear} + K_{rotational} + 0$$

$$E_{bottom} = \tfrac{1}{2} mv^2 + \tfrac{1}{2} I\omega^2$$

Final linear velocity is not given, but rather the final angular velocity is given.

Eliminate the linear velocity in favor of the angular velocity by applying the constraint that applies to a circular object rolling without slipping.

$$v = \omega r$$

$$E_{bottom} = \tfrac{1}{2}m\omega^2 r^2 + \tfrac{1}{2}I\omega^2$$

The moment of inertia of a disk is:

$$I = \tfrac{1}{2}mr^2$$

Thus:

$$E_{bottom} = \tfrac{1}{2}m\omega^2 r^2 + \tfrac{1}{2}(\tfrac{1}{2}\,mr^2)\omega^2$$

$$E_{bottom} = \tfrac{1}{2}m\omega^2 r^2 + \tfrac{1}{4}mr^2\omega^2$$

$$E_{bottom} = \tfrac{3}{4}m\omega^2 r^2$$

Combining results into the expression for conservation of energy:

$$mgh = \tfrac{3}{4}m\omega^2 r^2$$

or $$h = 3\omega^2 r^2 / 4g$$

Note that the mass has canceled, a common occurrence in mechanics problems.

The chance of error is reduced by proceeding algebraically (rather than plugging in numbers in the beginning), by which mass can be canceled.

Finally, note that diameter is given, not the radius:

$$r = d / 2 = 1.6 \text{ m}$$

$$h = [3(4.27 \text{ rad/s})^2 \cdot (1.60 \text{ m})^2] / [4(9.8 \text{ m/s}^2)]$$

$$h = 3.57 \text{ m}$$

24. A is correct.

The direction of angular velocity is taken by convention to be given by applying the right-hand rule to the rotation.

In the case of a wheel of a forward-moving bicycle, that direction is to the left of the rider.

25. A is correct.

Angular acceleration can be found if linear acceleration is calculated from:

$\alpha = a / R$

The linear acceleration follows from the kinematic relationship:

$v_f^2 - v_i^2 = 2ad$

In this case:

$v_f = 0$

$-v_i^2 = 2ad$

Only the absolute value of the acceleration is needed, so drop the minus sign and solve for a:

$a = v_i^2 / 2d$

The angular acceleration is:

$\alpha = v_i^2 / 2dR$

$\alpha = (8.4 \text{ m/s})^2 / [2(115.0 \text{ m})(0.34 \text{ m})]$

$\alpha = 0.90 \text{ rad/s}^2$

26. A is correct.

For a rotating object:

$K = \frac{1}{2}I\omega^2$

The moment of inertia of a cylinder is:

$I = \frac{1}{2}mr^2$

Combining these:

$K = \frac{1}{4}mr^2\omega^2$

The angular speed is given in rpm, but needs to be in rad/s:

33.4 rpm·(1 min / 60 s)·(2π rad/rev) = 3.498 rad/s

Thus:

$K = (0.25)·(3.0 \text{ kg})·(0.10 \text{ m})^2·(3.489 \text{ rad/s})^2$

$K = 0.091 \text{ J}$

27. A is correct.

The angular momentum of a spinning object can be written as:

$$L = I\omega$$

The moment of inertia of a long thin uniform object of length l about an axis through the center perpendicular to the long axis is:

$$I = (1/12)ml^2$$

Giving:

$$L = (1/12)ml^2\omega$$
$$L = (1/12) \cdot (0.1350 \text{ kg}) \cdot (1.000 \text{ m})^2 \cdot (3.5 \text{ rad/s})$$
$$L = 0.0394 \text{ kg} \cdot \text{m}^2/\text{s}$$

28. C is correct.

The period of a rotating object can be expressed as:

$$T = 2\pi / \omega$$

ω can be extracted from the definition of centripetal force:

$$F = mv^2 / r$$

Combining this with the relationship $v = \omega r$ gives:

$$F = mr\omega^2$$

Thus:

$$\omega = \sqrt{(F / mr)}$$

Then:

$$T = 2\pi\sqrt{(mr / F)}$$
$$T = 2\pi\sqrt{[(23.0 \text{ kg})(1.3 \text{ m}) / (51.0 \text{ N})]}$$
$$T = 4.8 \text{ s}$$

29. C is correct.

Angular acceleration is:

$$\alpha = \Delta\omega / \Delta t$$
$$\alpha = (38.0 \text{ rad/s} - 0.00 \text{ rad/s}) / (10.0 \text{ s})$$
$$\alpha = 3.80 \text{ rad/s}$$

The other information given in the question is not needed.

30. C is correct.

The magnitude of torque can be expressed as:

$$\tau = rF \sin \theta$$

where r is the distance from the origin (taken here to be the location of the pivot point) to the point of application of the force F, and θ is the angle between the position vector of the point of application and the force vector.

$$\tau = (0.63 \text{ m}) \cdot (17.0 \text{ N}) \cdot \sin (45°)$$

$$\tau = 7.6 \text{ N m}$$

31. D is correct.

Use conservation of energy.

Take the zero of potential energy to be the configuration in which the sphere is at the bottom. The potential energy at the bottom is zero.

The disk starts from rest, so the kinetic energy at the top is zero.

With that:

$$mgh = K_{\text{linear}} + K_{\text{rotation}}$$

$$mgh = \tfrac{1}{2}mv^2 + \tfrac{1}{2}I\omega^2$$

For a disk, $I = \tfrac{1}{2}mr^2$

Because the disk rolls without slipping, $v = r\omega$.

Substituting these into the conservation of energy equation:

$$mgh = \tfrac{1}{2}m(r^2\omega^2) + \tfrac{1}{2}(\tfrac{1}{2}mr^2)\omega^2$$

$$mgh = \tfrac{1}{2}mr^2\omega^2 + \tfrac{1}{4}mr^2\omega^2$$

$$mgh = \tfrac{3}{4}mr^2\omega^2$$

Isolating h:

$$h = 3r^2\omega^2 \,/\, 4g$$

$$h = [3 \cdot (1.60 \text{ m})^2 \cdot (4.27 \text{ rad/s})^2] \,/\, [4 \cdot (9.8 \text{ m/s}^2)]$$

$$h = 3.57 \text{ m}$$

32. D is correct.

The moment of inertia is proportional to the square of the distance of an object from the center of rotation.

As Paul moves toward the center, the moment of inertia decreases.

Angular momentum, $L = I\omega$ is conserved.

As I decreases, ω, the angular speed increases to compensate.

---

33. B is correct.

Converting units:

210.0 rpm·(1 min / 60 s)·(2π rad/revolution) = 22.0 rad/s

34. C is correct.

Use the conservation of energy:

$E_f = E_i$

$KE_f + PE_f = KE_i + PE_i$

Take the zero of potential energy at the initial height, so that PE_i is zero.

The kinetic energy of a rolling object is the sum of the kinetic energy of translation plus the kinetic energy of rotation:

$KE = \frac{1}{2}mv^2 + \frac{1}{2}I\omega^2$

If the object rolls without slipping, as is the case here, then:

$v = r\omega$, where R is the radius of the sphere.

The moment of inertia of a sphere is:

$I = (2/5)m\omega^2$

With these, write the kinetic energy of a sphere that rolls without slipping:

$KE = \frac{1}{2}mv^2 + \frac{1}{2}(2/5)mr^2(v/r)^2$

$KE = \frac{1}{2}mv^2 + (1/5)mv^2$

$KE = (7/10)mv^2$

Conservation of energy becomes:

$(7/10)mv_f^2 + mgh = (7/10)mv_i^2$

Canceling the mass and solving for the final speed:

$v_f = \sqrt{[v_i^2 - (10/7)gh]}$

The height, h, is related to the distance travelled and the angle of incline:

$h = d \sin \theta$

So:

$v_f = \sqrt{[v_i^2 - (10/7)gd \sin \theta]}$

$v_f = \sqrt{[(5.5 \text{ m/s})^2 - (10/7)·(9.8 \text{ m/s}^2)·(3.0 \text{ m})·\sin (25°)]}$

$v_f = \sqrt{[(5.5 \text{ m/s})^2 - (10/7)·(9.8 \text{ m/s}^2)·(3.0 \text{ m})·(0.4226)]}$

$v_f = 3.5 \text{ m/s}$

35. D is correct.

The dynamical relation for rotational motion is:

$\tau = I\alpha$

$I = \tau / \alpha$

where τ is the torque applied to the wheel, and α is the wheel's angular acceleration.

The torque is the product of the force and the radius of the pulley:

$\tau = FR$ (note that $\sin \theta = 1$, since $\theta = 90°$ [the problem mentions the force is applied tangentially]).

So:

$I = \tau / \alpha$

$I = FR / \alpha$

$I = (16.88 \text{ N})\cdot(0.340 \text{ m}) / (1.20 \text{ rad/s}^2)$

$I = 4.78 \text{ kg·m}^2$

36. B is correct. The energy required to bring a rotating object to rest is:

$E = \frac{1}{2}I\omega_0^2$

The moment of inertia of a cylinder is:

$I = \frac{1}{2}mr^2$

So, the energy needed to stop the object is:

$E = \frac{1}{4}mr^2\omega_0^2$

Solving for the mass:

$m = 4E / r^2\omega_0^2$

We are given the angular speed in rpm, but should be in rad/s:

$500.0 \text{ rpm}\cdot(1 \text{ min} / 60 \text{ sec})\cdot(2\pi \text{ rad} / 1 \text{ rev}) = 52.36 \text{ rad/s}$

The mass of the object is:

$m = 4(3900 \text{ J}) / (1.2 \text{ m})^2\cdot(52.36 \text{ rad/s})^2$

$m = 4.0 \text{ kg}$

37. C is correct. The torque at P_2 due to the weight of the billboard is:

$\tau = r_{perp}F = r_{perp}mg$

where r_{perp} is the perpendicular distance between P_2 and the line of application of the force.

Here, the weight of the billboard acts as if all of the mass is concentrated at the center of mass, which is the center of the billboard. Thus, the line of application of the force of gravity is P_1P_3, the vertical line that passes through P_1 and P_3.

The length r_{perp} is the length of the horizontal line segment between P_2 and the line of application of the force (P_1P_3). This line segment is perpendicular to P_1P_3 and intersects P_1P_3 at point P_4.

To find r_{perp} note that the triangle $P_1P_2P_3$ is similar to the triangle formed by $P_1P_4P_2$. The ratios of the lengths of corresponding sides of similar triangles are equal.

Apply this by forming the ratio of the length of the long side to the length of the hypotenuse of these two triangles:

$$h \,/\, \sqrt{(h^2 + w^2)} = r_{\text{perp}} \,/\, w$$

$$r_{\text{perp}} = hw \,/\, \sqrt{(h^2 + w^2)}$$

Giving an expression for torque:

$$\tau = mg[hw \,/\, \sqrt{(h^2 + w^2)}]$$

$$\tau = (5.0 \text{ kg}){\cdot}(9.8 \text{ m/s}^2){\cdot}(0.20 \text{ m}){\cdot}(0.11 \text{ m}) \,/\, \sqrt{[(0.20 \text{ m})^2 + (0.11 \text{ m})^2]}$$

$$\tau = 4.7 \text{ N m}$$

38. B is correct.

An object is rolling down an incline experiences three forces, and hence three torques.

The forces are the force of gravity acting on the center of mass of the object, the normal force between the incline and the object, and the force of friction between the incline and the object.

If the origin is taken to be the center of the object, the force of gravity provides zero torque.

This can be seen by noting that the distance between the origin and the point of application of the force is zero.

$$\tau_{\text{gravity}} = F_{\text{gravity}}r = mg(0) = 0$$

Similarly, the normal force contributes zero torque because the direction of the force is directed through the origin (pivot point).

$$\tau_{normal} = F_{normal}\,\text{r}\,\sin\theta = F_{normal}(R){\cdot}(\sin 180°) = F_{normal}(R){\cdot}(0) = 0$$

Use a coordinate system in which the x-axis is parallel to the incline and the y-axis is perpendicular. The object is rolling in the positive x-direction.

The dynamical equation for linear motion along the x-direction is:

$$F_{\text{net}} = ma$$

$$(mg \sin\theta - f) = ma$$

Note that the normal force is only in the y-direction, and thus does not directly contribute to the acceleration in the x-direction.

The dynamical equation for rotational motion is:

$\tau_{net} = I\alpha$

$fR = I\alpha$ (Note that the frictional force is perpendicular to the r vector; $\sin 90° = 1$)

where R is the radius of the object, f is the force of friction, and I is the moment of inertia.

A relation coupling these two dynamical equations is necessary.

The equation of constraint imposed by the restriction that the object rolls without slipping.

$\alpha = a / R$

To find the linear acceleration, use the equation of constraint to eliminate α from the rotational equation by replacing it with a / R:

$fR = I(a / R)$

The force of friction is of no interest, so rearrange this last expression:

$f = Ia / R^2$

Substitute this into the linear dynamic equation from above in place of f:

$(mg \sin \theta - Ia / R^2) = ma$

Solving this for a:

$a = mg \sin \theta / [m + (I / R^2)]$

$a = g \sin \theta / [1 + (I / mR^2)]$

For a sphere,

$I = (2/5)mR^2$

So: $\quad a_{sphere} = g \sin \theta / [1 + (2/5)]$

$a_{sphere} = (5/7)g \sin \theta$

$a_{sphere} = (0.714)g \sin \theta$

For the disk,

$I = \frac{1}{2} mR^2$

So: $\quad a_{disk} = g \sin \theta / (1 + \frac{1}{2})$

$a_{disk} = (2/3)g \sin \theta$

$a_{disk} = (0.667)g \sin \theta$

For the hoop,

$I = mR^2$

So: $\quad a_{hoop} = g \sin \theta / (1 + 1)$

$a_{hoop} = (1/2)g \sin \theta$

$a_{hoop} = (0.500)g \sin \theta$

The object with the largest acceleration will reach the bottom first.

The order is sphere, disk, hoop.

39. B is correct.

The kinetic energy of a rotation object is:

$K = \frac{1}{2}I\omega^2$

The moment of inertia is given in SI units, but the angular speed is in rpm, which is not an SI unit.

Convert:

96.0 rpm·(1 m/ 60 s)·(2π rad/rev) = 10.05 rad/s

$K = (0.5)\cdot(6.0 \times 10^{-3}$ kg·m^2)·(10.05 rad/s)^2

$K = 0.30$ J

40. D is correct. If a wheel of radius r rolls without slipping on the pavement, the relationship between angular speed ω and translational speed is:

$v = r\omega$

$\omega = v / r$

$\omega = (6.00$ m/s) / (0.120 m)

$\omega = 50.00$ rad/s

Converting this to rpm:

$\omega = (50.00$ rad/s)·(1 rev / 2π rad)·(60 s / 1 min)

$\omega = 477.5$ rpm = 478 rpm

41. C is correct. Her moment of inertia does not remain constant because the radial position of her hands is changing. Angular momentum does remain constant because there is no torque on her, assuming the ice is frictionless.

Her kinetic energy changes. To see this, notice that her hands initially execute uniform circular motion, and hence there is no tangential force. As long as this condition is maintained, her kinetic energy will be constant.

However, *as she pulls her hands in* they are no longer in a uniform circular motion. During this time, there will be a tangential component of force, and work will be done.

Another way to think about it is to recognize that because L is conserved,

$L_0 = L_f$

$I_0\omega_0 = I_f\omega_f$

I will decrease by some amount, and ω will multiply by that same amount, e.g., I halves and ω doubles.

When examining $KE = \frac{1}{2}I\omega^2$, I has gone down by half, but ω has doubled.

Since KE depends on ω squared, the change to ω has a greater impact on KE. KE will go up.

42. D is correct.

There are two perpendicular components to Tanya's acceleration. Centripetal acceleration:

$$a_c = r\omega^2$$

and tangential acceleration:

$$a_t = r\alpha$$

Since these two acceleration components are perpendicular to each other, find the magnitude of the total linear acceleration:

$$a = \sqrt{(a_c^2 + a_t^2)}$$
$$a = \sqrt{[(r\omega^2)^2 + (r\alpha)^2]}$$
$$a = r\sqrt{(\omega^4 + \alpha^2)}$$
$$a = (4.65 \text{ m})\cdot\sqrt{[(1.25 \text{ rad/s})^4 + (0.745 \text{ rad/s}^2)^2]}$$
$$a = 8.05 \text{ m/s}^2$$

43. C is correct.

For a rotating object:

$$\Delta\theta = \omega\Delta t$$

The angular speed is given in rpm, but needs to be in deg/s:

$$33.0 \text{ rpm}\cdot(1 \text{ min} / 60 \text{ s})\cdot(360 \text{ deg} / \text{rev}) = 198.0 \text{ deg/s}$$

$$\Delta\theta = (198.0 \text{ deg/s})\cdot(0.32 \text{ s})$$

$$\Delta\theta = 63°$$

44. C is correct.

The question asks to find the *magnitude* of the force of the floor on the bottom of the ladder. Two forces are acting on the bottom of the ladder: the normal force of the floor, N, which acts in the vertical direction, and the force of friction, f, which acts horizontally.

These two forces are directed in mutually perpendicular directions.

So, the magnitude of the net force of the floor on the bottom of the ladder is:

$$F_{\text{net, bottom}} = \sqrt{(N^2 + f^2)}$$

The values of N and f can be found by applying the laws of rotational and linear static equilibrium.

Assume the ladder is static (not moving), but this is not a valid assumption until it is known whether or not the force of friction exceeds the limit imposed by static friction. This will be verified at the end.

If the ladder is in equilibrium, the sum of the forces in both the x- and y-directions is zero, and the sum of the torques is zero:

$$\sum F_x = 0;$$

$$\sum F_y = 0;$$

$$\sum \tau = 0$$

The force equations are straightforward to fill in:

$$\sum F_x = F_w - f = 0$$

$$\sum F_y = N - Mg - mg = 0$$

where F_w is the normal force from the wall on the top of the ladder, M is the mass of the hanging block, and m is the mass of the ladder.

Note that since in the problem statement the wall is "smooth," there is no frictional force from the wall on the ladder.

The $\sum F_y$ equation has only one unknown quantity and can be solved for N:

$$N = (M + m)g = (80\text{kg} + 50\text{kg}) \cdot (9.8\text{m/s}^2) = 1{,}274 \text{ N}$$

For the torque equation, choose the origin to be the point where the top of the ladder touches the wall. With that choice, the torque due to the normal force of the wall is zero, and the torque due to the hanging block is also zero (since these forces are exerted right at the origin).

There are three non-zero torques.

One is the torque due to gravity on the ladder. This acts as if all of the mass of the ladder is concentrated at the center of mass.

The next torque is due to the normal force of the floor on the bottom of the ladder, and the third is the force of friction acting on the bottom of the ladder.

Using the general formula for torque:

$$\tau = Fr \sin \phi,$$

where F is the force, r is the distance from the origin to the point where the force is being applied, and ϕ is the angle between the force vector and the r vector (which points from the origin to the point where the force is being applied):

$$\sum \tau = 0 + 0 - mg(L / 2) \sin \beta - fL \sin \alpha + NL \sin \beta = 0$$

where m is the mass of the ladder and α and β are the angles in the figure shown.

Take counterclockwise torques to be positive and clockwise torques to be negative.

Use trigonometry to find α and β:

$$\alpha = \sin^{-1}(h / L) = \sin^{-1}(3.7 / 5) = 47.73°$$

$$\beta = 90° - \alpha = 42.27°$$

There is only one unknown quantity in the torque equation, so, dividing by L and rearranging, solve for f:

$$f \sin \alpha = N \sin \beta - \tfrac{1}{2}mg \sin \beta$$

$$f = [(N - \tfrac{1}{2}mg) \cdot \sin \beta] / \sin \alpha$$

$$f = [1274 \text{ N} - \tfrac{1}{2}(50 \text{ kg}) \cdot (9.8 \text{ m/s}^2) \cdot (\sin 42.27°)] / [\sin 47.73°]$$

$$f = 935.3 \text{ N}$$

Calculate the magnitude of the force on the bottom of the latter due to the floor:

$$F_{\text{net, bottom}} = \sqrt{(N^2 + f^2)}$$

$$F_{\text{net, bottom}} = \sqrt{[(1274 \text{ N})^2 + (935.3 \text{ N})^2]}$$

$$F_{\text{net, bottom}} = 1580 \text{ N}$$

Finally, check to see if the force of friction is lower than the limit imposed by static friction.

$$f_{\text{max}} = \mu_s N = (0.750) \cdot (1274 \text{ N}) = 955 \text{ N}$$

The calculated value for the force of static friction is 935.3 N, lower than the limit imposed by static friction, so the assumption that the system is in static equilibrium is valid.

If this number had been lower than the value of f, the static frictional force would *not* be able to hold the ladder stationary.

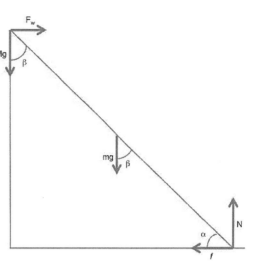

45. B is correct.

The maximum displacement occurs when the acceleration stops the forward motion, and the wheel reverses direction.

Since:

$$\theta_0 = 0, \, \Delta\theta = \theta - 0 = \theta$$

The kinematic relation is:

$$\omega_f^2 - \omega_i^2 = 2\alpha\theta$$

The final angular speed is zero at the instant that the wheel changes direction.

$$-\omega_i^2 = 2\alpha\theta$$

Thus, the angular displacement at that instant is:

$$\theta = -(\omega_i^2 / 2\alpha)$$

$$\theta = -(29.0 \text{ rad/s})^2 / [2 \cdot (-0.52 \text{ rad/s}^2)]$$

$$\theta = 809 \text{ rad}$$

46. C is correct.

The simplest way to determine the direction of the angular momentum for a rotating object is to use the *right-hand rule*.

Take the fingers of your right hand and curl them in the direction that the object is rotating, and stick your thumb out perpendicular to your fingers (as in a "thumbs-up" or "thumbs down" signal). The direction your thumb points in the direction of the angular momentum – in this case, down.

For a mathematical approach, use the definition $L = r \times p$ applied to a point on the outer edge of the object.

Taking a point on the disk along the positive *x*-axis, the position vector *r* is in the positive *x*-direction, and the momentum vector *p* is in the positive *z*-direction.

The cross-product of these two vectors points down in the negative *y*-direction.

Waves and Periodic Motion – Explanations

1. B is correct.

Frequency is the measure of the number of cycles per second a wave experiences, which is independent of the wave's amplitude.

2. D is correct.

Hooke's Law:

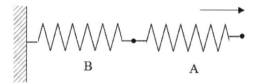

$$F = kx$$

It is known that the force on each spring must be equal if they are in static equilibrium, therefore:

$$F_A = F_B$$

Therefore, the expression can be written as:

$$k_A L_A = k_B L_B$$

Solve for the spring constant of spring B:

$$k_B = (k_A L_A) / L_B$$

3. D is correct.

In a longitudinal wave, particles of a material are displaced parallel to the direction of the wave.

4. C is correct.

$$\text{speed} = \text{wavelength} \times \text{frequency}$$

$$v = \lambda f$$

$$v = (0.25 \text{ m}) \cdot (1{,}680 \text{ Hz})$$

$$v = 420 \text{ m/s}$$

5. A is correct.

$$E_{stored} = PE = \tfrac{1}{2}kA^2$$

Stored energy is potential energy.

In a simple harmonic motion (e.g., a spring), the potential energy is:

$$PE = \tfrac{1}{2}kx^2 \text{ or } \tfrac{1}{2}kA^2,$$

where k is a constant and A (or x) is the distance from equilibrium

A is the amplitude of a wave in simple harmonic motion (SHM).

6. E is correct.

The spring will oscillate around its new equilibrium position (which is 3 cm below the equilibrium position with no mass hanging) with period $T = 2\pi\sqrt{(m / k)}$ since it's a mass-spring system undergoing simple harmonic motion.

To find k, consider how much the spring stretched when the mass was hung from it.

Since the spring found a new equilibrium point 3 cm below its natural length, the upwards force from the spring (F_s) must balance the downwards gravitational force (F_g) at that displacement:

$|F_s| = |F_g|$

$kd = mg$

$k(0.03 \text{ m}) = (11 \text{ kg}) \cdot (9.8 \text{ m/s}^2)$

$k = 3593 \text{ N/m}$

Now, solve for T:

$T = 2\pi\sqrt{(m / k)}$

$T = 2\pi\sqrt{(11 \text{ kg} / 3593 \text{ N/m})}$

$T = 0.35 \text{ s}$

The frequency is the reciprocal of the period:

$f = 1 / T$

$f = 1 / (0.35 \text{ s})$

$f = 2.9 \text{ Hz}$

7. C is correct. $T = 1 / f$

8. D is correct.

The period of a pendulum:

$T = 2\pi\sqrt{(L / g)}$

The period only depends on the pendulum's length and gravity.

In an elevator, the apparent force of gravity only changes if the elevator is accelerating in either direction.

9. A is correct. The period is the reciprocal of the frequency:

$T = 1 / f$

$T = 1 / 100 \text{ Hz}$

$T = 0.01 \text{ s}$

10. E is correct.

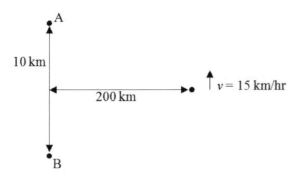

Convert *v* to m/s:

$v = (15 \text{ km}/1 \text{ h}) \cdot (1 \text{ h}/60 \text{ min}) \cdot (1 \text{ min}/60 \text{ s}) \cdot (10^3 \text{ m}/1 \text{ km})$

$v = 4.2 \text{ m/s}$

Convert frequency to λ:

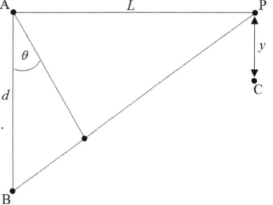

$\lambda = c / f$

$\lambda = (3 \times 10^8 \text{ m/s}) / (4.7 \times 10^6 \text{ Hz})$

$\lambda = 63.8 \text{ m}$

According to Young's Equation:

$\lambda = yd / mL$, where m = 0, 1, 2, 3, 4…

Solve for *y* by rearranging to isolate *y*:

$y = \lambda Lm / d$

y = distance travelled by the ship:

$y = vt$

Since the first signal came at the point of maximum intensity, m = 0 at that time, at the next maximum m = 1.

Therefore:

$t = L\lambda / vd$

$t = (200{,}000 \text{ m}) \cdot (63.8 \text{ m}) / (4.2 \text{ m/s}) \cdot (10{,}000 \text{ m})$

$t = 304 \text{ s}$

Convert time from seconds to minutes:

$t = (304 \text{ s}) \cdot (1 \text{ min}/60 \text{ s})$

$t = 5.06 \text{ min} \approx 5.1 \text{ min}$

For all m values greater than 1, the calculated times are beyond the answer choices so 5.1 min is the correct answer.

11. D is correct.

The tension in the rope is given by the equation:

$$T = (mv^2) / L$$

where v is the velocity of the wave and L is the length of the rope.

Substituting:

$$v = L / t$$

$$T = [m(L / t)^2] / L$$

$$T = mL / t^2$$

$$t^2 = mL / T$$

$$t = \sqrt{(mL / T)}$$

$$t = \sqrt{[(2.31 \text{ kg}) \cdot (10.4 \text{ m}) / 74.4 \text{ N}]}$$

$$t = \sqrt{(0.323 \text{ s}^2)} = 0.57 \text{ s}$$

12. A is correct.

$$\omega_A = 2\omega_B$$

$$\omega_B = \sqrt{g / l_B}$$

Therefore:

$$l_B = g / \omega^2_B$$

Similarly, for A:

$$l_A = g / \omega^2_A$$

$$l_A = g / (2\omega_B)^2$$

$$l_A = \frac{1}{4}g / \omega^2_B$$

$$l_A = \frac{1}{4}l_B$$

13. B is correct.

$$F = -kx$$

Since the motion is simple harmonic, the restoring force is proportional to displacement.

Therefore, if the displacement is 5 times greater, then so is the restoring force.

14. C is correct.

$$\text{Period} = (60 \text{ s}) / (10 \text{ oscillations})$$

$$T = 6 \text{ s}$$

The period is the time for one oscillation.

If 10 oscillations take 60 s, then one oscillation takes 6 s.

15. E is correct. Conservation of Energy:

total ME = ΔKE + ΔPE = constant

$\frac{1}{2}mv^2 + \frac{1}{2}kx^2$ = constant

16. B is correct.

A displacement from the position of maximum elongation to the position of maximum compression represents *half* a cycle. If it takes 1 s, then the time required for a complete cycle is 2 s.

$f = 1 / T$

$f = 1 / 2$ s

$f = 0.5$ Hz

17. C is correct. Sound waves are longitudinal waves.

18. E is correct.

speed = wavelength × frequency

speed = wavelength / period

$v = \lambda / T$

$\lambda = vT$

$\lambda = (362$ m/s$)\cdot(0.004$ s$)$

$\lambda = 1.5$ m

19. A is correct.

$a = -A\omega^2 \cos(\omega t)$

where A is the amplitude or displacement from the resting position.

20. D is correct. The acceleration of a simple harmonic oscillation is:

$a = -A\omega^2 \cos(\omega t)$

Its maximum occurs when $\cos(\omega t)$ is equal to 1

$a_{max} = -\omega^2 x$

If ω is doubled:

$a = -(2\omega)^2 x$

$a = -4\omega^2 x$

The maximum value of acceleration changes by a factor of 4.

21. B is correct.

Resonant frequency of a spring and mass system in any orientation:

$\omega = \sqrt{(k / m)}$

$f = \omega / 2\pi$

$T = 1 / f$

$T = 2\pi\sqrt{(m / k)}$

Period of a spring does not depend on gravity.

The period remains constant because only mass and the spring constant affect the period.

22. E is correct.

$v = \lambda f$

$\lambda = v / f$

An increase in v and a decrease in f must increase λ.

23. B is correct.

Frequency is the measure of oscillations or vibrations per second.

frequency = 60 vibrations in 1 s

frequency = 60 Hz

speed = 30 m / 1 s

speed = 30 m/s

24. A is correct.

$T = (mv^2) / L$

$m = TL / v^2$

$m = (60 \text{ N})\cdot(16 \text{ m}) / (40 \text{ m/s})^2$

$m = (960 \text{ N·m}) / (1{,}600 \text{ m}^2/\text{s}^2)$

$m = 0.6 \text{ kg}$

25. E is correct. Amplitude is independent of frequency.

26. C is correct.

$f = \text{\# cycles} / \text{time}$

$f = 60 \text{ drips} / 40 \text{ s}$

$f = 1.5 \text{ Hz}$

27. D is correct. Transverse waves are characterized by their crests and valleys, which are caused by the particles of the wave traveling "up and down" with respect to the lateral movement of the wave.

The particles in longitudinal waves travel parallel to the direction of the wave.

28. B is correct. The velocity vs. time graph shows that at $t = 0$, the velocity of the particle is positive, and the speed is increasing.

When speed increases, velocity and acceleration point in the same direction.

Therefore, the acceleration is non-zero and positive. Only graph B displays a positive acceleration at $t = 0$.

29. E is correct.

The speed of a wave is determined by the characteristics of the medium (and the type of wave). Speed is independent of amplitude.

30. A is correct.

$f = 1 / \text{period}$

$f = \text{\# cycles} / \text{second}$

$f = 1 \text{ cycle} / 2 \text{ s}$

$f = \frac{1}{2} \text{ Hz}$

31. B is correct.

$f = v / \lambda$

$\lambda = v / f$

$\lambda = (340 \text{ m/s}) / (2{,}100 \text{ Hz})$

$\lambda = 0.16 \text{ m}$

32. D is correct.

$\text{Period (T)} = 2\pi\sqrt{(L / g)}$

The period is independent of the mass.

33. E is correct.

$v = \omega x$

$\omega = v / x$

$\omega = (15 \text{ m/s}) / (2.5 \text{ m})$

$\omega = 6.0 \text{ rad/s}$

34. D is correct.

Unpolarized light on a polarizer reduces the intensity by ½.

$$I = (½)I_0$$

After that, the light is further reduced in intensity by the second filter.

Law of Malus:

$$I = I_0 \cos^2 \theta$$

$$(0.14\ I_0) = (0.5\ I_0) \cos^2 \theta$$

$$0.28 = \cos^2 \theta$$

$$\cos^{-1} \sqrt{(0.28)} = \theta$$

$$\theta = 58°$$

$I_0 = 1$ $I_1 = 0.5I_0$ $I_2 = 0.14I_0$

35. C is correct.

At a maximum distance from equilibrium, the energy in the system is potential energy, and the speed is zero.

Therefore, kinetic energy is also zero.

Since there is no kinetic energy, the mass has no velocity.

36. D is correct.

$$v = \lambda f$$

$$f = v / \lambda$$

$$f = (240 \text{ m/s}) / (0.1 \text{ m})$$

$$f = 2,400 \text{ Hz}$$

37. B is correct.

In a transverse wave, the vibrations of particles are perpendicular to the direction of travel of the wave.

Transverse waves have crests and troughs that move along the wave.

In a longitudinal wave, the vibrations of particles are parallel to the direction of travel of the wave.

Longitudinal waves have compressions and rarefactions that move along the wave.

38. C is correct.

$v = \sqrt{(T/\mu)}$

where μ is the linear density of the wire.

$T = v^2\mu$

$\mu = \rho A$

where A is the cross-sectional area of the wire and equals πr^2.

$\mu = (2,700 \text{ kg/m}^3)\pi(4.6 \times 10^{-3} \text{ m})^2$

$\mu = 0.18 \text{ kg/m}$

$T = (36 \text{ m/s})^2 \cdot (0.18 \text{ kg/m}) = 233 \text{ N}$

39. D is correct.

Refraction is the change in the direction of a wave, caused by the change in the wave's speed. Examples of waves include sound waves and light waves.

Refraction is seen most often when a wave passes from one medium to a different medium (e.g., from air to water and vice versa).

40. C is correct.

$f = \text{\# cycles / second}$

$f = 2 \text{ cycles / 1 s}$

$f = 2 \text{ Hz}$

41. A is correct.

Pitch is how the brain perceives frequency. Pitch becomes higher as frequency increases.

42. C is correct.

The KE is maximum when the spring is neither stretched nor compressed.

If the object is bobbing, KE is maximum at the midpoint between fully stretched and fully compressed because this is where all of the spring's energy is KE rather than a mix of KE and PE.

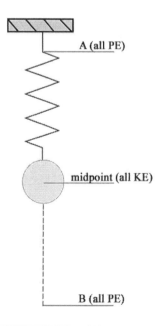

43. B is correct.

Torque = $rF \sin \theta$

$F = ma$, substitute mg for F

$\tau = rmg \sin \theta$

$\tau = (1 \text{ m}){\cdot}(0.5 \text{ kg}){\cdot}(10 \text{ m/s}^2) \sin 60°$

$\tau = (5 \text{ kg}{\cdot}\text{m}^2/\text{s}^2) \times 0.87$

$\tau = 4.4 \text{ N}{\cdot}\text{m}$

44. E is correct.

The Doppler effect can be observed to occur in all types of waves.

45. A is correct.

$v = \sqrt{(T / \mu)}$ where μ is the linear density of the wire.

$F_T = ma$

$F_T = (2{,}500 \text{ kg}){\cdot}(10 \text{ m/s}^2)$

$F_T = 25{,}000 \text{ N}$

$v = \sqrt{(25{,}000 \text{ N} / 0.65 \text{ kg/m})}$

$v = 196 \text{ m/s}$

The weight of the wire can be assumed to be negligible compared to the cement block.

46. B is correct.

$f = \frac{1}{2}\pi[\sqrt{(g / L)}]$

Frequency is independent of mass

47. A is correct.

$T = 2\pi\sqrt{(L / g)}]$

$T = 2\pi\sqrt{(3.3 \text{ m} / 10 \text{ m/s}^2)}$

$T = 3.6 \text{ s}$

48. C is correct.

$f = (1/2\pi)\sqrt{(k / m)}$

If k increases by a factor of 2, then f increases by a factor of $\sqrt{2}$ (or 1.41).

Increasing by a factor of 1.41 or 41%

49. D is correct.

In a simple harmonic motion, the acceleration is greatest at the ends of motions (points A and D) where velocity is zero.

Velocity is greatest at the nadir where acceleration is equal to zero (point C).

50. A is correct.

At the lowest point, the KE is at a maximum, and the PE is at a minimum.

The loss of gravitational PE equals the gain in KE:

$mgh = \frac{1}{2}mv^2$, cancel m from both sides of the expression

$gh = \frac{1}{2}v^2$

$(10 \text{ m/s}^2) \cdot (10 \text{ m}) = \frac{1}{2}v^2$

$(100 \text{ m}^2/\text{s}^2) = \frac{1}{2}v^2$

$200 \text{ m}^2/\text{s}^2 = v^2$

$v = 14$ m/s

51. A is correct.

Pitch is a psychophysical phenomenon when the sensation of a frequency is commonly referred to as the pitch of a sound.

A perception of high-pitch sound corresponds to a high-frequency sound wave, and a low-pitch sound corresponds to a low-frequency sound wave.

Amplitude plays no role, and speed is constant.

52. C is correct.

Because wind is blowing in the reference frame of both the train and the observer, it does not need to be taken into account.

$f_{observed} = [v_{sound} / (v_{sound} - v_{source})]f_{source}$

$f_{observed} = [340 \text{ m/s} / (340 \text{ m/s} - 50 \text{ m/s})] \cdot 500 \text{ Hz}$

$f_{observed} = 586$ Hz

$\lambda = v / f$

$\lambda = 340 \text{ m/s} / 586 \text{ Hz}$

$\lambda = 0.58$ m

53. B is correct.

$$PE = \frac{1}{2}kx^2$$

Doubling the amplitude x increases PE by a factor of 4.

54. E is correct.

The elastic modulus is given by:

E = tensional strength / extensional strain

$E = \sigma / \varepsilon$

55. D is correct.

Resonance is the phenomenon where one system transfers its energy to another at that system's resonant frequency (natural frequency).

Resonance is a forced vibration that produces the highest amplitude response for a given force amplitude.

Sound – Explanations

1. B is correct. Intensity is inversely proportional to distance (in W/m^2, not dB).

$$I_2 / I_1 = (d_1 / d_2)^2$$

$$I_2 / I_1 = (3 \text{ m} / 30 \text{ m})^2$$

$$100 \, I_2 = I_1$$

The intensity is 100 times greater at 3 m away than 30 m away.

Intensity to decibel relationship:

$$I \, (dB) = 10 \log_{10} (I / I_0)$$

The intensity to dB relationship is logarithmic. Thus, if I_1 is 100 times the original intensity then it is two times the dB intensity because:

$$\log_{10} (100) = 2$$

Thus, the decibel level at 3 m away is:

$$I \, (dB) = (2) \cdot (20 \text{ dB})$$

$$I = 40 \text{ dB}$$

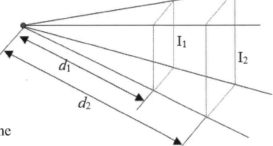

2. A is correct. distance = velocity × time

$$d = vt$$

$$t = d / v$$

$$t = (6{,}000 \text{ m}) / (340 \text{ m/s})$$

$$t = 18 \text{ s}$$

3. B is correct. Resonance occurs when a vibrating system is driven at its resonance frequency, resulting in a relative maximum of the vibrational energy of the system. When the force associated with the vibration exceeds the strength of the material, the glass shatters.

4. C is correct. The third harmonic is shown in the figure below:

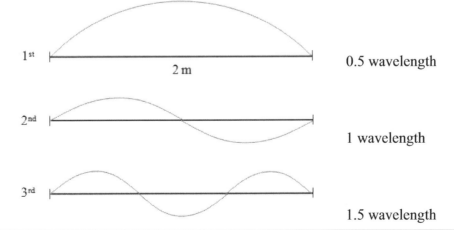

There are $(3/2)\lambda$ in the 2 m wave in the third harmonic

$L = (n / 2)\lambda$ (for n harmonic)

$L = (3 / 2)\lambda$ (for 3rd harmonic)

$L(2 / 3) = \lambda$

$\lambda = (2\ m)\cdot(2 / 3)$

$\lambda = 4/3$ m

5. B is correct.

High-pitched sound has a high frequency.

6. E is correct.

Snell's law:

$n_1 \sin \theta_1 = n_2 \sin \theta_2$

Solve for θ_2:

$(n_1 / n_2) \sin \theta_1 = \sin \theta_2$

$\sin \theta_1 = (n_1 / n_2) \sin \theta_2$

$\theta_2 = \sin^{-1}[(n_1 / n_2) \sin \theta_1]$

Substituting the given values:

$\theta_2 = \sin^{-1}[(1 / 1.5) \sin 60°]$

$\theta_2 = \sin^{-1}(0.67 \sin 60°)$

7. D is correct.

For a standing wave, the length and wavelength are related:

$L = (n / 2)\lambda$ (for n harmonic)

From the diagram, the wave is the 6th harmonic:

$L = (6 / 2)\lambda$

$\lambda = (2\ m)\cdot(2 / 6)$

$\lambda = 0.667$ m

$f = v / \lambda$

$f = (92\ m/s) / (0.667\ m)$

$f = 138$ Hz

8. A is correct.

$v = d / t$

$v = (0.6 \text{ m}) / (0.00014 \text{ s})$

$v = 4{,}286 \text{ m/s}$

$\lambda = v / f$

$\lambda = (4{,}286 \text{ m/s}) / (1.5 \times 10^6 \text{ Hz})$

$\lambda = 0.0029 \text{ m} = 2.9 \text{ mm}$

9. C is correct. The wave velocity is increased by a factor of 1.3.

$v^2 = T / \rho_L$

$T = v^2 \times \rho_L$

Increasing v by a factor of 1.3:

$T = (1.3v)^2 \rho_L$

$T = 1.69 v^2 \rho_L$

T increases by 69%

10. D is correct.

$\rho_L = \rho A$

$\rho_L = \rho(\pi r^2)$

Thus, if the diameter decreases by a factor of 2, then the radius decreases by a factor of 2, and the area decreases by a factor of 4. The linear mass density decreases by a factor of 4.

11. B is correct. The v and period (T) of wire C are equal to wire A so the ρ_L must be equal as well.

$\rho_{LA} = \rho_{LC}$

$\rho_A A_A = \rho_C A_C$

$A_C = (\rho_A A_A) / \rho_C$

$(\pi / 4) \cdot (d_C)^2 = (7 \text{ g/cm}^3)(\pi / 4) \cdot (0.6 \text{ mm})^2 / (3 \text{ g/cm}^3)$

$(d_C)^2 = (7 \text{ g/cm}^3) \cdot (0.6 \text{ mm})^2 / (3 \text{ g/cm}^3)$

$d_C^2 = 0.84 \text{ mm}^2$

$d_C = \sqrt{(0.84 \text{ mm}^2)} = 0.92 \text{ mm}$

12. A is correct.

$A = \pi r^2$

If d increases by a factor of 4, r increases by a factor of 4. A increases by a factor of 16.

13. E is correct.

Since the bird is moving toward the observer, the $f_{observed}$ must be higher than f_{source}.

Doppler shift for an approaching sound source:

$$f_{observed} = (v_{sound} / v_{sound} - v_{source})f_{source}$$

$$f_{observed} = [340 \text{ m/s} / (340 \text{ m/s} - 10 \text{ m/s})]f_{source}$$

$$f_{observed} = (340 \text{ m/s} / 330 \text{ m/s}) \cdot (60 \text{ kHz})$$

$$f_{observed} = (1.03) \cdot (60 \text{ kHz})$$

$$f_{observed} = 62 \text{ kHz}$$

14. C is correct. When an approaching sound source is heard, the observed frequency is higher than the frequency from the source due to the Doppler effect.

15. D is correct. Sound requires a medium of solid, liquid or gas substances to be propagated through. A vacuum is none of these.

16. E is correct.

According to the Doppler effect, frequency increases as the sound source moves towards the observer. Higher frequency is perceived as a higher pitch.

Conversely, as the sound source moves away from the observer, the perceived pitch decreases.

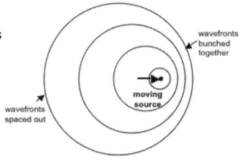

17. C is correct.

If waves are out of phase, the combination has its minimum amplitude of $(0.6 - 0.4) \text{ Pa} = 0.2 \text{ Pa}$.

If waves are in phase, the combination has its maximum amplitude of $(0.6 + 0.4) \text{ Pa} = 1.0 \text{ Pa}$.

When the phase difference has a value between in phase and out of phase, the amplitude will be between 0.2 Pa and 1.0 Pa.

18. B is correct.

$$I = P / A$$

$$I = P / \pi d^2$$

Intensity at $2d$:

$$I_2 = P / \pi(2d)^2$$

$$I_2 = P / 4\pi d^2$$

$$I_2 = \frac{1}{4}P / \pi d^2$$

The new intensity is ¼ the original.

19. A is correct.

  speed of sound = √[resistance to compression / density]

  $v_{sound} = \sqrt{(E / \rho)}$

Low resistance to compression and high density result in low velocity because this minimizes the term under the radical and thus minimizes velocity.

20. B is correct.

A pipe open at each end has no constraint on displacement at the ends. Furthermore, the pressure at the ends must equal the ambient pressure. Thus, the pressure is maximum at the ends: an antinode.

21. E is correct. For a pipe open at both ends, the resonance frequency:

  $f_n = nf_1$

  where n = 1, 2, 3, 4…

Therefore, only a multiple of 200 Hz can be a resonant frequency.

22. D is correct.

Unlike light, sound waves require a medium to travel through, and its speed is dependent upon the medium.

Sound is fastest in solids, then liquids and slowest in the air.

  $v_{solid} > v_{liquid} > v_{air}$

23. B is correct. Currents or moving charges induce magnetic fields.

24. C is correct.

  $\lambda = v / f$

  $\lambda = (5{,}000 \text{ m/s}) / (620 \text{ Hz})$

  $\lambda = 8.1 \text{ m}$

25. E is correct.

Sound intensity radiating spherically:

  $I = P / 4\pi r^2$

If *r* is doubled:

  $I = P / 4\pi(2r)^2$

  $I = \frac{1}{4}P / 4\pi r^2$

The intensity is reduced by a factor of ¼.

26. D is correct. As the sound propagates through a medium, it spreads out in an approximately spherical pattern. Thus, the power is radiated along the surface of the sphere, and the intensity can be given by:

$I = P / (4\pi r^2)$ ← for the surface area of a sphere

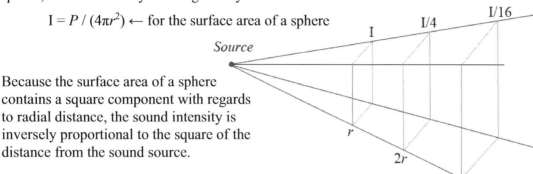

Because the surface area of a sphere contains a square component with regards to radial distance, the sound intensity is inversely proportional to the square of the distance from the sound source.

27. B is correct. The closed end is a node, and the open end is an antinode.

$\lambda = (4 / n)L$

where n = 1, 3, 5 …

For the fundamental n = 1:

$\lambda = (4 / 1) \cdot (1.5 \text{ m})$

$\lambda = 6 \text{ m}$

The 1.5 m tube (open at one end) is a quarter of a full wave, so the wavelength is 6 m.

28. A is correct. The 1.5 m is ¼ a full wave, so the wavelength is 6 m, for the fundamental.

$f = v / \lambda$

$f = (960 \text{ m/s}) / 6 \text{ m}$

$f = 160 \text{ Hz}$

29. E is correct.

For a closed-ended pipe, the wavelength to the harmonic relationship is:

$\lambda = (4 / n)L$

where n = 1, 3, 5…

For the 5th harmonic n = 5

$\lambda = (4 / 5) \cdot (1.5 \text{ m})$

$\lambda_n = 1.2 \text{ m}$

	Closed end tube			
Harmonic # (n)	# of waves in a tube	# of nodes	# of antinodes	Wavelength to length
1	1/4	1	1	$\lambda = 4 L$
3	3/4	2	2	$\lambda = 4/3 L$
5	5/4	3	3	$\lambda = 4/5 L$
7	7/4	4	4	$\lambda = 4/7 L$

30. A is correct.

$f = v / \lambda$

$f = (340 \text{ m/s}) / (6 \text{ m})$

$f = 57 \text{ Hz}$

31. C is correct.

Wavelength to harmonic number relationship in a standing wave on a string:

$\lambda = (2L / n)$

where n = 1, 2, 3, 4, 5 …

For the 3rd harmonic:

$\lambda = (2){\cdot}(0.34 \text{ m}) / 3$

$\lambda = 0.23 \text{ m}$

32. D is correct.

Beat frequency equation:

$f_{beat} = |f_2 - f_1|$

If one of the tones increases in frequency, then the beat frequency increases or decreases, but this cannot be determined unless the two tones are known.

33. A is correct.

For a closed-ended pipe, the wavelength to harmonic relationship is:

$\lambda = (4 / n)L$

where n = 1, 3, 5, 7…

The lowest three tones are n = 1, 3, 5

$\lambda = (4 / 1)L; \lambda = (4 / 3)L; \lambda = (4 / 5)L$

34. E is correct.

The sound was barely perceptible, the intensity at Mary's ear is $I_0 = 9.8 \times 10^{-12}$ W/m^2.

Since the mosquito is 1 m away, imagine a sphere 1 m in a radius around the mosquito.

If 9.8×10^{-12} W emanates from each area 1 m^2, then the surface area is $4\pi(1 \text{ m})^2$.

This is the power produced by one mosquito:

$P = 4\pi r^2 I_0$

$P = 4\pi(1 \text{ m})^2 \times (9.8 \times 10^{-12} \text{ W/m}^2)$

$P = 1.2 \times 10^{-10} \text{ W}$

energy = power × time

$E = Pt$

Energy produced in 200 s:

$Pt = (1.2 \times 10^{-10} \text{ W}){\cdot}(200 \text{ s})$

$E = 2.5 \times 10^{-8} \text{ J}$

35. A is correct.

$v = c / n$

where c is the speed of light in a vacuum

$v = \Delta x / \Delta t$

$\Delta x / \Delta t = c / n$

$\Delta t = n\Delta x / c$

$\Delta t = (1.33)\cdot(10^3 \text{ m}) / (3 \times 10^8 \text{ m/s})$

$\Delta t = 4.4 \times 10^{-6} \text{ s}$

36. E is correct.

When waves interfere constructively (i.e., in phase), the sound level is amplified. When they interfere destructively (i.e., out of phase), they cancel, and no sound is heard. Acoustic engineers work to ensure that there are no "dead spots" and the sound waves add.

An engineer should minimize destructive interference which can distort the sound.

37. B is correct.

Velocity of a wave on a string in tension can be calculated by:

$v = \sqrt{(TL / m)}$

Graph B gives a curve of a square root relationship which is how velocity and tension are related.

$y = x^{\frac{1}{2}}$

38. D is correct.

From the diagram, the wave is a 6th harmonic standing wave.

Find wavelength:

$\lambda = (2L / n)$

$\lambda = (2)\cdot(4 \text{ m}) / (6)$

$\lambda = 1.3 \text{ m}$

Find frequency:

$f = v / \lambda$

$f = (20 \text{ m/s}) / (1.3 \text{ m})$

$f = 15.4 \text{ Hz}$

1st

2nd

3rd

39. E is correct.

Soundwave velocity is independent of frequency and does not change.

40. C is correct.

First, find the frequency of the string, then the length of the pipe excited to the second overtone using that frequency.

The speed of sound in the string is:

$v_{string} = \sqrt{T/\mu}$

where T is the tension in the string, and μ is linear mass density.

$v_{string} = \sqrt{[(75 \text{ N}) / (0.00040 \text{ kg})]}$

$v_{string} = 433.01 \text{ m/s}$

The wavelength of a string of length L_{string} vibrating in harmonic n_{string} is:

$\lambda_{string} = 2L_{string} / n_{string}$

Therefore, the vibration frequency of the string is:

$f = v_{string} / \lambda_{string}$

$f = [(n_{string})(v_{string})] / 2L_{string}$

$f = [(6)(433.01 \text{ m/s})] / (2 \times 0.50 \text{ m})$

$f = (2{,}598.06 \text{ m/s}) / 1 \text{ m}$

$f = 2{,}598.1 \text{ Hz}$

Now, consider the open pipe.

The relationship between length, wavelength and harmonic number for an open pipe is the same as that for a string.

Therefore:

$L_{pipe} = n_{pipe} (\lambda_{pipe} / 2)$

However, since $\lambda_{pipe} = v_{air} / f$:

$L_{pipe} = n_{pipe} (v_{air} / 2f)$

Noting that the second overtone is the third harmonic ($n_{pipe} = 3$):

$L_{pipe} = (3 \times 345 \text{ m/s}) / (2 \times 2{,}598.1 \text{ Hz})$

$L_{pipe} = 0.20 \text{ m}$

Note that it is not necessary to calculate the frequency; its value cancels out.

There is less chance for error if the two steps that use frequency are skipped.

In $L_{pipe} = n_{pipe} (v_{air} / 2f)$ substitute $f = [(n_{string})(v_{string})] / 2L_{string}$, which gives:

$L_{pipe} = L_{string} (v_{air} / v_{string}) \cdot (n_{pipe} / n_{string})$

It yields the same answer but with fewer calculations.

41. A is correct.

$$v = \sqrt{(T / \mu)}$$
$$\mu = m / L$$
$$v = \sqrt{(TL / m)}$$
$$v_2 = \sqrt{(T(2L) / m)}$$
$$v_2 = \sqrt{2} \sqrt{(TL / m)}$$
$$v_2 = v\sqrt{2}$$

42. C is correct.

For a standing wave, the resonance frequency:

$$f_n = nf_1$$

where n is the harmonic number, n = 1, 2, 3, 4 …

Therefore, only a multiple of 500 Hz can be a resonant frequency.

43. D is correct.

The angle of incidence always equals the angle of reflection.

A light beam entering a medium with a greater refractive index than the incident medium refracts *toward* the normal.

Thus, the angle of refraction is less than the angles of incidence and reflection.

Snell's law:

$$n_1 \sin \theta_1 = n_2 \sin \theta_2$$

where $n_1 < n_2$

For Snell's law to be true, then:

$$\theta_1 > \theta_2$$

44. A is correct.

Speed of sound in gas:

$$v_{sound} = \sqrt{(yRT / M)}$$

where y = adiabatic constant, R = gas constant, T = temperature and M = molecular mass

The speed of sound in a gas is only dependent upon temperature and not frequency or wavelength.

45. B is correct.

Waves only transport energy and not matter.

46. E is correct.

$$v = \lambda f$$
$$\lambda = v / f$$
$$\lambda = (344 \text{ m/s}) / (700 \text{ s}^{-1})$$
$$\lambda = 0.5 \text{ m}$$

The information about the string is unnecessary, as the only contributor to the wavelength of the sound in air is the frequency and the speed.

47. C is correct. $v = \lambda f$

$$f = v / \lambda$$

Distance from a sound source is not part of the equation for frequency.

48. A is correct. Velocity of a wave in a rope:

$$v = \sqrt{[T / (m / L)]}$$
$$t = d / v$$
$$d = L$$
$$t = d / \sqrt{[T / (m / L)]}$$
$$t = (8 \text{ m}) / [40 \text{ N} / (2.5 \text{ kg} / 8 \text{ m})]^{\frac{1}{2}}$$
$$t = 0.71 \text{ s}$$

49. C is correct. Intensity to decibel relationship:

$$I \text{ (dB)} = 10 \log_{10} (I_1 / I_0)$$
where I_0 = threshold of hearing
$$dB = 10\log_{10}[(10^{-5} \text{ W/m}^2) / (10^{-12} \text{ W/m}^2)]$$
$$I = 70 \text{ decibels}$$

50. E is correct. The diagram represents the described scenario.

The wave is in the second harmonic with a wavelength of:

$$\lambda = (2 / n)L$$
$$\lambda = (2 / 2) \cdot (1 \text{ m})$$
$$\lambda = 1 \text{ m}$$
$$f = v / \lambda$$
$$f = (3.8 \times 10^4 \text{ m/s}) / (1 \text{ m})$$
$$f = 3.8 \times 10^4 \text{ Hz}$$

The lowest frequency corresponds to lowest possible harmonic number. For problem, $n = 2$.

51. D is correct.

The speed of light traveling in a vacuum is c.

$$c = \lambda v$$

$$c = \lambda f$$

$$f = c / \lambda$$

Frequency and wavelength are inversely proportional, so an increase in frequency results in a decreased wavelength.

52. B is correct.

Radio waves are electromagnetic waves while all other choices are mechanical waves.

53. D is correct.

Since the microphone is exactly equidistant from each speaker (i.e., equal path lengths), the sound waves take equal time to reach the microphone.

The speakers are emitting sound waves in phase with each other (i.e., peaks are emitted simultaneously), and since those peaks reach the microphone at the same time (because of the equal path length), they combine constructively and add, forming a large peak, or antinode.

54. C is correct.

Doppler equation for receding source of sound:

$$f_{observed} = [v_{sound} / (v_{sound} + v_{source})] f_{source}$$

$$f_{observed} = [(342 \text{ m/s}) / (342 \text{ m/s} + 30 \text{ m/s})] \cdot (1,200 \text{ Hz})$$

$$f_{observed} = 1,103 \text{ Hz}$$

The observed frequency is always lower when the source is receding.

55. E is correct.

$$f_1 = 600 \text{ Hz}$$

$$f_2 = 300 \text{ Hz}$$

$$f_2 = \tfrac{1}{2} f_1$$

$$\lambda_1 = v / f_1$$

$$\lambda_2 = v / (\tfrac{1}{2} f_1)$$

$$\lambda_2 = 2 (v / f_1)$$

The wavelength of the 300 Hz frequency is twice as long as the wavelength of the 600 Hz frequency.

Fluids – Explanations

1. C is correct.

Refer to the unknown liquid as "A" and the oil as "O."

$\rho_A h_A g = \rho_O h_O g$, cancel g from both sides of the expression

$\rho_A h_A = \rho_O h_O$

$h_A = 5$ cm

$h_O = 20$ cm

$h_A = \frac{1}{4} h_O$

$\rho_A(\frac{1}{4})h_O = \rho_O h_O$

$\rho_A = 4\rho_O$

$\rho_A = 4(850 \text{ kg/m}^3)$

$\rho_A = 3,400 \text{ kg/m}^3$

2. D is correct.

$P = \rho_{oil} \times V_{oil} \times g / (A_{tube})$

$P = [\rho_o \pi (r_{tube})^2 \times hg] / \pi(r_{tube})^2$

cancel $\pi(r_{tube})^2$ from both the numerator and the denominator.

$P = \rho_o g h$

$P = (850 \text{ kg/m}^3) \cdot (9.8 \text{ m/s}^2) \cdot (0.2 \text{ m})$

$P = 1,666$ Pa

3. A is correct.

$m_{oil} = \rho_{oil} V_{oil}$

$V = \pi r^2 h$

$m_{oil} = \rho_{oil} \pi r^2 h$

$m_{oil} = \pi(850 \text{ kg/m}^3) \cdot (0.02 \text{ m})^2 \times (0.2 \text{ m})$

$m_{oil} = 0.21$ kg $= 210$ g

4. A is correct.

Gauge pressure is the pressure experienced by an object referenced at atmospheric pressure. When the block is lowered its gauge pressure increases according to:

$P_G = \rho g h$

At $t = 0$, the block just enters the water and $h = 0$ so $P_G = 0$. As time passes, the height of the block below the water increases linearly, so P_G increases linearly as well.

5. E is correct.

Using Bernoulli's principle and assuming the opening of the tank is so large that the initial velocity is essentially zero:

$\rho gh = \frac{1}{2}\rho v^2$, cancel ρ from both sides of the expression

$gh = \frac{1}{2}v^2$

$v^2 = 2gh$

$v^2 = 2 \cdot (9.8 \text{ m/s}^2) \cdot (0.8 \text{ m})$

$v^2 = 15.68 \text{ m}^2/\text{s}^2$

$v = 3.96 \text{ m/s} \approx 4 \text{ m/s}$

Note: the diameter is not used to solve the problem.

6. C is correct.

The ideal gas law is:

$PV = nRT$

Keeping nRT constant:

If $P_{final} = \frac{1}{2}P_{initial}$

$V_{final} = \frac{1}{2}V_{initial}$

However, in an isothermal process there is no change in internal energy.

Therefore, because energy must be conserved:

$\Delta U = 0$

7. E is correct.

The object sinks when the buoyant force is less than the weight of the object.

Since the buoyant force is equal to the weight of the displaced fluid, an object sinks precisely when the weight of the fluid it displaces is less than the weight of the object itself.

8. A is correct.

$P = \rho gh$

$P = (10^3 \text{ kg/m}^3) \cdot (9.8 \text{ m/s}^2) \cdot (100 \text{ m})$

$P = 9.8 \times 10^5 \text{ N/m}^2$

9. C is correct.

Absolute pressure = gauge pressure + atmospheric pressure

$P_{abs} = P_G + P_{atm}$

$P_{abs} = \rho gh + P_{atm}$

Atmospheric pressure is added to the total pressure at the bottom of a volume of liquid.

Therefore, if the atmospheric pressure increases, absolute pressure increases by the same amount.

10. A is correct.

Surface tension increases as temperature decreases.

Generally, the cohesive forces maintaining surface tension decrease as molecular thermal activity increases.

11. A is correct.

The buoyant force upward must balance the weight downward.

Buoyant force = weight of the volume of water displaced

$$F_B = W_{object}$$

$$\rho V g = W_{object}$$

$$W_{object} = 60 \text{ N}$$

$$W_{object} = (\rho_{water}) \cdot (V_{water}) \cdot (g)$$

$$60 \text{ N} = (1,000 \text{ kg/m}^3) \cdot (V_{water}) \cdot (10 \text{ m/s}^2)$$

$$V_{water} = 60 \text{ N} / (1,000 \text{ kg/m}^3) \cdot (10 \text{ m/s}^2)$$

$$V_{water} = 0.006 \text{ m}^3$$

12. E is correct. Volume flow rate:

$$Q = vA$$

$$Q = (2.5 \text{ m/s}) \pi r^2$$

$$Q = (2.5 \text{ m/s}) \cdot (0.015 \text{ m})^2 \pi$$

$$Q = 1.8 \times 10^{-3} \text{ m}^3/\text{s}$$

13. C is correct.

Force equation for the cork that is not accelerating:

$$F_B - mg = 0$$

Let m be the mass and V be the volume of the cork.

Replace:

$$m = \rho V$$

$$F_B = (\rho_{water}) \cdot (V_{disp}) \cdot (g)$$

$$(\rho_{water}) \cdot (V_{disp}) \cdot (g) = (\rho_{cork}) \cdot (V) \cdot (g)$$

$V_{disp} = \frac{3}{4}V$

$\rho_{water}(\frac{3}{4}Vg) = (\rho_{cork})\cdot(V)\cdot(g)$, cancel g and V from both sides of the expression

$\frac{3}{4}\rho_{water} = \rho_{cork}$

$\rho_{cork} / \rho_{water} = \frac{3}{4} = 0.75$

14. D is correct. volume = mass / density

$V = (600\text{ g}) / (0.93\text{ g/cm}^3)$

$V = 645\text{ cm}^3$

15. C is correct. For monatomic gases:

$U = 3/2k_BT$

where U is average KE per molecule and k_B is the Boltzmann constant

16. B is correct. The object weighs 150 N less while immersed because the buoyant force is supporting 150 N of the total weight of the object.

Since the object is totally submerged, the volume of water displaced equals the volume of the object.

$F_B = 150\text{ N}$

$F_B = \rho_{water} \times V_{water} \times g$

$V = F_B / \rho g$

$V = (150\text{ N}) / (1,000\text{ kg/m}^3)\cdot(10\text{ m/s}^2)$

$V = 0.015\text{ m}^3$

17. C is correct.

$F_B / \rho_w = (m_c g) / \rho_c$

$F_B = (\rho_w m_c g) / \rho_c$

$F_B = [(1\text{ g/cm}^3)\cdot(0.03\text{ kg})\cdot(9.8\text{ m/s}^2)] / (8.9\text{ g/cm}^3)$

$F_B = 0.033\text{ N}$

$m_{total} = m_w + (F_B / g)$

$m_{total} = (0.14\text{ kg}) + [(0.033\text{ N}) / (9.8\text{ m/s}^2)]$

$m_{total} = 0.143\text{ kg} = 143\text{ g}$

18. D is correct.

$$v_1A_1 = v_2A_2$$

$$v_2 = v_1A_1 / A_2$$

$$v_2 = [v_1(\pi/4)d_1^2] / (\pi/4)d_2^2$$

cancel $(\pi/4)$ from both the numerator and denominator

$$v_2 = v_1(d_1^2 / d_2^2)$$

$$v_2 = (1 \text{ m/s}) \cdot [(6 \text{ cm})^2 / (3 \text{ cm})^2]$$

$$v_2 = 4 \text{ m/s}$$

19. E is correct.

Static fluid pressure:

$$P = \rho gh$$

Pressure is only dependent on gravity (g), the height (h) of the fluid above the object and density (ρ) of the fluid. It does depend on the depth of the object but does not depend on the surface area of the object.

Both objects are submerged to the same depth, so the fluid pressure is equal. Note that the buoyant force on the blocks is NOT equal, but pressure (force / area) is equal.

20. C is correct. Surface tension force acts as the product of surface tension and the total length of contact.

$$F = AL$$

For a piece of thread, the length of contact is l as shown:

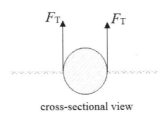

cross-sectional view

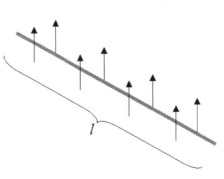

$L = 2L$ because the force acts on both sides of the thread.

Thus, for a thread rectangle, the total contact length is the total length times two.

$$L = 2(l + w + l + w)$$

$$F_{max} = 2A(l + w + l + w)$$

$$F_{max} = 2A(2l + 2w)$$

$$F_{max} = 4A(l + w)$$

21. D is correct.

Gauge pressure is the measure of pressure with respect to the atmospheric pressure.

So, if the pressure inside the tire is equal to the air pressure outside, the gauge reads zero.

22. E is correct.

Pressure is measured in force per unit area, which is the force divided by the area.

23. D is correct.

The shear stress is the force per unit area and has units of N/m^2.

24. B is correct.

Because the area of the reservoir is assumed to be essentially infinite, the velocity of the flow at the top of the tank is assumed to be zero.

Using Bernoulli's equation, find the speed through the 3 cm pipe:

$$(\frac{1}{2}\rho v^2 + \rho gh)_{out} = (\frac{1}{2}\rho v^2 + \rho gh)_{in}$$

$\frac{1}{2}\rho v^2 = \rho gh$, cancel ρ from both sides of the expression

$$\frac{1}{2}v^2 = gh$$

$$v^2 = 2gh$$

$$v = \sqrt{(2gh)}$$

$$v = \sqrt{[2(9.8 \text{ m/s}^2) \cdot (4 \text{ m})]}$$

$$v_{3cm} = 8.9 \text{ m/s}$$

To find the speed through the 5 cm pipe use the continuity equation:

$$A_{3cm}v_{3cm} = A_{5cm}v_{5cm}$$

$$(\pi / 4) \cdot (3 \text{ cm})^2 \cdot (8.9 \text{ m/s}) = (\pi / 4) \cdot (5 \text{ cm})^2 \cdot (v_{5cm})$$

$$v_{5cm} = 3.2 \text{ m/s}$$

25. E is correct.

The ideal gas law is:

$$PV = nRT$$

where n, R and T are constants.

P is pressure, V is volume, n is the number of particles, R is the ideal gas law constant, and T is temperature.

If $P \rightarrow 3P$, then $V \rightarrow (1/3)V$ to maintain a constant temperature.

26. D is correct.

$$F = PA + F_{cover}$$

$$P = \rho gh$$

$$F = \rho ghA + F_{cover}$$

$$F = [(1{,}000 \text{ kg/m}^3){\cdot}(10 \text{ m/s}^2){\cdot}(1 \text{ m}){\cdot}(1 \text{ m}^2)] + 1{,}500 \text{ N}$$

$$F = 11{,}500 \text{ N}$$

27. B is correct. The buoyant force on a totally submerged object is independent of its depth below the surface (since any increase in the water's density is ignored).

The buoyant force on the ball at a depth of 4 m is 20 N, the same as the buoyant force at 1 m.

When it sits at the bottom of the pool, the two upward forces (i.e., the buoyant force F_B and the normal force F_N), must balance the downward force of gravity.

$$F_B + F_N = F_g$$

$$(20 \text{ N}) + F_N = 80 \text{ N}$$

$$F_N = 80 \text{ N} - 20 \text{ N}$$

$$F_N = 60 \text{ N}$$

28. B is correct.

$$V_{Fluid\ Displaced} = \tfrac{1}{2} V_{block}$$

Buoyant force:

$$F_B = \rho gV$$

$\rho_F gV_F = \rho_B gV_B$, cancel g from both sides of the expression

$$\rho_F V_F = \rho_B V_B$$

$\rho_F(\tfrac{1}{2}V_B) = \rho_B V_B$, cancel V_B from both sides of the expression

$$\tfrac{1}{2}\rho_F = \rho_B$$

$$\rho_F = (1.6)\rho_{water}$$

$$\rho_B = (1.6){\cdot}(10^3 \text{ kg/m}^3){\cdot}(\tfrac{1}{2})$$

$$\rho_B = 800 \text{ kg/m}^3$$

29. A is correct. The pressure due to the density of a fluid surrounding an object submerged at depth d below the surface is given by:

$$P = \rho gd$$

Since the distance that the objects are below the surface is not specified, the only conclusion that can be drawn is that object B experiences less fluid pressure than object A.

This difference is because object B is higher off the floor of the container and thus its depth is less than object A.

30. B is correct.

$$A_1 v_1 = A_2 v_2$$

$$A = \pi r^2$$

$$A_2 = \pi (2r)^2$$

$$A_2 = 4\pi r^2$$

$$A_2 = 4A_1$$

If r is doubled, then area is increased by 4 times

$$A_1(14 \text{ m/s}) = (4A_1)v_2$$

$$v_2 = (A_1 \times 14 \text{ m/s}) / (4 \times A_1)$$

$$v_2 = (14 \text{ m/s}) / (4)$$

$$v_2 = 3.5 \text{ m/s}$$

Use Bernoulli's equation to find resulting pressure:

$$P_1 + \tfrac{1}{2}\rho v_1^2 = P_2 + \tfrac{1}{2}\rho v_2^2$$

$$(3.5 \times 10^4 \text{ Pa}) + \tfrac{1}{2}(1{,}000 \text{ kg/m}^3){\cdot}(14 \text{ m/s})^2 = P_2 + \tfrac{1}{2}(1{,}000 \text{ kg/m}^3){\cdot}(3.5 \text{ m/s})^2$$

$$P_2 = (13.3 \times 10^4 \text{ Pa}) - (6.1 \times 10^3 \text{ Pa})$$

$$P_2 = 12.7 \times 10^4 \text{ Pa}$$

31. D is correct.

The pressure due to the atmosphere is equal to its weight per unit area.

At an altitude of 2 km, there is less atmosphere pushing down than at the Earth's surface.

Therefore, atmospheric pressure decreases with increasing altitude.

32. C is correct.

The buoyant force:

$$F_B = \rho_{air} V_{disp} g, \text{ and } V_{disp} \text{ is the volume of the man } m / \rho_{man}$$

$$F_B = (\rho_{air} / \rho_{man})mg$$

$$F_B = [(1.2 \times 10^{-3} \text{ g/cm}^3) / (1 \text{ g/cm}^3)]{\cdot}(80 \text{ kg}){\cdot}(9.8 \text{ m/s}^2)$$

$$F_B = 0.94 \text{ N}$$

33. D is correct.

Graham's law states that the rate at which gas diffuses is inversely proportional to the square root of the density of the gas.

34. D is correct.

$A = \pi r^2$

$A_T v_T = A_P v_P$

$v_T = v_P A_P / A_T$

Ratio of the diameter^2 is equal to the ratio of area:

$v_T = v_P (d_1 / d_2)^2$

$v_T = (0.03 \text{ m/s}) \cdot [(0.12 \text{ m}) / (0.002 \text{ m})]^2$

$v_T = 108 \text{ m/s}$

35. B is correct.

Specific gravity:

$\rho_{object} / \rho_{water}$

Archimedes' principle:

$F = \rho g V$

$\rho_{water} = F / g(0.9V)$

$\rho_{object} = F / gV$

$\rho_{object} / \rho_{water} = (F / gV) / [F / g(0.9V)]$

$\rho_{object} / \rho_{water} = 0.9$

V_{water} is 0.9V because only 90% of the object is in the water, so 90% of the object's volume equals water displaced.

36. E is correct.

The factors considered are length, density, radius, pressure difference, and viscosity.

The continuity equation does not apply here because it can only relate velocity and radius to the flow rate.

Bernoulli's equation does not apply because it only relates density and velocity.

The Hagen-Poiseuille equation is needed because it includes all the terms except for density and therefore is the most applicable to this question.

Volumetric flow rate (Q) is:

$Q = \Delta P \pi r^4 / 8\eta L$

The radius is raised to the fourth power.

A 15% change to r results in the greatest change.

37. A is correct.

A force meter provides a force, and the reading indicates what the force is.

Since the hammer is not accelerating, the force equation is:

$$F_{meter} + F_B - m_h g = 0$$

$$m_h g = (0.68 \text{ kg}) \cdot (10 \text{ m/s}^2)$$

$$m_h g = 6.8 \text{ N}$$

The displaced volume is the volume of the hammer:

$$V_{disp} = m_h / \rho_{steel}$$

$$V_{disp} = (680 \text{ g}) / (7.9 \text{ g/cm}^3)$$

$$V_{disp} = 86 \text{ cm}^3$$

$$F_B = \rho_{water} \times V_{disp} \times g$$

$$F_B = (1 \times 10^{-3} \text{ kg/cm}^3) \cdot (86 \text{ cm}^3) \cdot (10 \text{ m/s}^2)$$

$$F_B = 0.86 \text{ N}$$

$$F_{meter} = m_h g - F_B$$

$$F_{meter} = 6.8 \text{ N} - 0.86 \text{ N}$$

$$F_{meter} = 5.9 \text{ N}$$

38. D is correct.

Pascal's Principle states that pressure is transmitted undiminished in an enclosed static fluid.

39. B is correct.

The normal force exerted by the sea floor is the net force between the weight of the submarine and the buoyant force:

$$F_N = F_{net}$$

$$F_{net} = mg - F_B$$

$$F_{net} = mg - \rho g V$$

$$F_{net} = mg - W_{water}$$

$$F_N = mg - W_{water}$$

40. E is correct.

$$P = \rho g h$$

Because the bottom of the brick is at a lower depth than the rest of the brick, it will experience the highest pressure.

41. A is correct.

Mass flow rate:

$\dot{m}$ = cross-sectional area × density × velocity

$\dot{m} = A_C \rho v$

$\dot{m}$ = (7 m)·(14 m)·(10^3 kg/m^3)·(3 m/s)

$\dot{m} = 2.9 \times 10^5$ kg/s

42. C is correct.

Since the object is motionless:

$a = 0$

$F_{net} = 0$

The magnitude of the buoyant force upward = weight downward:

$F = W$

$F = mg$

F = (3 kg)·(10 m/s^2)

$F = 30$ N

43. A is correct.

$P = P_{atm} + \rho gh$

$P = (1.01 \times 10^5$ Pa$) + (10^3$ kg/m^3)·(10 m/s^2)·(6 m)

$P = (1.01 \times 10^5$ Pa$) + (0.6 \times 10^5$ Pa$)$

$P = 1.6 \times 10^5$ Pa

44. B is correct.

density = mass / volume

45. E is correct.

The bulk modulus is defined as how much a material is compressed under a given external pressure:

$B = \Delta P / (\Delta V / V)$

Most solids and liquids compress slightly under external pressure.

However, gases have the highest change in volume and thus the lowest value of B.

46. B is correct.

Absolute pressure is measured relative to absolute zero pressure (perfect vacuum), and gauge pressure is measured relative to atmospheric pressure.

If the atmospheric pressure increases by ΔP, then the absolute pressure increases by ΔP, but the gauge pressure does not change.

Absolute pressure at an arbitrary depth h in the lake:

$$P_{abs} = P_{atm} + \rho_{water}gh$$

Gauge pressure at an arbitrary depth h in the lake:

$$P_{gauge} = \rho_{water}gh$$

47. D is correct.

By Poiseuille's Law:

$$v = \Delta Pr^2 / 8\eta L$$

$$\eta = \Delta Pr^2 / 8Lv_{effective}$$

$$\eta = (970 \text{ Pa}) \cdot (0.0021 \text{ m})^2 / 8 \cdot (1.8 \text{ m/s}) \cdot (0.19 \text{ m})$$

$$\eta = 0.0016 \text{ N·s/m}^2$$

48. C is correct.

Bernoulli's equation:

$$P_1 + \tfrac{1}{2}\rho_1v_1^2 + \rho_1gh_1 = P_2 + \tfrac{1}{2}\rho_2v_2^2 + \rho_2gh_2$$

There is no height difference, so the equation reduces to:

$$P_1 + \tfrac{1}{2}\rho_1v_1^2 = P_2 + \tfrac{1}{2}\rho_2v_2^2$$

If the flow of air across the wing tip is v_1 then:

$$v_1 > v_2$$

Since the air that flows across the top has a higher velocity, as it travels a larger distance (curved surface of the top) over the same period, then:

$$\tfrac{1}{2}\rho_1v_1^2 > \tfrac{1}{2}\rho_2v_2^2$$

To keep both sides equal:

$$P_1 < P_2$$

$$\Delta P = (P_2 - P_1)$$

Thus, the lower portion of the wing experiences greater pressure and therefore lifts the wing.

Electrostatics – Explanations

1. C is correct. Since charge is quantized, the charge Q must be a whole number (n) times the charge on a single electron:

Charge = # electrons × electron charge

$Q = n(e^-)$

$n = Q / e^-$

$n = (-1 \text{ C}) / (-1.6 \times 10^{-19} \text{ C})$

$n = 6.25 \times 10^{18} \approx 6.3 \times 10^{18}$ electrons

2. C is correct. Coulomb's law: $F_1 = kQ_1Q_2 / r^2$

If r is increased by a factor of 4:

$F_e = kQ_1Q_2 / (4r)^2$

$F_e = kQ_1Q_2 / (16r^2)$

$F_e = (1/16)kQ_1Q_2 / r^2$

$F_e = (1/16)F_1$

As the distance increases by a factor of 4, the force decreases by a factor of $4^2 = 16$.

3. D is correct. Use a coordinate system in which a repulsive force is in the positive direction, and an attractive force is in the negative direction.

Gravitational Force: F_g

$F_g = -Gm_1m_2 / r^2$

$F_g = -[(6.673 \times 10^{-11} \text{ N·m}^2/\text{kg}^2) \cdot (54{,}000 \text{ kg}) \cdot (51{,}000 \text{ kg})] / (180 \text{ m})^2$

$F_g = -0.18 \text{ N·m}^2 / (32{,}400 \text{ m}^2)$

$F_g = -5.7 \times 10^{-6} \text{ N}$

Electrostatic Force: F_e

$F_e = kQ_1Q_2 / r^2$

$F_e = [(9 \times 10^9 \text{ N·m}^2/\text{C}^2) \cdot (-15 \times 10^{-6} \text{ C}) \cdot (-11 \times 10^{-6} \text{ C})] / (180 \text{ m})^2$

$F_e = (1.49 \text{ N·m}^2) / (32{,}400 \text{ m}^2)$

$F_e = 4.6 \times 10^{-5} \text{ N}$

Net Force:

$F_{net} = F_g + F_e$

$F_{net} = (-5.7 \times 10^{-6} \text{ N}) + (4.6 \times 10^{-5} \text{ N})$

$F_{net} = 4 \times 10^{-5} \text{ N}$

F_{net} is positive, which means there is a net repulsive force on the asteroids. In other words, the repulsive electrostatic force between them is stronger than the attractive gravitational force.

4. B is correct. Newton's Third Law states for every force there is an equal and opposite reaction force. This also applies to electrostatic forces.

Electrostatic Force:

$$F_1 = kQ_1Q_2 / r^2$$
$$F_2 = kQ_1Q_2 / r^2$$
$$F_1 = F_2$$

5. E is correct.

charge = # electrons × electron charge

$$Q = ne^-$$
$$n = Q / e^-$$
$$n = (-10 \times 10^{-6} \text{ C}) / (-1.6 \times 10^{-19} \text{ C})$$
$$n = 6.3 \times 10^{13} \text{ electrons}$$

6. C is correct. Coulomb's law:

$$F_e = kQ_1Q_2 / r^2$$

If the separation is halved, then r decreases by ½:

$$F_2 = kq_1q_2 / (\tfrac{1}{2}r)^2$$
$$F_2 = 4(kq_1q_2 / r^2)$$
$$F_2 = 4F_e$$

7. E is correct. Coulomb's law:

$$F = kQ_1Q_2 / r^2$$

Doubling both the charges and distance:

$$F = [k(2Q_1)\cdot(2Q_2)] / (2r)^2$$
$$F = [4k(Q_1)\cdot(Q_2)] / (4r^2)$$
$$F = (4/4)[kQ_1Q_2 / (r^2)]$$
$$F = kQ_1Q_2 / r^2, \text{ remains the same}$$

8. A is correct.

Coulomb's law:

$$F = kQ_1Q_2 / r^2$$

The Coulomb force between opposite charges is attractive.

Since the strength of the force is inversely proportional to the square of the separation distance (r^2), the force decreases as the charges are pulled apart.

9. B is correct.

Coulomb's Law:

$$F_1 = kQ_1Q_2 / r^2$$
$$F_2 = kQ_1Q_2 / r^2$$
$$F_1 = F_2$$

Newton's Third Law: the force exerted by one charge on the other has the same magnitude as the force the other exerts on the first.

10. E is correct.

$$F_e = kQ_1Q_2 / r^2$$
$$F_e = (9 \times 10^9 \text{ N·m}^2/\text{C}^2) \cdot (-1.6 \times 10^{-19} \text{ C}) \cdot (-1.6 \times 10^{-19} \text{ C}) / (0.03 \text{ m})^2$$
$$F_e = 2.56 \times 10^{-25} \text{ N}$$

11. C is correct.

Charge = # electrons × electron charge

$$Q = ne^-$$
$$n = Q / e^-$$
$$n = (8 \times 10^{-6} \text{ C}) / (1.6 \times 10^{-19} \text{ C})$$
$$n = 5 \times 10^{13} \text{ electrons}$$

12. A is correct.

An object with a charge can attract another object of opposite charge or a neutral charge.

Like charges cannot attract, but the type of charge does not matter otherwise.

13. D is correct.

$$W = Q\Delta V$$
$$V = kQ / r$$

Consider the charge Q_1 to be fixed and move charge Q_2 from initial distance r_i to final distance r_f.

$$W = Q_2(V_f - V_i)$$
$$W = Q_2[(kQ_1 / r_f) - (kQ_1 / r_i)]$$
$$W = kQ_1Q_2(1 / r_f - 1 / r_i)$$
$$W = (9 \times 10^9 \text{ N·m}^2/\text{C}) \cdot (2.3 \times 10^{-8} \text{ C}) \cdot (2.5 \times 10^{-9} \text{ C}) \cdot [(1 / 0.01 \text{ m}) - (1 / 0.1 \text{ m})]$$
$$W = 4.7 \times 10^{-5} \text{ J}$$

14. D is correct.

Equilibrium:

$$F = kq_1q_2 \, / \, r_1^2$$

$$F_{\text{attractive on } q2} = F_{\text{repulsive on } q2}$$

$$kq_1q_2 \, / \, r_1^2 = kq_2Q \, / \, r_2^2$$

$$q_1 = Qr_1^2 \, / \, r_2^2$$

$$q_1 = (7.5 \times 10^{-9} \text{ C}) \cdot (0.2 \text{ m})^2 / (0.1 \text{ m})^2$$

$$q_1 = 30 \times 10^{-9} \text{ C}$$

15. A is correct.

The strength of the electrostatic field due to a single point charge is given by:

$$E = kQ \, / \, r^2, \text{ assumes that the source charge is in vacuum}$$

E depends on both the magnitude of the source charge Q and the distance r from Q.

The sign of the source charge affects only the direction of the electrostatic field vectors.

The sign of the source charge does not affect the strength of the field.

16. C is correct.

Coulomb's law:

$$F_e = kQ_1Q_2 \, / \, r^2$$

$$1 \text{ N} = kQ_1Q_2 \, / \, r^2$$

Doubling charges and keeping distance constant:

$$k(2Q_1) \cdot (2Q_2) \, / \, r^2 = 4kQ_1Q_2 \, / \, r^2$$

$$4kQ_1Q_2 \, / \, r^2 = 4F_e$$

$$4F_e = 4(1 \text{ N}) = 4 \text{ N}$$

17. D is correct.

The Na^+ ion is positively charged and attracts the oxygen atom. Oxygen is slightly negative because it is more electronegative than the hydrogen atoms to which it is bonded.

18. C is correct.

Charge = # of electrons × electron charge

$$Q = ne^-$$

$$Q = (30) \cdot (-1.6 \times 10^{-19} \text{ C})$$

$$Q = -4.8 \times 10^{-18} \text{ C}$$

19. B is correct.

The repulsive force between two particles is:

$$F = kQ_1Q_2 / r^2$$

As r increases, F decreases

Using $F = ma$, a also decreases

20. C is correct.

The Coulomb is the basic unit of electrical charge in the SI unit system.

21. A is correct.

By the Law of Conservation of Charge, a charge cannot be created nor destroyed.

22. B is correct.

Coulomb's Law:

$$F = kQ_1Q_2 / r^2$$

If both charges are doubled,

$$F = k(2Q_1)\cdot(2Q_2) / r^2$$
$$F = 4kQ_1Q_2 / r^2$$

F increases by a factor of 4.

23. C is correct.

Coulomb's law:

$$F = kQ_1Q_2 / r^2$$
$$Q_1 = Q_2$$

Therefore:

$$Q_1Q_2 = Q^2$$
$$F = kQ^2 / r^2$$

Rearranging:

$$Q^2 = Fr^2 / k$$
$$Q = \sqrt{(Fr^2 / k)}$$
$$Q = \sqrt{[(4 \text{ N})\cdot(0.01 \text{ m})^2 / (9 \times 10^9 \text{ N·m}^2/\text{C}^2)]}$$
$$Q = 2 \times 10^{-7} \text{ C}$$

24. C is correct.

Coulomb's law:

$$F = kQ_1Q_2 / r^2$$

When each particle has lost ½ its charge:

$$F_2 = k(\tfrac{1}{2}Q_1){\cdot}(\tfrac{1}{2}Q_2) / r^2$$

$$F_2 = (\tfrac{1}{4})kQ_1Q_2 / r^2$$

$$F_2 = (\tfrac{1}{4})F$$

F decreases by a factor of ¼

25. A is correct.

$$W = Q\Delta V$$

$$V = kq / r$$

$$W = (kQq){\cdot}(1 / r_2 - 1 / r_1)$$

$$W = (kQq){\cdot}(1 / 2 \text{ m} - 1 / 6 \text{ m})$$

$$W = (kQq){\cdot}(1 / 3 \text{ m})$$

$$W = (9 \times 10^9 \text{ N·m}^2/\text{C}^2){\cdot}(3.1 \times 10^{-5} \text{ C}){\cdot}(-10^{-6} \text{ C}) / (1 / 3 \text{ m})$$

$$W = -0.093 \text{ J} \approx -0.09 \text{ J}$$

The negative sign indicates that the electric field does the work on charge q.

26. D is correct.

charge = # electrons × electron charge

$$Q = ne^-$$

$$n = Q / e^-$$

$$n = (-600 \times 10^{-9} \text{ C}) / (-1.6 \times 10^{-19} \text{ C})$$

$$n = 3.8 \times 10^{12} \text{ electrons}$$

27. D is correct.

An object that is electrically polarized has had its charge separated into opposites and thus rearrange themselves within distinct regions.

Electric Circuits – Explanations

1. B is correct.

$R = \rho L / A$, where ρ is the resistivity of the wire material.

If the length L is doubled, the resistance R is doubled.

If the radius r is doubled, the area $A = \pi r^2$ is quadrupled, and resistance R is decreased by ¼.

If these two changes are combined:

$R_{new} = \rho(2L) / \pi(2r)^2$

$R_{new} = (2/4) \cdot (\rho L / \pi r^2)$

$R_{new} = (2/4)R = ½R$

2. D is correct.

Internal resistance of battery is in series with resistors in circuit:

$R_{eq} = R_1 + R_{battery}$

where R_{eq} is equivalent resistance and R_1 is resistor connected to battery

$V = IR_{eq}$

$V = I(R_1 + R_{battery})$

$R_{battery} = V / I - R_1$

$R_{battery} = (12\ V / 0.6\ A) - 6\ \Omega$

$R_{battery} = 14\ \Omega$

3. C is correct.

An ohm Ω is defined as the resistance between two points of a conductor when a constant potential difference of 1 V, applied to these points, produces in the conductor a current of 1 A.

A series circuit experiences the same current through all resistors regardless of their resistance.

However, the voltage across each resistor can be different.

Since the light bulbs are in series, the current through them is the same.

4. D is correct.

$V = kQ / r$

$V_B = kQ / r_B$

$V_B = (9 \times 10^9\ N \cdot m^2/C^2) \cdot (1 \times 10^{-6}\ C) / 3.5\ m$

$V_B = 2{,}571\ V$

$V_A = kQ / r_A$

$$V_A = (9 \times 10^9 \, \text{N·m}^2/\text{C}^2) \cdot (1 \times 10^{-6} \, \text{C}) \, / \, 8 \, \text{m}$$

$$V_A = 1{,}125 \, \text{V}$$

Potential difference:

$$\Delta V = V_B - V_A$$

$$\Delta V = 2{,}571 \, \text{V} - 1{,}125 \, \text{V}$$

$$\Delta V = 1{,}446 \, \text{V}$$

5. E is correct.

The capacitance of a parallel place capacitor demonstrates the influence of material, separation distance and geometry in determining the overall capacitance.

$$C = k \mathcal{E}_0 A \, / \, d$$

where k = dielectric constant or permittivity of material between the plates, A = surface area of the conductor and d = distance of plate separation

6. A is correct.

$$E = qV$$

$$E = \tfrac{1}{2} m (\Delta v)^2$$

$$qV = \tfrac{1}{2} m (v_f^2 - v_i^2)$$

$$v_f^2 = (2qV \, / \, m) + v_i^2$$

$$v_f^2 = [2(1.6 \times 10^{-19} \, \text{C}) \cdot (100 \, \text{V}) \, / \, (1.67 \times 10^{-27} \, \text{kg})] + (1.5 \times 10^5 \, \text{m/s})^2$$

$$v_f^2 = (1.9 \times 10^{10} \, \text{m}^2/\text{s}^2) + (2.3 \times 10^{10} \, \text{m}^2/\text{s}^2)$$

$$v_f^2 = 4.2 \times 10^{10} \, \text{m}^2/\text{s}^2$$

$$v_f = 2.04 \times 10^5 \, \text{m/s} \approx 2 \times 10^5 \, \text{m/s}$$

7. C is correct.

$$\text{Power} = \text{current}^2 \times \text{resistance}$$

$$P = I^2 R$$

Double current:

$$P_2 = (2I)^2 R$$

$$P_2 = 4(I^2 R)$$

$$P_2 = 4P$$

Power is quadrupled

8. D is correct. A magnetic field is created only by electric charges in motion.

A stationary charged particle does not generate a magnetic field.

9. B is correct.

Combining the power equation with Ohm's law:

$$P = (\Delta V)^2 / R \text{, where } \Delta V = 120 \text{ V is a constant}$$

To increase power, decrease the resistance.

A longer wire increases resistance, while a thicker wire decreases it:

$$A = \pi r^2$$

$$R = \rho L / A$$

Larger radius of the cross-sectional area means A is larger (denominator) which lowers *R*.

10. E is correct.

$$W = k q_1 q_2 / r$$

$$r = \Delta x$$

$$r = 2 \text{ mm} - (- 2 \text{ mm})$$

$$r = 4 \text{ mm}$$

$$W = [(9 \times 10^9 \text{ N·m}^2/\text{C}^2)·(4 \times 10^{-6} \text{ C})·(8 \times 10^{-6} \text{ C})] / (4 \times 10^{-3} \text{ m})$$

$$W = (0.288 \text{ N·m}^2) / (4 \times 10^{-3} \text{ m})$$

$$W = 72 \text{ J}$$

11. A is correct.

$$V = IR$$

$$I = V / R$$

$$I = (220 \text{ V}) / (400 \ \Omega)$$

$$I = 0.55 \text{ A}$$

12. E is correct.

A parallel circuit experiences the same potential difference across each resistor.

However, the current through each resistor can be different.

13. D is correct.

$$E = qV$$

$$E = \tfrac{1}{2}mv^2$$

$$qV = \tfrac{1}{2}mv^2$$

$$v^2 = 2qV / m$$

$$v^2 = [2(1.6 \times 10^{-19} \text{ C})·(990 \text{ V})] / (9.11 \times 10^{-31} \text{ kg})$$

$$v^2 = 3.5 \times 10^{14} \text{ m}^2/\text{s}^2$$

$$v = 1.9 \times 10^7 \text{ m/s}$$

14. B is correct.

Calculate magnetic field perpendicular to loop:

$B_{Perp2} = (12 \text{ T}) \cos 30°$

$B_{Perp2} = 10.4 \text{ T}$

$B_{Perp1} = (1 \text{ T}) \cos 30°$

$B_{Perp1} = 0.87 \text{ T}$

Use Faraday's Law to calculate generated voltage:

$V = N\Delta BA / \Delta t$

$V = N\Delta B(\pi r^2) / \Delta t$

$V = [(1)\cdot(10.4 \text{ T} - 0.87 \text{ T})\cdot(\pi(0.5 \text{ m})^2)] / (5 \text{ s} - 0 \text{ s})$

$V = [(1)\cdot(10.4 \text{ T} - 0.87 \text{ T})\cdot(0.785 \text{ m}^2)] / (5 \text{ s})$

$V = 1.5 \text{ V}$

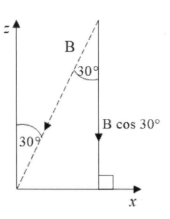

Use Ohm's Law to calculate current:

$V = IR \text{ or } I = V / R$

$I = (1.5 \text{ V}) / (12 \text{ }\Omega)$

$I = 0.13 \text{ A}$

15. C is correct. Ohm's Law:

$V = IR$

$V = (10 \text{ A})\cdot(35 \text{ }\Omega)$

$V = 350 \text{ V}$

16. A is correct. The magnitude of the acceleration is given by:

$F = ma$

$a = F / m$

$F = qE_0$

$a = qE_0 / m$

Bare nuclei = no electrons

^{1}H has 1 proton, and ^{4}He has 2 protons and 2 neutrons

Thus, ^{1}H has ½ the charge and ¼ the mass of ^{4}He.

$a_H = q_H E_0 / m_H$

$a_{He} = q_{He} E_0 / m_{He}$

$a_H = (½q_{He})E_0 / (¼m_{He})$

$a_H = 2(q_{He}E_0 / m_{He})$

$a_H = 2a_{He}$

17. B is correct.

The current will change as the choice of lamp arrangement changes.

Since $P = V^2 / R$, power increases as resistance decreases.

To rank the power in increasing order, the equivalent resistance must be ranked in decreasing order.

For arrangement B, the resistors are in series, so:

$R_{eq} = R + R = 2R$

For arrangement C, the resistors are in parallel, so:

$1/R_{eq} = 1/R + 1/R$

$R_{eq} = R/2$

The ranking of resistance in decreasing order is B to A to C, which is, therefore, the ranking of power in increasing order.

18. D is correct.

$C = k\varepsilon_0 A / d$

where k = dielectric constant or permittivity of material between the plates, A = area and d = distance of plate separation

$C = (2.1)\cdot(8.854 \times 10^{-12}\ \text{F/m})\cdot(0.01\ \text{m} \times 0.01\ \text{m}) / (0.001\ \text{m})$

$C = (1.9 \times 10^{-15}\ \text{F/m}) / (0.001\ \text{m})$

$C = 1.9 \times 10^{-12}\ \text{F} = 1.9\ \text{pF}$

19. C is correct.

Resistor R_1 is connected directly across the battery. Thus, the voltage across R_1 is V and is held constant at that value regardless of whatever happens in the circuit.

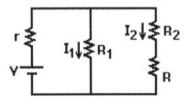

Similarly, the voltage across the series combination of R and R_2 is also held constant at V.

Since the voltage across R_1 will always be V, the current I_1 through R_1 will be unchanged as R changes (since R_1 didn't change, so $I_1 = V / R_1$ remains the same).

Since the voltage across the combination of R and R_2 will always be V, when R is decreased the effective resistance of the series combination $R + R_2$ will decrease, and the current I_2 through R_2 will increase.

20. C is correct.

$$V = IR$$

$$I = V / R$$

Ohm's law states that the current between two points is directly proportional to the potential difference between the points.

21. E is correct. Root mean square voltage equation:

$$V_{rms} = V_{max} / \sqrt{2}$$

$$V_{rms} = 12 / \sqrt{2}$$

$$V_{rms} = (12 / \sqrt{2}) \cdot (\sqrt{2} / \sqrt{2})$$

$$V_{rms} = (12\sqrt{2}) / 2$$

$$V_{rms} = 6\sqrt{2} \text{ V}$$

22. C is correct.

By definition:

$$V_{rms} = V_{max} / \sqrt{2}$$

Therefore:

$$V_{max} = V_{rms}\sqrt{2}$$

$$V_{max} = (150 \text{ V})\sqrt{2}$$

$$V_{max} = 212 \text{ V}$$

23. D is correct.

Kirchhoff's junction rule states that the sum of all currents coming into a junction is the sum of all currents leaving a junction. This is a statement of conservation of charge because it defines that no charge is created nor destroyed in the circuit.

24. A is correct. The capacitance of capacitors connected in parallel is the sum of the individual capacitances:

$$C_{eq} = C_1 + C_2 + C_3 + C_4 = 4C$$

The relationship between the total charge delivered by the battery and the voltage of the battery is:

$$V = Q / C_{eq} = Q / 4C$$

The charge on one capacitor is:

$$Q_1 = CV$$

$$Q_1 = C (Q / 4C)$$

$$Q_1 = Q / 4$$

25. B is correct.

If two conductors are connected by copper wire, each conductor will be at the same potential because current can flow through the wire and equalize the difference in potential.

26. C is correct.

Electromagnetic induction is the production of an electromotive force across a conductor.

When a changing magnetic field is brought near a coil, a voltage is generated in the coil thus inducing a current.

The voltage generated can be calculated by Faraday's Law:

$\text{emf} = -N\Delta\phi / \Delta t$

where N = number of turns and $\Delta\phi$ = change in magnetic flux

27. A is correct.

Current is constant across resistors connected in series.

28. D is correct.

By convention, the direction of electric current is the direction that a positive charge migrates.

Therefore, current flows from the point of high potential to the point of lower potential.

29. E is correct.

$PE_e = PE_1 + PE_2 + PE_3$

$PE_e = (kQ_1Q_2) / r_1 + (kQ_2Q_3) / r_2 + (kQ_1Q_3) / r_3$

$PE_e = kQ^2 [(1 / r_1) + (1 / r_2) + (1 / r_3)]$

$r_1 = 4$ cm and $r_2 = 3$ cm are known, use Pythagorean Theorem to find r_3:

$r_3{}^2 = r_1{}^2 + r_2{}^2$

$r_3{}^2 = (4 \text{ cm})^2 + (3 \text{ cm})^2$

$r_3{}^2 = 16 \text{ cm}^2 + 9 \text{ cm}^2$

$r_3{}^2 = 25 \text{ cm}^2$

$r_3 = 5$ cm

$PE_e = (9.0 \times 10^9 \text{ N·m}^2/\text{C}^2){\cdot}(3.8 \times 10^{-9} \text{ C})^2 \times [(1 / 0.04 \text{ m}) + (1 / 0.03 \text{ m}) + (1 / 0.05 \text{ m})]$

$PE_e = (1.2 \times 10^{-7} \text{ N·m}^2){\cdot}(25 \text{ m}^{-1} + 33 \text{ m}^{-1} + 20 \text{ m}^{-1})$

$PE_e = (1.2 \times 10^{-7} \text{ N·m}^2){\cdot}(78 \text{ m}^{-1})$

$PE_e = 1.0 \times 10^{-5} \text{ J}$

30. A is correct.

The magnetic force acting on a charge q moving at velocity v in a magnetic field B is given by:

$F = qv \times B$

If q, v, and the angle between v and B are the same for both charges, then the magnitude of the force F is the same on both charges.

However, if the charges carry opposite signs, each experiences oppositely-directed forces.

31. C is correct. By convention, the direction of electric current is the direction that a positive charge migrates.

Electrons flow from regions of low potential to regions of high potential.

Electric Potential Energy:

$U = (kQq) / r$

Electric Potential:

$V = (kQ) / r$

Because the charge of an electron (q) is negative, as the electron moves opposite to the electric field, it must be getting closer to the positive charge Q. As this occurs, an increasingly negative potential energy U is produced; thus, potential energy is decreasing.

Conversely, as the electron approaches Q, the electric potential V increases with less distance. This is because the product is positive and reducing r increases V.

32. E is correct. Magnets provide magnetic forces.

Generators convert mechanical energy into electrical energy, turbines extract energy from fluids (e.g., air and water), and transformers transfer energy between circuits.

33. B is correct. The potential energy of a system containing two point charges is:

$U = kq_1 q_2 / r$

In this problem, one of the charges is positive, and the other is negative. To account for this, write:

$q_1 = +|q_1|$ and $q_2 = -|q_2|$

The potential energy can be written as:

$U = -k|q_1||q_2| / r$

Moreover, the absolute value of the potential energy is:

$|U| = k|q_1||q_2| / r$

All quantities are positive. The absolute value of the potential energy is inversely proportional to the orbital radius.

Therefore, the absolute value of the potential energy decreases as the orbital radius increases.

34. C is correct.

$$R = (\rho L) / (\pi r^2)$$
$$R_A = (\rho L) / (\pi r^2)$$
$$R_B = [\rho(2L)] / [\pi(2r)^2]$$
$$R_B = (2/4) \cdot [(\rho L) / (\pi r^2)]$$
$$R_B = \tfrac{1}{2}[(\rho L) / (\pi r^2)]$$
$$R_B = \tfrac{1}{2}R_A$$

35. D is correct.

By convention, current flows from high to low potential, but it represents the flow of positive charges.

Electron flow is in the opposite direction, from low potential to high potential.

36. C is correct.

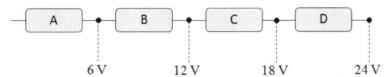

6 V   12 V   18 V   24 V

Batteries in series add voltage like resistors in series add resistance.

The resistances of the lights they power are not needed to solve the problem.

37. B is correct.

$$C = (k\mathcal{E}_0 A) / d$$
$$k = (Cd) / A\mathcal{E}_0$$

If capacitance increases by a factor of 4:

$$k_2 = (4C)d / A\mathcal{E}_0$$
$$k_2 = 4(Cd / A\mathcal{E}_0)$$
$$k_2 = 4k$$

38. E is correct.

$$C = (k\mathcal{E}_0 A) / d$$
$$C = [(1) \cdot (8.854 \times 10^{-12} \text{ F/m}) \cdot (0.4 \text{ m}^2)] / (0.04 \text{ m})$$
$$C = 8.854 \times 10^{-11} \text{ F}$$
$$V = Q / C$$
$$V = (6.8 \times 10^{-10} \text{ C}) / (8.854 \times 10^{-11} \text{ F})$$
$$V = 7.7 \text{ V}$$

39. A is correct.

Since force is the cross-product of velocity and magnetic field strength:

$$F = qv \times B$$

The force is at a maximum when v and B are perpendicular:

$$F = qvB \sin 90°$$

$$\sin 90° = 1$$

$$F = qvB$$

40. E is correct.

Ampere is the unit of current, which is defined as the rate of flow of charge. The current describes how much charge (in Coulombs) passes through a point every second.

So, if the current is multiplied by the number of seconds (the time interval), one can measure just how much charge passed by during that time interval.

Mathematically, the units are expressed as:

$$A = C / s$$

$$C = A \cdot s$$

41. C is correct.

$$\Delta V = \Delta E / q$$

$$\Delta V = (1 / q) \cdot (\tfrac{1}{2}mv_f^2 - \tfrac{1}{2}mv_i^2)$$

$$\Delta V = (m / 2q) \cdot (v_f^2 - v_i^2)$$

$$\Delta V = [(1.67 \times 10^{-27}\,\text{kg}) / (2) \cdot (1.6 \times 10^{-19}\,\text{C})] \times [(3.2 \times 10^5\,\text{m/s})^2 - (1.7 \times 10^5\,\text{m/s})^2]$$

$$\Delta V = 384\,\text{V}$$

42. E is correct. $Q = VC$

Even though the capacitors have different capacitances, the voltage across each capacitor is inversely proportional to the capacitance of that capacitor.

Like current, the charge is conserved across capacitors in series.

43. A is correct.

Calculate capacitance:

$$C = k\varepsilon_o A / d$$

$$C = [(1) \cdot (8.854 \times 10^{-12}\,\text{F/m}) \cdot (0.6\,\text{m}^2)] / (0.06\,\text{m})$$

$$C = 8.854 \times 10^{-11}\,\text{F}$$

Find potential difference:

$$C = Q / V$$

$$V = Q / C$$
$$V = (7.08 \times 10^{-10} \text{ C}) / (8.854 \times 10^{-11} \text{ F})$$
$$V = 8 \text{ V}$$

44. B is correct.

"In a perfect conductor" and "in the absence of resistance" have the same meanings, and current can flow in conductors of varying resistances.

A semi-perfect conductor has resistance.

45. C is correct.

Faraday's Law: a changing magnetic environment causes a voltage to be induced in a conductor. Metal detectors send quick magnetic pulses that cause a voltage (by Faraday's Law) and subsequent current to be induced in the conductor.

By Lenz's Law, an opposing magnetic field will then arise to counter the changing magnetic field. The detector picks up the magnetic field and notifies the operator.

Thus, metal detectors use Faraday's Law and Lenz's Law to detect metal objects.

46. E is correct.

$$E = qV$$
$$E = (7 \times 10^{-6} \text{ C}) \cdot (3.5 \times 10^{-3} \text{ V})$$
$$E = 24.5 \times 10^{-9} \text{ J}$$
$$E = 24.5 \text{ nJ}$$

47. B is correct.

$$R_1 = \rho L_1 / A_1$$
$$R_2 = \rho (4L_1) / A_2$$
$$R_1 = R_2$$
$$\rho L_1 / A_1 = \rho (4L_1) / A_2$$
$$A_2 = 4A_1$$
$$(\pi / 4)d_2^{2} = (\pi / 4) \cdot (4)d_1^{2}$$
$$d_2^{2} = 4d_1^{2}$$
$$d_2 = 2d_1$$

48. D is correct.

The total resistance of a network of series resistors increases as more resistors are added.

$$V = IR$$

An increase in the total resistance results in a decrease in the total current through the network.

49. A is correct.

This is a circuit with two resistors in series.

Combine the two resistors into one resistor:

$$R_T = R + R_{int}$$
$$R_T = 0.5\ \Omega + 0.1\ \Omega$$
$$R_T = 0.6\ \Omega$$

Ohm's law:

$$V = IR$$
$$I = V / R$$
$$I = 9\ \text{V} / 0.6\ \Omega$$
$$I = 15\ \text{A}$$

50. C is correct.

Energy stored in capacitor:

$$U = \tfrac{1}{2}(Q^2 / C)$$

Capacitance:

$$C = k\varepsilon_0 A / d$$
$$U = \tfrac{1}{2}(Q^2 d) / (k\varepsilon_0 A)$$
$$Q = \sqrt{[(2U \times k\varepsilon_0 A) / d]}$$
$$Q = \sqrt{\{[(2)\cdot(10 \times 10^3\ \text{J})\cdot(1)\cdot(8.854 \times 10^{-12}\ \text{F/m})\cdot(2.4 \times 10^{-5}\ \text{m}^2)] / 0.0016\ \text{m}\}}$$
$$Q = 52\ \mu\text{C}$$

51. B is correct.

Potential energy:

$$U = (kQq) / r$$

Electric Potential:

$$V = (kQ) / r$$

As r increases, the potential energy U decreases as does the electric potential V.

Movement in the direction of the electric field is movement away from a positive charge.

52. D is correct.

Electric field energy density:

$$\eta_E = \tfrac{1}{2}E^2 \times \varepsilon_0$$
$$\eta_E = \tfrac{1}{2}(8.6 \times 10^6\ \text{V/m})^2\cdot(8.854 \times 10^{-12}\ \text{F/m})$$
$$\eta_E = 330\ \text{J/m}^3$$

53. A is correct.

Resistance = Ohms

$$\Omega = V / A$$

$$\Omega = [(kg \cdot m^2/s^2)/C] / [C/s]$$

$$\Omega = kg \cdot m^2/(C^2/s)$$

54. E is correct.

Ohm's Law:

$$V = IR$$

If V is constant, then *I* and *R* are inversely proportional.

An increase in *R* results in a decrease in *I*.

55. D is correct. Electric Potential:

$$V = kQ / r$$

All other positions on the square (1, 2 or 3) are equidistant from point *p*, as is charge +*Q*.

Thus, a negative charge placed at any of these locations would have equal magnitude potential but an opposite sign because the new charge is negative.

Thus: $|V| = |-V|$

$$V + (-V) = 0$$

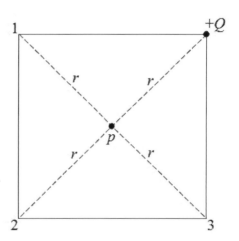

Light and Optics – Explanations

1. A is correct.

Soap film that reflects a given wavelength of light exhibits constructive interference.

The expression for constructive interference of a thin film:

$2t = (m + \frac{1}{2})\lambda$

where t = thickness, m = 0, 1, 2, 3… and λ = wavelength

To find the minimum thickness set m = 0:

$2t = (0 + \frac{1}{2})\lambda = \frac{1}{2}\lambda$

$t = \frac{1}{4}\lambda$

2. A is correct.

By the law of reflection, the angle of incidence is equal to the angle of reflection.

Thus, as the angle of incidence increases, the angle of reflection increases as well to be equal to the angle of incidence.

3. B is correct.

If image is twice her height and upright, then:

$2h_o = h_i$

$m = h_i / h_o$

$m = -d_i / d_o$

$m = 2h_o / h_o$

$m = 2$

$2 = -d_i / d_o$

$-2d_o = d_i$

Use lens equation to solve:

$1 / f = 1 / d_o + 1 / d_i$

$1 / 100 \text{ cm} = 1 / d_o + (-1 / 2 d_o)$

$1 / 100 \text{ cm} = 1 / 2 d_o$

$2d_o = 100 \text{ cm}$

$d_o = 50 \text{ cm}$

4. D is correct.
If a person's eye is too long, the light entering the eye is focused in front of the retina causing myopia. This condition is also referred to as nearsightedness.

Hyperopia is also referred to as farsightedness.

5. E is correct.

Visible light:

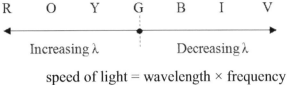

speed of light = wavelength × frequency

$$c = \lambda f$$

Wavelength to frequency:

$$f = c \, / \, \lambda$$

Frequency and wavelength are inversely proportional:

As λ increases, f decreases.

As λ decreases, f increases.

Thus, because $E = hf$:

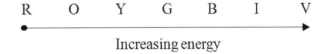

6. B is correct.

The lens equation:

$$1 \, / \, f = 1 \, / \, d_o + 1 \, / \, d_i$$

$$1 \, / \, d_i = 1 \, / \, f - 1 \, / \, d_o$$

$$1 \, / \, d_i = -1 \, / \, 3 \text{ m} - 1 \, / \, 4 \text{ m}$$

$$1 \, / \, d_i = (-3 \text{ m} - 4 \text{ m}) \, / \, 12 \text{ m}$$

$$1 \, / \, d_i = -7 \text{ m} \, / \, 12 \text{ m}$$

$$d_i = -12 \, / \, 7 \text{ m}$$

Magnification:

$$m = -d_i \, / \, d_o$$

$$m = -(-12 \, / \, 7 \text{ m}) \, / \, 4 \text{ m}$$

$$m = 3 \, / \, 7$$

Height of the candle image:

$$h_i = m h_o$$

$$h_i = (3/7) \cdot (18 \text{ cm})$$

$$h_i = 54 \, / \, 7 \text{ cm}$$

$$h_i = 7.7 \text{ cm}$$

7. C is correct.

$\theta_{syrup} = \tan^{-1}(0.9 \text{ m} / 0.66 \text{ m})$

$\theta_s = \tan^{-1}(1.36)$

$\theta_s = 53.7°$

$\theta_{oil} = \tan^{-1}[(2 \text{ m} - 0.9 \text{ m}) / 1.58 \text{ m}]$

$\theta_o = \tan^{-1}(0.7)$

$\theta_o = 34.8°$

$n_o \sin \theta_o = n_{air} \sin \theta_{air}$

$n_o \sin 34.8° = (1) \sin 90°$

$n_o = 1 / (\sin 34.8°)$

$n_o = 1.75$

8. D is correct.

$\theta_{syrup} = \tan^{-1}(0.9 \text{ m} / 0.66 \text{ m})$

$\theta_s = \tan^{-1}(1.36)$

$\theta_s = 53.7°$

$\theta_{oil} = \tan^{-1}[(2 \text{ m} - 0.9 \text{ m}) / 1.58 \text{ m}]$

$\theta_o = \tan^{-1}(0.7)$

$\theta_o = 34.8°$

$n_o \sin \theta_o = n_{air} \sin \theta_{air}$

$n_o \sin 34.8° = (1) \sin 90°$

$n_o = 1 / (\sin 34.8°)$

$n_o = 1.75$

$n_s \sin \theta_s = n_o \sin \theta_o$

$n_s = n_o \sin \theta_o / \sin \theta_s$

$n_s = (1.75) \cdot (\sin 34.8°) / (\sin 53.7°)$

$n_s = 1.24$

9. A is correct.

The photoelectric effect (i.e., emission of electrons when light shines on a material) cannot be explained with the wave theory of light.

The photoelectric effect is the phenomenon where light incident upon a metallic surface causes electrons to be emitted.

The photoelectric effect is described by the equation:

$KE_{max} = hf - \phi$, where h = Planck's constant, f = frequency and ϕ = work function.

10. D is correct.

Geometrical optics, or ray optics, describes light propagation in terms of rays and fronts to approximate the path along which light propagates in certain circumstances.

11. D is correct.

First find the critical angle:

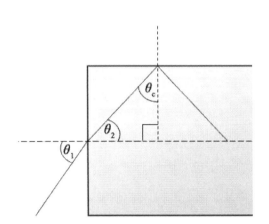

$$n_{fiber} \sin \theta_c = n_{air} \sin \theta_{air}$$

$$(1.26) \sin \theta_c = (1) \sin 90°$$

$$\sin \theta_c = 1 / 1.26$$

$$\theta_c = \sin^{-1} (1 / 1.26)$$

$$\theta_c = 52.5°$$

Find θ_2:

$$\theta_2 + \theta_c + 90° = 180°$$

$$(\theta_2 + 52.5° + 90°) = 180°$$

$$\theta_2 = 37.5°$$

Find θ_1:

$$n_{air} \sin \theta_1 = n_{fiber} \sin \theta_2$$

$$(1) \sin \theta_1 = (1.26) \sin 37.5°$$

$$\sin \theta_1 = 0.77$$

$$\theta_1 = \sin^{-1} (0.77)$$

$$\theta_1 = 50°$$

12. A is correct.

If the power of the lens is 10 diopters,

$$1 / f = 10 \text{ D}$$

where f is the focal length in m

Thin Lens Equation:

$$1 / f = 1 / d_o + 1 / d_i$$

$$10 \text{ m}^{-1} = 1 / 0.5 \text{ m} + 1 / d_i$$

$$1 / d_i = 10 \text{ m}^{-1} - 1 / 0.5 \text{ m}$$

$$1 / d_i = 8 \text{ m}^{-1}$$

$$d_i = 1 / 8 \text{ m}$$

$$d_i = 0.13 \text{ m}$$

13. D is correct.

Most objects observed by humans are virtual images or objects which reflect incoming light to project an image.

14. E is correct.

An image from a convex mirror will always have the following characteristics, regardless of object distance:

- located behind the convex mirror
- virtual
- upright
- reduced in size from the object (image < object)

15. A is correct.

The mirror has a positive focal length which indicates that the mirror is concave.

The object is at a distance greater than the focal length. Therefore, it is inverted.

Use lens equation to solve image distance:

$1 / f = 1 / d_o + 1 / d_i$

$1 / 10 \text{ m} = 1 / 20 \text{ m} + 1 / d_i$

$d_i = 20 \text{ cm}$

The image distance is positive so the image is real.

Use the magnification equation to determine if it is upright or inverted.

$m = -d_i / d_o$

$m = h_i / h_o$

$-(20 \text{ m} / 20 \text{ m}) = h_i / h_o$

$-1 = h_i / h_o$

The object height h_o is always positive so the image height h_i must be negative to satisfy the equation.

A negative image height indicates an inverted image.

16. E is correct.

For a converging lens, if an object is placed beyond $2f$ from the lens, the image is real, inverted and reduced.

Use the lens equation to determine if the image is real (or vitual):

Assume $f = 1 \text{ m}$ and $d_o = 3f$ (because $d_o > 2f$)

$1 / f = 1 / d_o + 1 / d_i$

$1 / f = 1 / 3f + 1 / d_i$

$d_i = 1.5$

A positive d_i indicates a real image.

Use the magnification equation to determine if the image is inverted and reduced.

$m = -d_i / d_o$

$m = -(1.5 \text{ m} / 3 \text{ m})$

$m = -\frac{1}{2}$

$|m| = \frac{1}{2}$

$|m| < 1$

A negative magnification factor with an absolute value less than 1 a reduced and inverted image.

17. C is correct.

Radio waves range from 3 kHz to 300 GHz, which is lower than all forms of radiation listed.

Since the energy of radiation is proportional to frequency ($E = hf$), radio waves have the lowest energy.

18. B is correct.

A medium's index of refraction is the ratio of the speed of refracted light in a vacuum to its speed in the reference medium.

$n = c / v$

$n = 2.43$

$2.43 = c / v_{\text{diamond}}$

$c = 2.43(v_{\text{diamond}})$

19. D is correct.

$1 / f = 1 / d_o + 1 / d_i$

$1 / 20 \text{ cm} = 1 / 15 \text{ cm} + 1 / d_i$

$3 / 60 \text{ cm} - 4 / 60 \text{ cm} = 1 / d_i$

$-1 / 60 \text{ cm} = 1 / d_i$

$d_i = -60 \text{ cm}$

The negative sign indicates that the image is projected back the way it came.

20. B is correct.

Red paper absorbs all colors but reflects only red light giving it the appearance of being red. Cyan is the complementary color to red, so when the cyan light shines upon the red paper, no light is reflected, and the paper appears black.

21. B is correct.

$$1/f = 1/d_o + 1/d_i$$

If $d_i = f$,

$$1/d_o = 0$$

Thus, d_o must be large.

22. E is correct.

Since the index of refraction depends on the frequency, and the focal length depends on the refraction of the beam in the lens, dispersion causes the focal length to depend on frequency.

23. C is correct. Use the equation for magnification:

$$m = -d_i/d_o$$

$$d_i = d_o$$

$$m = 1$$

Thus, there is no magnification, so the image is the same size as the object.

24. E is correct.

When viewed straight down (90° to the surface), an incident light ray moving from water to air is refracted 0°.

25. C is correct.

The rotating of one polarized lens 90° with respect to the other lens results in complete darkness, since no light would be transmitted.

26. C is correct.

First, find the angle that the ray makes with the normal of the glass:

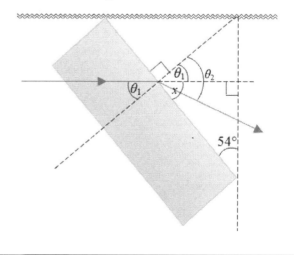

$$180° = x + 90° + 54°$$

$$x = 36°$$

Find θ_1:

$$\theta_1 = 90° - 36°$$

$$\theta_1 = 54°$$

Referring to the diagram, $\theta_1 = 54°$

Snell's Law:

$$n_1 \sin \theta_1 = n_2 \sin \theta_2$$

$$\sin^{-1}[(n_1/n_2) \sin \theta_1] = \theta_2$$

$$\theta_2 = \sin^{-1}[(1.45/1.35) \sin 54°]$$

$\theta_2 = 60°$

Solve for the angle with the horizontal:

$\theta_H = 60° - 54°$

$\theta_H = 6°$

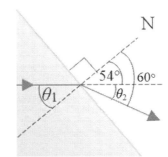

27. A is correct.

The angle at which the ray is turned is the sum of the angles if reflected off each mirror once:

$\theta_{turned} = \theta_1 + \theta_2 + \theta_3 + \theta_4$

By law of reflection:

$\theta_1 = \theta_2$

$\theta_3 = \theta_4$

Note the triangle formed (sum of interior angles is 180°):

$30° + (90° - \theta_2) + (90° - \theta_3) = 180°$

$\theta_2 + \theta_3 = 30°$

Given:

$\theta_2 + \theta_3 = \theta_1 + \theta_4$

Thus:

$\theta_{turned} = 30° + 30°$

$\theta_{turned} = 60°$

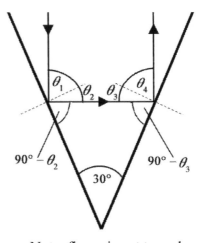

Note: figure is not to scale

In general: for two plane mirrors that meet at an angle of $\theta \leq 90°$ the ray that is deflected off both mirrors is deflected through an angle of 2θ.

28. E is correct.

All of the following statements about light are true: a packet of light energy is known as a photon, color can be used to determine the approximate energy of visible light and light travels through space at a speed of 3.0×10^8 m/s.

29. A is correct.

The angle of incidence is < the angle of refraction if the light travels into a less dense medium.

The angle of incidence is > the angle of refraction if the light travels into a denser medium.

The angle of incidence is = the angle of refraction if the densities of the mediums are equal.

30. E is correct.

Plane mirrors do not distort the size or the shape of an object since light is reflected at the same angle the mirror received it.

Magnification equation:

$$m = h_i / h_o$$

For a plane mirror m = 1:

$$1 = h_i / h_o$$

$$h_i = h_o$$

Therefore, the image size is the same as object size, and the image is virtual since it is located behind the mirror.

31. C is correct.

A spherical concave mirror has a focal length of:

$$f = R / 2$$

32. B is correct.

Refracted rays bend further from the normal than the original incident angle when the refracting medium is optically less dense than the incident medium. Therefore, $n_1 > n_2$.

The index of refraction for a medium can never be less than 1.

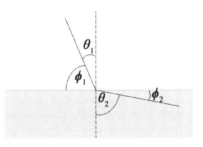

33. B is correct.

If a person's eye is too short, then the light entering the eye is focused behind the retina causing farsightedness (hyperopia).

34. A is correct.

Hot air is less dense than cold air. Light traveling through both types of air experiences refractions, which appear as shimmering or "wavy" air.

35. E is correct.

Chromatic aberration occurs when a lens focuses different wavelengths of color at different positions in the focal plane.

It always occurs in the following pattern for converging lens:

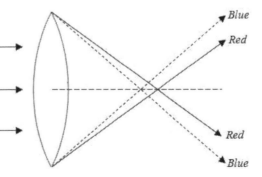

36. B is correct.

$$1 / f_{total} = 1 / f_1 + 1 / f_2$$
$$1 / f_{total} = 1 / 2 \text{ m} + 1 / 4 \text{ m}$$
$$1 / f_{total} = 3 / 4 \text{ m}$$
$$f_{total} = 4 / 3 \text{ m}$$

37. C is correct.

The angle in the water respective to the normal:

$$\theta = \tan^{-1}(37.5 \text{ ft} / 50 \text{ ft})$$
$$\theta = \tan^{-1}(0.75)$$
$$\theta = 36.9°$$
$$n_{air} \sin(90 - \theta) = n_{water} \sin \theta$$
$$(1) \sin(90 - \theta) = (1.33) \sin 36.9°$$
$$\sin(90 - \theta) = 0.8$$
$$(90 - \theta) = \sin^{-1}(0.8)$$
$$(90 - \theta) = 52.9$$
$$\theta = 37.1° \approx 37°$$

38. A is correct.

Violet light has the highest energy and frequency, and therefore has the shortest wavelength.

39. E is correct.

Objects directly in front of plane mirrors are reflected in their likeness since plane mirrors are not curved and therefore reflect light perpendicularly to their surface.

40. B is correct.

A virtual image is always upright and can be formed by both a diverging lens and a converging lens.

Diverging lens → reduced and virtual image

Converging lens → enlarged and virtual image

41. B is correct. Neon light is the light emitted from neon atoms as their energized electrons cascade back down to ground level. When this occurs, energy is released in the form of light at very specific wavelengths known as the emission spectrum.

When this light is passed through a prism, a series of bright discontinuous spots or lines will be seen due to the specific wavelengths of the emission spectrum of neon.

42. E is correct.

The law of reflection states that the angle of incidence is equal to the angle of reflection (with respect to the normal) and is true for all mirrors.

$\theta_i = \theta_r$

43. C is correct.

A concave lens always forms an image that is virtual, upright and reduced in size.

44. B is correct.

Virtual images are always upright.

There is no correlation between the size and nature – virtual or real – of an image.

Images may be larger, smaller, or the same size as the object.

45. E is correct.

From all choices listed, red is the light with the lowest frequency (longest wavelength) detected by your eyes. (ROY G BIV)

46. D is correct.

$1/f = 1/d_o + 1/d_i$

$1/6 \text{ m} = 1/3 \text{ m} + 1/d_i$

$1/d_i = 1/6 \text{ m} - 1/3 \text{ m}$

$1/d_i = -1/6 \text{ m}$

$d_i = -6 \text{ m}$

where the negative sign indicates the image is on the same side as the object.

The image is upright and virtual since the rays must be extended to intersect.

47. A is correct. A diverging lens (concave) always produces an image that is virtual, upright and reduced in size.

48. C is correct.

Thin lens formula:

$1/f = 1/d_o + 1/d_i$

d_i is negative because the image is virtual

$1/f = 1/14 \text{ cm} + 1/-5 \text{ cm}$

$f = -7.8 \text{ cm}$

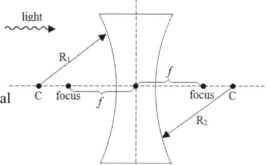

The focus is negative because the lens is diverging.

Lensmaker's formula:

$$1 / f = (n - 1)\cdot(1 / R_1 - 1 / R_2)$$

R_1 is negative by convention because the light ray passes its center of curvature before the curved surface.

$$1 / (-7.8 \text{ cm}) = (n - 1)\cdot(1 / -15 \text{ cm} - 1 / 15 \text{ cm})$$

$$(1 / -7.8 \text{ cm})\cdot(15 \text{ cm} / -2) + 1 = n$$

$$n = 2$$

49. E is correct.

The magnification equation relates the image and object distance:

$$m = -d_i / d_o$$

or

The magnification equation relates the image and object height:

$$m = h_i / h_o$$

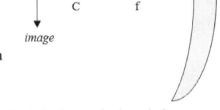

50. D is correct. (see image)

For a concave mirror, if an object is located between the focal point and center of curvature, the image is formed beyond the center of curvature.

In this problem, Mike does not see his image because he is in front of where it forms.

51. D is correct.

For a concave spherical mirror, the produced image characteristics depend upon the placement of the object in relation to the focal point and center of curvature.

The image can be smaller, larger or the same size as the object.

52. A is correct.

Lens power is the reciprocal of the focal length in meters:

$$P = 1 / f$$

If the effective focal length of the lens combination is less than the focal length of either individual lens, then the power of the combination must be greater than the power of either individual lens.

53. B is correct.

A medium's index of refraction is the ratio of the speed of refracted light in a vacuum to its speed in the reference medium.

$$n = c / v$$

54. E is correct.

As it is a plane mirror, the image is not distorted.

Only some of the light rays are reflected, the others create an image behind the mirror's surface.

For a plane mirror:

$$m = 1$$

$$m = -d_i / d_o$$

$$1 = -d_i / d_o$$

$$d_o = -d_i$$

The negative indicates the image is virtual and behind the mirror.

55. C is correct.

The radius length is the center of curvature, $r = 50$ cm

Find the focal length:

$$f = r / 2$$

$$f = 50 \text{ cm} / 2$$

$$f = 25 \text{ cm}$$

For a concave mirror with an object between the center of curvature and the focal length, the resulting image is real and inverted.

Heat and Thermodynamics – Explanations

1. B is correct.

Ideal gas law:

$$PV = nRT$$

$$P_0 = nRT / V_0$$

If isothermal expansion, then n, R and T are constant

$$P = nRT / (1/3 \; V_0)$$

$$P = 3(nRT / V_0)$$

$$P = 3P_0$$

2. C is correct.

Area expansion equation:

$$\Delta A = A_0(2\alpha\Delta T)$$

$$\Delta A = (\pi / 4)\cdot(1.2 \; cm)^2\cdot(2)\cdot(19 \times 10^{-6} \; K^{-1})\cdot(200 \; °C)$$

$$\Delta A = 8.6 \times 10^{-3} \; cm^2$$

$$\Delta A = A_f - A_0$$

$$8.6 \times 10^{-3} \; cm^2 = (\pi / 4)\cdot[d_f^2 - (1.2 \; cm)^2]$$

$$d_f = 1.2 \; cm$$

3. D is correct.

$$1 \; Watt = 1 \; J/s$$

$$Power \times Time = Q$$

$$Q = mc\Delta T$$

$$P \times t = mc\Delta T$$

$$t = (mc\Delta T) / P$$

$$t = (90 \; g)\cdot(4.186 \; J/g\cdot°C)\cdot(30 \; °C - 10 \; °C) / (50 \; W)$$

$$t = 151 \; s$$

4. A is correct.

Convert 15 minutes to seconds:

$$t = (15 \; min/1)\cdot(60 \; s/1 \; min)$$

$$t = 900 \; s$$

Find total energy generated:

$$Q = P \times t$$
$$Q = (1{,}260 \text{ J/s}) \cdot (900 \text{ s})$$
$$Q = 1{,}134 \text{ kJ}$$

Find mass of water needed to carry away energy:

$$Q = mL_v$$
$$m = Q / L_v$$
$$m = (1{,}134 \text{ kJ}) / (22.6 \times 10^2 \text{ kJ/kg})$$
$$m = 0.5 \text{ kg}$$
$$m = 500 \text{ g}$$

5. C is correct.

Phase changes occur at a constant temperature. Once the phase change is complete the temperature of the substance then either increases or decreases.

For example, water remains at 0 °C until it has completely changed phase to ice before the temperature decreases further.

6. E is correct.

The amount of energy needed to melt a sample of mass m is:

$$Q = m \, L_f$$

Where L_f is the latent heat of fusion.

$$Q = (55 \text{ kg}) \cdot (334 \text{ kJ/kg})$$
$$Q = 1.8 \times 10^4 \text{ kJ}$$

7. D is correct.

Metals are good heat and electrical conductors because of their bonding structure.

In metallic bonding, the outer electrons are held loosely and can travel freely.

Electricity and heat require high electron mobility.

Thus, the looseness of the outer electrons in the materials allows them to be excellent conductors.

8. A is correct.
Find heat of phase change from steam to liquid:

$$Q_1 = mL_v$$

Find heat of phase change from liquid to solid:

$$Q_2 = mL_f$$

Find heat of temperature from 100 °C to 0 °C:

$$Q_3 = mc\Delta T$$

Total heat:

$$Q_{net} = Q_1 + Q_2 + Q_3$$

$$Q_{net} = mL_v + mL_f + mc\Delta T$$

To find mass:

$$Q_{net} = m(L_v + c\Delta T + L_f)$$

$$m = Q_{net} / (L_v + c\Delta T + L_f)$$

Solve:

$$Q_{net} = 200 \text{ kJ}$$

$$Q_{net} = 2 \times 10^5 \text{ J}$$

$$m = (2 \times 10^5 \text{ J}) / [(22.6 \times 10^5 \text{ J/kg}) + (4{,}186 \text{ J/kg·K}){\cdot}(100 \text{ °C} - 0 \text{ °C}) + (33.5 \times 10^4 \text{ J/kg})]$$

$$m = 0.066 \text{ kg}$$

9. C is correct.

Fusion is the process whereby a substance changes from a solid to liquid (i.e., melting).

Condensation is the process whereby a substance changes from a vapor to liquid.

Sublimation is the process whereby a substance changes directly from a solid to the gas phase without passing through the liquid phase.

10. E is correct.

$$Q = mc\Delta T$$

$$Q = (0.2 \text{ kg}){\cdot}(14.3 \text{ J/g·K}){\cdot}(1{,}000 \text{ g/kg}){\cdot}(280 \text{ K} - 250 \text{ K})$$

$$Q = 86{,}000 \text{ J} = 86 \text{ kJ}$$

11. B is correct.

Heat needed to raise temperature of aluminum:

$$Q_A = m_A c_A \Delta T$$

Heat needed to raise temperature of water:

$$Q_W = m_W c_W \Delta T$$

Total heat to raise temperature of system:

$$Q_{net} = Q_A + Q_W$$

$$Q_{net} = m_A c_A \Delta T + m_W c_W \Delta T$$

$$Q_{net} = \Delta T(m_A c_A + m_W c_W)$$

$$Q_{net} = (98 \text{ °C} - 18 \text{ °C}){\cdot}[(0.5 \text{ kg}){\cdot}(900 \text{ J/kg·K}) + (1 \text{ kg}){\cdot}(4{,}186 \text{ J/kg·K})]$$

$$Q_{net} = 370,880 \text{ J}$$

Time to produce Q_{net} with 500 W:

$$Q_{net} = (500 \text{ W})t$$

$$t = Q_{net} / (500 \text{ W})$$

$$t = (370,880 \text{ J}) / 500 \text{ W}$$

$$t = 741.8 \text{ s}$$

Convert to minutes:

$$t = (741.8 \text{ s}/1)\cdot(1 \text{ min}/60 \text{ s})$$

$$t = 12.4 \text{ min} \approx 12 \text{ min}$$

12. A is correct.

When a substance goes through a phase change, the temperature doesn't change.

It can be assumed that the lower plateau is L_f and the upper plateau is L_v.

Count the columns: $L_f = 2$, $L_v = 7$

$$L_v / L_f = 7 / 2$$

$$L_v / L_f = 3.5$$

13. B is correct.

Specific heat is the amount of heat (i.e., energy) needed to raise the temperature of the unit mass of a substance by a given amount (usually one degree).

14. E is correct.

Find ½ of KE of the BB:

$$KE = \tfrac{1}{2}mv^2$$

$$\tfrac{1}{2}KE = \tfrac{1}{2}(\tfrac{1}{2}mv^2)$$

$$\tfrac{1}{2}KE_{BB} = \tfrac{1}{2}(\tfrac{1}{2})\cdot(0.0045 \text{ kg})\cdot(46 \text{ m/s})^2$$

$$\tfrac{1}{2}KE_{BB} = 2.38 \text{ J}$$

The $\tfrac{1}{2}KE_{BB}$ is equal to energy taken to change temperature:

$$Q = \tfrac{1}{2}KE_{BB}$$
$$Q = mc\Delta T$$

$$mc\Delta T = \tfrac{1}{2}KE_{BB}$$

$$\Delta T = \tfrac{1}{2}KE_{BB} / mc$$

Calculate to find ΔT:

$$\Delta T = (2.38 \text{ J}) / (0.0045 \text{ kg})\cdot(128 \text{ J/kg·K})$$

$$\Delta T = 4.1 \text{ K}$$

15. C is correct.

Vaporization is the process whereby a substance changes from a liquid to a gas. The process can be either boiling or evaporation.

Sublimation is the process whereby a substance changes from a solid to a gas.

16. A is correct.

Carnot efficiency:

η = work done / total energy

$\eta = W / Q_H$

$\eta = 5\,J / 18\,J$

$\eta = 0.28$

The engine's efficiency:

$\eta = (T_H - T_C) / T_H$

$0.28 = (233\,K - T_C) / 233\,K$

$(0.28) \cdot (233\,K) = (233\,K - T_C)$

$65.2\,K = 233\,K - T_C$

$T_C = 168\,K$

17. D is correct. Heat needed to change temperature of a mass:

$Q = mc\Delta T$

Calculate to find Q:

$Q = (0.92\,kg) \cdot (113\,cal/kg\cdot°C) \cdot (96\,°C - 18\,°C)$

$Q = 8,108.9\,cal$

Convert to joules:

$Q = (8,108.9\,cal) \cdot (4.186\,J/cal)$

$Q = 33,940\,J$

18. B is correct.

During a change of state, the addition of heat does not change the temperature (i.e., a measure of the kinetic energy). The heat energy added only adds to the potential energy of the substance until the substance completely changes state.

19. E is correct.

For a pressure vs. volume graph of the work done for a cyclic process carried out by a gas, it is equal to the area enclosed by the cyclic process.

20. A is correct.

Specific heat of A is larger than B:

$$c_A > c_B$$

Energy to raise the temperature:

$$Q = mc\Delta T$$

If m and ΔT are equal for A and B:

$$Q_A = m_A c_A \Delta T_A$$

$$Q_B = m_B c_B \Delta T_B$$

$$Q_A > Q_B$$

This is valid because all other factors are equal and the magnitude of Q only depends on c.

21. D is correct.

Find kinetic energy of meteor:

$$KE = \tfrac{1}{2}mv^2$$

$$KE = \tfrac{1}{2}(0.0065 \text{ kg}) \cdot (300 \text{ m/s})^2$$

$$KE = 292.5 \text{ J}$$

Find temperature rise:

$$Q = KE$$

$$Q = mc\Delta T$$

$$mc\Delta T = KE$$

$$\Delta T = KE \,/\, mc$$

Convert KE to calories:

$$KE = (292.5 \text{ J}/1) \cdot (1 \text{ cal}/4.186 \text{ J})$$

$$KE = 69.9 \text{ cal}$$

Calculate ΔT:

$$\Delta T = (69.9 \text{ cal}) \,/\, [(0.0065 \text{ kg}) \cdot (120 \text{ cal/kg·°C})]$$

$$\Delta T = 89.6 \text{ °C} \approx 90 \text{ °C}$$

22. A is correct.

When a liquid freezes it undergoes a phase change from liquid to solid. For this to occur heat energy must be dissipated (removed).

During any phase change, the temperature remains constant.

23. B is correct.

For an isothermal process:

$$\Delta U = 0$$

$$\Delta U = Q - W$$

$$Q = W$$

Work to expand an ideal gas in an isothermal process:

$$W = nRT \ln(V_f / V_i)$$

From the ideal gas law, $nRT = P_f V_f$, giving:

$$W = P_f V_f \ln(V_f / V_i)$$

$$W = (130 \text{ kPa}) \cdot (0.2 \text{ m}^3) \ln[(0.2 \text{ m}^3) / (0.05 \text{ m}^3)]$$

$$W = 36 \text{ kJ}$$

$$Q = W$$

$$Q = 36 \text{ kJ}$$

The process is isothermal, so there is no change in the internal energy.

Since the surroundings are doing negative work on the system:

$$\Delta E = 0 = Q + W = Q - 36 \text{ kJ}$$

Therefore:

$$Q = 36 \text{ kJ}.$$

24. D is correct.

Find the potential energy of 1 kg of water:

$$PE = mgh$$

$$PE = (1 \text{ kg}) \cdot (9.8 \text{ m/s}^2) \cdot (30 \text{ m})$$

$$PE = 294 \text{ J}$$

Assume all potential energy is converted to heat for maximum temperature increase:

$$PE = Q$$

$$Q = mc\Delta T$$

$$mc\Delta T = PE$$

$$\Delta T = PE / mc$$

$$\Delta T = (294 \text{ J}) / [(1 \text{ kg}) \cdot (4{,}186 \text{ J/kg/K})]$$

$$\Delta T = 0.07 \text{ °C}$$

For temperature differences it is not necessary to convert to Kelvin because a temperature change in Kelvin is equal to a temperature change in Celsius.

25. A is correct.

Find heat from phase change:

$$Q = mL_f$$

$$Q = (0.75 \text{ kg}) \cdot (33,400 \text{ J/kg})$$

$$Q = 25,050 \text{ J}$$

Because the water is freezing, Q should be negative due to heat being released.

$$Q = -25,050 \text{ J}$$

Find change in entropy:

$$\Delta S = Q / T$$

$$\Delta S = -25,050 \text{ J} / (0 \text{ °C} + 273 \text{ K})$$

$$\Delta S = -92 \text{ J} / \text{K}$$

A negative change in entropy indicates that the disorder of the isolated system has decreased.

When water freezes the entropy is negative because water is more disordered than ice.

Thus, the disorder has decreased.

26. A is correct.

Copper has a larger coefficient of linear expansion than iron, so it expands more than iron during a given temperature change.

The bimetallic bar bends due to the difference in expansion between the copper and iron.

27. D is correct. Calculate heat needed to raise temperature:

$$Q = mc\Delta T$$

$$Q = (0.110 \text{ kg}) \cdot (4,186 \text{ J/kg} \cdot \text{K}) \cdot (30 \text{ °C} - 20 \text{ °C})$$

$$Q = 4,605 \text{ J}$$

Calculate time needed to raise temperature with 60 W power source:

$$Q = P \times t$$

$$Q = (60 \text{ W})t$$

$$t = Q / (60 \text{ W})$$

$$t = (4,605 \text{ J}) / (60 \text{ W})$$

$$t = 77 \text{ s}$$

28. B is correct. During a change of state, the addition of heat does not change the temperature (i.e., a measure of the kinetic energy).

The heat energy added only adds to the potential energy of the substance until the substance completely changes state.

29. E is correct.

Convert to Kelvin:

$$T = -243\ °C + 273$$
$$T = 30\ K$$

Double temperature:

$$T_2 = (30\ K)\cdot(2)$$
$$T_2 = 60\ K$$

Convert back to Celsius:

$$T_2 = 60\ K - 273$$
$$T_2 = -213\ °C$$

30. D is correct.

If a researcher is attempting to determine how much the temperature of a particular piece of material would rise when a known amount of heat is added to it, knowing the specific heat would be most helpful.

31. B is correct.

Convert units:

$$1.7 \times 10^5\ J/kg = 170\ kJ/kg$$

Change in internal energy = heat added (Q)

$$Q = mL_v$$
$$Q = (1\ kg)\cdot(170\ kJ/kg)$$
$$Q = 170\ kJ$$

32. D is correct.

$$Q = mc\Delta T$$

If m and c are constant, the relationship is directly proportional. To double Q, T must be doubled:

$$5\ C + 273 = 278\ K$$
$$278\ K \times 2 = 556\ K$$
$$556\ K - 273 = 283\ C$$

33. E is correct.

The mass of each material is required to determine the time the system takes to reach thermal equilibrium.

34. B is correct.

Body heat gives energy to the water molecules in the sweat. This energy is transferred via collisions until some molecules have enough energy to break the hydrogen bonds and escape the liquid (evaporation).

However, if a body stayed dry, the heat would not be given to the water, and the person would stay hot because the heat is not lost due to the evaporation of the water.

35. D is correct.

Calculate heat released when 0 °C water converts to 0 °C ice:

$Q_1 = mL_f$

$Q_1 = (2,200 \text{ kg}) \cdot (334 \times 10^3 \text{ J/kg})$

$Q_1 = 734,800 \text{ kJ}$

Calculate heat released for temperature drop ΔT

$Q_2 = mc\Delta T$

$Q_2 = (2,200 \text{ kg}) \cdot (2,050 \text{ J/kg K}) \cdot [(0 \text{ °C} - (-30 \text{ °C})]$

$\Delta K = \Delta °C$, so units cancel:

$Q_2 = 135,300 \text{ kJ}$

Add heat released to get Q_{net}:

$Q_{net} = Q_1 + Q_2$

$Q_{net} = (734,800 \text{ kJ}) + (135,300 \text{ kJ})$

$Q_{net} = 870,100 \text{ kJ}$

36. E is correct.

Object 1 has three times the specific heat capacity and four times the mass of Object 2:

$c_1 = 3c_2$; $m_1 = 4m_2$

A single-phase substance obeys the specific heat equation:

$Q = mc\Delta T$

In this case, the same amount of heat is added to each substance, therefore:

$Q_1 = Q_2$

$m_1 c_1 \Delta T_1 = m_2 c_2 \Delta T_2$

$(4m_2)(3c_2)\Delta T_1 = m_2 c_2 \Delta T_2$

$12 m_2 c_2 \Delta T_1 = m_2 c_2 \Delta T_2$

$12 \Delta T_1 = \Delta T_2$

37. C is correct.

Conduction is a form of heat transfer in which the collisions of the molecules of the material transfer energy through the material. Higher temperature of the material causes the molecules to collide with more energy which eventually is transferred throughout the material through subsequent collisions.

Radiation is a form of heat transfer in which electromagnetic waves carry energy from the emitting object and deposit the energy to the object that absorbs the radiation.

Convection is a form of heat transfer in which mass motion of a fluid (i.e., liquids and gases) transfers energy from the source of heat.

38. A is correct.

From the ideal gas law:

$$p_3 V_3 = nRT_3$$
$$T_3 = p_3 V_3 \,/\, nR$$
$$T_3 = 1.5 p_1 V_3 \,/\, nR$$
$$T_3 = 1.5 V_3 (p_1 \,/\, nR)$$

Also from the ideal gas law:

$$(p_1 \,/\, nR) = T_1 \,/\, V_1$$
$$(p_1 \,/\, nR) = (293.2 \text{ K}) \,/\, (100 \text{ cm}^3)$$
$$(p_1 \,/\, nR) = 2.932 \text{ K/cm}^3$$

Calculate T_3:

$$T_3 = 1.5 V_3 \,(2.932 \text{ K/cm}^3)$$
$$T_3 = 1.5 \,(50 \text{ cm}^3){\cdot}(2.932 \text{ K/cm}^3)$$
$$T_3 = 219.9 \text{ K}$$
$$T_3 = -53.3 \text{ °C} \approx -53 \text{ °C}$$

Calculate T_4:

$$T_4 = 1.5 V_4 \,(2.932 \text{ K/cm}^3)$$
$$T_4 = 1.5 \,(150 \text{ cm}^3){\cdot}(2.932 \text{ K/cm}^3)$$
$$T_4 = 659.6 \text{ K}$$
$$T_4 = 386.5 \text{ °C} \approx 387 \text{ °C}$$

39. B is correct.

Steel is a very conductive material that can transfer thermal energy very well.

The steel feels colder than the plastic because its higher thermal conductivity allows it to remove more heat and thus makes touching it feel colder.

40. B is correct.

An isobaric process involves constant pressure.

An isochoric (also isometric) process involves a closed system at constant volume.

An adiabatic process occurs without transfer of heat or matter between a system and its surroundings.

An isothermal process involves the change of a system in which the temperature remains constant.

An isentropic process is an idealized thermodynamic process that is adiabatic of a frictionless system where work is transferred such that there is no transfer of heat or matter.

41. E is correct.

Carnot coefficient of performance of a refrigeration cycle:

$C_P = T_C / (T_H - T_C)$

$C_P = Q_C / W$

$Q_C / W = T_C / (T_H - T_C)$

$W = (Q_C / T_C) \cdot (T_H - T_C)$

$W = (20 \times 10^3 \text{ J} / 293 \text{ K}) \cdot (307 \text{ K} - 293 \text{ K})$

$W = 955.6 \text{ J} = 0.956 \text{ kJ}$

Power = Work / time

$P = W / t$

$P = 0.956 \text{ kJ} / 1 \text{ s}$

$P = 0.956 \text{ kW} \approx 0.96 \text{ kW}$

42. C is correct.

Heat energy is measured in units of Joules and calories.

43. B is correct.

Convection is a form of heat transfer in which mass motion of a fluid (i.e., liquids and gases) transfers energy from the source of heat.

44. A is correct.

Radiation is the transmission of energy in the form of particles or waves through space or a material medium.

Examples include electromagnetic radiations such as X-rays, alpha particles, beta particles, radio waves, and visible light.

45. D is correct.

Convert P_3 to Pascals:

$P_3 = (2 \text{ atm} / 1) \cdot (101,325 \text{ Pa} / 1 \text{ atm})$

$P_3 = 202,650 \text{ Pa}$

Use the ideal gas law to find V_3:

$PV = nRT$

$V = (nRT) / P$

$V_3 = [(0.008 \text{ mol}) \cdot (8.314 \text{ J/mol·K}) \cdot (2,438 \text{ K})] / (202,650 \text{ Pa})$

$V_3 = 8 \times 10^{-4} \text{ m}^3$

Convert to cm^3:

$V_3 = (8 \times 10^{-4} \text{ m}^3 / 1) \cdot (100^3 \text{ cm}^3 / 1 \text{ m}^3)$

$V_3 = 800 \text{ cm}^3$

46. C is correct.

An adiabatic process involves no heat added or removed from the system.

From the First Law of Thermodynamics:

$\Delta U = Q + W$

If $Q = 0$, then:

$\Delta U = W$

Because work is being done to expand the gas, it is considered negative, and then the change in internal energy is negative (decreases).

$-\Delta U = -W$

47. E is correct.

Standing in a breeze while wet feels colder than when dry because of the evaporation of water off the skin. Water requires heat to evaporate, so this is taken from the body making a person feel colder than if they were dry and the evaporation did not occur.

48. A is correct.

Conduction is a form of heat transfer in which the collisions of the molecules of the material transfer energy through the material. Higher temperature of the material causes the molecules to collide with more energy which eventually is transferred throughout the material through subsequent collisions.

49. D is correct.

An isobaric process is a constant pressure process, so resulting pressure is always the same.

50. B is correct.

This question is asking which type of surface has a higher emissivity than others and therefore can radiate more energy over a set period. A blackbody is an idealized radiator and has the highest emissivity. As such, a surface most similar to a blackbody (the black surface) is the best radiator of thermal energy.

A black surface is considered to be an ideal blackbody and therefore has an emissivity of 1 (perfect emissivity). The black surface will be the best radiator as compared to another surface which cannot be considered as blackbodies and have an emissivity of <1.

51. E is correct.

Calculate gap between the rods:

The gap in between the rods will be filled by both expanding, so total thermal expansion length is equal to 1.1 cm.

$$\Delta L = L_0 \alpha \Delta T$$

$$\Delta L_{tot} = \Delta L_B + \Delta L_A$$

$$\Delta L_{tot} = (\alpha_B L_B + \alpha_A L_A) \Delta T$$

Rearrange the equation for ΔT:

$$\Delta T = \Delta L_{tot} / (\alpha_B L_B + \alpha_A L_A)$$

$$\Delta T = 1.1 \text{ cm} / [(2 \times 10^{-5} \text{K}^{-1}) \cdot (59.1 \text{ cm}) + (2.4 \times 10^{-5} \text{K}^{-1}) \cdot (39.3 \text{ cm})]$$

$$\Delta T = 517.6 \text{ K} \approx 518 \text{ K}$$

Measuring difference in temperature in K is the same as in °C, so it is not required to convert:

$$\Delta T = 518 \text{ °C}$$

52. A is correct.

Find seconds in a day:

$$t = (24 \text{ h} / 1 \text{ day}) \cdot (60 \text{ min} / 1 \text{ h}) \cdot (60 \text{ s} / 1 \text{ min})]$$

$$t = 86,400 \text{ s}$$

Find energy lost in a day:

$$E = \text{Power} \times \text{time}$$

$$E = (60 \text{ W})t$$

$$E = (60 \text{ W}) \cdot (86,400 \text{ s})$$

$$E = 5,184,000 \text{ J}$$

Convert to kcal:

$$E = (5,184,000 \text{ J}/1) \cdot (1 \text{ cal}/4.186 \text{ J}) \cdot (1 \text{ kcal}/10^3 \text{ cal})$$

$$E = 1,240 \text{ kcal}$$

53. D is correct.

Conduction is a form of heat transfer in which the collisions of the molecules of the material transfer energy through the material.

Higher temperature of the material causes the molecules to collide with more energy which eventually is transferred throughout the material through subsequent collisions.

54. B is correct.

Heat given off by warmer water is equal to that absorbed by the frozen cube. This heat is split into heat needed to melt the cube and bring the temperature to equilibrium.

$$Q_{H2O,1} + Q_{alcohol,Temp1} + Q_{alcohol,Phase1} = 0$$

$$(mc\Delta T)_{H2O,1} + (mc\Delta T)_{alcohol,Temp1} + (mL_f)_{alcohol} = 0$$

$$Q_{H2O,2} + Q_{alcohol,Temp2} + Q_{alcohol,Phase2} = 0$$

$$(mc\Delta T)_{H2O,2} + (mc\Delta T)_{alcohol,Temp2} + (mL_f)_{alcohol} = 0$$

Set equal to each other to cancel heat from phase change (since they are equal):

$$(mc\Delta T)_{H2O,1} + (mc\Delta T)_{alcohol,Temp1} = (mc\Delta T)_{H2O,2} + (mc\Delta T)_{alcohol,Temp2}$$

$$(m_{alcohol})(c_{alcohol}) \cdot (\Delta T_{alcohol1} - \Delta T_{alcohol2}) = c_{H2O}(m\Delta T_{H2O,2} - m\Delta T_{H2O,1})$$

$$c_{alcohol} = (c_{H2O} / m_{alcohol}) \cdot [(m\Delta T_{H2O,2} - m\Delta T_{H2O,1}) / (\Delta T_{alcohol1} - \Delta T_{alcohol2})]$$

Solving for $c_{alcohol}$:

$$c_{alc} = [(4{,}190 \text{ J/kg·K}) / (0.22 \text{ kg})] \cdot [(0.4 \text{ kg}) \cdot (10 - 30 \text{ °C}) - (0.35 \text{ kg}) \cdot (5 - 26 \text{ °C})]$$
$$/ [(5 \text{ °C} - (-10 \text{ °C}) - (10 \text{ °C} - (-10 \text{ °C})]$$

$$c_{alc} = (19{,}045 \text{ J/kg·K}) \cdot [(-0.65 \text{ °C}) / (-5 \text{ °C})]$$

$$c_{alc} = 2{,}475 \text{ J/kg·K}$$

55. D is correct.

Using the calculated value for c_{alc} in the problem above:

$$Q_{H2O,1} + Q_{alcohol,Temp1} + Q_{alcohol,Phase1} = 0$$

$$(mc\Delta T)_{H2O,1} + (mc\Delta T)_{alcohol} + (mL_f)_{alcohol} = 0$$

$$L_{f \, alcohol} = [-(mc\Delta T)_{H2O,1} - (mc\Delta T)_{alcohol}] / m_{alcohol}$$

Solve:

$$L_{f \, alcohol} = -[(0.35 \text{ kg}) \cdot (4{,}190 \text{ J/kg·K}) \cdot (5 \text{ °C} - 26 \text{ °C})$$
$$- (0.22 \text{ kg}) \cdot (2{,}475 \text{ J/kg·K}) \cdot (5 \text{ °C} - (-10 \text{ °C})] / (0.22 \text{ kg})$$

$$L_{f \, alcohol} = (30{,}796.5 \text{ J} - 8{,}167.5 \text{ J}) / (0.22 \text{ kg})$$

$$L_{f \, alcohol} = 103 \times 10^3 \text{ J/kg} = 10.3 \times 10^4 \text{ J/kg}$$

We want to hear from you

Your feedback is important to us because we strive to provide the highest quality prep materials. Email us if you have any questions, comments or suggestions, so we can incorporate your feedback into future editions.

Customer Satisfaction Guarantee

If you have any concerns about this book, including printing issues, contact us and we will resolve any issues to your satisfaction.

info@sterling-prep.com

We reply to all emails – please check your spam folder

Thank you for choosing our products to achieve your educational goals!

Made in the USA
Middletown, DE
18 November 2019